INTERACTIONAL SUPERVISION

INTERACTIONAL SUPERVISION

LAWRENCE SHULMAN

National Association of Social Workers
Washington, DC

Barbara W. White, PhD, ACSW
President

Sheldon R. Goldstein, ACSW, LISW
Executive Director

NASW PRESS

First impression, December 1992
Second impression, September 1994
Third impression, December 1995
Fourth impression, June 1998
Fifth impression, August 2000

© 1993 by the NASW Press

Library of Congress Cataloging-in-Publication Data

Shulman, Lawrence.
   Interactional supervision / Lawrence Shulman.
     p.   cm.
   Includes bibliographical references and index.
   ISBN 0-87101-220-0
   1. Social workers—Supervision of.   2. Social interaction.   3. Interpersonal communication.   4. Social workers—Supervision of—United States.
   I. Title.
   HV40.54.S58   1992   92-32359
   361.3'2'0683–dc20   CIP

Printed in the United States of America

CONTENTS

FOREWORD

Supervision is a key process in social work. Skilled supervisors are responsible for the protection of clients, for the advancement of social work practice, and for the professional development of the individual worker. In the complex environments in which social workers function, the supervisor must work effectively on many different levels, often simultaneously. Making assignments, resolving disputes, implementing an unpopular administrative policy, taking disciplinary action, finding funds for important continuing education, and establishing priorities are just some of the activities a supervisor may carry out in a day's work. All of these actions require skill.

The National Association of Social Workers (NASW) places such importance on supervision that it is a criterion for all NASW credentials. Two years postgraduate supervision is a requirement for the bachelor's-level credential—the Academy of Certified Baccalaureate Social Workers—as well as for the master's-level credentials—the School Social Work Specialist Credential and the Academy of Certified Social Workers. Two years supervision also is required for listing in the *NASW Register of Clinical Social Workers*. NASW does not view supervision as a requirement only for beginning professionals. On the contrary, our clinical standards (NASW, 1989) and our guidelines for private practice (NASW, 1991) both call for periodic consultation for practitioners with all levels of experience. Each of us needs supervision to ensure quality assurance for our clients or constituents and our own personal growth and development.

As an association devoted to advancing the practice of social work and assuring the quality of service delivery, NASW clearly has an interest in helping supervisors enhance their skills. Lawrence Shulman's *Interactional Supervision* is a superb tool for doing so. The techniques Shulman outlines, although they are carefully grounded in theory, are not so esoteric or amorphous. Instead, they are directly related to the circumstances and the situations that frontline supervisors face. Shulman writes about what happens in the real world, and he offers solid skills-building material for helping the supervisor deal with those realities. Furthermore, he understands that all professionals must work on dual tracks—within the formal systems that surround them and in the informal systems where they may accomplish most of their important work. Because Shulman has tested all of the techniques and processes he outlines in practice situations as well as in empirical research, the reader can feel assured that the techniques can be effective.

I am very pleased that the NASW Press is publishing *Interactional Supervision*. Having watched Lawrence Shulman teach supervision in workshops and seminars, I recommend this book highly to all supervisors and would-be supervisors.

Sheldon R. Goldstein, ACSW, LISW
Executive Director, NASW

References

National Association of Social Workers. (1989). *NASW standards for the practice of clinical social work*. Silver Spring, MD: Author.
National Association of Social Workers. (1991). *NASW guidelines on the private practice of clinical social work*. Silver Spring, MD: Author.

ACKNOWLEDGMENTS

I would like to acknowledge the contributions of the many people who have made this work possible.

William Schwartz developed the interactionist perspective on which much of my work has been based. He died a number of years ago and is still very much missed.

The first supervision study cited in this book was a joint project conducted with two colleagues, Elizabeth Robinson and Anna Luckyj (Shulman, Robinson, & Luckyj, 1981). This project was supported by the P. A. Woodward Foundation, of Vancouver, British Columbia, and the Welfare Grants Directorate of Health and Welfare Canada. From the P. A. Woodward Foundation, the late Dr. Jack McCreary was most helpful in encouraging my early preparatory work, which led to the project grant provided by the Welfare Grants Directorate. I am particularly indebted to J. Evariste Theriault, who provided advice and encouragement for this early study.

The most recent supervision research project reported in this book was a subdesign of a larger, holistic study of social work practice (Shulman, 1991). This study was made possible by a generous grant from the Edna McConnel-Clark Foundation. In particular, I thank Peter Forsyth, vice president, for providing encouragement.

Various colleagues have offered help along the way. At the School of Social Work of the University of British Columbia, a number of colleagues participated in colloquia on my work in progress and offered their valuable advice. Colleagues at the Boston University School of Social Work were also helpful through colloquia and individual consultations. Don Oellerich was available when I needed statistical advice. His help in exploring the use of Lisrel (Jöreskog & Sörbom, 1988a, 1988b) for statistical analysis was particularly important. My wife Sheila provided specific editing assistance and general support during the many years of work on the project from conception to publication.

Many staff members worked on the major research project during its various stages. April Hamilton and Lavone Stanfield provided crucial administrative and support services from the start of the study to its completion. Reisa Schneida and Anna Luckyj did much of the key informant pilot testing of instruments.

The original Statistical Package for Social Services X data file was created at the University of British Columbia by Reid Spencer and then transferred to the Boston University computer system by Richard Rasulis. John Hoolihan of the Boston University Computer Center staff was also very helpful. Student research assistants at Boston University who were involved in the finishing stage of the project included Laura Clere, Barbara Lewis, and Jody Yonigihara.

The study was implemented in the Ministry of Human Resources of the Canadian Province of British Columbia (now called the Ministry of Housing and Community Services). I am indebted to the many members of the ministry staff, both in the central office and the field, who contributed to the study with their suggestions during the preparatory stage and who responded during the data-gathering stages. Special thanks to John Noble, deputy minister at that time, Liaison Executive Director Dick Butler (currently deputy minister), Gerry Merner, Leslie Arnold, and Elizabeth Robinson.

Finally, I thank the staff and clients who participated in both studies. As will become clear in the chapters that follow, both staff and clients experienced tremendous stress during the years we examined their work together. Both groups gave generously of their time and energy.

PART I

INTERACTIONAL SUPERVISION

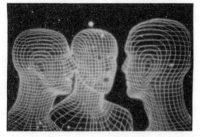

CHAPTER 1

INTRODUCTION, OVERVIEW, AND BASIC ASSUMPTIONS

After six years of front-line work with a large child welfare agency, a worker was promoted on the retirement of the previous supervisor. On the first Monday morning in her new role, she walked into the common room for coffee and suddenly her former peers became quiet. Two of them had also applied for the supervisory job. She knew they were talking about her because she used to talk about the former supervisor with them. She wondered if this meant the end of her friendship with them.

A new supervisor was brought into an agency from the outside. The administrator warned her that her department had experienced poor supervision and needed some shaking up. A male front-line worker, with more experience than she, who had been turned down by the administrator when he applied for the supervisor's job, told her in their first conference that he had not been supervised by a woman before and that the previous supervisor had generally left him alone to do his work. The supervisor felt a gut-tightening sensation as she wondered what she had gotten herself into.

After six months on the job, a supervisor decided that the evaluation process would be a good time to level with a long-term staff member about his inadequate performance. The supervisor had left the problem alone, hoping it would just go away. Instead, it had become increasingly worse. He reviewed the staff member's personnel record and discovered that previous supervisors had given the employee consistently positive evaluations. He dreaded the approaching conference with what he knew would be an angry worker. It did not help knowing that the worker was also the local union steward.

A clerical support staff worker stormed into the supervisor's office and insisted that the supervisor had to "do something" about a front-line social worker who was always late with his work but still expected her to respond

immediately. He was rude to her, and she did not want to tolerate it any-
more. In addition, the social worker regularly told her to lie to clients on the
phone and to tell them that he was not in. As a result, she had to deal with
angry people when he would not return their calls. The supervisor indicated
that it sounded like a real problem and suggested they meet to discuss and
resolve it. The support worker, shocked at the suggestion, insisted that the
supervisor not tell the worker she had complained. "After all, we have to
have coffee together." The supervisor felt frustrated and angry at both staff
members.

An executive director revealed in a management team meeting that
agency funding was about to be cut severely. As a result, all salaries would
be reduced by 5 percent, and some staff would be let go. Because the
agency could not cut intake or reduce the caseloads, supervisors were told
that their staff members must take on more cases for less money. The
administrator asked the supervisors to "back her up" and to let her know if
any staff members made trouble. When a memo to staff members announced
the cutbacks and new caseload policies, they reacted with anger. At a team
meeting, one worker, who appeared to be speaking for the rest, said to the
supervisor, "You are going to be with us on this one, aren't you?" The
supervisor felt caught in the middle and wondered why she had left her
front-line worker's position to take the job.

A recently promoted, African American supervisor heard through the
grapevine that many members of the largely white staff in the office thought
he had obtained the promotion because of the agency's affirmative action
program. Although he recognized that affirmative action had been a factor,
he believed he was competent for the job and would have had a good chance
of getting it regardless of his color. Nothing was said directly; however, he
could sense tension in the staff group. He felt angry, hurt, and bitter at the
racist element in his reception, and as a result, he maintained a formal and
distant relationship with his staff members. He felt increasingly isolated at
the agency, and because he was the only person of color on the management
team, he did not feel free to raise the issue openly.

These are just a few examples raised by participants in my supervision
and management workshops and addressed in this book. What the presenters had in common was that they felt ill-prepared to deal with their
problems, and they did not have access to either administrative or peer
support for help. If any training was offered, it tended to be theoretical (for
example, identify your style of management on a matrix; what is the hierarchy of human needs?) and unrelated to the day-to-day, nitty-gritty issues
faced by supervisors and managers. The theory presented in this book is
grounded in the realities of life in human services agencies and tested
through experience and empirical research. Most human services supervi-

sors eventually learn to cope with, or at least to adapt to, many of the stresses associated with supervision. This can be a painful process because some issues are suppressed and never directly dealt with. The goal of this book is to speed up learning, to provide specific next steps and strategies for supervisors, and to make the process less painful.

FOCUS OF THE BOOK

Although administrators and supervisors have a pivotal impact on the effective provision of services, they receive surprisingly little training in the skills necessary to carry out their function. Training programs often concentrate on the managerial aspects of the job (for example, budgeting, time management, report writing, setting objectives) but give little attention to the interpersonal skills needed for implementing supervisory and administrative functions.

This state of affairs seems to be the result of assuming that professionals who can do their jobs well as social workers, nurses, psychologists, child care workers, and so on should be able to make the transition to supervisory positions on their own. There is some truth to the idea that direct practice experience with clients, patients, and others can be useful (as will be illustrated in this text); however, it is a fallacy to assume that this parallel between practice and supervision will be apparent to the neophyte. New supervisors need clear, simple models of supervision practice that will help them learn how to implement their complex human relations tasks. These models can also help experienced supervisors conceptualize what they already do well so that they can function more efficiently and consistently. In addition, good models can help experienced supervisors adjust to the changing demands in the field. The presentation of such a framework is the task to which this book is directed.

Much of the book's content is drawn from the author's practice experience and from discussions with thousands of human services supervisors and administrators in workshops and consultation sessions. The issues selected for discussion have repeatedly been identified as central problems. This fact enhances the book's practical value and relates it to the daily problems experienced by supervisors. To make it easier to refer to the discussion of particular problems or issues (for example, dealing with defensive staff members, adjusting to the position of supervisor when one is promoted from the ranks, effectively implementing affirmative action hiring programs, helping staff cope with a traumatic incident such as a suicide on a caseload), subjects and illustrations are cross-referenced by topic in the Index.

In attempting to understand the dynamics of the problems, as well as to develop an approach for dealing with the issues, a practice theory developed by William Schwartz (1961) has been applied. Schwartz first developed the theory for the social work practitioner. He suggested that this powerful practice theory could have applications to other helping relationships, such as supervision, administration, and teaching (Schwartz, 1968). Although the approach described in this book is rooted in the work of Schwartz and draws on his written and verbally communicated ideas, the content reflects this author's elaboration.

THREE ASSUMPTIONS

Three assumptions underlie the approach used in this book. First is the belief that a number of common dynamics and core skills are central to all supervision processes. Although the examples draw on a range of settings (for example, social welfare agencies, hospitals, residential treatment centers) and include the work of many different professionals (social work supervisors, hospital administrators, nursing supervisors, consultants, child care supervisors), the common elements of the practice are stressed. It is recognized that there are also variant elements to supervision practice that may be specific to the particular setting and actors involved.

A second assumption is that many of these dynamics and skills are universal to the various modes of interaction within which supervisors operate. For example, some key skills are equally relevant to working with staff members individually or in groups. There are, of course, important differences between individual and group sessions, and these differences are identified. There are also similar dynamics when working with staff members during a formal conference or when providing informal supervision in short, focused discussions on specific issues.

In addition to being responsible for formal group meetings (for example, staff or team conferences), supervisors are also responsible for coordinating the work of staff members in the informal system. This part of their task is often the most frustrating and difficult because interpersonal and professional conflicts can lead to a lack of cooperation. These same skills and dynamics can also be applied to the work of supervisors as they represent staff concerns to the administration, deal with other supervisors (for example, department heads) on issues of conflict between units, or relate to outside agencies. Examples will illustrate the skills involved in working with individual staff members, the staff as a group, and the system as a whole, and they will deal with both the formal and informal contexts of this work.

The third assumption is that there are parallels between the dynamics of supervision and any other helping relationship. Therefore, the skills that are important in direct practice with clients or patients are also important to the supervisory relationship. These similarities have been identified by a number of authors (Arlow, 1963; Doehrman, 1972; Schwartz, 1968). It is not suggested, however, that supervision should become a therapeutic relationship. The staff member is not a client of the supervisor. Indeed, it is absolutely essential that this relationship does not happen and that the work of supervision remains focused on helping staff members carry out their work-related tasks. Nevertheless, much of what is known about effective communication and relationship skills can be useful in implementing diverse aspects of the supervisory function, such as coordination, education, and evaluation.

In addition, the way the supervisor demonstrates the helping relationship with workers will influence the manner in which staff members relate to clients. For example, when supervisors attempt to help staff members develop a greater capacity for empathy with difficult clients, they ought also to simultaneously demonstrate their own empathy for their staff members. Examples in later chapters will illustrate the importance of "being with" a worker at exactly the moment the supervisor is asking the worker to "be with" the client. Supervisees learn what a supervisor really feels about helping by observing the supervisor in action. More is "caught" by staff than "taught" by the supervisor. This will be referred to as the *parallel process* in which a supervisor models a view of helping relationships through his or her interaction with staff.

This assumption of the parallel process suggests that even a new supervisor who has recently been promoted from the practitioner role already knows more than he or she realizes about the skills needed for effective supervision. This text will demonstrate how one can harness to the supervisory role one's understanding and skills developed in direct practice.

ORGANIZATION OF THE BOOK

The book is organized into four parts. Part I includes this chapter, as well as a chapter that describes the conceptual groundwork for the interactional approach to supervision. Part II includes three chapters that use time as an organizing principle; it borrows the framework of the phases of work from Schwartz's (1976) practice theory. Skills needed for the preparatory and beginning phases of supervisory work are examined in chapter 3, starting with the skill of tuning in, or developing preliminary sensitivity to staff members' potential concerns and issues about the new relationship. An underlying assumption of the beginning phase model is the importance of developing a clear working contract at the start. Both the problems of beginning as a new supervisor from outside the system and those of the new supervisor who is promoted from within are examined. Issues associated with the introduction of affirmative action hiring and promotion policies are also examined.

Chapter 3 also explores the skills of recontracting. Many experienced supervisors, who have held their position for years, find that they may still be struggling with unfinished business from the beginning phase. Finally, another section describes the contracting and preparatory work needed to incorporate a new staff member into the working unit.

Chapter 4 focuses on the work phase in individual supervision. Reviewed are the core interactional and communication skills required in ongoing work with staff regardless of the issue or problem under discussion. The skills of empathy, sharing one's own feelings, providing data, and making a "demand for work" are among those described in this context. A number of common situations in the work phase are used to illustrate the theory, such as the problem of how authority affects the supervisory relationship and how to deal with a defensive staff member who mistrusts the supervisor. Resistance is also explored, both active ("Yes, but . . .") and passive ("You are absolutely right about that, and I am definitely going to do something about it").

Chapter 5 completes Part II by focusing on the dynamics and skills involved in the ending and transition phase of supervision. It highlights the phenomenon observed in so many human services setting in which staff members tend to have difficulty in dealing with endings (for example, cleaning out an office on a Saturday and not saying good-bye).

Part III deals with supervision of the practice of front-line staff. Chapter 6 examines the educational function of the supervisor in helping staff members develop the skills needed for carrying out their work. Although specific issues connected with student supervision are included in this chapter, the general purpose is to identify core issues involved whenever one person attempts to help another master new skills. Chapter 6 also examines the issues involved in working with staff on matters associated with the growing emphasis on multiculturally sensitive practice. The argument is made that skillful supervision is crucial in these areas because of the norms and taboos that make it difficult to discuss these issues openly. If staff reactions, fears, and concerns are not dealt with, the potential for active and passive resistance, even on the part of generally supportive staff, may increase.

Chapter 7 focuses on one of the most important and difficult aspects of supervision—holding staff members accountable for their work through ongoing feedback and evaluation. Evaluation is presented as a potentially effective tool for helping staff members grow in the work situation.

In Part IV, the focus is on working with the staff group. Chapter 8 explores the skills needed for effective leadership of both formal and informal staff systems. This includes such diverse tasks as leading staff meetings and helping staff members deal with conflicts. In chapter 9, the specific focus is on mobilizing the potential for mutual aid and social support in staff groups in response to traumatic agency events. These may include, for example, the death of a client (for example, child abuse, patient suicide), as well as the impact of the illness or death of a colleague and the impact of cutbacks and cost-containment efforts.

Part V examines the role of the supervisor in the middle position, between the staff group and the external systems that powerfully affect its work. The common phrase used to describe the feelings of middle managers is "caught in the middle," as both staff and administration appear to be asking, "Which side are you on?" Chapter 10 explores how a supervisor can avoid the trap of identifying with staff versus the administration or the reverse, siding with the administration versus staff. A "third-force," or "buffer," role is described and illustrated. In chapter 10, examples include how to relate to staff when introducing changes in policy that may generate resistance and how to provide feedback to higher authorities on the feelings and concerns of staff members. The mediation function suggested by Schwartz (1968) provides a framework for discussing this critical and difficult supervisory task. Many of the dynamics and skills described in the preceding chapters are directly relevant to this work, and these connections are stressed. Chapter 10 also addresses the unique aspects of the role of the administrator, who is often one or more levels removed from the work of the staff.

EMPIRICAL BASE

Related research findings are shared in this book in the context of the discussion in each chapter. These include findings from a general review of supervision and management studies in the human services, findings from a study by this author and colleagues (Shulman et al., 1981), and specific findings of a subdesign of a more recent study conducted by this author designed to develop and test a holistic theory of practice (Shulman, 1991). This more recent study served, in part, as a replication of the first study. Instruments developed and tested in the first study were used again in the more recent project.

The first study involved a mailed survey to supervisors and their staff members in social work agencies (child welfare workers), hospitals (nurses), and residential treatment centers (counselors) in three provinces of Canada. A total of 109 supervisors and 671 front-line workers were included in the final sample. The second study was a subdesign of a major, holistic study conducted in a provincial child welfare agency in British Columbia. Five executive directors (responsible for macroareas of the province), 10 managers (responsible for regional offices), 68 supervisors (responsible for district offices), and 168 front-line workers participated in the supervision subdesign of this study.

The reader is referred to the Appendix for a summary of the designs of both studies. In particular, the limitations of each study should be reviewed and kept in mind when evaluating the findings reported in this text.

SUMMARY

This book focuses on the interactional supervision and management skills needed to work in the increasingly complex and stressful human services field. It examines what supervisors and managers actually do in interacting with staff, clients, administrators, the community, and other systems important to their work. Three assumptions underlie the approach to this text. The first is that a core set of dynamics and skills forms the constant element of supervision observable in different settings and with different professionals. Variant elements can also be identified. The second is that the supervision process has a number of universals that are common to different modes of supervision—for example, individual and group, formal and informal. The third assumption is of a parallel process between the supervisor–supervisee relationship and the interaction between front-line workers and clients or patients. Supervisors are seen as modeling their views of the helping process through their interaction with staff.

Through its five-part organization, the book explores the theoretical base, the four phases of supervision practice (preliminary, beginning, middle, and endings and transitions), evaluation, the educational and case consultation functions of supervision, working with staff groups, and the supervisor's third-force role between staff and administration.

The empirical base of supervision practice is explored by reviewing the general supervision and management literature, as well as the results of two major studies conducted by the author. The design of these studies are briefly summarized in the Appendix.

CHAPTER 2

AN INTERACTIONAL APPROACH TO SUPERVISION

This chapter sets out some central ideas of the interactional approach to supervision, describes a model for understanding the supervisee as interacting with a number of vital systems (for example, the client, agency, colleagues), and includes a statement of the supervisor's functional role with respect to that interaction. These ideas form the basic building blocks of the interactional model.

It is important to note that the ideas presented in this book are still evolving. They represent a form of practice wisdom derived from the analysis of hundreds of anecdotes prepared by supervisors and administrators. In analyzing these examples and theorizing about the supervision process, the major elements of the practice theory developed by Schwartz (1968, 1969, 1977) was used, as well as a number of other theoretical constructs and models from the behavioral and social sciences. These are shared as tools that can be helpful in studying the dynamics of supervision. This author's research findings (Shulman, 1991; Shulman, Robinson, & Luckyj, 1981) and those of others are described, but it must be acknowledged that the empirical basis of the understanding of supervision is still evolving. The ideas presented in this text, therefore, should always be considered in the light of personal experiences. The final test of the value of each idea must be whether it can help supervisors deal with specific concerns more effectively or can explain why their current approach to supervision does or does not work.

TERMINOLOGY

In developing the framework for his model of practice for the social work professional, Schwartz (1962) defined a practice theory as a system of concepts integrating three conceptual subsystems: one which organizes the appropriate aspects of social reality, as drawn from the findings of science; one which defines and conceptualizes specific values and goals, which we might call the problems of policy; and one which deals with the formulation of interrelated principles of action. (p. 270)

In this view, a practice theory of the supervision process must identify underlying assumptions (corresponding to current knowledge) about human behavior and social organization, set out specific practice goals based on these assumptions, and describe the supervisory behaviors that might achieve these goals.

Accordingly, this book first identifies what is known about the supervision relationship, as expressed in such sources as group dynamics and organizational theory. For example, in discussing the way in which a new supervisor begins to relate to staff, some principles that guide people's behavior in new situations, especially when dealing with people in authority, are examined. On the basis of these assumptions, goals for the beginning phase of supervision are suggested, and the skills (such as contracting) designed to achieve these goals are identified and discussed. As another example, what is known about organizational theory and the process of change provides the theoretical basis for exploring the dynamics involved when a supervisor attempts to introduce a new policy or procedure to a resistant staff group. On the basis of this knowledge, particular goals for the staff meeting that are designed to lower defenses and to encourage open communications are identified, together with the skills needed to achieve them.

Taken as a whole, the book represents an effort to develop a practice theory of supervision designed to assist supervisors in facing day-to-day problems with a clear idea of what we know, what we might hope to achieve, and what skills are required. This is the sense in which the term *practice theory* is used in this book.

The term *model* is used to describe a representation of reality. A number of such models are presented to simplify the presentation of the complex process of supervision. For example, models are used to describe the relationship between a supervisor and supervisee, the operations of staff groups, the organizational dynamics of the work setting, and the process through which supervisors have an impact on their staff members.

The term *skill* describes behaviors used by supervisors in the execution of their professional tasks. Many of these skills, such as empathy and listening, have been identified as the core relationship, communication, and problem-solving skills that are important in all human contacts. The focus in this book, however, is on their use in the context of supervision and management.

Another term of significance is the *working relationship*. This relationship between supervisor and supervisee, which parallels the relationship between worker and client, is defined in this text as consisting of three elements: rapport (general ability to get along), trust (the ability of the worker to be open with the supervisor and to share mistakes and failures, as well as successes), and role (the function played by the supervisor with the worker and the availability of the supervisor). Specific findings from the associated study (Shulman, 1991) on the importance of the working relationship as the medium through which supervisory influence is exerted will be shared throughout the text.

The terms *worker* and *agency* are frequently used in describing the supervisee and the setting of supervision because social work practice encompasses a wide range of settings in the helping professions. Moreover, the study of supervision that forms the research basis for this text is an extension of the author's study of social work practice. Although the terms *worker* and *agency* often have broader meanings in this book, they can be interpreted as synonymous with *staff member* and the *institutional setting*. In most cases, the term *supervisor* is used to refer to all levels of administration and all managers. This is done to avoid repeating "supervisors and managers" throughout the text. In those cases involving particular issues associated with supervising at a higher level than front-line supervisor, the terms *manager* and *administrator* are used.

TASK DEFINITION

Almost 50 years ago, Robinson (1936) defined supervision in the context of social work as "an educational process in which a person with a certain equipment of knowledge and skill takes responsibility for training a person with less equipment" (p. 53). This emphasis on the educational aspect of supervision has been combined over the years with a second emphasis on the administrative aspect of the work, such as efforts to control and coordinate workers in order to get the job done. In a more recent definition of supervision, Kadushin (1976) added to these two sets of tasks the "expressive–supportive leadership function," which focuses on the problem of sustaining workers by offering emotional support and making efforts to assist them when they have "job-related discouragements and discontents." "This," Kadushin said, "gives supervisees a sense of worth as professionals, a sense of belonging in the agency, a sense of security in their performance" (p. 20).

By combining these three major functions, Kadushin (1976) provided a definition of supervision that serves well the purposes of this book:

> A social work supervisor is an agency administrative staff member to whom authority is delegated to direct, coordinate, enhance, and evaluate on-the-job performance of the supervisees for whose work he [or she] is held accountable. In implementing this responsibility the supervisor performs administrative, educational, and supportive functions in interaction with the supervisee in the context of a positive

relationship. The supervisor's ultimate objective is to deliver to agency clients the best possible service, both quantitative and qualitatively, in accordance with agency policies and procedures. (p. 21)

A crucial aspect of this definition is the emphasis on carrying out these tasks in interaction with the supervisee "in the context of a positive relationship." An important assumption throughout this book is that the supervisees have a key part to play in the supervision process, and the supervisor will be unable to implement his or her functions without their active involvement.

Schwartz (1968) stressed this interactional nature of supervision in describing his ideas about working with staff. After pointing out that the final effectiveness of an agency is determined by the skills with which the practitioners implement its services, he described supervisory tasks as "designed to enrich these skills, increase the efficiency with which each worker manages his job, and coordinate many workers and their functions into a smoothly articulated whole" (p. 358). Thus, he identified supervisory tasks as concerned with skill, efficiency, and coordination.

Schwartz (1968) also highlighted the supervisor's limitations in implementing these functions:

> The interesting thing about these administrative tasks is that they cannot be accomplished by administrators, that is, they cannot be "legislated" or "administered" from on high, but depend almost entirely on the interest and energy that the staff members themselves are able and willing to throw into them. Thus, the quality of staff education is determined by the extent to which workers feel free to reveal their problems, share their mistakes, and use the wisdom and experience of both their supervisors and their peers. So, too, morale is a group product, involving a sense of group support, a feeling of being "in the same boat," and an atmosphere in which workers can draw strength from each other as they face common problems. (p. 358)

From the supervisor's viewpoint, Schwartz (1968) said, organizing human beings into a harmonious and effective work group depends on the ability of the workers to lend themselves wholeheartedly (privately as well as publicly) to their task, which essentially is "making policies and procedures come alive in action" (p. 358). He suggested that the adage about the horse—one can lead it to water but not make it drink—is demonstrated in "the complexities of an agency culture, where the subtle operation of hostilities, confusions, and simple ignorance can so effectively undercut policies on which everybody is in apparent agreement" (p. 358).

As all supervisors soon discover, the process of carrying out the administrative, educational, and supportive aspects of the job is complicated by the inherent necessity of involving staff members. Many supervisors experience a sinking feeling as they attempt to educate a low-performing staff member who sits passively at the conference, arms folded, nonverbally signaling, "Go ahead, change me!" A similar feeling is the panic before a meeting when supervisors must deal with a touchy administrative issue that they know will be greeted by active or passive resistance. This fear often leads them to place the item last on the agenda and then subtly to conspire with the staff to ensure that there is no time left to discuss it. Such an effort to move quickly past the issue, or, conversely, to act heavy handedly and demand conformity, is usually met by direct or indirect resistance. Moments such as these lead supervisors to wonder why they ever left direct practice for the often-frustrating job of helping others work effectively.

Although the interactional work generates the most difficulty in implementing the supervision function, it is also the part that can prove most challenging and satisfying. The fact is that supervision is not a mechanical process; it requires a positive working relationship with staff. Supervisors must develop their communication and relationship skills, applying those they already have to the new situation and learning new ones to fit the unique aspects of their jobs. The very qualities of work that initially attracted the supervisor to work with people can be rediscovered in ongoing relationships with staff members. The satisfactions derived from direct practice, such as positive feedback from clients or the excitement of observing growth and change as a part of the process, can be realized from supervision as well.

One goal of this book is to suggest new ways of looking at situations that supervisors have reported as being most difficult for them. An essential feature is identification and discussion of the communication and relationship skills that are helpful in dealing with these problems. A first step is a model for conceptualizing worker–system relationships relevant to supervision and the functional role of the supervisor in these interactions.

WORKER–SYSTEM INTERACTION

In the helping professions, a useful model of supervision conceptualizes staff members as constantly interacting with a number of systems that are directly related to their work (Figure 2.1). A social worker in a child welfare agency, for example, must deal with numerous systems, including clients, foster parents, agency administrators, the supervisor, professional colleagues, clerical staff, and other agencies or institutions, such as the schools.

At any moment in their workday, workers could be called on to participate in one or more of these systems. This interactional model can be applied to helping professionals in any setting, although the particular systems differ; for example, the work of a hospital-based nurse involves patients, other health disciplines, housekeeping, and so on. The point is

Figure 2.1
Worker–System Interaction

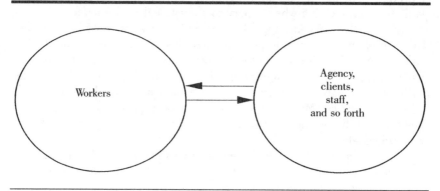

that it is possible to conceptualize any worker as being involved in interactions with a number of work-related systems. The relationship with each system places specialized demands on the worker and requires specific knowledge and skills if the worker is to function effectively.

An underlying assumption of the interactional perspective is that this relationship is always reciprocal. That is, the movements of the worker are affected, moment by moment, by the influence of the other system (for example, the client). In turn, the reactions of the other person are constantly influenced by the behaviors of the worker. Because the system is dynamic, it is impossible ever to understand fully the behavior of one member of the system without understanding that behavior as influenced by other parts of the system.

The interactional assumption of reciprocal influence is elaborated throughout the book on many levels. For example, chapter 7, which deals with case consultation, explains how the supervisor helps the worker understand the client's behavior by using an interactional perspective. The common example of the child in the family who plays the family's "scapegoat" role is one illustration. In the chapters in Part IV, which deals with the staff group, the behavior of individual members of the staff group is examined from the same dynamic systems approach. For example, the negative staff member who is perceived as the "deviant member" of the group by the supervisor may be understood in a new way as actually expressing the concerns and issues of the staff group as a whole. This difficult staff member, often perceived by the supervisor as the "enemy," may be transformed by this perspective into the supervisor's "ally." In Part V, the behavior of the agency or organization, as well as the behavior of departments or staff subgroups, will be viewed through an interactional, dynamic systems perspective. For example, a particularly stressed department in a large agency or institution may be seen as "acting out" the stress felt by the institution as a whole in reaction to cutbacks of resources. Throughout the book, as interactions between supervisors and workers are examined, the same interactional, reciprocal, and dynamic perspective will help explain the supervisor's behavior as affected by and affecting the behaviors of his or her workers.

If we return to the model of the worker–system interaction, using a child welfare example, then effective agency service requires that workers understand the dynamics of worker–client interaction and that they develop relationship and communication skills. In addition, a specific worker's knowledge of the unique problems facing specific clients, the research findings related to effective child welfare practice, and the systems of community support available to clients will affect the success of his or her work. Many of the communication and relationship skills are also important in dealing with other agencies or systems that are important to clients. An unskilled or heavy-handed worker who intervenes in the school system on behalf of a foster adolescent, for example, can create problems for both the client and the agency.

The worker's tasks in the agency consist of a number of components. First, there is the matter of job management. A worker must be able to work within the structure of the agency in terms of time (for example, being on time for work and meetings, meeting deadlines on reports, and developing the skills needed for effective management of caseloads). A second important area is the worker's ability to relate effectively to agency policy and procedures. Workers must implement policies and follow established procedures while they are developing the skills necessary to influence them. Effective practice also requires workers to develop skills to deal with professional colleagues, support staff, and supervisors. As workers attempt to deliver a service, their efforts must be coordinated with those of other staff members. Harmonious work relationships are required to help staff members relate to each other effectively in providing help to clients. When breakdowns occur in team relationships, the outcome is almost an inevitable deterioration of client service. In addition, workers must deal with supervisors, a symbol of authority, and learn how to use this relationship to their advantage.

Even this brief analysis reveals how complicated the systems facing a worker can be. Fortunately, all systems are not operating at every moment, and some are more urgent than others. By viewing the worker's function as dynamic and interacting with systems, supervisors can partialize the tasks and begin to develop the supervisory agenda with specific workers or the work group as a whole. In addition, this conceptualization of tasks helps take the focus off of analyzing the worker and places it on the worker's activities. It is better for the supervisor to deal with the way a worker relates to various authorities in the agency, for example, than to try to help with the worker's "problem with authority." The approach of analyzing the worker's personality, which is rooted in some early misconceptions of helping processes with clients, can lead to resistance by workers and to complaints that they are being "social worked" by a supervisor.

OBSTACLES TO WORKER–SYSTEM INTERACTION

The interactions between workers and the systems they deal with do not always go well. In fact, because the relationships can break down in so many ways, the supervisor's function is required. These breakdowns emerge from a number of sources. For example, the complexity of the process or the system may lead to difficulties. Giving and receiving help is a complex human relationship, and there are a number of ways in which the process can go wrong. The source of the difficulty may be the worker, the client, or, as in most cases, both. An agency, for example, is a complex system, and it is easy for workers to feel overwhelmed by the bureaucracy or for administrators to lose track of the realities of workers' experiences.

The difficulty of maintaining accurate communications is another major source of trouble in a work situation. People often hear and remember only what they want or expect to hear. Misinterpretation of messages based on the stereotypes that workers and clients or supervisors and workers hold about one another is the rule rather than the exception. Some subjects, such as authority, dependency, and race, cannot easily be discussed openly in our society. A staff angry at a supervisor for something said, done, or not done may express that anger in a number of indirect ways such as passivity at staff meetings, lateness, or the silent treatment. Even more powerful may be the norms that govern communications between peers. Normal work-related strains, which are to be expected in any working relationship, may lead to antagonisms that remain beneath the surface. These emerge indirectly to block effective collaborative efforts, but they are rarely discussed openly because of general injunctions against direct confrontations.

A third area of potential problems in interactions results from the difficulty the staff may have in understanding and acting on the common ground they hold with the various systems within which they interact. For example, an agency administration's stake in the positive morale of staff can have a profound impact on the achievement of agency goals. In turn, staff members need an administration that operates effectively, is in tune with the realities of practice, and is able to make the work situation more supportive. Supervisors depend on staff to carry out their tasks; workers need supervisors who are knowledgeable and supportive and whose expectations of them will help them undertake their work. In addition, staff members need peers who can offer mutual support as they tackle their common tasks.

These examples suggest lines of mutual dependence in the staff–system interaction that can easily be obscured by the pressures of self-interest. In some areas, the needs of the staff and the needs of the administration may not overlap or, in fact, may be clearly divergent. It is easy to understand, for instance, why social workers might not want to work nights and weekends, but the realities of agency staffing requirements may make this necessary.

The problems inherent in conceptualizing the staff as interacting with key systems will be expanded on throughout this book. This interactive model is used to begin the analysis in each example, and the ability to identify the people or systems that are on the right side of the interaction is a powerful aid in theorizing about supervision practice. The breakdowns described are often normal in the staff–system relationship; indeed, all of these problems and others can be encountered in any complex organization. In fact, the existence of the obstacles and the difficulty in coping with them establish the need for the supervisor's functional role.

SUPERVISION FUNCTION

The definition of the term *supervision* and the description of the general supervisory tasks of administration, education, and support in the preceding section are helpful in clarifying the responsibilities of a supervisor, but they are too general to be of assistance in the many instances of staff–system interaction described in this chapter. For example, how does a supervisor execute administrative and coordinating tasks when faced with a serious conflict between workers that is blocking effective service? Or how is the educational role implemented when a worker is struggling to deal with an angry and defensive client—and the worker is angry and defensive as well? Or, in an even more common example, what is the functional role of the supervisor when caught in the middle between a staff that is angry at a new hospital administration policy and an administration that expects the supervisor to "sell" the idea? Both the staff group and the administration expect the supervisor to identify with them rather than with the other side in the dispute.

It could be argued that there is no one supervisory function that holds true for each of these cases, and the function varies according to the supervisor's style and the circumstances (for example, whether the supervisor agrees with the policy). This is an attractive argument because there is some truth to it. Nevertheless, it would be helpful if some widely applicable statement of function could be developed for many of the circumstances encountered by supervisors. If this statement were activity oriented—that is, if it said something about the supervisor's part in the proceedings (what he or she actually does)—it could provide a framework for making sense of complicated situations and for developing a strategy for action.

Although there are some important limitations in the functional statement developed for social work practice by Schwartz (1960, 1968, 1977),

Figure 2.2
The Mediating Function for Supervisors

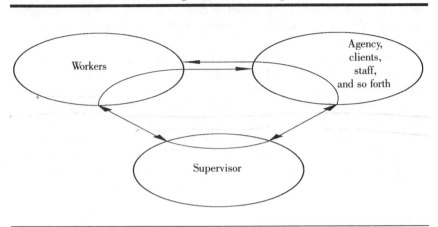

this author will borrow it and test it in analyzing the many practical supervisory situations described in this text. Schwartz described the client–system interaction in terms similar to those this author has used to describe staff–system relationships. He then proposed that the general function of the social work profession is to "mediate the process through which the individual and society reach out for each other through a mutual need for self-fulfillment" (Schwartz, 1961, p. 15). This mediation, or third-force, function is central to Schwartz's practice theory. Its application to the supervision model is illustrated in Figure 2.2.

To the two elements in the model of a worker relating to the various systems of demand shown earlier in Figure 2.1, this figure adds a third element, the supervisor. It suggests that the functional role of the supervisor may be best explained as mediating the engagement between the worker and the systems. This idea may be more true of some situations than others, however. For example, if there are two workers interacting with each other, it is easy to argue that the supervisor must help them talk to and listen to each other and discuss their differences, without losing sight of their common interest. In other situations, such as at a point of conflict between staff members and the agency itself, more doubts might be raised. These would be particularly strong if mediation is interpreted as simply reducing or covering up conflict, not taking sides on an issue (being neutral), or in some other way trying to avoid or smooth over conflict. But as later chapters will show, none of these commonly expressed criticisms of mediation apply to the view of the process described here. In fact, the opposite is often true because supervisors using mediation bring issues out in the open rather than leaving them, and the accompanying feelings, hidden and festering. Another reservation has to do with those situations in which the supervisor must exercise authority, ranging from

Interactional Supervision

demanding that work be produced by a certain date to the extreme of recommending dismissal of a nonproductive employee. What does mediation have to do with these functions?

These doubts are important, and they will be examined as examples are presented in the following chapters. In some cases, it will be clear that other functional responsibilities, in addition to those suggested by the mediation idea, are carried by supervisors. In other cases, implementing this third-force function will appear to be the only way to help—for example, the only way to identify with the staff and the administration at exactly the same time. In this discussion, it is argued that the power of this theoretical idea, indeed of any theory, rests in its ability to help us understand a situation in a new way and to provide alternatives for action. If a theory cannot do that, then it is not useful, regardless how elegantly it is stated. In the last analysis, this is a crucial criterion for testing the validity of any set of new ideas.

RESEARCH FINDINGS

The findings on the role of the supervisor, the context of supervision, and job stress and manageability presented in this section were principally derived from two studies. The first is the subdesign of the study described briefly in the Appendix (Shulman, 1991). A brief discussion of an earlier study (Shulman et al., 1981), on which the most recent research was built, is also included. Other research, particularly a study of sources of satisfaction for workers and supervisors by Kadushin (1973), is also reported.

Role of the Supervisor

In one study dealing with the role of the supervisor, Kadushin (1973) reported the responses of 469 supervisors and 384 social workers.[1] When supervisors were asked to rate factors that were strong sources of job satisfaction, two of the top three factors were helping supervisees grow and develop as professionals (88 percent) and sharing social work knowledge and skills (63 percent).

When workers were asked to indicate their sources of satisfaction with their supervisors, 27 percent indicated that the stimulation provided by supervisors for their thinking about social work theory and practice was a strong source of satisfaction. When asked to indicate their major source of dissatisfaction with supervisors, 25 percent indicated that the supervisors' failure to provide real help in dealing with the problems they faced with their clients was a strong reason to be dissatisfied. Thus, both super-

---

[1]An early contributor to the examination of the changing role of the social work supervisor was Lucille N. Austin (see Austin, 1956, 1960, 1961).

visors and workers appeared to agree on a desire for an increase in their investment in the supervision–consultation and teaching aspects of their work.

In another early study of supervision (Shulman et al. 1981), workers indicated they would most prefer that their supervisors spend more time teaching practice skills, followed by discussing information from research that would be helpful on the job, and then providing feedback on ongoing job performance. The areas on which workers wished supervisors would spend less time were discussing administrative requirements, performing other tasks, and planning on individual cases. The negative response to planning on individual cases may be a reflection of the workers' feelings about the type of supervision and consultation received. The focus on this type of consultation is usually the case, with little attention paid to the worker's performance, such as the skills used in interviews.

Heppner and Roehlke (1984), who examined supervision in the related field of counseling psychology, used data from surveys of counselors in training. Their findings were similar to those of the studies just cited. Supervisor roles that included behaviors that helped trainees assess their strengths and increase their self-confidence were positively associated with the trainee's perceptions of the supervisor's competence, the trainee's satisfaction with supervision, and the trainee's perception of the supervisor's contribution to his or her increased counseling ability.

In a 1979 study of 16 supervisors and 31 practicum students in counseling psychology, Worthington and Roehlue examined the associations between 42 supervisory behaviors and perceptions of effective supervisory behavior. They found that supervisors generally perceived good supervision as providing feedback to the students. Beginning students, however, rated their supervision as good if a personal and pleasant supervisory–supervisee relationship existed; if the supervisors structured conferences, especially during the early sessions; and if the supervisor taught how to counsel (by example, the literature, and didactic presentation) and then encouraged the student to try out the skills.

Similar findings were also observed by Pincus (1986) in a questionnaire surveying 327 hospital nurses. A positive communications climate between supervisor and worker and feedback on skills were associated with job satisfaction and job performance. In a study by Gondolfo and Brown (1987), 102 clinical psychology interns rated the supervision they were receiving and determined what their ideal would be. They viewed a model supervisor as one who served in a collaborative role, who functioned as a facilitator, and who promoted problem solving. They also indicated that they wanted to observe more of their supervisors' clinical work, wanted their supervisors to observe their work, and desired a more open process of evaluative feedback. Ideal supervisors were seen as warm, active, confrontive, and direct with feedback.

In a more recent study (Shulman, 1991), five area executive direc-

Table 2.1
Percentage of Time Allocated to Different Roles

Role	Executives (N = 5)	Managers (N = 10)	Supervisors (N = 68)
Consultation	34	24	40
Management	21	30	23
Dealing with personnel	9	17	11
Coordinating	33	18	18
Other	3	11	8

Source: Data from Shulman, L. (1991). *Interactional social work practice: Toward an empirical theory.* Itasca, IL: Peacock.

tors, 10 managers, and 68 front-line supervisors were asked to indicate what percentage of their time they gave to each of their different roles (see Table 2.1). The consultation role, from which supervisors indicated they achieve the most satisfaction and which workers indicated they most appreciate, constituted only 40 percent of the front-line supervisor's time and only 24 percent of the manager's time.

For another type of analysis in the 1981 study (Shulman et al.), the authors created a number of scales consisting of the average score on two or more variables for each supervisor. The supervisors were then ranked in order of their scores on these scales, and the top 25 percent (approximately) and the bottom 25 percent of the supervisors for each scale were identified. These two contrasting groups were then compared on the scores they received from their workers on another scale that combined relationship ("In general, how satisfied are you with your working relationship with your supervisor?") and helpfulness ("In general, how helpful is your supervisor?").

One scale was an index of supervisors' satisfaction with their role. The percentage of time supervisors reported they would like to invest in each task was subtracted from the percentage they indicated they actually did invest. The absolute differences (disregarding positive or negative signs) for each task were summed to produce the index of role satisfaction. When the group of 18 supervisors who were highly satisfied with their role was compared with the group of 21 who indicated low satisfaction, there was no difference in their workers' responses on the relationship–helpfulness scale. Thus, the supervisors' satisfaction with their roles did not seem to affect how the workers judged their working relationship and helpfulness.

The findings were different when these authors examined worker satisfaction with supervision content. Using a similar procedure, they summed the absolute differences between the actual content of supervision and the preferred content and computed an index of worker satisfaction with content. Then the authors ranked the supervisors from those with the least satisfied workers to those with the most satisfied workers. When the

25 supervisors with the most satisfied workers were compared with the 28 with the least satisfied workers, a significant difference was found on the relationship–helpfulness scale in favor of the supervisors with more satisfied workers ($p = .02$).

Thus, the data appeared to support the argument that the workers' satisfaction with the content of supervision was a factor in how they judged their supervisors, whereas the supervisors' role satisfaction did not seem to have any impact on their workers' satisfaction. Because the theoretical model guiding the study assumed that factors associated with the content, context, and process of supervision would be important contributors to supervision effectiveness, these findings offer some support for the model.

Supervisory Models

Various models of supervision have emerged from the literature. They range from traditional, authoritarian models in which the supervisor's authority emerges from agency sanction to collaborative models in which the authority emerges essentially from the supervisor's competence.

Munson (1981) surveyed 65 supervisees and 64 supervisors. He focused on models of supervision in three areas: structure (traditional/individual, group, and independent), authority (sanction versus competence), and teaching (Socratic, growth, and integrative). He examined the impact of the use of different models on worker satisfaction with supervision and integration. His findings supported Kadushin's (1974), which questioned the traditional view in which the supervisor's authority flows from agency sanction. Munson pointed to "the need to encourage greater independence and autonomy" (p. 68). He also found that a competency model of supervision, in which the supervisor's authority flows from her or his competency rather than agency sanction, was the most effective in all respects.

Similar findings were reported in a study of counseling trainees (Stoltenberg, Pierce, & McNeill, 1987), which found that as trainees develop over time, they perceive a greater need for "more peer/collegial type of supervision presented in a fairly unstructured/egalitarian environment" (p. 30).

Context of Supervision

The 1981 (Shulman et al.) study examined a number of variables related to the context of supervision. Workers responded to questions dealing with the frequency of supervision, both individual and group, and the supervisor's general availability. The scale used on these items contained six responses: (1) "none of the time," (2) "a little of the time," (3) "sometimes," (4) "a good part of the time," (5) "most or all of the time," and (6) "undecided."

The average supervisor in this study set aside regularly scheduled time for individual supervision from "a little of the time" to "sometimes," and these sessions were, on average, held monthly. Group sessions were "sometimes" regularly scheduled, with a reported average of twice a month. On a related question, when workers were asked to report on their supervisors' availability when needed, the mean reply was that the supervisors were available "a good part of the time." The following workers' comments on the questionnaire provide a sample of the most frequent statements:

- I feel regular individual supervision would be helpful.
- Peer group supervision can be very helpful.
- Most of my concern centers on not getting enough scheduled time for myself.
- My supervisor stresses the team approach and encourages his staff to give input on almost all aspects of our work.
- Supervision at the start of the job should be more frequent, and as the worker progresses, he should have the option to request it when he needs it.

Workers were also asked to describe their supervisors' investment of time in different tasks. There were associations between the supervisors' regular scheduling of individual sessions and their implementing the consultant role ($r = .29$) and the teacher role ($r = .33$). Holding regularly scheduled individual conferences correlated negatively with the role of manager ($r = -.39$). Similar correlations occurred among these three roles (consultant, teacher, and manager) and the frequency of individual sessions. Of the four settings in the study (child welfare, residential treatment, nursing, and other social work), only child welfare correlated positively with reports of regular individual sessions ($r = .39$) and increased frequency of individual sessions ($r = .47$).

There were some interesting findings with respect to the issue of holding regularly scheduled group sessions. Holding more group sessions correlated positively with a harmonious working relationship between worker and supervisor ($r = .34$), the supervisor's role as teacher ($r = .36$), and the supervisor's skill in helping workers discuss taboo subjects ($r = .29$). These findings are discussed more fully in the chapters on the educational function of supervision and the group work skills of the supervisor.

The question of supervisor availability was an important one in this analysis, and it correlated with a large number of other variables. For example, availability correlated positively with working relationship ($r = .40$), ability of the worker to talk openly with the supervisor ($r = .41$), the provision of a supportive atmosphere ($r = .35$), and the supervisor's helpfulness ($r = .47$). In addition, supervisors who were available were also seen as demonstrating an ability to clarify the role of the supervisor ($r =$

.26), help the worker discuss taboo subjects ($r = .31$), understand the worker's feelings ($r = .39$), articulate the worker's feelings ($r = .25$), partialize the worker's concerns ($r = .28$), and provide relevant data ($r = .33$). These skills are discussed in more detail in the next two chapters.

In considering the meaning of these correlations, the problem of not being able to determine the direction of influence must be recognized. Are supervisors who are available able to demonstrate their capacity for empathy, for example, whereas those who are not available cannot do so? Or do supervisors who are more empathic make themselves more available? The author's own experience suggests that both statements are partially true. These findings raise a question as to how the workers actually interpreted the phrase "available when I need him/her." Although the question was meant to determine the supervisors' allocation of time, for some workers it may have meant being emotionally available when needed.

Whatever the inferences—and different ones are possible and reasonable—the findings suggest that the context of supervision does have some impact on supervisors' effectiveness, although it may not be simply a question of how much regularly scheduled time is provided. Although regularly scheduled individual and group time appears to be important, no specific pattern is identified as the correct one. I can imagine a supervisor holding regularly scheduled individual conferences with a worker, but because of the worker's lack of satisfaction with content or the supervisor's lack of skill, the worker might still say, "My supervisor was not there when I needed him/her." Another supervisor might meet on a less regular schedule and yet always be perceived as being there when needed.

Comparing groups of supervisors on context factors produced results that support these inferences. For example, a scale on contact regularity was computed by combining a worker's responses to the questions on the regularity of individual and group sessions. The 26 supervisors with the lowest scores on regularity were compared with the 26 supervisors with the highest scores. There was a significant difference in their levels on the relationship–helpfulness scale, and the results favored the supervisors with the higher levels of regularity ($p = .000$). A second scale on supervisor availability was constructed by combining the contact regularity items with the item specifically asking if the supervisor was available when needed. This scale also produced significant differences between the 26 supervisors with the lowest scores and the 26 with the highest; again, results favored those who were considered the most available ($p = .000$).

Analysis of similar variables in a more recent study (Shulman, 1991) supported these general findings on the importance of contextual variables such as frequency of meetings and the availability of the supervisor when needed across all three levels of management (executive/manager, manager/supervisor, supervisor/worker). One difference indicated that the lower the level of the supervision pair, the greater the supervisor's availability when needed.

Job Stress and Job Manageability

The issues of job stress and job manageability are crucial in supervision. Although the emphasis may vary in different settings, in all of the author's workshops the theme most commonly stressed by supervisors has been the difficulty of the job. In a workshop for child welfare supervisors, one supervisor put it this way:

> The public just doesn't understand the stress we are under. They don't realize that some days, when I drive to work, I feel physically sick thinking about the decisions I am going to have to make that day: whether to leave a child in a home or take the child away. When you have a child killed by a client on your caseload, the feeling is simply terrible. You always wonder, could I have done something different?

Similar comments have been voiced by nursing supervisors dealing with the pressures of emergency or operating room procedures and by those concerned about patients receiving the proper medication. Child care supervisors describe the pressure of feeling that they are often a child's last resort, and they fear the not-uncommon teenage suicide.

In addition to the stress concerning the decisions to be made, supervisors also cite workload stress. They often feel stretched too thin, with too much management and coordinating responsibility and not enough time for consultation and supervision. Some of the supervisors' written comments on the questionnaire in Shulman et al. (1981) study addressed these problems:

- The number and kinds of service that the agency provides—the standard of service expected versus the level of service possible—the span of control is currently too wide.
- Often I feel I'm not as available to workers as perhaps I should be because of many other meetings, high-risk case involvement, and policy and planning projects.
- The amount of paperwork and heavy demands on social work staff detract from time available for effective case consultation.

Supervisors usually raise these issues when explaining why they cannot be available to their workers as much as they would like, why they cannot provide regularly scheduled conferences, or why they cannot focus on the consultation and teaching roles. For many supervisors, this is clearly a serious problem. To obtain data in this area in the 1981 study, the authors asked supervisors to respond to two statements: "My job as a supervisor is stressful," and "My job as a supervisor is manageable." The scaling was the same as described earlier, ranging from (1) "none of the time" to (5) "most or all of the time." The two questions resulted from key-informant interviews in which supervisors indicated that their jobs could be both stressful and manageable at the same time.

The average score on stress indicated that the job was considered

Table 2.2
Percentage of Reported Job Stress across Four Levels of Staff

Reported Frequency	Executives (N = 5)	Managers (N = 10)	Supervisors (N = 68)	Workers (N = 149)
Most of the time	0	0	7.9	26.2
Part of the time	75	70	19.0	57.7
Sometimes	25	30	65.1	6.7
A little of the time	0	0	6.3	7.4
None of the time	0	0	1.6	2.0

Source: Data from Shulman, L. (1991). *Interactional social work practice: Toward an empirical theory.* Itasca, IL: Peacock.
Note: Percentages may not add to 100 because of rounding.

stressful between "sometimes" and "a good part of the time" by most of the supervisors. The average score on manageability indicated that they considered the job manageable "a good part of the time."

In the later study (Shulman, 1991), the average stress score for front-line supervisors was again between "sometimes" and "a good part of the time." The score for job manageability, however, was much lower, dropping from "a good part of the time" to slightly below "sometimes." It should be kept in mind that the sample for the 1991 study was all child welfare supervisors, whereas the 1981 sample included nursing and residential treatment supervisors as well. However, in the 1981 study, there were no significant differences between these professions, a fact suggesting that a supervisor's job, at least in child welfare, may have become less manageable. This finding supports comments from supervisors about their increased span of control and the greater complexity of their jobs and the more serious nature of the problems on their caseloads.

This later study also provided an interesting comparison of how stress and job manageability were experienced across all four levels of staff, from executive directors to front-line workers (see Table 2.2).

Workers reported significantly more stress on the job than did any of the supervisory levels; there was an apparent decrease in stress as one moved higher up in the system. None of the five executives or the 10 managers reported their jobs to be stressful "most of the time." One explanation as to the difference in stress levels relates to the nature of the work. Dealing with a staff member in supervision, for example, is rarely physically threatening, whereas facing a hostile child welfare client may be stressful in this regard.

Another contributor to front-line worker stress may be related to the increased stress associated with being closer to an actual problem. For example, all levels of the ministry staff were concerned and felt stress about the problem of obtaining enough suitable foster homes and emergency residential placements for special needs children. But as one social worker put it, "The administrators may also feel stress about this problem, but on Friday afternoon at 4:30 P.M., when I have this kid sitting in my

Table 2.3
Percentage of Reported Job Manageability across Four Levels of Staff

Reported Frequency	Executives ($N = 5$)	Managers ($N = 10$)	Supervisors ($N = 63$)	Workers ($N = 149$)
Most of the time	100	40	49.2	6.2
Part of the time	0	40	38.1	61.0
Sometimes	0	20	11.1	12.3
A little of the time	0	0	0	15.8
None of the time	0	0	1.6	4.8

Source: Data from Shulman, L. (1991). *Interactional social work practice: Toward an empirical theory.* Itasca, IL: Peacock.
Note: Percentages may not add to 100 because of rounding.

office and the resource department tells me there is no place for him, I can't just walk out and say, 'Sorry, it's Friday afternoon and I'm off.' I mean, exactly what do I do with him?"

Similar findings were reported when job manageability was examined across the four levels of staff (Table 2.3): More than 20 percent of the front-line workers reported their jobs to be manageable only "a little" or "none of the time."

Further analysis indicated that for the degree of stress experienced by the front-line supervisor, a pattern of low to moderate associations with other variables emerged. First, one source of the supervisors' stress was suggested by the negative correlations with their rating of their executive directors' ($r = -.18$) and their regional managers' ($r = -.19$) abilities to communicate their concerns to the administration. Stress may have come from the supervisors' feelings of impotence in their system and from their perceptions that their concerns were not being passed along.

Positive significant associations between lower supervisor stress and availability to the social workers ($r = .19$), implementation of the consulting role ($r = .36$), capacity to empathize with workers ($r = .22$), and the workers' ability to talk openly to their supervisors ($r = .18$) all supported the hypothesis that lower stress for the supervisor is associated with the supervisor's effectiveness.

Other studies have also pointed to stress and job manageability as important factors. In one study of workloads of supervisors in a public welfare agency, Galm (1972) found that supervisors simply did not have enough time to supervise. In the Kadushin (1973) study of 469 supervisors, 53 percent indicated that not having time to supervise was one of the strongest sources of their dissatisfaction with the job. For 27 percent, having to make decisions without clear guidelines was a strong source of dissatisfaction.

In spite of the data on the reality of job stress and job manageability difficulties, some supervisors may use the stress and manageability issues to explain their lack of activity in certain areas of supervision when other factors, such as lack of confidence or skills, are also blocking them. When

I have pressed supervisors in workshops, many (although not all) of them have admitted that they could provide more help, even within the limitations of the job. This experience led me to assume that stress and manageability by themselves are not crucial factors affecting supervision effectiveness for most supervisors. For some supervisors, they might be the only factors, but on the whole other factors might also be important. Some stressed supervisors with jobs they often found unmanageable could nevertheless provide significant help to their workers, whereas some unstressed supervisors with manageable jobs provided little help.

SUMMARY

This chapter sets out some of the central ideas of the approach to supervision presented in this book, starting with Kadushin's (1976) definition of the supervisor. The supervisor's general tasks include administrative, educational, and supportive functions. Especially important is the interactional nature of the process: The supervisor is dependent on the active involvement of the staff, just as the staff is dependent on the supervisor.

In the model for viewing staff–system interactions described here, the staff member interacts with certain key systems according to his or her professional function and the setting. Examples of such systems are clients, patients, the agency or organizational setting, the supervisor, colleagues, and professionals from other disciplines or settings. The nature of the interaction is reciprocal at all levels, with each part of the system affecting and being affected by the other part on a moment-to-moment basis.

A number of obstacles can complicate the interactions between staff members and these important systems, including problems associated with complexity (for example, problems inherent in large organizations), difficulties in maintaining accurate communications, and the ease of overlooking the common ground between workers and their relevant systems.

The mediation practice theory first developed by Schwartz (1961) for the social work profession has been adapted to the supervision context. It is proposed as a useful framework for analyzing many of the complicated situations supervisors find difficult to handle.

A number of key factors related to the role of the supervisor and the context of supervision were identified in a review of research as having a significant impact on the supervision process. These included the implementation of a consultation role, the use of individual and group supervision, and the availability of the supervisor when needed by the worker. Stress was found to increase and job manageability to decrease the closer a staff member was to the front line. Social workers reported the highest levels of stress and the lowest levels of job manageability. Stress appeared to affect somewhat a front-line supervisor's availability to workers, capacity for empathy, and ability to implement a consultation role and the ability of the worker to talk openly to the supervisor.

PART II

SUPERVISION AND THE PHASES OF WORK

CHAPTER 3

PREPARATORY AND BEGINNING SKILLS IN SUPERVISION

The beginning phase of a supervisory relationship is critical in establishing an appropriate structure for the working relationship. Many of the problems supervisors encounter can be traced back to issues that arose in the beginning phase and were ignored or not handled well. The difficulties in this phase are compounded by the fact that these issues must be addressed at precisely the time when both supervisors and staff are most tense and uncertain about their relationship. One supervisor who had been faced with a group of resistant and angry staff members at her first unit meeting agreed that an alternative response might have helped her deal with the problem directly. But, she asked, "How can you say something like that when all you feel is scared spitless?"

Her point is well taken. The feelings of new supervisors greatly affect how well they can deal with a particular problem, and their skill may be demonstrated in efforts to catch and correct a mistake an hour, a day, a week, or even months later. Preparatory work, an understanding of the dynamics of new relationships, and clarity about the requisite core skills can help speed up the process.

This chapter explores the dynamics and skills of preparing for and beginning a supervisory relationship. It addresses the problems of starting as a new supervisor, as well as those of helping new staff members begin. It also examines common variations on the themes, including the special dynamics involved when a new supervisor is brought in from outside the system or when a staff member is promoted from within.

SUPERVISION AND THE PHASES OF WORK

Supervision of staff and work with clients are both helping relationships, and significant parallels exist between the two. Although many of the dynamics and skills involved are similar in the two helping relationships, there are also important differences. The purpose of supervision is to get the work of the agency or other institutional setting accomplished, and the functions of a supervisor, as described in chapter 2, differ in important ways from those of a social worker or other helping professional. It would not be appropriate, for example, for a supervisor to provide counseling for a staff member who has a personal problem that is interfering with work. However, listening, understanding, and trying to help the staff member obtain any necessary assistance from another source would be appropriate. In the work of supervision, helping staff members examine how personal problems are affecting their ability to work is a legitimate function. The supervisor's ability to be empathic and yet set expectations that can aid a staff member's performance are extremely important. These are the same skills that are important for the worker's effective practice with clients.

The parallels between work with clients and work with staff members suggest that the complex skills of supervision and staff management can be approached in the same framework as can the skills of direct practice. The approach is similar to the one used in *The Skills of Helping Individuals, Families and Groups* (3rd ed.; Shulman, 1992). It uses time as an organizing structure, an idea Taft (1949) applied to her helping theory. In this structure, the work is divided into consecutive segments; thus, the process can be traced through a series of phases from beginning to end. Schwartz (1961) described the phases of social work as (1) preliminary, (2) beginning, (3) work, and (4) endings and transitions.

This chapter is concerned with the particular dynamics and skills involved in the first two phases. But the framework is also useful for analyzing each brief supervisory encounter with staff, every staff meeting and individual conference, whenever they might occur. In the work phase (see chapter 4), when skills of the other phases are called for, they are described as *sessional skills* (for example, sessional contracting). Throughout the book, the model of the phases of work provides an introduction to explicit examples of how the skills of the various phases of supervisory work can be developed and applied.

Preliminary Phase of Supervision: Tuning In

The work of the *preliminary phase*, as the term suggests, takes place before the initial encounter between supervisor and staff. For a new supervisor entering a system, preliminary-phase work involves personal preparation for the first individual or group sessions. One of the key skills of the preliminary phase is described by Schwartz (1976) as *tuning in*, or trying to develop some preliminary empathy by putting oneself in the place of the other person. The goal is to sensitize oneself to the concerns, feelings, and issues that may be present in a relationship but that are not easily communicated. When supervisors begin this process by tuning in to their own feelings, they often find parallels between their fears and concerns and those that are probably troubling staff members.

The importance of tuning in is emphasized by the indirect nature of many of the communications that staff members have with supervisors. Human communication can be difficult under any circumstances. The process of encoding ideas into words (or nonverbal behaviors such as gestures and facial expressions) is complex in even the simplest of situations. The many obstacles to direct communications that can arise in an engagement between a supervisor and a supervisee often lead staff members to use indirect means of sending their signals. Most people learn in childhood that there are certain risks involved in being honest with people in authority—especially when negative feedback is possible.

An Example of Tuning In: The New Hospital Supervisor

The experience of Eleanor, a new social work supervisor in a hospital social services department, provides an example of how tuning in works. The supervisor had responsibility for social workers assigned to the pediatric oncology service. During her first meeting with workers from this service, she was asked if she had had much experience in working with pediatric cancer patients. At a workshop for supervisors, I asked Eleanor how she felt when the question was asked. She replied that she was embarrassed and uncomfortable; the worker apparently was challenging her competency because her experience in hospital social work had not included this population. She felt as if she had been put on the spot. In response, she said that although she had not worked on this service, her general experience more than qualified her to be helpful in this setting. The discussion immediately changed to a new subject, although the supervisor sensed that her response had not been well received.

It is easy to understand why this supervisor had responded as she did. She had been extremely nervous about beginning, and the question about her past experience with pediatric cancer patients struck right at the heart of her own fears, doubts, and questions of competency. Had she tuned in to her own fears and concerns before her first encounter, she would have been less vulnerable when the question was raised.

This supervisor could also have tuned in to the concerns that the staff members might be expected to have, such as whether she, as a new supervisor, would understand how they felt about working with children and their families who were facing a terminal illness. Possibly they had experienced other supervisors who were harsh and judgmental, who did not seem to appreciate how difficult the work was or how worn out they could be after particularly tough emotional encounters.

Given such circumstances, the question "Have you had much experience with pediatric cancer patients?" might not be an attack on Eleanor's competence but rather an indirect way of raising this concern. A supervisor who had tuned in to the possible meaning of this comment could have avoided making a defensive comment. Instead, a skill described by Schwartz (1976) as responding directly to an indirect cue could have been used. The exact form of this response would vary according to the particular style of the supervisor. One version might be to say something like this:

> Although I have supervised before in a hospital setting, I haven't had much experience in working with this population. Why do you ask? Are you concerned that I might not understand what it's really like to work on this service, how hard it is to deal with dying children and their families, and how it feels for you? Because, frankly, I am concerned about that as well. If I'm to be helpful as a supervisor, I am going to have to understand, and you will have to help me.

When this alternative response was role played in a supervision workshop, the participants felt more responsive to the supervisor, liked her honesty, appreciated that she understood their concerns, and, most important, thought that they might be able to "educate her." The direct response to the indirect cue, based on the supervisor's tuning in during her preparation for the preliminary phase, would give the staff members permission to discuss an important but difficult area. Her message would be that it was all right with her to deal even with this tough issue. Her honesty could help open up the relationship rather than close it off through responses that the staff might immediately interpret as defensive.

Some Reservations about Tuning In

It is not easy to tune in to the feelings of staff members or to have the courage to open up a potentially touchy subject early in a new relationship. This is why it is important for the supervisor to tune in to his or her own feelings as well. Too often supervisors are thrust into their positions without preparation. Department heads or administrators can be insensitive to the many fears or doubts a supervisor might have. Because the supervisor does not want to appear unsure or incompetent, these fears may be withheld in discussions with the administrator. A later illustration will show how new supervisors can be helped to develop some comfort and skill in becoming aware of their own feelings.

There is also the possibility of tuning in to the wrong issues. The classic example is of the supervisor who anticipates that the staff is going to be upset and angry because he has been selected for the job rather than a popular staff member. He tunes in to this anger and at the first hint of an indirect cue says, "I realize you must be angry at my selection." His staff members look blank and say, "No, we're really not upset about that." He replies, "Look, I can appreciate that you would be upset that I got the job instead of Frank." One of the members quickly reassures him, but the supervisor stubbornly persists, insisting that they must be angry at him. Finally, one of the staff members says, "Damn it, now I am mad!"

The advantage of tuning in is that it is tentative: The supervisor must be ready to abandon preconceived notions and respond to the reality of the present. There may be other issues that are more important to the staff members, or the supervisor may be projecting feelings that do not really exist. If the subject is in a particularly taboo area, such as authority, and if the supervisor is fairly certain that the concerns or feelings are present, it would be appropriate to reach for them a second time gently and tactfully so that the staff members do not feel defensive about having refused the first offer. For example, the supervisor could say, "I know you all like Frank quite a bit, and it would not surprise me if you were disappointed when he didn't get the job." By reaching a second time, the supervisor sends the message that it really is all right to discuss their feelings in this manner. Staff members will often accept a second invitation so long as it is not phrased as an accusation. If they do not, then the supervisor must drop the issue and not engage in a battle of wills that may provoke angry feelings. Staff members have heard the invitation to discuss the matter, and if it is a real concern that needs to be aired, they may take the supervisor up later when they have developed greater trust.

Another potential problem with tuning in is that if purpose and function are not clear, the supervisor will be seen as trying to use therapeutic techniques with the staff. A worker's reaction is likely to be, "Don't social work me!" When staff members say this, I believe they are referring to poorly applied social work skills that can cause clients to view workers' intellectual interpretations as mechanical or artificial. If the supervisor is genuinely tuned in to the staff members' feelings, the staff will not resent the interaction. Intellectual interpretations or statements about the staff's supposed feelings that really disguise the supervisor's own fears or hostility will always meet resistance. The classic case is the defensive supervisor who responds to an angry staff member with the punishing accusation that he or she "seems to have a problem with authority."

Advantages of Tuning In

One of the most important arguments for tuning in and acknowledging workers' feelings is that the staff can learn a great deal about a supervisor's view of the helping process from the way the supervisor deals with them. For the staff working with the new social work supervisor in the earlier example, for instance, tuning in and responding directly is a critical skill they must develop in their work with clients. Clients facing a traumatic illness such as cancer often send indirect cues of their real feelings, and if these are missed by the workers, they will lose an opportunity to be helpful. The supervisor can help by modeling an alternative way of responding to indirect cues.

Although tuning in and responding directly to indirect cues are critical skills for a supervisor who is new to a setting and who is in the preliminary phase, these skills are also essential for encouraging honest communications in all situations and in every phase of supervision. A supervisor who is introducing a new and somewhat controversial agency policy at a staff meeting, for example, could benefit from tuning in to potential reactions from staff members and considering some of the indirect ways these may emerge. Planning how to reach for an honest expression of negative responses, rather than leaving them to fester beneath the surface, can give the supervisor a beginning handle for work. Of course, this is not always easy to do. As one workshop participant commented, "First, I have to decide just how much honesty I really want." Facing this question is the first step in developing the courage to take the risk.

Beginning Phase of Supervision: Contracting

A staff anticipating the appearance of a new supervisor wonders what kind of person he or she will be. They also wonder about the new supervisor's sense of the purpose of supervision, the role of the supervisor, and how the supervisor's authority will be implemented, although they probably would not express these concerns in those words.

The supervisor's idea of the purpose of supervision determines the content of supervisory contacts. Staff members may wonder, for example, what kind of questions can be brought up in conferences or staff meetings. They may wonder what areas of work this new supervisor will want to deal with and what kinds of expectations will be placed on them. Even though they have had prior experiences with supervisors, they know that each one has personal ideas about the purpose of the work. And because the supervisor has such an important impact on their work life, they are anxious to know how this one will operate.

Staff members may also speculate about how this particular supervisor will play his or her role in the relationship as they deal with the content. This raises the question of function. The purpose of supervision and the role carried out by the supervisor are separate matters because it is entirely possible for supervisors to implement different functional roles in relation to the same supervisory purposes. For example, one purpose of supervisory conferences may be case management discussions, but for one supervisor this can mean, "Tell me what is going on, and I will tell you what to do," whereas for another it means, "Tell me what is going on, and I will help you figure out what you are going to do." Much of what happens in supervision will be affected by the supervisor's and the staff's sense of purpose and function, as derived from past experiences.

Another concern for the staff members is the supervisor's authority and how it will be implemented. Because supervisors are powerful influences on a worker's life, their use of power is of central concern at the start of a relationship. Supervisors can evaluate a worker and recommend promotions, merit raises, dismissals, or changes in assignments. As in all new relationships with people in authority, tension is inevitable until the questions are answered and the uncertainties are resolved.

The questions of purpose, role, and authority are the crucial areas cited by Schwartz (1977) in his analysis of the importance of the contracting process in social work practice, whereby worker and client develop a mutual understanding that provides a structure for the work. This structure is essential in giving both of them the freedom necessary to carry out their parts in the proceedings. Although these are central questions of the beginning phase, often they are not dealt with directly by either worker or client (Shulman, 1991, 1992).

The same is true in the supervisory relationship. I have found that there is often little direct conversation on the issues, and the result is a prolonged period of testing during which the staff members have to figure out what the supervisor is going to do. Lack of clarity in these areas causes heightened anxiety for the staff and frustrations in the development of the early working relationship. In addition, supervisees find it difficult to use the supervisor's help effectively unless they are clear about what that help can be. Thus, the supervisory relationship may be haunted by unanswered, underlying questions as long as it lasts.

This section explores some of the reasons why the issues of purpose, role, and authority are often ignored by supervisors and are raised only indirectly by the staff. The specific skills that help a supervisor deal with these critical areas are described and illustrated with an example of a new supervisor in a hospital.

Contracting Skills   4 skills

Four key skills of contracting in the beginning phase of work include the supervisor sharing his or her sense of purpose, describing the supervisor's role, eliciting feedback from the workers on their perceptions, and discussing the mutual obligations and expectations related to the supervisor's authority. These tasks may sound simple, but the process is actually complex.

In workshops for supervisors, I often role play a naive new worker and ask the assembled supervisors to describe their role to me and explain the kind of help I can get from them. A long silence usually follows before one of them asks, "What kind of help do you want from me?" In response I point out that my question has been answered with a question, and if I understood what kind of help there was to offer, I might have a better idea of what kind of help I needed. Another supervisor will then usually suggest, "I'm going to help do your job better." When I ask, "How, exactly, will you do that?" it is obvious that this supervisor's answer to my question was provided in terms of her own expectations for the outcome of our work together, rather than as a description of what our work would actually be. A third group member may then say something like this: "I'm going to discuss your work with you, and, through a mutual learning process in which you will have an opportunity for individual inquiry, I will facilitate your growth as a worker, enhance your job performance, and enable you to work more effectively with clients." I would credit this supervisor for mentioning that we would discuss the work together (the first hint of the purpose of supervision), but I would point out that the statement is so full of jargon—"facilitate," "enhance," and "enable"—that a worker probably would not have understood it.

It is difficult to describe the purpose of supervision and the supervisor's role in simple phrases that do not use overworked terms like *enhance*, *enable*, or *facilitate*. This is not surprising because supervisors are often given unclear, if not mixed, messages from administrators about what they are supposed to do. In one study of supervisors, Olyan (1972) found that most described learning how to do the job from role models, without any specific directions. If the purpose of supervision and the role of the supervisor are not clearly defined by these role models or by the administration that hired the supervisor, then lack of clarity will persist. The supervisor's uncertainty here can lead to hesitancy in discussing purpose and role.

Staff members seldom raise such questions directly. In fact, because the discussion of authority issues is generally taboo in our society, such concerns are usually raised indirectly. A worker who says, "One of the things we really liked about our old supervisor was that she let you make some of your own decisions" may be asking, "Will that be the way you will supervise?" The worker's lack of directness allows the supervisor to avoid open discussion in this area.

Supervisors also may feel uncomfortable about discussing the authority aspects of their work. A new supervisor wants to be liked by the staff and may fear that raising authority-related issues casts him or her as an adversary. Staff members, in turn, may be wary of being direct in this area or may find it convenient not to be direct. They may think that if they do not ask questions about what they can do on their own, then they will not hear the answers they do not want to hear. Thus, both the supervisor and the staff members may have a stake in avoiding direct discussions.

Some supervisors hesitate to be direct in contracting with the staff in certain areas because they are afraid that the members might take them up on their offer. One purpose, for example, could be helping workers develop their practice skills in relation to work with clients. As part of a contracting statement of purpose by a supervisor, this could be stated simply thus: "I will go over the specifics of your work with clients and try to help you develop your skills for dealing with the tough parts of the work." Supervisors may be concerned that if the worker asks for help, they will not be able to give it. This concern stems from viewing the supervisor as the one with all the answers, an unrealistic expectation supervisors often assume for themselves.

Thus, lack of clarity about role and purpose, the taboo nature of authority issues, the possibility of avoiding direct discussion by using professional jargon, the discomfort experienced in direct discussion of authority, and the fear of making an offer one cannot back up are all reasons why the working contract can remain vague. As in work with clients, the lack of a clear contract will frustrate efforts at almost every turn. Workers will perceive the supervisor as a stereotyped personality because of their own past experiences with people in authority and with past supervisors in a particular setting.

An Example of Contracting: The New Supervisor

There are many variations in the way contracting proceeds, depending on the context within which the work takes place, the definition of the supervision role provided by the administration, the particular style of the supervisor, and the specific needs of the staff. In the following example, a new supervisor in a hospital setting reported her attempts to clarify the purpose of supervision, her role, and the authority issues at an early staff meeting:

> I thought it would help us to get off to a good start if I took a few minutes to describe how I approach supervision. You probably have some of your own ideas about supervisors, so I would like to get your comments as well. The way I see it, it's my job to try to help the rest of you provide a good quality service. To do this, I will meet with you regularly, both individually and as a group, to discuss our work. I'll let you know if I have any ideas about how you can improve the quality of your work, and I'll want to know your ideas about what we can do around here to make your work easier and more satisfying. I also see it as my job to help you work well with each other, so if there are problems and you need help in sorting them out, you can come to me about them.
>
> If you have specific questions about patients or procedures, I'll try to answer them or find out where you can get your answers. If you have any feedback you want to see passed along to the administration, I'll do my best to see that they hear what you have to say. Finally, this work can be very demanding, and there maybe some days when you feel you have had it and want a chance to unload—I'll try to be available to listen if it's any help. That's about it, as I see it. Now it's your turn. How does that sound, any questions, any reactions? Is that what supervision has been like around here before?
>
> There was a short silence as they seemed to be taking it all in. I waited, and finally Rita responded by saying it sounded all right and would be a nice change. I asked what she meant, and she proceeded to describe how the last supervisor was really a "snoopervisor." I asked her to explain what she meant by that, and she described how my predecessor had always hovered over them, constantly complaining if they were talking to each other or taking a few extra minutes on coffee breaks. I said I thought I could

understand what she meant and that perhaps I should say something about my approach in this area. I didn't think it helped to have someone always on your back, and so I try to treat my staff as responsible adults. However, if a pattern of a problem exists—that is, a staff member is always late, or not taking her share of the responsibility, or sloughing off—then it was my business, and I would raise it directly with the staff member. It was part of my responsibility to evaluate job performance, and I took that part seriously. I thought, however, that it could be done in a constructive and helpful way. If they ever felt it wasn't being handled well, that I seemed to be "snoopervising," then I'd like to hear about it from them.

They nodded and Rita laughed and said: "Don't worry, you'll know." I laughed with them and asked if there were any other comments or reactions. There were none, so we moved on to the next question on our agenda.

Just because these words were spoken by the supervisor does not mean that they were heard, understood, or remembered. Probably each staff member heard something a little different, depending on her own circumstances, background, and prior experiences with people in authority. In addition, they might not believe that the supervisor really meant what she said. Perhaps other supervisors had invited feedback and then shot them down when they provided it. They will have to test this new one to see what she is really like in action.

Rita, who might be an internal leader for the staff group (see chapter 8) began the testing process when she raised the issue of "snoopervision." The supervisor passed the first test of supervision by opening up the discussion and relating it directly to herself. In addition, she did not pretend she did not have responsibility for their work or would not be holding them accountable. Instead, she described under what circumstances she would have to call them to task and in what way she would try to do it.

The contracting process is not begun and finished in the same session, or even in the beginning phase of work. Clarification of purpose, role, and authority will come in the day-to-day operations. As the implications of the process take on meaning in the daily routine, the supervisor will have to discuss again the role she has described. But at least she has stated her views, and her staff can watch how she implements them. They can also take her up on problems with which she has offered help.

Of particular importance in this example are the supervisor's comments about being available to support the staff when the going gets rough. One of the major contributions supervisors can make comes through their ability to empathize with the feelings of staff. This skill, which will be discussed in more detail in chapter 4, can be briefly described as the capacity to genuinely feel, as closely as possible, what the staff member may be experiencing and to communicate that understanding through words, expressions, respectful silence, or other appropriate means.

Most staff members have experienced so many different responses to their emotions from people in positions of authority that they are reluctant to reveal their vulnerability. They have been taught that dependency is a sign of weakness and that one should be able to handle problems and feelings on one's own. When their ambivalence meets the ambivalence of the supervisor, the result may well be a supervision process that deals with the symptoms of the underlying feelings but provides little in the way of support for the worker or satisfaction for the supervisor. By directly mentioning her availability to the staff when things are difficult, this supervisor issued a clear invitation that the members needed to hear. As with other aspects of the contract, it is likely that they will test her in this area by limited sharing of a concern. They may raise what is called in the literature a "near problem" and may wait to see how the supervisor handles it. If she picks up the hint, takes the time to listen, is supportive and nonjudgmental, and appears to be genuinely trying to understand, then the staff will get the message that she meant her original offer.

Supervisors in my workshops often ask themselves whether they really want their staff members to take them up on the offer to share feelings. They are afraid that they will not know what to do once feelings are shared, that feelings will be about personal problems, or that they will hear their own feelings coming back to them from the staff. Although the supportive function of supervision and particularly the skills of dealing with feelings in pursuit of purpose are discussed in a later chapter, the point here is that, one way or another, a supervisor has to deal with feelings. A television advertisement for an autombile repair service makes the point directly: "You can pay me now, or you can pay me later." The feelings of staff members have a powerful impact on the operations of a service, and the supervisor simply chooses whether to deal with the problems themselves or to struggle over the results of having ignored them. Lowered staff morale, sharp drops in levels of performance, conflicts between staff members that prevent them from working together, increased use of sick leave, and complaints of poor service from consumers are all possible results of the powerful forces operating in the emotional underlife of the work situation.

THE NEW SUPERVISOR:
SOME VARIATIONS ON THE THEME

The examples of the new hospital social work supervisor and nursing supervisor illustrate the importance of (1) tuning in and responding directly to indirect cues; (2) the contracting skills of dealing with purpose, role, and authority; and (3) inviting staff feedback. Each situation has unique characteristics, however. The following examples illustrate the same dynamics and skills in a number of different contexts. The problems illustrated have been raised often in supervision workshops, an indication that they involve universal issues. They include a new supervisor who is promoted from within the ranks and has to deal with a staff with whom she has had a social relationship, an office manager who began to work at the agency in the year the supervisor was born, and a colleague who thought he should have gotten the job. In two other examples, the supervisors are brought into the job to straighten out a problem with a poorly performing staff.

From Practitioner to Supervisor

The point at which the helping professional makes the role shift from direct practice to supervision is both an exciting and a trying time. Even under the best of circumstances the transition can be difficult. Schwartz (1968) described a training group of assistant supervisors in a welfare department who reported feeling "shaky about role-switch from social investigator to supervisor, teacher and—most frightening—'boss' " (p. 360). Even though they may have actively sought their jobs, new supervisors inevitably face doubts about competency as they try out a new role.

The beginning period is complicated by the experiences supervisors have had as supervisees. They know the usual feelings toward supervisors, having felt them themselves. They also have participated in after-work discussions, when a supervisor's most minute faults can be the topic for hours. Inevitably, the first time they enter a staff room and the conversation falls suddenly silent, they wonder what is being said about them. Although the supervisor's judgment of the staff member is powerful, so is the combined judgment of the staff on the supervisor. Kadushin (1976) noted the dependency of the supervisor on the supervisees for some psychic rewards: "Approbation from supervisees, expressions of commendation, and appreciation from supervisees are a source of intrinsic job satisfaction for the supervisor" (p. 107).

The problem can be even more complicated if a staff member is promoted from within. In one workshop, Fran, a recently promoted supervisor in a child welfare agency, reported being faced with the problems of a strain in her social relationships with former colleagues, a much older office manager, and a more experienced colleague who had applied for the same job and had been passed over. When the workshop members were asked to help her with these issues, one of them laughed and suggested, "Given that situation, have you considered quitting?" Fran replied, "Actually, I have given serious thought to telling them I have changed my mind." I suggested taking a look at the problems one at a time to see if the members could come up with any alternatives for Fran; she could always quit later.

Social Relationships with Staff

Fran began with the social relationships, the most painful area for her. She described having been part of a small group of staff members who had lunch regularly, went for drinks after work on Fridays, and had out-of-work contacts such as going to movies. This all had changed in the past few weeks, and the invitations had stopped. She had missed some lunches to catch up on all of the reading of manuals she had to do, and suddenly she found herself going for lunch on her own. She said she felt miserable about this change in her relationships: "Actually, I'm finding myself feeling all alone in the office, and it's just not as much fun." She indicated that she had made some joking comments to her colleagues about cutting her out, and they had joked back about her being the "boss" now, but they had not really discussed the issue. She was just too uncomfortable and did not want to seem as if she were forcing herself on them.

All of the supervisors in the workshop group could identify with the poignancy of the problem. A middle-range supervisor is half in and half out of the group, close enough to identify with the staff and yet removed enough to feel that a significant change has occurred in the relationship. Such problems are not easy to sort out clearly, particularly the dilemma of still wanting to be a friend while understanding the need also to be the boss. The group did some tuning in to how the staff might feel, and it was soon obvious that they were probably just as uncomfortable in knowing how to relate to Fran. Using the tuning in as a basis, members role played how Fran might use the next opportunity to open up the direct discussion of the role change by sharing her own feelings and asking the staff to share theirs. The role play went this way:

> Fran: I wanted to take a few minutes to talk about something on my mind since I switched jobs and became a supervisor. I have always felt close to all of you and thought we had a good friendship going, but recently it seems to have been strained. I have been trying to figure out how to still be friends with you while carrying out this supervisor job—and it has not been easy. I just know I value your relationship too much to lose it. How about you? Has it been on your mind too?
>
> Louise: We felt things were more uncomfortable, but we figured you were just cutting yourself off now that you were a supervisor—you know, not wanting to have as much to do with us.
>
> Terry: Frankly, it's not as easy to talk in front of you anymore. I mean, we used to be able to share all the dirt about what was going on—you know, the gossip about who was doing what or goofing off. Now, it would feel like squealing. It's hard enough already, knowing what you know about what we do around here.
>
> Fran: You know, that's my problem, too. Those same conversations would have a different meaning for me now because I'm responsible for that stuff.
>
> Louise: Maybe we just have to sort out what we can talk about with you and what is so work related that we need to separate it from the social part. Just knowing that you still want our friendship is important to me, because I felt a loss as well.

After the role play, Fran said she realized she had been avoiding an uncomfortable issue, and she felt that with the help of the group she might be able to handle it. The group gave her a great deal of support, and when she reported back at the next session, she indicated that her friends had been relieved that she had brought up the problem. She said she felt much better because she realized that although the friendships might make some aspects of the work more difficult, such as setting limits if staff members got out of line, it was not necessary to give up the personal relationships completely.

Avoiding Stereotypes

The work on the other two parts of her problem moved quickly as the same analysis was applied—the tuning-in and role-playing skills were used to practice a more direct response. Fran's written notes of her conversation with Ellen, the long-term office manager whom Fran said "began to work at the agency the year I was born," were presented at a follow-up workshop. This office manager had had ongoing problems with the professional staff, who always seemed to be in conflict with her clerical workers. Her relationship with the previous supervisor had not been good. He had handled the strains by sometimes attempting to appease her and by at other times doing an end run around her and setting policies or procedures that stripped her of some of her authority.

Fran's previous relationship with Ellen had been reasonably cordial, if not close. Shortly after becoming supervisor, though, Fran had noticed that Ellen was becoming more reserved in her contacts. Using the tuning-in and role-playing skills practiced in the workshop, Fran attacked the problem head on:

> I had asked Ellen in to discuss how we would work together now that I was the supervisor. I told her I realized that there were tensions in the office between the clerical staff and the professional staff and that she often found herself in the middle, having to protect her workers. I told her I hoped we could find a way to work together on the problems, because I felt I genuinely needed her help and support if I were to do my job properly. I continued by saying I realized she had been part of the office a long time and had seen lots of young supervisors like me come along, some of whom made her job more difficult. I didn't want that to happen with us. I asked her what she thought about this. She replied that it would certainly be a change from the way supervisors had worked with her in the past. I asked her to fill me in on the details, because I heard only one side of the story.
>
> She described with great feeling how she had continually been rebuffed by my predecessor whenever she tried to bring up problems between the professional and clerical staffs. He would attempt to smooth things over, but sometimes he didn't even listen to her. She finally gave up and decided she would just have to protect her staff as best she could. She went on to describe, with bitterness, the ways in which he had reduced her responsibility in a number of important areas, often without talking to her

about it. I told her that after having worked so long in the job it must have felt as if he was wiping out her contribution to the office. She said that was exactly what it felt like.

I told her I wanted to try to deal with these problems in the hope we might clear some of them up but that, frankly, I was a bit wary of jumping in too fast because I was just starting. I said I certainly couldn't see how I could have any impact unless I had her help and support. I wanted to see if we could erase the battle lines and the we-versus-they mentality in the office. But, first, I thought we had to make sure we had sorted things out between ourselves. I asked her how she felt about it. She told me anything would be better than the way it was now. I suggested she make a list of the issues she thought we should tackle and that we could meet again the next day to see where to go from there. She smiled and said that was fine with her and that she hoped my good intentions were not just part of being a new supervisor. I said I realized that she wondered if I would change after a while, and frankly, I was worried about that as well. I told her I would count on her to keep me honest.

The key factor in this first interview is that Fran did not treat this office manager as if she fit the stereotype that everyone else had accepted. She avoided the trap of treating Ellen as if she had a "personality problem" but instead dealt with her behavior as a symptom of a problem in the system and as the result of previous interactions with supervisors. Thus, Fran was able to elicit a different response.

"Deviant behavior" by a staff member (see chapter 8) is an often misunderstood communication, and the kind of work that follows a beginning effort to deal with long-term office conflicts, such as those between clerical and professional staffs, is examined in later chapters. The point here is that by not treating Ellen as a stereotypical defensive, hostile staff member, Fran made it impossible for Ellen simply to dismiss her as a stereotypical new supervisor. Each had to deal with the other as a complex, rather than one-dimensional, personality.

This example reflects a serious mistake that new supervisors often make: They believe the "grapevine's" description of a problem staff member. In many ways, doing so is a convenient defense for not dealing with a problem ("Everyone else has problems with Ellen too"). By tuning in and addressing the problem directly, it is often (but not always) possible to break the patterns of miscommunication that can create a vicious cycle and inspire a self-fulfilling prophecy.

Skillful intervention by a supervisor will not always produce a positive response. It is important to recognize the interactional nature of the supervision process: The supervisor has a part in the proceedings, and so does the person being supervised. Therefore, although using the skills and strategies suggested in this book can lead to positive results, it is entirely possible to conceive of situations in which, for any number of reasons, the supervisee does not respond as expected. A worker might not find it possible, for instance, to lower defenses, to admit to vulnerability, or to trust the supervisor's intentions. This is why it is sometimes necessary to give up on an employee and recommend dismissal or other job action. The focus of this discussion is on how the supervisor can do his or her part as skillfully as possible and thereby bring out the strength in most, if not all, workers.

Continued Resistance

The dynamic of continued resistance was illustrated when Fran reported back to the workshop group on her efforts to deal with John, the colleague with seniority who was angry when he did not get the supervisory job. Fran described verbal and nonverbal communications from this worker that bordered on outright hostility. She had been hurt by his reaction but again had kept her feelings inside and had not confronted him. Her written report of her efforts to engage him directly on this sensitive issue, after she had tuned in and role played the interview in the workshop, follows:

> I had asked John to meet with me to review his current caseload so I could be in touch with any problems he felt I should know about. He missed the first appointment, apologizing later and telling me he had forgotten. He was 10 minutes late for the second appointment and had not brought his files with him, even though that was the usual procedure for reviewing cases. I was getting the distinct feeling that he was not too happy about meeting with me. Taking my courage in hand, and strengthened by my other experiences, I decided to try to get at the problem directly.
>
> I told him I had the feeling he was not too anxious to talk with me about the cases—at least he certainly didn't seem enthusiastic. He said he didn't really see the need for the discussion because, as he told me before, there were no problems on his caseload that he needed help with right now. I told him I could appreciate that he had his caseload in order, but I felt that, as a new supervisor, it was important for me to get a feel for the work that all of the staff was doing. He told me that Sam [the previous supervisor] had respected his competence and had left him to do his work alone.
>
> At this point, I felt stuck and frustrated, as if we were going around in circles. I finally leveled with him and told him that I felt there was more to this than just a change in procedures. I told him I had felt some tension from him since I had received the promotion, and, particularly because I knew he had applied for the same job, I was worried about what it meant. I told him I had felt uncomfortable about the whole situation. I had even avoided raising it with him—which was a mistake. I realized he was an experienced caseworker and had even been at the agency longer than I, and yet I got the job. I was frankly afraid he would be mad at me, and that was what I was sensing.
>
> He told me he didn't understand what I was talking about. He was not angry at me, although he didn't feel he had received completely fair treatment in the selection process. I asked him what he meant by that, and he responded by saying he did not want to talk about it; it was all over. I told him that I was feeling upset about their having to make the choice between

us. Therefore, I wouldn't have been surprised if he had some feelings as well.

He got angry at me and said, "Look, if you feel people are angry at you for getting the job, that's your problem, not mine. Maybe you feel guilty about having gotten it in the first place." I told him I wasn't feeling guilty, just worried about how we would get along in these circumstances. He told me that if I let him alone, there should be no problems. I told him I couldn't do that and feel comfortable about the job, so we had just better work out what we could expect from each other. I told him I would expect to be informed about his work, as I would with all staff. He could, however, expect that I would respect his competency and give him a good deal of leeway in the way he handled cases. In those situations in which I differed with him, and I thought they would be few, I would have to take responsibility for the final decision because that came with the job. I asked if he would make another appointment, and this time I would like him to bring the folders. He said he would do that, and our conference ended. I was glad because by this time, my knees were shaking so hard I was sure he must be able to hear them.

Although the session was difficult and although Fran did not think she was much further along with John, some important steps had been taken. First, she had declared the formally taboo subject of authority as legitimate for discussion. Second, John actually had become angry at Fran, while simultaneously denying he felt any anger at all. It is possible that John was not in touch with how he felt in the situation and meant the denial. At any rate, the quarrel was out in the open, and it might get picked up at a later date when John felt more free to discuss it. Even if it were not raised again, simply pointing out the obstacle in this way might effectively diminish its effect.

Fran had confronted the issue of their working relationship and had made it clear that she would not be intimidated by John into pretending she was not his supervisor. This was important for John to hear, because now that she had made it clear she would not just disappear, he was going to have to deal with her in one way or another. At the same time that she made this part of the contract clear, she offered recognition of her respect for his experience and competency, something that he also needed to hear—although his feelings might have made it hard for him to understand this just now.

The workshop group offered support to Fran for her courage in the exchange. It was significant that she did not close the door because of John's first response. Often, a staff member needs time to think things over before being able to engage in a dialogue. It would be a mistake to assume that the question was closed forever or that John would not become more responsive as the work progressed. Fran would have to achieve the delicate balance of remaining sensitive to his feelings while not letting up on her demands and expectations.

The group members also tuned in to the problem of gender, because this was the first time John was supervised by a woman. They agreed that Fran should keep this in mind until a better working relationship was established; it would not be wise at this point to raise yet another potential obstacle. Fran ended the discussion by saying that although it had been rough going in this case and although she still saw problems ahead, she felt strengthened by having at least confronted the problem and finding that the whole world did not collapse.

This is an important observation, and it recurs in the examples given throughout this book. It is often true that the problems we fear the most turn out to be less potent the moment we start to face them.

The Hired-Gun Syndrome

Another common variation on the theme of the new supervisor appears when the supervisor is brought in from outside the unit for the express purpose of straightening out perceived problems. I call this the *hired-gun syndrome* because that is the way the staff members often see this type of new supervisor. This is the most extreme version of the problem of a new authority figure, an outsider, entering any system. The discussion in this section, therefore, is relevant even in situations in which serious problems are not apparent.

When a new supervisor enters an established system, staff members are concerned about how this authority figure will judge them. All helping professionals have some concern about their effectiveness, and any system, even the best, has unresolved problems in its operations. Staff members are well aware of the blemishes and weaknesses in the program, and this awareness heightens their concern about how the new supervisor will judge them.

If a staff group has been formally or informally identified as operating poorly or if it presents some other problem for the system, its concerns and defensiveness are usually accentuated. Most helping systems have subgroups of staff members that are so identified: the regional office to which all of the "losers" have been transferred, the ward in the hospital that contains the "negative" staff, the department in the agency whose staff members are the "sweathogs" of the system, the residential treatment center in which the staff seems to have lost any sense of control over residents, or the transition house that has been recently incorporated into the formal welfare system but is rebelling against any form of accountability. In a discussion on administration skills in chapter 6, the functional role often played by such staff groups in the system as a whole is considered. Here, the concern is only with the problems that such a group presents for the new supervisor in the beginning phase.

A common mistake made by new supervisors in this situation is trying to lay down the law at the very beginning. This is often the result of poor preparation, in which the supervisor may be charged by an administrator with "cleaning up the mess." The supervisor is made to feel that early progress is required and that the sole reason for his or her involvement in the situation is to bring about change. Another factor that leads the supervisor to be authoritarian in the beginning is his or her own anxiety about the situation. Because resistance and anger are expected, the supervisor moves in a way that brings them about quickly. Still a third reason is the supervisor's feelings about having been selected for this "choice" role. One supervisor was transferred from an extremely well-run hospital ward to the trouble spot in the system. Because of the poor way in which the assignment was discussed with her, she experienced it as a punishment rather than as a recognition of her superior abilities. She directed her anger at the administration toward her new staff.

In another case in which the assignment was handled well, the supervisor really did not want to leave her unit in a child welfare agency, even though she recognized the validity of the administrator's appeal and clearly understood it as a demonstration of faith in her competence. At a workshop, when I challenged her on her real feelings about beginning with this new group of staff and pointed out that it sounded as if she were really upset about leaving her old staff, she broke into tears, revealing the depth of her feelings about the endings. It is often true that beginnings are infused with many unresolved feelings about endings.

Whatever the reasons for being aggressive in the beginning, it is usually a mistake, as is illustrated in the following example from a child care treatment home. A problem in the home had received public notice through a story in the press. A teenager had been acting out in the community, and the police had charged that because the staff in the home was not providing enough structure, the youths were being allowed to run free. This precipitated an agency investigation into the home, some confirmation of the problems, the transfer of the child care supervisor to a new position, and his temporary replacement (for a few months) by a supervisor from another home that had a reputation for strong discipline. Will, the new supervisor, described his first staff meeting as tense. When he walked into the meeting room, he could see that many of the staff members were angry or upset. Some were sitting with their arms folded in a posture that seemed to challenge, "Go ahead—change me!" Will had prepared himself for the tough job, however, so he just put his head down and ploughed ahead:

> I told them I realized things had been rather lax around here and that they should realize this was not the way I wanted to see the house run. I pointed out that they had run into many problems that we were not experiencing at my other home and that I thought lack of proper discipline was at the bottom of the troubles. I told them I thought we could straighten that out fairly quickly, making the place better for the kids and for them.

The response he received was a sullen silence. He quickly changed the subject and raised some questions about staff rotations and other policy issues. Things went "miserably" after that; Will said, "They hardly even talk to me, and I feel like it's uphill going all the way."

This new supervisor had made the classic mistake of attacking the staff members at a time when they were most vulnerable. He would have been helped by Hollander's (1961) analysis of how leaders build up "idiosyncratic credits" through a process of conforming to the group's norms before presenting any challenges to them. In a modified version, this means that any new supervisor is wise to spend some time with the staff, learning to understand the problems through the eyes of its members before attempting to initiate changes.

It is important to develop a working relationship based on understanding on which to draw when the time comes to make a demand for work (Schwartz, 1961). The same holds true in any new staff contact. Because these staff members seemed to feel so vulnerable, what they needed at this point was not a lecture on how to straighten out their house but rather some understanding of how stressful the past few weeks must have been for all of them. Without such a relationship, defenses are heightened by an attack. The results might have been different if Will had begun another way, perhaps as follows:

> I know you have all been going through a rough time in the past few weeks, what with the publicity, a change of supervisors, and everyone coming down hard on you. I also realize you're probably worried about my being transferred in here to make some changes. I wanted you to know I realize I need to find out a great deal from you about what goes on around here, what parts of the program you value, and where you see the problems. So don't worry. Although I was asked to help you examine the program, I'm clear that I can't do a thing without your cooperation and involvement—and so I won't try. Now it's your turn to speak, and I'll listen.

It is important for the supervisor to be genuine in such comments. If the staff finds out it is really a con job—that is, that he is setting them up and does not really mean what he is saying—the reaction will be negative. In reality, it is impossible to make serious changes in a program without the cooperation of the staff. And if the staff has been having difficulty in the area of setting limits, then exploring the issues involved and trying to understand why such discipline is hard for them is the first step in helping them make changes. A supervisor who simply makes demands without providing support will be experienced by the staff as harsh and uncaring.

In the case of Will, members of the workshop role played how he might go back to the staff and admit his mistake, asking for a chance to start over. They suggested Will might say something like this:

> I wanted to talk to you about the way I began at this place. Frankly, I was nervous about starting under pressure to bring about changes. As a

result, I came on heavy and probably put you all off just at the time you were already reeling from everyone coming down on your backs. It certainly didn't help our working relationship, which I feel is not in great shape right now. I would like a chance to start over. How about it?

The workshop participants felt this might help. They thought the staff members would appreciate the honesty and the admission of a mistake. It is interesting that this particular approach—admitting a mistake—usually provokes an important discussion among supervisors. Many say they have felt that to be effective, they should not admit to having faults. They view it as exposing a weakness that would lower their status in the eyes of their workers. But when asked to think about important authority figures in their lives, most realize that this kind of honesty made these people seem more real, less like cardboard figures, more vulnerable, and less threatening. In fact, workers are relieved when supervisors make and admit mistakes. Indeed, it is the supervisor who always seems to be perfect, in control, and never flustered who is hard to live with.

There is another important reason for showing more honesty and understanding. Staff members often relate to their clients in a manner parallel to the way the supervisor relates to them. Two interesting studies have highlighted this phenomenon. In a study of the training of psychotherapists, Doehrman (1972) found that therapists act out with patients the effects of the conflicts engendered in them by their supervisors. And, in a study of training students for social work, Mayer and Rosenblatt (1975) found that the students' security with their clients was directly associated with how secure they themselves felt with their supervisors.

Thus, the supervisor in this child care setting has an opportunity to demonstrate to the staff, through his work with them, a way of dealing with residents. With acting-out teenagers in a residential setting, who are there because other forms of help such as foster homes have not worked, it is critical for the staff to begin with support and understanding. This can develop a working relationship that allows the youngsters to accept the limitations the staff must set for them. The ability of the staff to understand deviant behavior by residents as a form of communication and to reach for the underlying feelings is crucial.

In addition, the staff should feel free to admit mistakes they may make with residents. This is an essential skill when working with youngsters, who will respond with a battle of wills to any adult they perceive as arbitrary and unfair. To carry the parallel further, it is precisely the ability to admit mistakes and to take responsibility for one's own actions, that the staff wishes to develop in the youngsters. Thus, the modeling of adult behavior really begins with the supervisor, continues with the staff, and gets picked up by the clients. The importance of such modeling in the setting as a whole is described in chapter 6.

Another example of the hired-gun syndrome concerns a new supervisor who took responsibility for a transition house for women in crisis that had recently been incorporated into a large government agency. It had operated independently on grants and had constantly been in financial trouble until, after a campaign for public recognition of the service, it was accepted into the agency's structure. This house had operated without a supervisor, through a form of group democracy that had been popularized as an alternative leadership style involving collegial decision making and shared authority. Thus, a supervisor was being sent in from the outside to take responsibility for a setting that had been independent and without a supervisor for its first year of operation. The issues and problems involved with leaderless groups or teams are described in chapter 8.

This example was presented in a supervision workshop before Betty, the new supervisor, joined the group; thus, the members were able to anticipate a number of problems and develop a strategy for dealing with them. As in all situations, the tuning in began with the supervisor, who was feeling concerned about rejection and hostility. Betty was pleased about the assignment because she felt a strong commitment to the service provided, but she was worried that she would not be accepted and would always be viewed as the "agency's person."

In the tuning-in exercise, the workshop group focused mostly on the negatives in the situation. They were skillful at anticipating the problems but did not tune in at all to the possibility that some staff members might feel pleased at the arrival of the supervisor. This is a common mistake; when I point it out in workshops, many participants admit that the problems scare them so much that they simply cannot respond to the advantages in the situation.

People's feelings, in most situations, are ambivalent. Staff members in the transition house might be worried about their freedom, concerned about being co-opted by the system, and fearful of the new supervisor's efforts to direct them. But they might also feel relieved at the end of their funding problems, pleased to be recognized as an important service, and hopeful that a new supervisor can help them with some of the difficulties of the job.

Whenever there is a leaderless team, I have found, a number of serious problems are created in the work situation, and these problems are rarely dealt with. There are complex reasons for this, but basically they stem from the difficulty peers have in confronting one another and the resultant problems of organizing cooperative efforts without a clearly recognized leadership role. In addition, although staff members can be supportive of and helpful to each other on the technical issues associated with the work (that is, in this example, the skills of working effectively with women in crisis), they need a supervisor for some forms of help that they will not provide for each other, such as making demands in difficult areas. These dynamics are discussed later in the book. The important point here is that a new supervisor should also tune in to positive feelings.

The following extract describes Betty's beginning efforts at contracting as she attempted to deal with purpose and function while opening up the issue of authority:

I began by telling the staff I was pleased to get this job. I told them I had a strong commitment to their service to women and was pleased to have the opportunity to work with them. I told them I realized they had mixed feelings about the agency takeover and my being there. I wanted to tell them my views on the matter, which I had given a great deal of thought to, and then hear some of theirs.

I told them I felt the takeover was a tribute to their efforts during the past year to establish this kind of service as meeting a real and persistent need. At least they would not have to worry about whether they are going to exist beyond the end of the month. At this point, Lill interrupted me and said, "Now we have to worry about whether we are still going to be operating in the same way at the end of the month." I asked her what she meant, and she replied that integration was a mixed blessing, and they were worried about what the agency had in mind for them. I said I could appreciate that because I realized they had had fairly free rein. I told them that, as far as I knew, there were no plans for changing the service as they had established it. I explained that I saw my function as partly being in the middle between them and the agency, and if there was anything they wanted me to communicate to the administration, I would try to do that, as well as keep them informed on what was in the works on the administration's part.

I then told them that I realized that the biggest change they had to face was my involvement and that they probably had mixed feelings about that. They had operated without a supervisor for 1½ years, had done a fine job in establishing an important new service, and now they had to take me along with the money. I was worried about their feelings at having an outsider move into this role.

Hazel spoke up and indicated they were not too happy about it at all. I asked what they were worried about, specifically. Rhoda said that most of them had been attracted to this job partly because of the kind of work it was, but, also, to get out from under authoritarian supervisors who were on power trips. I asked if they were concerned about my going on a power trip. They nodded in agreement.

I told them I was new to this setting, and so I would have to learn a lot about their work from them. I did not come in with preconceived ideas and changes in mind. I told them I did not feel I could operate effectively without their cooperation, [and so] how I planned my role would, in part, depend on our discussions. I saw my job as carrying out some of the coordinating functions, which meant I would pay attention to how they worked together to deliver this service. Whenever it seemed helpful, I would draw their attention to issues or questions that needed to be addressed to maintain its effectiveness or improve it. As I had already explained, I also saw this coordinating function in relation to the agency, for example, in making sure we get our resources or in improving communications with referring agencies. I couldn't do this work myself but, rather, would coordinate our joint efforts in these areas or others that they identified as troublesome.

They agreed that it might be helpful to have someone pay attention to these areas, because they sometimes fell between the cracks. I asked what they meant, and they described some of the administrative foul-ups with other agencies and even some of the internal communications problems.

Zoey, who had been looking most closed during the discussion, said with some force: "All of this sounds terrific, but why don't we cut the bullshit and get to the real issue? If you're the supervisor, you're the boss, and what is that going to mean?" I said I guessed we had all been trying to avoid getting to the toughest part. I knew it was the part I had lost sleep over for the past few nights. As I saw it, I was responsible to the agency for the operations of this house, and that included supervision of staff, seeing that the house conformed to general policies, and evaluating general and individual work performances. However, I was free to develop the way I carried out these jobs, and, as I had said earlier, I didn't think I could do them alone without their active involvement.

Zoey said that at least I was straight about it. I told her that I did not think power tripping was the answer and that if I did get out of line in that way, I would want to know about it. Hazel said, "Don't worry—with this group you would hear about it fast enough." She laughed, as did the rest of us, breaking the tension a bit. I continued by [telling them] that while [I was] new to the house itself, I did bring some experience to the situation that they might find helpful. Part of my job, as I saw it, was to help them strengthen their work skills. I knew they did lots of group work in the house, and I thought I could be helpful in that area by providing a sounding board for examining the dynamics of the groups and suggesting ideas about how to work with them.

I also said I thought it would be my job to try to give them some emotional support when they needed it. I realized they gave a great deal to the women and the kids and that having to deal with broken and battered families took a toll on them. I knew they helped each other during the tough times, but, as a supervisor, I would see that as my job as well. I asked them what they thought about that. There was silence for a while, and Hazel said, "I hope you're prepared for calls at 2 A.M. from the hospital emergency ward." I told them I guessed because they had to be ready for those calls, I should be too. They were quiet for a while and then began to talk about the impact of all of the brutality on them. I just listened.

Our meeting time was almost over when I asked them what they thought. Zoey said she still didn't think they needed a supervisor, but she knew they really had no choice. I said I guessed we were stuck with each other now. I asked them to give me a fair chance, because I very much wanted things to work out and realized it was not possible without their support. The meeting ended on that note.

This discussion did not resolve the issues, but it did establish a beginning working relationship. Betty won the respect of the staff members, if not their acceptance. It would be in future weeks, as she demonstrated her sense of her function and purpose, that the relationship would have a chance to deepen. A critical factor in this beginning was her honesty, as well as her direct recognition of the pain involved in carrying out this kind of work. These attributes gave the staff a glimpse of what might be available for them if they could bring themselves to trust and accept her.

AFFIRMATIVE ACTION IN PROMOTION AND HIRING: ISSUES FOR THE SUPERVISOR

Systematic efforts are under way in many human services organizations to increase the number of minority group members and women in management roles. In some cases, these efforts are designed to redress imbalances created through direct and indirect discriminatory policies that restricted access to management positions. The "glass ceiling" that prevented women and minorities from moving into significant management positions existed in human services organizations, as well as in business. In other situations, the affirmative action effort is designed to encourage and strengthen the presence of women and minority group members in positions of influence in recognition of the fact that the large majority of the clients served, particularly in public agencies, are members of these population groups. Concern over developing culturally sensitive practice and policies has also led to efforts to infuse management levels with professionals who are members of the population groups being served. Language issues are also central in many urban areas as the percentage of clients who have English as a second language grows. This has led to affirmative action hiring policies for front-line staff as well.

Most human services professionals would agree that these efforts are long overdue. However, the implementation of these policies always has a powerful impact on staff. Unfortunately, the effects of these practices are often ignored or are dealt with badly. Consider the following scenario.

> As the result of the changing racial and ethnic composition of a community, a district office of a statewide child welfare agency had an all-white staff dealing with a population that consisted of more than 60 percent Hispanic clients. A supervisory position opened up in the office, and a senior social worker, well respected by her colleagues, applied for the job but was passed over. Instead, the job was offered to a Hispanic worker from another office. The area administrator did not meet with the worker who was not chosen or with the rest of the staff to discuss the decision. The new supervisor quickly became aware of a hostile attitude toward her in the office. She heard through the grapevine that staff members were suggesting that the only reason she got the job was because of her race. She was deeply hurt by the charges. She realized that affirmative action was a factor in her selection, but she also knew she was competent and was not being given a fair chance by staff. The issue and the associated feelings stayed beneath the surface because race is one of the most taboo and painful of subjects. Her relationship with staff remained cold and distant, and her ability to exert a postive influence on their practices with Hispanic clients was negated

because race and ethnicity were never discussed. As the only Hispanic in the office, she felt increasingly isolated, lonely, and bitter.

This scenario is not uncommon. When handled this way, the affirmative action program appears to be successful because the administration can point to the increase in workers and supervisors of color. However, it is merely an illusion of success because the actual goals of the policy are not achieved. This negative scenario could have been avoided, or at least its impact could have been buffered, if the implementation of the policy had been handled differently. For example, some of the anger directed at the new supervisor was really anger at the administration for the decision and for the way it was handled. Instead of simply imposing a solution on the staff, the administrator could have met with front-line staff before the decision was made and discussed openly the concerns in relation to the racial composition of the staff group and the changing nature of the client population. By tuning in before the meeting, the administrator could have been prepared to deal with the problem directly.

Consider the following example of a similar situation in which an affirmative action program for promoting African Americans to supervisory jobs was handled differently. In this illustration, the administrator had the advantage of preparing for this meeting in a workshop. He had tuned in to the underlying issues and had even role played how he would handle the session. The administrator began by making a direct, opening statement, broaching the taboo subject directly and acknowledging its impact on staff. He also clearly defined the parameters of the discussion so as not to mislead the staff by pretending that this was a democratic process in which they had equal votes.

> I began the meeting by telling the staff that I wanted to discuss the competition that had just opened for the supervisory job created by Frank's retirement. I suspected they had a number of questions and feelings about how it would be implemented and felt it was important that we discuss them openly. One issue, I am sure, would be the agency's affirmative action program and how it would affect the decision. The office was all white, the community and our client population was becoming increasingly African American, and they all knew the policy was to make more management and front-line positions open to people of color. I wanted to be honest with them up front, because the administration was not prepared to put the policy before staff for a vote. We would have to make the final decision in this matter. I did, however, want to hear their views and to discuss how best to handle the process.
>
> Ted wanted to know if this meant the job was reserved for a person of color. I said that it was not reserved, but that given the importance of the issue, race would be a factor in the decision. If it came down to two candidates of equal ability, an African American would have an edge for the job. We would, however, not promote someone we did not feel was competent just to meet the affirmative action goals. Louise asked how important would familiarity with the office be—would someone who worked here have any

chance at all? (I knew that both Ted and Louise were close to Jane, who would be an obvious candidate for the job.) I told them that I knew of at least two staff members whom I suspect we all felt would make good supervisors. I would encourage them to apply although I wanted them to be clear about their chances up front. I also said that even if they applied and lost out on this job, that would not mean they have no chance to move up in the agency. We value their contribution and would be sure to keep them near the top of the list for other openings in which affirmative action might not be as crucial a factor in the decision. I said, "I realize the situation is a painful one for potential candidates, as well as the rest of you who would look forward to having these workers as their supervisor. I wouldn't be surprised if there was some anger at us for this policy. If so, I would rather hear it myself than have you give it to a new supervisor if we do decide to go to an outside candidate of color."

It is important that the administrator be honest with other potential candidates for the job. It is also important that the agency really mean to implement the policy in this way so that the reassurance is not artificial. The honesty in the discussion is crucial for creating trust. If the administrator tried to soft-pedal the impact of the policy, then the staff members would not believe the second part of his statement—that current workers did have a chance in this competition and could have an even better chance for future openings. The tuning in allowed the administrator to reach for both the pain and the anger and to invite their direct expression by staff. By pointing out the possibility of their projecting their anger onto a new supervisor, the administrator gave them an opportunity to deal with their feelings and to take control of them.

I asked if they wanted to comment at this point. There was silence. I waited a few moments and then recognized this was tough to talk about, and they might need to do some thinking before we could discuss it. I would check back in with them as the process proceeded to both keep them informed and give them an opportunity to keep me informed. In the meantime, I would be pleased to meet with any one of them who wanted to discuss this individually or who might want to discuss their own chances for this job. I thanked them for their time.

This conversation would not have resolved the issue. At least, however, the administrator had opened the door for discussion and had dealt with it in a straightforward manner. Staff members might still be upset about the policy, partly because of their feelings for their colleagues and partly because of their underlying racism, which may be difficult for them to admit to themselves. As products of a white, European, male-dominated culture, we have all experienced both subtle and direct forms of racism, sexism, homophobia, and so forth, which have caused us to internalize oppressive attitudes. This is one of the reasons why affirmative action policies are so important for modifying these strongly entrenched biases.

However, if these policies are not implemented well, as in the first scenario described in this section, they may further exacerbate the problem.

Regardless of whether an administrator has handled the preliminary work well, the new supervisor of color will be faced with subtle issues in the development of the working relationship. Staff will be reluctant to raise these themes directly, in part because of their fear of the authority of a new supervisor. In addition, white staff members who are aware of their own underlying attitudes and who struggle with them as part of their personal and professional development, may also be reluctant to open up any conversations related to race. As one staff member described the concern, "I'm afraid if I say anything at all, and I don't say it well, and I will be immediately jumped on for being racist. It's like walking on egg shells, so I don't say a thing."

On the side of the new supervisor, the issue is also one that is difficult to address. If one has experienced racism consistently throughout life, there is a sensitivity to its subtle expressions, as well as a vulnerability to its impact. As one supervisor put it, describing the need for self-protection, "My antenna is always up." As a result, it is not unusual for the issue to be ignored and to remain just beneath the surface, as the societal norms of behavior and the shared sense of taboo block discussion.

In the example described in the first scenario, the new Hispanic supervisor adopted the policy of ignoring the tension in hopes that the problem would eventually go away by itself. In some situations, this can happen; however, when the transition has been mishandled by the administration, as in this case, the feelings are not likely to disappear by themselves.

Ignoring the issue will not only create obstacles for effective supervision, but it may also influence the ability of workers to discuss issues of race in their practice with this supervisor. Also, the parallel process needs to be considered because the supervisor will be modeling for staff how *not* to handle cross-cultural practice. Hispanic clients may also have some feelings about dealing with white workers, who may not understand them and their culture. Given the inherent authority in the child welfare context, where a worker's perception might influence a court to remove a child from the home, issues of race and culture often remain beneath the surface. If the supervisor wishes to be helpful to staff in developing strategies for dealing openly with clients' feelings in this area, she will have to first demonstrate her own willingness to take risks.

In this example, the supervisor presented her problem in a workshop I conducted for managers in the agency. This followed a day of discussion about a number of sensitive areas, with examples presented by other supervisors. When an element of trust emerged in the workshop, the Hispanic supervisor decided to risk sharing her example because the stress of dealing with the ongoing problem was greater than was her fear of exposing herself. Workshop members were supportive; they helped her to understand the problems she faced and the source of the difficulties, as well as to strategize about how to reopen the discussion with her staff.

One incident she described took place in the staff coffee room, where she could overhear front-line workers describing problems they were having with Hispanic clients. The discussion indicated a number of negative stereotypes about Hispanics held by the workers, as well as a lack of understanding of cultural issues. She described how she finally decided to intervene to correct their misunderstandings by providing a minilecture on cultural diversity. She admitted, when asked, that she did not think they heard a word and that, in fact, her comments were met with stony silence. She and the workshop participants could quickly see how the workers would have interpreted her comments as a scolding that would intimidate them. When I asked her how she had felt as she had listened to their discussion, she revealed she had been hurt by the negative stereotypes and was actually angry at the workers. She had taken the comments personally as a reflection of their unstated feelings toward her. It was easy to see how her pain and anger emerged indirectly.

The workshop participants and I were very supportive in acknowledging her vulnerability. When I asked her what she had really felt like saying to them if she could have been spontaneous, she replied, "I want you to know that as a Hispanic myself, it is very painful for me to hear you discuss Hispanic clients in such a stereotyped manner. If I were your client, I would feel angry at your lack of understanding of my life, your lack of caring and concern. A wall would begin to build for me—just as I think we have had a wall between us since I got the job." As she spoke, her strong emotions began to emerge, and the workshop participants could feel her pain and the emotional price she was paying in making this statement.

I asked the group how they might have reacted to these comments if she had shared them in the coffee room, as compared with the intellectual lecture on multicultural practice. One participant said, "You have just gotten my attention." Another said, "I think, for the first time, I'm starting to feel what it must have been like for you in this office." A third indicated that she would be taken aback by the comments and would feel a bit guilty about how she had reacted to the new supervisor. Another worker who had been uncomfortable about the way her colleagues had discussed their Hispanic clients replied that she would have appreciated her honesty and would have been relieved. She had not had the courage to confront them herself because she was afraid she might be isolated as a result. She thought that the supervisor's comments would help her to be more honest in the future.

After a long silence at this point, I asked the supervisor what she was thinking and feeling. She said, "It's been six months like this. Can I still go back and start again?" The other supervisors encouraged her to try and provided examples from their own work of going back to deal with unfinished business. With the help of the group, the Hispanic supervisor role played an opening statement for her next staff meeting:

> I wanted to spend some time this morning discussing our relationship. I feel there was some strain right from the start because I got the job, and many of you felt it was because I was a Hispanic. I realize you were disappointed that it did not go to one of your colleagues and were angry because the whole process was handled badly. To be honest, I believed I was competent for this job, but I was deeply hurt that you felt I was given it only because of race. I hid my hurt feelings, as you tried to hide yours, only I think they are still with us and may be blocking our ability to work effectively together. I think it is time to talk.

The comments in the workshop were greeted with silence. I asked everyone to describe what might be inside of this silence. A number of reactions were shared, ranging from shock that the supervisor had been so direct in sharing her fear that it might be risky to speak out. The supervisor role played various ways she might reach inside of the silence to encourage discussion.

> I suspect you are all quite right now for different reasons. Some of you may just be shocked that I am raising this—and let me tell you it is not easy for me. Some of you may be worried that if you are honest with me, I might get angry and punish you. I realize this is a risky conversation, but I really want to clear the air, if possible, so I hope you will give me a chance.

The workshop members literally applauded the supervisor and told her that she had a lot of courage to take this issue on directly. Some offered their telephone numbers and said she could call them if she wanted to talk further. She thanked them for their support and promised to let us know at the next workshop session what had happened. I credited her for her work and pointed out that she was not alone and that she could use her supervisory peer group for help. At a later session, she reported that she had opened up the discussion and that although it had not gone exactly as we role played, nevertheless she felt that the tension in the office had lessened and that she was making some progress. Some workers were still angry and closed, but others had come to her support and made her feel less alone.

Whenever an issue of race emerges in examples such as these, I am continually impressed with the courage required by a supervisor to address the taboo subject directly. A member of a visible minority will experience racism, in some form, almost every day. Emotional survival may depend on developing a tough exterior and protecting oneself against the pain associated with vulnerability. All supervisors take some risks when they expose their vulnerability to their staff. For a person of color, dealing with race introduces singular and powerful factors that require a support system—from administrators or colleagues—to help make the true goals of affirmative action a reality, not just a statistic. Later chapters will explore how a supervisor can help a new front-line worker of color to become integrated more effectively into a white staff group and how a significant impact on ethnic-sensitive practice can be achieved.

SUPERVISORY BEGINNINGS WITH NEW WORKERS

Another type of beginning is necessary when the supervisor is already established in a system and the staff member is new. Supervisory skills in the preliminary and beginning phases are examined in four different situations in this section. The first involves beginning work with a new and inexperienced worker. In the second situation, the new worker has had some prior experience. In the third, the worker is new to the field but has just completed professional training and wants everyone to realize just how "professional" he really is. The fourth is an example of beginning with a student placed for a practicum experience by a school of social work.

The Inexperienced New Worker

In some settings, it is not unusual for a staff member to begin to fill a position with little or no prior experience. This lack of experience can accent the difficulties in adjustment, which, in turn, can significantly delay effective integration into the service. New workers in child welfare settings, for example, have described a beginning at an agency at which they were given an orientation to policies, procedures, and forms that left them completely overwhelmed and bewildered. This was followed by a traumatic entry into the system in which a harried supervisor merely handed them files of cases to be seen. Often, there was little preparation. If there was discussion, it was usually on case management issues and rarely on practice skill questions (such as how to handle the first contact with a client). Little attention, if any, was paid to the reactions and feelings of the worker. Workers have described how they ended their first day on the job in a daze, close to tears, or ready to quit—or all three.

Although this is admittedly an extreme example, some elements of it are often part of the beginning process. One of the serious implications of such a beginning is what it says to a new social worker about the way in which new relationships are handled in the agency. This can have an impact on the worker's future practice with clients. In many ways, the worker's beginning at the agency offers an excellent teaching opportunity to make the worker sensitive to the parallel relationship with a client.

Although the beginnings described in this section are often expressed in terms of workers and agencies, many of the ideas are applicable to assisting new employees to become integrated into any system in the helping professions. And though they are expressed in terms of new, inexperienced workers, they are applicable to all new workers, regardless of their experience.

Beginning Phase for Inexperienced Workers

In the supervision model illustrated in Figure 2.2, the worker is viewed as interacting with a number of significant systems, and the supervisor is seen as mediating these interactions. In the beginning phase of the supervision process with a new social worker, for example, the key areas for attention are the agency and its policies and procedures, including personnel practices and physical facilities; the staff unit or department in which the worker will do most of his or her work; the larger staff system that relates to this unit; the supervisor; and the client or receiver of services. It is easy to see how a new worker can feel anxious and uncertain about so many unknowns. An established supervisor can forget just how complicated and confusing the system must appear at the beginning.

This is especially true when early efforts at orienting new workers consist of providing a deluge of information that is impossible to integrate, particularly when they have other concerns about the job. A two-week orientation that attempts to teach the whole policy manual to a worker who has no idea how to use the information, for example, will usually engender more anxiety than it relieves.

With a little advance planning, the supervisor should be able to segment the problem of beginning into its component pieces and to help new workers tackle each one, a step at a time. In relation to the agency, going over personnel questions such as payroll procedures and benefits can answer some urgent personal questions. Location is also important; having a desk ready provides some reassurance that the supervisor has thought about making the worker comfortable. If the supervisor simply is free on the first morning to take the new worker around, introduce colleagues, and point out key spots such as the cafeteria or local eating places, this helps to begin the orientation process. In each case, the supervisor should resist the temptation to tell new workers everything they need to know for the entire first year and should concentrate instead on helping them get through the first day and the first week.

Orientation to agency policies and procedures should be designed to make workers aware of the availability of manuals and how to use them, rather than expecting workers to memorize their contents. A supervisor who watches the eyes of a new worker during orientation quickly notices when the worker has had enough. Simply acknowledging that there is a lot to learn but that it does not have to be learned all at once can help a great deal.

In addition to such orientation, a worker who is new to the area may have a number of important personal questions about housing, schools for children, and so on for which the supervisor can suggest answers or sources of help. The more quickly new workers get settled in their personal lives, the faster they will have the energy available to make the necessary adaptation to the agency.

Orientation to the staff group is also important on the first day. Workers have reported the sinking feeling they experienced on their first day at work as noon approached and they did not know if they should go to lunch on their own, wait for someone to ask them to join them, or initiate a contact themselves. Some thoughtfulness on such simple matters can be helpful. The supervisor can appreciate the importance of the way in which a worker begins with the peer group if the staff group is considered as an informal, as well as a formal, system. The informal system (which is described in more detail in chapter 8) is characterized by a well-developed set of rules of behavior, certain commonly accepted norms, taboo subject areas that members agree not to discuss, and subgroups. In many ways, the operation of the informal system can have a more powerful effect on the effectiveness of services than can the formal, recognized system. In the beginning phase, a new worker is making a start at becoming integrated into this informal system.

Schwartz (1961) described the anxieties about beginning a new relationship as part of the authority theme. He used the term *intimacy theme* to refer to the dynamics that take place between members of a peer group (this theme is explored in some detail in later chapters). A supervisor who is conscious of this aspect of the beginning process may help to ease this integration. Sometimes this can be accomplished by calling attention to the arrival of a new staff member and asking the staff group to take some responsibility for the beginning phase. A simple question such as, "Any ideas on how we can make it comfortable for Frank on his first day here?" can set the process in motion.

The smaller staff unit is usually set within the context of a larger system (for example, the hospital ward in relation to the hospital or the unmarried parents' department in relation to the child welfare agency). Because it is not possible to provide services to clients within the smaller unit without considering relationships with staff in the larger system, it is helpful in the beginning phase if the supervisor identifies key individuals in related systems and helps the new worker make the initial contacts. The first weeks might involve learning about the system, the people in it who help make it work, and some of the formal and informal ways it operates. This information should be shared in manageable doses, and it should be related to the worker's current tasks.

In some settings, the new worker may have to take some time to learn about the community in which the work takes place. A new child care worker who visits the local school attended by the children in a group care home can make personal contacts that will be invaluable later. A community health nurse who stops in to meet the staff at a family services agency may be able to make more effective referrals as they become necessary.

Attendance at an interprofessional committee meeting can attach a face to a name that will become important when service is delivered. Although the specifics of this aspect of orientation differ according to the setting and the helping professional's role, the general idea of orientation to the larger system within which the working system is set is important in any beginning.

The process of orienting the new worker to the supervisor was described in the section on contracting skills. As soon as possible, time should be set aside for a discussion of the purpose of supervision and the role of the supervisor. This provides an opportunity for the supervisor to answer questions, as well as to explore how the worker is feeling about the beginning. Simply acknowledging the strain of so much new information in such a short time means a great deal to the new worker. In addition, the supervisor can open up the question of client contact and can recognize the worker's probable concerns about being thrown into first interviews without some preparation. A discussion of the possible early caseload might help, and any efforts to reduce the pressure would be reassuring.

Helping a new worker prepare for work with clients is one of the educational functions of supervision (see chapter 6), but some consideration of questions and concerns in this area is important in the beginning. In a hospital setting, for example, it is reassuring to let a new nurse know that the supervisor will provide some direct help with patients for the first few days. In the social work or counseling setting, supervisors might invite new workers to sit in on their own interviews as observers in order to get some ideas on how to begin. Workers usually appreciate the willingness of supervisors to share their work in this way. The workers not only get a chance to begin to relate with clients without the pressure of responsibility, but they also can observe the supervisors' own style of work.

Integrating New Staff Members

The techniques for helping new social workers begin can be applied by supervisors to ease the integration of new staff members in all the helping professions. Admittedly, devoting so much attention to this phase does take time; also it must be recognized that there are pressures facing both new staff members and supervisors. Sometimes supervisors have to carry workers' caseloads or perform staff services in addition to their own responsibilities for months while awaiting the arrival of new staff members. By the time a new employee arrives, the supervisor is under great pressure, both to put the worker to work quickly and to deal with his or her own piled-up tasks. This presents the question of how to attempt to influence policy on the handling of short-term vacancies and orientation procedures for new staff. (Providing feedback on the implications of policy for practice is discussed in chapter 6.)

Although the time available for effective beginning work may be affected by factors beyond the supervisor's control, being conscious of the possibilities can help many supervisors provide more effective orientations for their staffs. Supervisors often orient beginners in precisely the same way that they themselves were oriented, even though they know that the process did not meet their own needs. Time spent in a more careful orientation process can save time later because the new member will be able to move more quickly into the staff system. In the beginning phase, as in all the others, good practice saves time in the long run. Overlooked key issues always come back to haunt the supervisor.

A supervisor may be able to tap the resources of the staff group to provide much of the help described in this section. Experienced staff members often are glad to help with the orientation of new members if they are asked, and they may appreciate recognition of their abilities. An office manager or ward clerk also can provide some important information needed by new employees. Asking the staff to reflect on their own beginnings at the setting and then to share in developing an effective orientation program for new staff members might help distribute the labor. Even more important, it could make the orientation process more effective.

The Experienced New Worker

When new staff members are experienced, there are some particular variations in the orientation process. Experienced staff members may have even more concerns about beginning a new job than may those who are inexperienced. If their past encounters with supervisors have been unsatisfactory, they may have a stereotyped idea of supervision that is not helpful.

New staff members may also be concerned that the skills and understandings they have acquired in their previous jobs may not be relevant in the new setting. The normal questions of competency are intensified as they prepare to test themselves in a new context. Adding to the stress may be concerns about what will be expected of them because of their experience. They may feel more reluctant to ask for help or to reveal their ignorance because they believe they are supposed to understand already.

Two examples of this kind of relationship are given here. In the first example, a nursing supervisor for an emergency unit was engaged in dialogue with a new nurse. The supervisor attempted to develop the proper balance between recognizing the nurse's prior experience, while allowing her to feel free to be a learner:

> Supervisor: First of all, welcome to the unit. I want to tell you about the unit and about how we work around here. But before that, I want to find out a bit more about your prior work experience. I realize you have had four years on a general ward, and I'm really pleased to get someone with that kind of background. At the same time, you probably have a lot of questions about how to fit in on emergency, how it will be the same, and what will be different. Maybe we can start there.

Nurse: Actually, I was kind of worried about that. You know I took training on emergency, but that was a long time ago. I'm sure things have changed now. I wasn't even sure I wanted emergency, but as you know, that was the only opening.

Supervisor: It's always a lot easier if you can find a place in a service you're already comfortable with. Also, there are a lot of advantages for us to have an experienced emergency room nurse. However, up here in the boon-docks you don't have any other hospitals to choose from, and we don't get applicants with exactly the experience we want. We're really pleased to have gotten you, though. What are some of the things you're worried about?

Nurse: Things can happen fast on emergency—maybe too fast for someone learning on the job.

Supervisor: I'm not going to expect you to be able to handle situations on your own for a while. Until you feel more comfortable, you will work along with me or another nurse on serious situations. On the other hand, you have a lot of experience that will be helpful, so you should be able to pick up independently on much of the routine stuff. I will make a point of checking with you as we go along, and when you feel OK about handling something, just do it. If you're not sure, or I'm not sure, then we will do it together. The important thing is that I don't expect you to simply jump in and act like you have worked here for years. How does that sound?

Nurse: That's a relief. You know, I was really scared about reporting this morning. It felt just like my first day on a ward back at nursing school.

Supervisor: Let me show you around and introduce you to the other staff. That will help you feel a little more at home.

The second example concerns an experienced social worker who joins a community mental health team after having worked for years on a similar team in another part of town. In this case, the worker was less concerned about the setting and the job than about the type of supervision he would be receiving. Close supervision of practice skill development is important in the early years of practice, but workers with substantial experience are usually ready to take a more active responsibility for setting the continued learning agenda. They need a supervisor who can serve as a practice consultant; the supervisor should recognize this and should avoid relating to these workers as if they were inexperienced. In the following report, the supervisor described how she tuned into this issue and raised it directly.

I told Frank I thought we were particularly lucky to have gotten him on staff. I said I was looking forward to working with him and thought it would help if we discussed our relationship. I explained that I was responsible for monitoring his cases with him and also wanted to provide whatever help I could on the tough ones. [But] I felt he was experienced enough to work independently and have a say in which areas I might need to become involved. I saw myself somewhat as a practice consultant for him, with him taking responsibility for developing his own agenda and deciding how best to use me. I asked him how that sounded to him.

Frank smiled and told me he was glad to hear what I had just said. He had been concerned about that, having changed jobs from one in which he did have a good deal of professional autonomy and independence. I asked if he had worried that I might not recognize that. He replied that he had been somewhat concerned about what my approach would be. He described other supervisors he had known who seemed to feel that a worker never got past the dependent stage. He felt this was a serious problem in social work, which has a strong tradition of smothering workers.

I laughed and told him I knew what he meant, having experienced some of that in my own early practice. I said we would have to develop a balance between my being involved and knowing what is going on and, at the same time, giving him some freedom of action. Most important, I wanted him to feel free to use any help I might be able to give, even if I acted only as a sounding board for his own thinking. I might like to use him in a similar way. He agreed it would be helpful to talk with someone about the practice.

The Abrasive New Worker

In a supervisors' workshop, Jim, a supervisor in a child welfare agency in a rural area, described a first conference with a new worker who had just graduated from a professional program in social work. Most of the staff, including Jim, had not had professional training. In the midst of the conference, the new worker asked whether he would be able to use his professional training in that agency. He said he had really enjoyed the "reality therapy" approach, combined with an "ecological view" of the client and the relevant systems. Jim said he felt like telling the worker that a few weeks in the agency would be a real "reality therapy" for him, and what he really wanted to suggest was what the worker could do with his ecological approach.

Others in the workshop shared incidents in which graduates of professional schools had immediately attacked the agency on the first day of work. One supervisor described how a new worker made it clear that he thought the government-run agency was simply a "tool of the oppressor class" and that the social workers were being used to "suppress dissent."

These incidents precipitated a more general attack on professional training by the workshop group members, who said that they thought it often was far removed from the realities of the field. These supervisors, and others I have worked with in related fields such as nursing, education, and counseling, have strong feelings about professional training programs that seem to turn new graduates into "agency haters." That they have some valid arguments is evident in the literature of the profession, much of which attacks helping systems without appreciating their strengths, as well as their weaknesses. Because agency staff supervisors often judge their own services harshly, these attacks are felt even more strongly.

In the workshop, I pointed out that when recent graduates articulate highly theoretical positions or arguments that tend to denigrate the services of the agency, they put the supervisor on the defensive, and this often leads to an initial battle of wills. Jim, the supervisor with the new worker who wanted to combine reality therapy and an ecological approach, said he had expressed his anger by letting the worker know in no uncertain terms that they did not operate with fancy theories in that agency; although that might have been all right at school, here he would have to deal with reality. This led Jim and the worker to undertake an hour-long argument on the questions of the relation between theory and practice, the professionalism of the agency, and the freedom of action available to workers. It became clear that the supervisor felt put on the spot by such a staff member, and he responded angrily and defensively. Because Jim also had worked up through the ranks and lacked professional training, it was little wonder that the new worker was able to nettle him so quickly.

Similar examples were presented by nursing supervisors who had new staff members who wanted to institute a "team nursing approach" on their second day at the hospital and by residential treatment home supervisors who had encountered recent graduates who claimed to have found "the answer" in their training—behavior modification, reality therapy, or remotivation theory, for example—and were prepared to educate the rest of the staff at the first staff meeting they attended. In part, this represents a natural desire for recent graduates to apply in practice the theories they have learned in school. It is also helpful to think that the worker's pattern of behavior may be a form of indirect communication to the supervisor. Such "deviant" (that is, departing from the group norm) beginnings may be a signal of the new worker's concerns about his or her own effectiveness in the system but may raise the concerns in such a manner that makes it difficult for them to be understood. When the supervisor's own feelings of anger and defensiveness are so strong, it is difficult to understand the staff member's behavior as a call for help. A parallel exists in practice; clients feeling pressure from the agency often handle their anxiety about the new contact by appearing hostile and defensive. A worker who responds only to the anger will often miss the clients' concerns that lie just below the surface.

In the case described earlier, if Jim had understood how such "deviant" communications from the new worker might be such a signal, then instead of responding quickly with an angry remark, the conversation might have gone like this:

> New worker: I really enjoyed using reality therapy and an ecological approach in working with my clients in my previous job.
> Supervisor (Jim): Sounds like you developed some ideas about what you can do with clients, and you feel comfortable with them. Are you worried that you won't be able to use what you know in this setting, that is, that the demands will be so much different?

There is at least a chance that the conversation might have taken a different turn had the supervisor understood and reached further for the worker's concerns. It is not unusual for students graduating from a professional school to be anxious about their ability to put theory into practice. New workers who sound extremely sure of themselves may actually be sending a signal of opposite feelings. Supervisory skill involves taking time to find out what the workers are really saying before responding. (This skill is described in chapter 4 as sessional contracting.)

Many new workers have misconceptions about the services, fear becoming stereotyped social workers, or worry about being co-opted by the system. They may even be anxious about all three. An abrasive new worker who is critical of the agency may simply be expressing the same concerns felt by all new workers fresh out of school but may be doing it in a way that makes it hard for the supervisor to understand. Because the worker will be facing many clients who handle their anxiety in new situations in precisely the same manner, it is important for the supervisor to model an effective response that reaches behind the facade for the real feelings.

The Student as New Worker

For social work students placed in a field practicum experience, the receptivity of the setting can be a particular problem. A decision to accept a student is sometimes reached between an administrator and the school, with only a superficial involvement of agency staff. If the situation has not been handled well by the supervisor, the student may not be received favorably by the staff and, in fact, may be frozen out of the system. The signals of such a rejection are often subtle. A common one is that repeated requests by the student's supervisor for appropriate referrals to the student's caseload result in many promises but no cases. The problem is often rooted in the fact that the staff agreed to accept the student without openly expressing their reservations.

A student must be seen as the responsibility of the whole staff, not the exclusive problem of the agency supervisor. Thus, a supervisor anticipating this relationship would be wise to explore the feelings of other staff members in some detail before agreeing to accept a student. In the following report, Susan, an agency field instructor for a social work student, described the staff meeting at which she raised the possibility of taking a student for the first time:

> After I had explained what would be involved if we took a student, I asked if there were any questions. Lou asked me if I thought I would have enough time for a student on top of everything else. I said I thought I could fit it into my schedule. There was a brief silence, and then someone suggested that there didn't seem to be a problem and that we should move on to the next item on the agenda.

There was a problem, but it was lurking just beneath the surface, and the prospective student supervisor did not want to reach for it. In a workshop for school field instructors, she admitted that she had sensed the lack of enthusiasm, but she felt that it would change after the student had arrived. It did not, and that was why she was raising the problem. The student was an outsider at the agency, no referrals had been made, and Susan did not know what to do about it.

The problem really began in that silence when she sensed their ambivalence but did not address it. She could have said something like this: "You all don't seem that enthusiastic about the idea of a student, and because I am going to need your help if we decide to take one, maybe we should have your doubts out in the open." Schwartz (personal communication, April 1975) described this skill as "looking for trouble when everything is going your way."

This skill is important because people often have difficulty talking to each other directly about controversial areas. It is easier to hold back negative comments than to risk disagreeing with a colleague. (This issue is dealt with in relation to the culture of the staff group in chapter 8.) Because of this general tendency to withhold honest communications, Susan needed to give permission to her colleagues to open up so that they would say what they really felt rather than what they thought she wanted them to say. Otherwise, the negative feelings beneath the surface would be more powerful in their effect on the student than would those that were brought out into the open. By inviting honest discussion, she could genuinely involve the staff in weighing the pros and cons of having a student at the agency. If they then agreed to the placement, it would be their student and not just the supervisor's responsibility.

Schwartz (1968) noted this dynamic of the illusion of work in his experience with supervisors, many of whose presentations, he said, illustrated

> the problem of the "false consensus," in which staff workers agree on a course of action, only to fail repeatedly to implement it. Here the supervisor's frustration is borne of the fact that he can raise neither disagreement nor compliance, but only acceptance of the logic of the official position and an implacable inability to do anything about it. In most of the meetings reported—on instituting new forms, keeping dictation up to date, carrying out new service decisions and others— it was not open, or even conscious, defiance that held up the action. Rather, it was a kind of blind passivity that muffled the feelings and immobilized the energy either for or against the move. What had happened was that the "rightness" of the decision had been so incontrovertibly established—by both supervisor and workers—that one would require great courage to mention any of the lurking negatives, even though they were there, and would thereafter proceed to work underground. In this climate, the staff had made what we came to call a "New Year's resolution," in which the will is registered, but the work necessary to make it function has been left out. (p. 359)

The task for the supervisor is to reach past this artificial agreement and to make a demand that the conversation be real. When Susan returned to the agency, she opened up the issue directly with the staff in the following manner:

> I told the staff that I had sensed some resistance toward having the student. I quickly pointed out that I thought it had been there right from the beginning but that I had been so anxious to get a student that I had ignored it. I didn't think it was too late to talk about it, even though I had pushed ahead, and I wanted to hear their real feelings on the matter.
>
> There was a silence, and then Lou began by saying he had wondered if they were in good enough shape as a unit to carry a student. He then went on to describe some of the problems we were experiencing, because we were only recently formed, and made a case for us needing to straighten out our own work before we taught others.
>
> This opened up a flood of comments, and it became clear that I had missed a lot of negatives. We discussed some of the pros and cons of having a student. I had to resist the temptation to jump in all the time with "yes, buts . . ." As the conversation continued, I was surprised to find other staff arguing the positive aspects of a student's involvement—bringing in new ideas from the university and a fresh perspective on practice, asking questions that forced them to think more clearly about our work, and so on. June pointed out that we all have a responsibility to train new workers, just as we had been taken on by agencies for our training.
>
> After the discussion had proceeded for a period, I asked them where we stood now. I realized it was rather late, but if they felt it really wasn't go for this year, maybe I should raise the question at the school and we could consider a transfer. I would be disappointed, but that was a reality. Lou thought that we could handle the situation this year but that we should evaluate it at the end of the year before we decided about going ahead again. I laughed and said, "Don't worry, I won't make that mistake again."
>
> I then told them that if we were going to keep the student, I wanted her to be their student as well. I would need their help in thinking about her program, I would need referrals, and I would need their active involvement. They nodded their heads in agreement, and we discussed the specifics of how we could proceed.

Susan reported a marked change in attitudes toward the student after the meeting. She said that she had initially not really wanted them to discuss having a student because she had been afraid they would say no. She now realized how important it was to negotiate the contract with the staff system, as well as with the student, so that the acceptance of a student was a real one. To do this, the hidden negative and ambivalent feelings had to be honestly explored, or they would trouble both her and the student throughout the year.

RESEARCH FINDINGS

The ability of supervisors to put themselves in the shoes of workers and to develop a preliminary empathy with them is an important skill in the first

...s of supervision. By developing this sensitivity to the indirect cues of the worker, the supervisor is better able to respond directly to indirect cues. In the studies of the author and colleagues (Schulman, 1982, 1991; Shulman, Robinson, & Luckyj, 1981), there was no way to determine the supervisor's use of the tuning-in skill, but it was possible to measure a skill that should be enhanced by tuning in: the skill of putting the worker's feelings into words. The item on the workers' questionnaire designed to measure this skill was worded as follows: "My supervisor can sense my feelings without my having to put them into words." In my 1991 study, the worker could select a response from among the following: (1) "strongly agree," (2) "agree," (3) "uncertain," (4) "disagree," and (5) "strongly disagree." The same response categories were used to measure most of the skill items.

A number of workers in my 1982 study identified the importance of this skill with comments such as, "It is important that the qualities of empathy for both client and worker are in a supervisor." Other workers commented on their supervisors' lack of being tuned in, for example, "Many times I have the feeling that my supervisor is not really interested in what I have to say—is preoccupied."

In the 1991 study, 40 percent of the managers strongly agreed or agreed that their supervisors were able to put their feelings into words—whereas only 21 percent of the supervisors agreed (none strongly) that their supervisors demonstrated that same skill. As for workers, only 4 percent strongly agreed and 22.5 percent agreed that supervisors articulated their feelings for them. All three levels of administration scored lower on the use of this skill than did their workers when rated by their clients. This may be a reflection of the confusion cited earlier in this chapter over the appropriate place of the empathic skills in supervision and the concern over not "social working" the staff.

When correlations between the use of this skill by front-line supervisors and supervisory outcomes were examined in the 1991 study, a pattern of significant positive associations emerged. These included positive correlations with the social worker's perception of rapport with the supervisor ($r = .79$) and trust ($r = .75$). In addition, a positive association with the social worker's morale ($r = .49$) and perception of availability of peer group support ($r = .44$) was noted. The strong associations between the use of this skill and rapport and trust were also found when the manager–supervisor level of interaction was examined.

SUMMARY

In the preliminary and beginning phases of supervisory work in the helping professions, preparatory empathy (tuning in) can help a supervisor to enter a new system, as well as to integrate a new worker into the system. The contracting skills help the supervisor clarify the purpose of supervision and his or her sense of function, reach for feedback from staff members, and deal with issues arising from authority.

New supervisors face particular problems in moving from practitioner to supervisor within an agency or in being brought in from outside the system to deal with staff problems. Other problems are involved in integrating new workers into a setting, including inexperienced workers, experienced workers, abrasive workers, and students in a field practicum.

The next chapter examines the work phase in supervision; it combines a skills model of the work phase with examples of problems common in this phase.

CHAPTER 4

WORK-PHASE SKILLS IN SUPERVISION

The middle, or work phase, of supervision can be even more difficult than the beginning phase. One reason is that concern over beginning a new relationship directs the supervisor's attention to the supervision process. As the working relationship settles down during the work phase, it is easier to take the process for granted and to direct less energy and attention toward thinking about supervision. Routine aspects of the work are handled superficially, as indeed they must be in some cases. Existing problems may not be recognized precisely because of the supervisor's tendency to be lulled by the commonplace activity of the work phase.

In addition, as other priorities call for the supervisor's attention, the temptation to ignore the more subtle cues of supervision problems is increased. A lower performance level by a staff member could signal a serious personal problem, but it may not be low enough to attract the attention of the supervisor or indicate the need for dealing with it. The policy of leaving it alone and hoping it will go away is tempting to supervisors who have to deal with the many other demands of their jobs. It is not uncommon for a supervisor to avoid confronting a difficult staff member, particularly one who is not too much of a problem, and then have to raise troublesome issues for the first time during a formal evaluation conference (see chapter 7).

Another problem complicating the work phase of supervision is that staff members often express their concerns in indirect ways; thus, it is hard for supervisors to know what really may be troubling them. The illusion of work described in the preceding chapter can cause staff members and supervisors to ignore serious problems, while maintaining the misleading perception that the work is proceeding well when they encounter one another during individual conferences and staff meetings. The combination of indirect communications and the ability of staff and supervisor to

Figure 4.1
Model of the Work Phase of Supervision

Sessional tuning-in skills

Sessional contracting skills

Elaborating skills

Empathic skills

Skills in sharing own feelings

Skills in making a demand for work

Skills in pointing out obstacles

Skills in sharing data

Sessional ending skills

tolerate the illusion in place of real work can frustrate the growth and movement needed in any supervisory situation.

As an aid to solving these problems, this chapter examines the special dynamics of the work phase. A model of communication, relationship, and problem-solving skills for the work phase of supervision is described. Examples drawn from supervision practice of how the various skills can be applied in common work-phase problem situations are then presented. The dynamics of the problems are explicated, and the application (or nonapplication) of appropriate skills is discussed in each case.

WORK-PHASE MODEL

The skills of the work phase in supervision described in this chapter have been grouped into general categories called *skill factors*. Each skill factor consists of a set of closely related behaviors in which the common element is the general intent of the supervisor using the skill. In the model of the work phase of supervision (Figure 4.1), all behaviors associated with the supervisor's efforts to deal with the worker's affect, or emotional responses, for example, are grouped in *empathic skills*.

The skill factors in this work-phase model include adaptations of the tuning-in and contracting skills from the preliminary and beginning phases described in chapter 3, as well as the ending skills described in chapter 5. Because these skills are associated with single sessions during which much of the work of supervision proceeds, they are described as *sessional skills*. The other supervisory skill factors listed in the model give the supervisor a framework for dealing with day-to-day problems in staff supervision. An overview of the process follows, and then each element is examined in more detail.

Staff members often raise their concerns, particularly those in taboo areas, in indirect ways. They may raise an issue in a factual manner, for example, even though they are experiencing very strong associated feelings. An example might concern a worker discussing a child welfare case in which the worker has just found out that a child placed in a foster home has been seriously abused. The facts of the case may be presented while the worker's associated feelings are withheld. Before an individual conference or team meeting, the supervisor considers, or tunes in to, potential themes that may emerge during the work. This involves sessional tuning in to develop a preliminary empathy with the staff's concerns and feelings in preparation for indirect communication of the issues. The supervisor also develops strategies for responding directly to the indirect cues.

At the start of each session, one of the supervisor's central tasks is to determine the concerns of the staff members. Sessional contracting skills are used to clarify the immediate work at hand. For many conferences or staff meetings, the supervisor prepares an agenda in advance. Sessional contracting requires that the supervisor not move too quickly into the set agenda before determining the staff member's sense of urgency. The supervisor should also refrain from proposing a solution for the problem before it has been completely understood from all points of view. In effect, the supervisor does not answer the worker's question until she or he knows what the question is. The work-phase skills of elaboration and empathy are helpful in this stage to encourage staff members to explore their concerns. In the child welfare example mentioned earlier, the supervisor might immediately inquire about how the worker is feeling before moving into the details of what to do about the case.

When the sessional contract has been tentatively identified, other skills facilitate the supervisory work of the session. Important in achieving results is the supervisor's use of empathic skills and readiness to share his or her own feelings spontaneously. For instance, a supervisor who experiences some feelings about a traumatic event such as abuse of a child in foster care should be prepared to share her or his own reactions.

As the work progresses, it is not unusual to encounter some resistance from staff members, who often are of two minds about proceeding in difficult areas of work. In part, they want to enter the taboo areas, while at the same time, they want to pull back. Evidence of this ambivalence often emerges just as the session starts to go well. It can be seen in the staff's evasive reactions (for example, jumping from one issue to another), defensiveness, expressions of hopelessness, or other forms. For the child welfare worker, the supervisor's inquiries may touch a painful place and may cause the worker to change the subject and return the focus to the case. Resistance is both normal and to be expected. It can be a sign that the work is going well. The supervisor must have the ability to read this resistance and to make a demand for work that will help the worker take the important next steps. If the supervisor joins in the evasion of work, because the issue has strong emotional impact on him or her, then the worker receives the message that the supervisor is also reluctant to face the worker's pain.

Throughout the work phase, obstacles may emerge to frustrate the staff's efforts. Staff's reactions to the demands of the supervisor, for example, can generate negative feelings that affect the working relationship. As the supervisor and the staff members deal with the task facing them, reactions to the process (the way in which they approach the task) may become important. The supervisor must be able to point out obstacles such as the authority theme and must be prepared to discuss them openly.

The staff members must have access to the supervisor's "relevant data"—facts, beliefs, and values, as well as information on policies and practices. Sharing such knowledge and judgments is an important part of the supervision process, and how it is shared can have far-reaching effects on its usefulness to the staff.

The dynamics of ending a session must also be considered by the supervisor. Issues that may have been only hinted at during a session can emerge when the staff is about to leave the office. Attention must also be paid to the transitions involved in each ending. If, for example, an agreement has been reached at the end of a team meeting to undertake a course of action, then it must be established who will implement the next steps.

Although this complex model of the work phase of supervision has been discussed in terms of formal individual conferences and group staff meetings, the same skills can be applied in brief contacts, informal talks, and hallway meetings between supervisors and staff members. The description has been oversimplified, of course; the work session seldom proceeds simply or directly from skill factor to skill factor, and the factors are not mutually exclusive. During sessional contracting, for example, the supervisor will often use both the empathic and elaborating skills, as noted earlier.

Sessional Tuning-in Skills

The principles of tuning in during the preliminary phase of supervision described in chapter 3 are equally applicable to every session or encounter with the staff. In sessional tuning in, the supervisor anticipates concerns and feelings of the staff that may emerge during the session, as well as his or her own feelings about the encounter that could affect the work.

Consider, for instance, the problems supervisors face in reporting unpopular policy decisions to their workers (see Part V). Supervisors, feeling caught in the middle between their staffs and the administration, often dread such a session. As a result, they place the crucial issue at the end of the agenda so that there will be little time available for discussion or adverse reactions. This is a mistake because the staff's real reactions and feelings will emerge later in indirect forms such as absenteeism, apathy, or less commitment to work.

Instead of avoiding the problem, the supervisor should concentrate on the particular meaning the decision will have for the staff. One way is to tune in not only to the staff's probable anger at the policy but also to the underlying feelings staff members often have but do not always express. They may feel that the administration does not appreciate them or understand their problems. In one hospital, for example, staff shortages and the opening of a new wing meant that some of the most experienced nurses were going to have to take weekend supervisory shifts, which they had not had to do for some 18 months. In the opinion of these nurses, going back to weekend shift work represented a drop in hard-won status, and they felt less valued. In addition, the changes involved major complications in their family situations. But by tuning in to these reasons for their anger, the supervisor was able to help the staff discuss the effects of the change on them, the reality of the situation that necessitated the change, and the measures they might take to minimize its impact.

Although this discussion by itself would have been helpful, the supervisor also tuned in to another key issue, one that could have gone unnoticed. The change also meant that these nursing supervisors would have to master some unfamiliar, difficult practices, and they would be called on to learn and demonstrate new techniques. Therefore, they also felt professionally threatened. Through her tuning-in preparation, the supervisor was able to anticipate this reaction. The ensuing discussion helped the nurses by letting them discover that they were not alone and that others were in the same predicament. The staff group then discussed training that would help the nurses feel more comfortable with these new demands.

The staff's perceived need to maintain a professional image often causes them to mask fears about new procedures by expressing strong feelings about other real, but relatively less important, issues. Social workers in a child welfare agency, for example, expressed strong objections to being asked to approach parents of teenage children who had been taken into care about their ability to make support payments. They raised a number of ethical objections and insisted that this would turn them into collection agents, and it would turn natural parents away from the children and the agency. Although there was an element of truth to these objections, the agency's position that maintaining a reasonable financial involvement was an important way of keeping parents connected to their children was also valid. When supervisors reached past the initial objections, they found that some workers were embarrassed and concerned about how to handle the interview with the parents. Money is often a taboo subject in our society, and staff members needed help in dealing with their own feelings about the interview. Once this help was given and a number of interviews had been attempted, staff members were more inclined to accept the new procedure. Their fears would never have been discussed in a staff meeting if the supervisor had not tuned in.

In both the nursing and child welfare examples, the first step was for the supervisors to tune in to their own mixed feelings about the policy in question and the effects it would have on their efforts to help their staffs. It soon became clear that because they had many of the same feelings that their staff members did, they could easily identify with the staff's opposition to the administration and the policy. This identification might have prevented them from dealing with key staff issues, but their tuning-in skills made their affective identification with the staff an important tool rather than a potentially serious impediment to their effectiveness.

In addition to tuning in to specific reactions to events, a supervisor can use the skill to understand a staff member's pattern of behavior. For example, supervisors often report workers who appear to be suffering from *burnout*, a term in the professional language referring to the worker's development of apathy, among other symptoms, as a response to excessive stress and limited sources of support. Burnout may result, for example, when a worker feels ineffective with a range of clients and, in particular, with a specific current client. A supervisor who can tune in to this reason for burnout can seek the particular causes of the syndrome. The supervisor might identify the current tough cases, try to help the worker see them in a new way, and then develop a next step to be taken. As in all cases, the first step is for the supervisor to tune in to his or her own feelings, which often mirror the feelings of the worker.

Tuning in can also help a supervisor deal with the staff's reaction to a specific traumatic event. For example, a social worker in a psychiatric setting had a strong emotional reaction to the suicide of a patient for whom she had carried major responsibility. By tuning in to the worker's feelings, the supervisor was able to help her deal with her sense of guilt and gain a clearer perspective on the situation. The supervisor also tuned in to the impact of the suicide on herself and on other staff members as well. (The issue of helping staff cope with a trauma is discussed in chapter 9.) Although such discussions usually do not resolve these feelings, because the effects of such traumatic events are long lasting, at least this social worker could talk to someone who understood what she was going through. In addition, specific help was provided on how to manage the impact of trauma.

Sessional Contracting Skills

Sessional contracting differs from contracting in the beginning phase, as described in chapter 3, in that it identifies the specific agenda for the immediate encounter, individual conference, or group meeting. In its simplest form, the supervisor uses the beginning of the session to introduce the agenda items he or she proposes, while inquiring what the staff would like to discuss. By leaving some room at the beginning of each formal session for this agenda-setting operation, the supervisor allows the staff to. place urgent questions on the table. The mere act of paying attention to these concerns sends a message to staff members that the time belongs to them as well.

Allowing staff members to voice their concerns at the beginning of the session has the added value of freeing them to invest themselves in the total agenda. A worker at a staff meeting who is obsessed by certain issues or anxieties is unlikely to hear or respond to the topics under discussion. A common example of the illusion of work is when conversation takes place, but nothing really happens. The real agenda is just below the surface of the session, and all of the worker's energy is committed there. Simply recognizing the concerns and placing them on the agenda may be all that is necessary to free the worker for the task at hand. At other times, the issues may need to be discussed, the feelings shared, and if it is not possible to deal fully with them then, an appropriate time must be set aside for a follow-up meeting. A supervisor who ignores the staff's concerns in the interests of covering the agenda may find that the original agenda is not covered at all.

The importance of sessional contracting is underlined by the fact that the staff's sense of urgency may change according to current circumstances. If, for example, agreement was reached at a prior conference to discuss a particular case or work problem but the worker experiences a stressful interview on the morning of the conference, then this particular interview may require immediate attention. If sessional contracting is ignored, the issue often is raised either directly or indirectly at the end of the meeting, as the staff member leaves—the supervisory equivalent of what is described in direct practice as "door-knob therapy." At this point, it may be too late to deal with the issue.

Another reason why sessional contracting skills are required is the staff's indirect ways of communicating its concerns. In some situations, the agenda appears to be set and the work begins, but the real agenda is not on the table, perhaps because the worker is ambivalent about raising it, is fearful of the supervisor's response, or is not even clear about what the agenda is. The worker may then simply hint at the agenda. Until the sessional contract is clear, the supervisor is wise to be tentative in the beginning phase of each encounter.

An example is the following report of a brief conversation between a worker responsible for financial aid in a public welfare agency and his supervisor:

> Frank came into my office appearing agitated and somewhat upset. He asked if I had a minute for an interpretation of a policy question. I said, "Sure, what is it?" He described the problem, which related to eligibility for special funds. I interpreted the policy as I understood it, and he nodded his head vigorously, agreeing with me.
> I said he really seemed agitated by this question, and I wondered why. He then went on to describe an interview he had just had with a client who had been abusive when he had explained the policy. The client had

verbally attacked him, a new experience for this worker. I said I thought that was upsetting and wondered if he wanted to spend a minute talking about it. He said he did, because he hadn't really known how to handle it and wasn't feeling too good about what had happened.

Although this worker had raised the policy question, his nonverbal cues and evidence of strong emotions indicated another agenda for the supervisor. Possibly, Frank may have simply been waiting to see if the supervisor would be willing to deal with the issue. Had the supervisor been hard pressed for time, he could have at least identified the issue, acknowledged the feelings, and set another time to discuss it. If the supervisor had simply ignored the underlying message, Frank would have understood that he could not get help in this area from this supervisor.

The indirect raising of concerns in the beginning phase of any session or meeting is common. Through verbal or nonverbal methods, the staff alerts the supervisor to important issues. Sometimes these issues emerge slowly because the workers themselves are not sure of their feelings. It is helpful if the supervisor can maintain a tentative attitude in the beginning stage until the sessional contract is fully understood. In moment-by-moment encounters with staff members, the supervisor should resist the temptation to offer immediate answers to their questions until he or she knows exactly what the questions are. The skills for determining the sessional themes often involve the skills of elaboration.

Elaborating Skills

When workers begin to share a particular concern, they often present the problem in a fragmentary way. These initial descriptions give the supervisor a handle to use for deepening the work. The elaboration skills are important in this stage because they help the worker tell his or her own story. The focus of the supervisor's questions and comments is on helping the staff members elaborate and clarify specific concerns. Some examples of the elaboration skills that are explored in this section include moving from the general to the specific, containment, focused listening, questioning, and reaching inside silences.

Moving from the General to the Specific

When staff members raise a general concern that is related to a specific event, their statement is best seen as a first offering. It may be presented in universal terms because the worker experiences it that way at the moment. Its general expression may also represent the worker's ambivalence about dealing with it in depth.

In one of the most common situations in which this skill is crucial, a worker brings a practice problem to the supervisor's attention. Note how the issue is expressed in general terms in the following report of a supervisory conference in which a psychiatric social worker raised a problem she was having with a "defensive client":

> Louise began the conference by saying she would like to discuss the problem of defensiveness. When I asked her what she meant, she explained she needed help on how to get clients to admit they have problems and not just blame the problems on their wives or kids. I told her that defensiveness was normal if people felt threatened, and she shouldn't be discouraged by it. I felt that after clients got to know her better, they might let down their defenses.
>
> She looked doubtful, and I asked her if she disagreed with me. She said that some people don't want to change, and no matter what a worker does, they would not own up to having problems. I agreed that there were unmotivated clients, and it was tough to give up on them, but sometimes it was necessary. She pointed out that it was easy to say that but hard to do, especially if there are kids involved. I agreed that workers often feel guilty if they can't bring about changes and then pointed out that the client had responsibilities as well. She agreed.

When a concern is presented generally, it is easy for the supervisor to enter into a general discussion of the problem. Unfortunately, at the end of this conversation, the worker is no better off, in terms of ideas for what to do next, than at the beginning. Consider the following contrasting example, wherein a supervisor of a family support worker responded to a similar opening comment by using the skill of moving from the general to the specific:

> Worker: You know, some people are just impossible to work with. They don't want to change.
> Supervisor: Did you have a tough interview?
> Worker: It's the Gruber family. I don't think they will ever admit they have any problems. As far as Mr. Gruber is concerned, I should just straighten out their teenage daughter, make her listen to them, and everything will be okay.
> Supervisor: Sounds like you hit a bit of a stone wall. Give me some details of the interview, and maybe we can discuss this whole business of defensiveness. At what point did you sense the wall go up?
> Worker: He seemed a little distant right from the beginning, the first session, but he really closed up this time. I wanted to get at his parenting skills, but he kept saying that kids have no respect for their parents any more.
> Supervisor: How had you tried to get at his parenting skills? What did you actually say?
> Worker: Well, he described how his daughter was a tramp, didn't listen to him, stayed out late at night, the whole business. He was coming down heavy on her, and I could see that she was close to tears.
> Supervisor: Were you feeling upset for her and angry at him for not understanding her feelings?

Worker: Exactly! I was thinking that if he handles her that way all the time, no wonder she doesn't listen to him.

Supervisor: It's easy to understand how you would feel that way. Probably at that moment you identified strongly with his daughter. I wonder, if you were with his daughter, who was with him?

Worker (after a brief silence): I guess he was alone.

Supervisor: You know, he probably already feels pretty guilty and defensive about his part in the problem. He may figure that everyone else, you included, is against him and is siding with his daughter. If he is going to let the barriers down, he needs to know that you understand his feelings and that you don't judge him too harshly. After all, if he could handle his daughter differently, he wouldn't need your help. What did you say to him?

Worker: I'm embarrassed to say that I told him that things are different here and that kids have more freedom than they did in the Old Country. Wow! I guess he really knew then whose side I was on.

Supervisor: Exactly! The interesting part is that if you want him to have more understanding for his daughter, you are probably going to have to model what you mean by having more understanding for him. You can't ask him to be empathic with her while at precisely the same time you won't empathize with him.

Not only did the supervisor begin this interview by asking if the worker had had a tough session, she also persisted in getting the specific details of the interaction between this worker and the defensive client. This process is called "memory work," in which the worker is asked to recall, from memory, some of the interaction and the associated worker affect. Memory work is discussed in more detail in chapter 6. In this example, the general discussion of defensiveness turned into a much more productive discussion of one specific defensive client and the worker's part in the proceedings. The supervisor was able to be helpful only after she had used the skill of moving from the general to the specific. After some work on this specific example, the supervisor could then generalize with the worker about the problem of defensiveness. As in this case, supervision work often moves from the general to the specific and back to the general, then back to the specific, and so on.

By handling the discussion in this way, the supervisor also modeled the very same skill that the worker needs to use. The next time Mr. Gruber makes a comment about how hard it is to raise teenagers these days, instead of engaging in a general discussion of cultural differences between countries, the worker might ask, "Did you and your daughter have an argument this week?" Thus, just as the supervisor helped to focus the discussion on the details of the interview, the worker can help to focus the discussion on the details of the family encounter. This is an illustration of the powerful ways supervisors teach through example and of the importance of paying attention to the parallel process.

In workshops for supervisors, when I suggest the use of this skill, a comment such as the following is common: "If I reach for the specifics in the case, then the worker is going to expect me to have some ideas on how to help. In a lot of situations, I don't have the foggiest idea about what to do." This raises the important issue of the supervisor's ability to understand practice issues, to conceptualize the dynamics and skills, and to teach them effectively. It is indeed hard to teach while one is still learning. In addition, some skills have been learned from experience but have never been articulated in a way that makes them teachable.

Even if supervisors do not have all the answers, it is helpful for them to explore practice problems with their staff members. Specific discussions often lead staff and supervisors to clarify and develop their ideas. The professional literature, which is giving more attention to method—that is, what helping professionals actually do—can also be helpful to both. It is possible to find clearly articulated descriptions of skills and dynamics that can be shared and reports of findings from practice and empirical research that help to develop keener insights into how to do the job.

By being specific, supervisors sometimes learn as much (perhaps more) from their teaching as do those they try to teach. I found, for example, that teaching practice to students forced me to sharpen my ability to articulate what I did in an easily understandable way. In turn, this helped me to be more consistent in my own direct practice.

Containment

As the staff describes its concerns, a supervisor may be tempted to begin to help before the whole story has been told. New supervisors, who very much want to be helpful, find this a special problem. They often rush in with suggestions that are not helpful because they are not directed at the staff's actual concerns. In effect, the supervisor begins to answer the worker's question before she or he really knows what the question is. The elaboration skill of containment, that is, refraining from action and remaining quiet, is an active skill.

The following example is a nursing supervisor's record of her discussion of a new recording system with a nurse who had been on the staff for 15 years. The supervisor, new to the hospital, had found some general resistance to the introduction of this system, which included daily dictation of notes by the nursing staff. The supervisor tried to overcome the initial resistance by providing a "solution" to the problem:

> I mentioned that I was concerned that Janice had not started to use the new system. I told her she was the only one on the ward who had not begun. She said it was hard to find the time to do the dictation. I told her that was no problem; I would arrange for her relief to pick up a few minutes earlier so she could have a few minutes to herself. She then pointed out that there was a rush for the equipment at 4 P.M., with everyone wanting to get their notes done at the same time. I told her I could easily arrange for

another machine on the ward. She agreed that would help and promised to get her recordings started.

This is an example of a "New Year's resolution"; both the supervisor and the nurse knew that the agreement would not be implemented. After tuning in, the supervisor reopened the conversation on an occasion when the records had not been prepared. This time, instead of rushing in with solutions, she contained herself and probed for the real concerns:

> When I mentioned I was still not getting her recordings, Janice apologized and said she had had a hard time getting the recording machine to work. She had tried to dictate but found she had not pressed the "record" button. I resisted the temptation to show her how to operate the machine and instead asked if there was something about this whole recording business that was bothering her. I told her I realized it was new to most of the staff, and she might have some feelings about it.
>
> There was a period of silence, and then Janice told me that she had never recorded on a dictating machine before. She froze up when she tried and couldn't think of a thing to say. She always had had this problem; she couldn't even leave a message on a telephone answering machine when she encountered one. She just hung up. I also asked her if knowing what to say and being able to compose her ideas as she spoke was a part of the problem. She agreed that it was and said she had been too embarrassed to bring it up.
>
> I then proposed to work with her on how to put an oral report together and on how to dictate on the machine. She said she thought that would help a great deal.

Focused Listening

Although listening is something everyone does all the time, focused listening concentrates on a specific part of the staff's message. Even the simplest of communications can be complex. Particularly in sensitive areas, the staff may send so many messages all at once that the key concern is buried in the words. A simple analogy describes the difficulty. In the evening, it is sometimes possible to hear two radio stations with close frequencies simultaneously. To hear either one clearly, the listener has to fine tune the set, tuning one station out and the other one in more clearly. In another example, when walking into a crowded room filled with people in conversation, one first hears a general noise or din in which individual conversations are inaudible. Simply focusing on one pair of people brings their conversation out of the background noise into the foreground. In a similar way, the supervisor must tune in to the central concerns and eliminate the "noise."

A worker beginning a conference on a specific practice problem, for example, might begin with an apparently personal story. At first the supervisor may dismiss this as idle chatter, preliminary to getting down to work, but if he or she listens with awareness of the purpose of the conference, the connection to the work may become clear. It is often the case that the introductory story is related to the content of the meeting or conference.

Questioning

Questioning, as an elaboration skill, means requesting more information on the nature of the problem. In moving from the general to the specific, the supervisor uses questioning to help the worker elaborate the details of the interview: "And what did you say at that point?" or "Can you tell me more about what was bothering you?" The questions help the worker amplify the content of the presentation so that the supervisor has a clearer idea of the details.

Questioning is particularly important when the worker raises an issue or states a concern that puts the supervisor on the spot. The natural reaction is defensive, but often a question is a better response: "Why are you asking that question?" or "You seem really angry at me; why?"

Questions designed to encourage a clearer definition of the concern at the start of an exchange can be useful, particularly because the use of jargon in the helping professions can be confusing. For example, if a worker asks about handling transference in working with a client, the supervisor should determine, before replying, precisely what the worker means by that term and why it is being raised at this conference.

Reaching inside Silences

Silence can be an important form of communication during a conference or meeting. The difficulty is that it is often unclear exactly what the staff member is "saying" with such a response. A worker may be reflecting on the implications of the conversation or may be dealing with powerful emotions that have been released by the discussion. Silence can indicate a moment of uncertainty as the worker pauses, deciding whether to plunge headlong and risk a difficult area of work. Silence can also indicate that the supervisor's previous response did not address the worker's concerns. Or it can indicate that the worker has not understood the supervisor; these silences are usually accompanied by a glassy-eyed look. Frequent silences in a conference can be a systematic attempt to express anger passively.

Because silences mean many things, the supervisor's response must be equally flexible. The supervisor's own feelings during the silence are important. If, for example, the silence represents the emergence of difficult feelings, such as when staff members share personal tragedies, their nonverbal communications of posture, facial expression, and body tension can speak loudly to the observing supervisor and can trigger empathic responses. At times like these, the supervisor can respond to the silence with silence or with some nonverbal expression of support. All of these responses offer support to the staff members while allowing them time to experience the feelings.

If the supervisor believes that staff members are silent because they are thinking about a key point, then silence in response gives them time to think and demonstrates respect for their work. Allowing a long period of silence can be a mistake, however, because it can turn into a battle of wills over who will speak first.

One main reason supervisors have trouble with silences, like the deadly silence at a staff meeting after a question, is that they often interpret them as negative feedback. They feel that they must have done or said something wrong. This interpretation of silence may lead the supervisor to respond by changing the subject, which could cut off an important communication. The message sent to the staff might be, "I don't really want to hear what you have to say."

Reaching inside the silence involves exploring its meaning. Thus, the supervisor who responds to a silence by saying, "You've grown quiet in the last few moments. What are you thinking about?" is encouraging the staff members to share their thoughts. Alternatively, a supervisor could try to articulate what the silence might be saying. To a worker who hesitates as he describes a particularly difficult experience, the supervisor might say, "I can see this is hard for you to talk about." Or, in the face of silence that apparently is a negative reaction, the supervisor might say, "I get the feeling you're not too happy about what I just said, but you're not sure you can let me know. Is that what you're thinking?" The supervisor's own feelings should guide attempts to explore the silence, although she or he must be open to the possibility that the guess is wrong and should encourage the staff to feel free to say so.

The importance of dealing with silences was brought home to me in a research project on social work practice with child welfare clients (Shulman, 1977, 1978). The skill of reaching inside of silences was one of the five skills used least often of the 27 studied, although another analysis showed it to be one of the most significant. The 15 workers with the most positive overall skill scores had more positive working relationships and were more helpful than those with negative scores. When the practice skill profiles of these two groups of workers were compared according to their scores on the 27 skills, the skill of reaching inside silences was one of the three most important in which the positive skill group of workers differed from the negative skill group. Similar findings emerged in a more recent replication of this part of the earlier study (Shulman, 1991). Although it cannot be inferred that the same skill would be as important for supervision relationships as it was in practice, nevertheless, these findings suggest that there are important communications within silences that can lead to more effective work.

Empathic Skills

It is important for a supervisor to pay attention to the staff's feelings, as well as to the facts involved in any situation. Kadushin (1976) introduced empathy by pointing out that both staff and supervisors face a variety of job-related stresses. Some resource must be available to help them deal with these stresses, or their work and agency effectiveness will suffer. This resource, he suggested, is empathy for the other person's position in the supervisory relationship:

> The supervisor is responsible for helping the supervisees adjust to job-related stress. Higher administrators are usually responsible for support to first-line supervisors. The ultimate objective of this component of supervision is to enable the workers, and the agency through the workers, to offer the client the most effective and efficient service. (p. 198)

Kadushin (1976, p. 201) listed a number of sources of job-related tension for a staff member. They include the following:

1. Administrative pressures—requirements for work assessment and evaluation; demands of agency policies and procedures.
2. Educational supervision challenges to long-held positions; situations that cause the worker to be uncertain.
3. The supervisor–supervisee relationship; the intimate, personal, and demanding relationship with a person in authority leading to elements of transference; the acting out within the supervision relationship of problems encountered with clients.
4. Client relationship pressures—the raw emotions expressed by many clients under strain and in crisis; hostile and resistant clients.
5. The nature and context of the task—the work setting; constant changes in directions; particular problems facing clients.

The power of affect on all aspects of clients' or consumers' lives is generally acknowledged in the helping professions. Taft (1933) was one of the early theorists to stress the importance of feelings:

> There is no factor of personality which is so expressive of individuality as emotion. . . . The personality is impoverished as feeling is denied, and the penalty for sitting on the lid of angry feelings or feelings of fear is the inevitable blunting of capacity to feel love and desire. For to feel is to live, but to reject feeling through fear is to reject the life process itself. (p. 105)

Rogers (1961) directed the helping person to listen for the affective component of a communication and try to understand rather than evaluate or judge a message. According to Rogers,

Real communication occurs when the evaluative tendency is avoided, when we listen with understanding. . . . It means to see the expressed idea and attitude from the other person's point of view, to sense how it feels to him, to achieve his frame of reference in regard to the thing he is talking about. (pp. 331–332)

Research evidence on the relevance of the empathic skills to work with people has been cited in studies in a number of the helping professions. These skills have been found to be important, for example, in teaching (Flanders, 1970), psychotherapy (Berenson & Carkhuff, 1967; Truax, 1966), social work (Shulman, 1978, 1991), and medicine (Charney, 1967; Shulman & Buchan, 1982).

Barriers to Empathic Responses

In spite of a growing emphasis on the importance of empathy in work with clients, use of these skills is often lacking in work with staff in the supervision process. There are a number of reasons for this. One is that the capacity of supervisors to be in touch with the feelings of the staff is related to the supervisors' ability to acknowledge their own feelings. Supervisors also may have difficulty expressing empathy with feelings of the staff that are similar to their own. Being only human, they face the same stresses experienced by workers. They must receive support from administrators or colleagues, or both, if their capacity for empathy is not to be blunted.

Another major obstacle to empathy may be the supervisor's authority over the staff. Many supervisors accept the myth that it is unprofessional to get too close to workers. They think that they must "remain objective" to implement the part of their role that sets expectations and makes demands on the staff. Because they are afraid of becoming too friendly with individual workers, they try to maintain a detached, clinical, cold front. As a result, when they must make demands on a worker, as in raising questions about performance, they may withhold their empathic responses. At such times when a worker needs support the most, it is not forthcoming.

For effective supervision, it is necessary to develop the capacity to be both supportive and demanding at the same time, rather than separating the two elements of the helping relationship. As later examples in this section show, this ability to integrate support and demand is the hallmark of effective practice, both in work with staff and in work with clients. This synthesis of two apparent opposites is one important skill for supervisors to master in their professional and personal activities.

Another barrier to the use of empathic skills by supervisors is the notion that these are "therapeutic techniques" and that applying them is akin to turning the staff into clients. Some supervisors with extensive counseling experience and a well-developed ability to express empathy are nevertheless reluctant to empathize with their workers. They do not want a staff member to say, "Don't social work me!"

The major reason for this kind of staff reaction is that the supervisor is using a mechanical empathic technique, such as automatically reflecting everything that a staff member says without really understanding what he or she is experiencing. Consider, for example, the social worker who says, "I don't know if I can take any more verbal abuse from Mr. Smith. He has made me really angry now." A supervisor who responds by saying, "So, Mr. Smith has made you really angry now" is risking a negative response from the worker. The worker probably will experience this response, often described in the literature as *reflection*, as mechanical and devoid of real feelings and will resent it. It would also be resented by a client, who would have every reason to respond angrily by saying to the worker, "I just told you I was really angry!"

The key issue is whether the supervisor's expressed empathy is genuine. There are so many technique-focused training approaches that it is easy to understand how empathy could become a ritual. Phrases such as "I hear you saying that . . .," followed by the supervisor's interpretation of the worker's feelings can easily lead to the perception that one is being "social worked." Of course, this kind of response is also poor practice for a social worker with a client. To avoid this, the supervisor must try to actually experience, as fully as possible, the underlying feelings of the staff member and acknowledge them by putting these unstated feelings into words. In response to the social worker's expression of anger at the client, the supervisor might reach for the worker's accompanying feelings by saying, "You really sound frustrated and at the end of your rope." The worker has named the feeling of anger, and the supervisor has articulated the frustration and feelings of hopelessness that may also be present. This specific skill will be discussed in more detail in the next section, but in whatever ways the supervisor expresses empathy, the worker must experience it as genuine.

Another reason why supervisors with clinical experience may avoid using their empathic skills in work with staff is their lack of clarity about their function and the purpose of supervision. When a staff member raises, directly or indirectly, a personal problem affecting job performance, some supervisors do not like suddenly discovering themselves in the role of counselor. This can be avoided if the supervisor is clear that the purpose of supervision is to get a job done and that supervision is not a therapeutic role. If the functional differences between supervision and counseling are clearly recognized, the supervisor is free to empathize with the staff member's feelings and also to discuss the implications of the problem for job performance.

Supervisors who understand these issues can help staff members find other appropriate sources of help for their personal problems. They deal with staff members' feelings; however, they do so in pursuit of purpose. All feelings are not appropriate for work, and empathy must be used as a tool for implementing the supervisory function and the working contract.

Reaching for Feelings

By reaching for feelings, the supervisor asks the staff member to share the affective portion of the message. As pointed out earlier, this request must not be handled in a routine manner, such as asking "How do you feel about that?" Rather, the supervisor must be prepared to experience the other person's feelings.

An example involves the way a nursing supervisor dealt with a nurse on a hospital ward whose work performance was being affected by a marital crisis. After two years of satisfactory performance, Jan, the nurse, had started coming in late and missing work and while on the job seemed to be in a daze. The staff was aware of her personal problems, which included physical violence by her husband, and had tried to cover up for her poor performance. Eventually, the supervisor seemed to become part of the conspiracy to ignore the work problems; she did not want to mention the personal problems for fear of invading the nurse's privacy. As the problems increased, they became impossible to ignore, however, because the safety of patients could be jeopardized.

Once a personal problem affects performance on the job, it is no longer just personal. A staff member facing great personal strain may be sending an indirect message to colleagues by diminished work performance. In this case, with Jan's personal life in a shambles, it was little help to allow her professional life to go to pieces also. It would be better to confront the problem in a supportive manner so that she would be helped to keep control of her work world. Being able to maintain herself effectively in the work situation could be the very thing Jan needed to strengthen her ability to deal with her personal problems.

At a supervisors' workshop, the supervisor in this situation admitted that by her embarrassment at raising personal concerns she was really protecting herself, not the worker. At the same time, she and the other nurses were starting to feel guilty about the problems on the ward and a bit angry at Jan for not carrying her load. The group role played how the supervisor might handle a conference with this staff member, how she might honestly draw out an admission of the problems and reach for the associated feelings. Here is her report of the conference with Jan, presented at a follow-up workshop:

> Supervisor: I wanted to talk to you about your work performance. There have been a lot of problems with being late, missing days, and generally seeming out of it.
> Jan: I know things have been going badly, but I have been under some strain. I'll be able to handle it.

Supervisor: I've heard you've been having troubles at home, and I figured that must have been making it tough for you here as well. I didn't raise the issue because I felt it was your personal business, and it is personal. However, I wanted you to know that I have been concerned for you. Has it been very rough for you?

Jan (starting to cry): It's been the toughest time of my life.

This example is continued in the discussion of the other empathic skills in this section. The key point here is that the supervisor has given Jan permission to discuss the feelings that are affecting her ability to work. The question, "Has it been very rough for you?" both reaches for these feelings and communicates her acceptance of Jan.

Although this example concerns a personal problem, the same skill can be used in asking a worker for an affective response while discussing a practice problem. When a worker describes a hostile or aggressive client, the supervisor might enquire, "What were your feelings while he was coming on so strong?" Or when a child care worker describes how a teenager cried while talking about the recent death of his father, the supervisor could ask, "How did it hit you while John was telling you all this?"

Acknowledging Feelings

The skill of acknowledging the staff's feelings involves indicating—through words, gestures, expression, physical posture, or touch—the supervisor's understanding of the workers' expressed affect. Supervisors must attempt to understand how workers feel about experiences, even if they believe that a situation does not warrant such a reaction or that the workers are being too harsh on themselves or are taking too much responsibility for the problem. They may think that the workers should not have such feelings, but the important point is that the workers do have them.

A common mistake is to rush in with reassurances, to tell the worker "not to feel so bad." This merely indicates to the worker that the supervisor has failed to understand. We have all had moments when we felt like saying to friends or loved ones, "If you really understood how bad I felt, you wouldn't be trying to cheer me up."

In the example of Jan, the nurse whose marriage was in crisis, the supervisor attempted to display her understanding of the feelings in this way:

Jan (starting to cry): It's been the toughest time of my life.

Supervisor (sitting quietly for a few moments and then putting her hand on Jan's shoulder): This has really hit you hard, hasn't it?

Thus, through words, expression, and physical touch, the supervisor maintained closeness with the nurse, indicating her understanding of the feelings involved.

This is the true meaning of support: to share another's feelings as much as possible. Jan responded to this invitation by describing her current crisis with her husband. She described how he had recently beaten her during an argument. The supervisor listened for a while as Jan aired her problems. But the supervisor displayed her clarity of purpose and role by refraining from exploring the problem to offer counseling. Even if the staff member requests this help from a supervisor, providing it is a subversion of the supervision process. Supervisors who feel more comfortable counseling than supervising can easily be drawn into this more familiar role, and they may turn the worker into a client. This is not the purpose of supervision. The supervisor who makes this mistake and begins to "treat" the worker often neglects those aspects of supervision that are the supervisor's responsibility.

In this case, the supervisor tried first to discuss sources of help that might be available for the worker:

> Supervisor: It sounds like you've been going through a very stressful time. Have you had anyone to talk to?
> Jan: I've been too ashamed to tell people. I mean, I'm not the kind of person who gets beaten up by a man. That happens to other people. I didn't come in for four days until my black eye could be covered up by makeup.
> Supervisor: So you have been all alone during this.
> Jan: That's right.
> Supervisor: I think you are going through a tough time, and no one should have to do that by themself. Have you considered seeing someone about this—for example, the family services agency or perhaps the women's center? You're not the only one to go through this experience. Just talking about it may give you some relief.

Two elements of the supervisor's response are particularly important. First, she encouraged Jan to seek out help for the problem. In some cases, the staff members may not be aware of such services; in others, such as this one, they may be ashamed to talk to other people and may need some support to do so. The supervisor won Jan's confidence by being understanding and nonjudgmental. This made it easier for the nurse to seek help elsewhere.

In some large agencies or settings, specific staff members may be available for those seeking help with personal problems. For example, they may provide alcohol and drug counseling or psychiatric aid. Whether staff members actually follow up on this course of action is their responsibility. They must make the decisions related to their own lives.

Second, she began to explore the implications of this crisis for the nurse's ability to do the job.

Articulating Workers' Feelings

At times, a staff member comes close to expressing emotions but stops just short of it. The individual might not fully understand the feeling and thus might be unable to articulate it, or the individual might not be sure that it is all right either to have such a feeling or to share it with a supervisor. The use of this supervisory skill involves articulating the worker's affect just before the worker does so. The stage is set when the supervisor's tuning in and intense efforts to empathize during the session result in associations to his or her own experiences as the worker elaborates a concern.

In the example of Jan, when the supervisor suggested that she consider some sources of help, Jan hesitated and did not respond. The supervisor sensed her reluctance and tried to articulate the feelings:

> Supervisor: You seem thoughtful right now. Are you feeling you would be too ashamed to go for help?
> Jan: I'm a professional myself. I shouldn't have this happening to me.
> Supervisor: Look, this is your life and your problem. I can't tell you what to do about it. However, this can happen to anyone, and it's nothing to be ashamed about. The important thing is getting the help you need so you don't have to go through this alone. The only reason I raised this issue is that I thought it might be part of what was making things so rough for you here at the hospital. Now that is my business. Can we talk about what's been going on?

At this point in the interview the supervisor's clear sense of function and purpose takes her to the question of job performance. Rather than being seduced into helping the nurse deal with the problem, she must deal with how the problem is affecting the nurse's work. Although Jan must make her own decision about how to handle her personal life, it is the supervisor's responsibility to hold her accountable for her work performance. Had the supervisor begun this discussion of accountability without first exploring the family crisis, the discussion would have had a different and, I believe, less productive effect. Note how the supervisor continued to articulate the nurse's feelings:

> Jan: This thing has hit me so hard I find myself thinking about it all the time. Some mornings I just don't want to get out of bed.
> Supervisor: I can understand how bad you must feel and how that would make it difficult to work. However, I'm getting worried, particularly about the safety of our patients. In addition, I can't believe you feel too good about being late, being absent, and having the rest of staff cover for you. It's bad enough having problems at home; it must make it worse when the job goes badly as well.
> I'd like to try to help you pull yourself together on the work side. I realize it will be hard, and we may have to work things out to make it a bit easier, but I know you're a good nurse, and I think we can deal with this thing. What do you think?
> Jan: I could tell people were giving me funny looks on the ward.
> Supervisor: That must have made you feel even worse, and more like staying home. I think at first everyone, including me, just felt sorry for you,

and they were afraid to say anything. We all just hoped it would go away. That really wasn't very helpful, and that is why I'm [talking about] it today. Can you tell me how you see it affecting your job and what we can do to help?

The ensuing discussion explored some of the specific responsibilities and problems experienced by the nurse, and an arrangement was made to modify her duties for a time until she felt better able to cope. The supervisor said she would make some time available for Jan to see a counselor. They agreed to see how things worked out for a week and to check with each other then. At the end of the session, Jan thanked the supervisor for raising the issue directly with her and for giving her a chance to do something about it.

Skills in Sharing One's Feelings

The supervisory skill of sharing one's feelings is another method that supervisors can use to present themselves to the staff as human beings. In some theories of supervision, the model of a supervisor is that of an objective, clinical, detached, knowledgeable professional. In such an approach, direct expression of a supervisor's personal feelings—anger, fear, ambivalence, caring—is viewed as "unprofessional." Many staff members hold a parallel view of their work with clients. This narrow concept of professionalism forces both staff and supervisor to choose between being personal or being professional. As one worker put it, "I was taught to take my professional self to work and to leave my personal self at home."

The injunction against expressing personal feelings was deeply rooted in a therapeutic model of practice in which the clinician allows the transference process to emerge by remaining neutral in the relationship. Also, concern about the possibility of countertransference, in which the helping professional reacts inappropriately to the person receiving help, was another factor. Expression of open emotion could lead to "acting out." The authority of the supervisor (or worker) was such that caution had to be exercised because of the increased impact of emotions such as anger. All of the problems and concerns that led to this separation between the clinician's personal and professional selves were valid and should not be ignored. Unfortunately, the proposed solution created an artificial dichotomy between the personal and the professional—a false dualism that generated new problems. The model suggested here is that the supervisor must learn to integrate his or her personal and professional selves. Mistakes will be made along the way. The supervisor must learn to catch these mistakes and apologize when appropriate. He or she will be engaging in an ongoing process of discovery about those conditions that tend to lead to inappropriate responses. As one learns from these mistakes, a natural synthesis of personal self and professional role will emerge. The quality was described nicely by one worker, while referring to her supervisor: "I like my supervisor. She's not like a supervisor. She's more like a real person."

Research on sharing of feelings has been undertaken recently in a number of helping professions. There are indications that this skill, sometimes called *self-disclosure*, plays as important a part in the helping process as do the empathic skills (Carkhuff, 1969). The key characteristic is that the helping person appears to have a congruent personality, in which his or her external actions and expressions coincide with his or her real inner feelings. In my studies of social work practice, the worker's ability to share personal thoughts and feelings was a powerful correlate with both developing working relationships and being helpful (Shulman, 1978, 1991, 1992).

A supervisor who appears to be always under self-control, who always has everything all worked out, who is never at a loss or flustered, and who sets impossible standards is a difficult person to relate to or to please.

Showing Vulnerability

Some feelings are particularly difficult to show. Supervisors describe vulnerability as one of these. In one example, a supervisor was strongly attacked by his staff members at a unit meeting for failing to stand up enough to the agency on a policy issue. This supervisor had had a good relationship with the staff, and he felt deeply hurt at their anger and unwillingness to understand his position. He expressed none of this at the meeting, however, and instead sat passively, in stony silence, taking the punishment. Later, he said he did not think it was right to let the staff know they had hurt him. He held back so that he could think about it later and deal with it in a more rational way.

This supervisor encouraged his staff members to share their feelings with him, but when they took him up on that offer, he was not willing to share his own feelings with them. He seemed to be saying, "You should take risks with me and allow yourself to be vulnerable, but don't expect me to do the same." His staff must have sensed his discomfort and the discrepancy between the way he felt and the way he acted. Supervisors agree that it is hard to be candid with staff in such circumstances. Observation of their own supervisors often has taught them not to express their feelings honestly. Many report they have trouble being open with others in all relationships, not just professional ones.

One of the most important reasons for more honest, spontaneous expression of feeling by the supervisor is the consequent release of energy needed to empathize with the worker. In the example cited, there was important work to be done with the staff members on their feelings and the policy decision, but the supervisor could not begin to empathize with the staff while he was sitting there unhappily, trying to manage his own feelings. At his next staff meeting, the supervisor caught his mistake nicely and reopened the issue as follows:

> I wanted to talk about how I felt last week when you all attacked me. I didn't level with you then because I felt I couldn't—that I had to keep my cool. Now I think that was a mistake. You should know how I really feel. At that meeting I felt lousy and disappointed. I know you had every right to be upset because I couldn't get that decision changed, but I thought you owed me a little understanding of the bind I have been in and a little more concern for my feelings. You can get angry at me, and sometimes I will deserve it, but last week, you just dumped all over me.

This opening was followed by a long silence, and then the discussion began. It turned out that the staff had felt guilty about attacking him. They went on to explain how upset and frustrated they had felt, how the agency did not seem to appreciate how difficult it was for them, and how they had probably taken it all out on him. After acknowledging their feelings, they discussed what possibilities remained for further action on the issue with the agency.

It is interesting to examine the nature of the feelings described by the workers; in many ways, they were similar to those felt by the supervisor at the time of the attack. This similarity is meaningful beause one way staff people communicate their own feelings is by making their supervisor feel the same way. Bion (1961) identified this process in practice with clients as *projective identification*. Rather than simply describing their feelings, the workers may act in a way that evokes a similar response by the supervisor. When the supervisor can respond with an expression of his or her own feelings, it is easier to acknowledge the staff's feelings. The supervisor's affect thus becomes an indicator of the affect of the staff. When a supervisor is made to feel cornered and insecure, for example, the cause may be the staff's own insecurity.

Showing Anger

Another feeling that supervisors find hard to express is anger; more specifically, they find it hard to express anger openly and directly. They express anger all the time but usually through indirect, "professional" means. A supervisor who is angry at a worker for voicing negative feedback too strongly is clearly expressing that anger in suggesting that the worker has a "problem with authority." The difficulty with this kind of expression of anger is that it cuts off communications and intensifies the worker's negative feelings. The difficulty of openly expressing anger is common in our society, wherein we are taught early in life that it is not polite to be angry. We also learn that open expressions of anger can be dangerous, especially if they are directed at people in authority. If we are openly angry at another person, we may get an angry response.

The problem with this suppression of anger, both personally and professionally, is that the feelings are nevertheless there. If they are left unexpressed, they work under the surface and can have a powerful underground effect on a relationship. When anger is suppressed, the result often is apathy, depression, or transference of the anger onto a safer object.

Anger is as much a part of any relationship between supervisor and staff as is caring. There are times when a supervisor's legitimate demands will make the staff angry. In fact, the effectiveness of supervisors whose workers are never angry at them might well be questioned. (In workshops, some supervisors greet this observation with expressions such as, "Great! Then I must be doing something right, because my staff sure gets angry at me.") There are also times when a supervisor has every right to be angry at a staff member, and honest expression of this anger can have a positive effect.

The following example concerns Marge, a staff member nearing retirement (in two years) who was obviously slacking off in her work in a child welfare agency. She was often late or absent, complained of constant medical problems, and was becoming a general nuisance in the agency. Other staff members were covering for her. Until recently, Marge had been an effective contributor to the work of the agency and had much to offer younger workers. In effect, the staff had prematurely retired her, saying, "We might as well wait until she quits." The supervisor had made the same decision but felt uncomfortable about it.

At a workshop session, members tuned in to Marge's feelings about retirement and ending her work life. The supervisor could see then that she had avoided discussing this area. In role play, she practiced how she could stimulate discussion and explore the work-related issues facing Marge. The workshop participant who role played Marge's position presented an image of a woman overwhelmed by the situation. The supervisor responded with a proposal to rework her job description to include more opportunities to train other staff. She suggested that this might help make the last few years more interesting and productive for Marge, and it would give the agency a chance to draw on her years of experience. The worker in the role play kept coming up with excuses why she could not accept the suggestions, however, and it became a classic "Yes, but . . ." encounter.

When the supervisor was asked how she felt as the worker stubbornly insisted on her helplessness to change or to try something new, she replied, "I feel like wringing her neck!" I pointed out that she could have fooled us: None of that had come through. I argued that feelings respond to feelings, and Marge might perceive a direct, honest expression of the supervisor's anger as her really caring. The cycle might be broken if the supervisor could be honest. In response to a suggestion that she go back into the role play and say exactly what was on her mind, instead of censoring it until it sounded professional, her first line was, "Damn it, no matter what I suggest, you find another reason why you can't do it. I'm really angry because you already have one foot out the door, and I think you have so much to give here at the agency. I don't want just to give up on you." The participant who was role playing the worker sat in stunned silence. She said that she was not sure how she would feel just then, but the supervisor surely had her attention.

Possibly the supervisor might be honest with Marge and still get no response. This depends on Marge's ability to respond to the demand for work and the caring. In this case, the anger came from the supervisor's real concern for Marge. If Marge could perceive that, it might make it easier for her to respond. The supervisor is saying, "You have something to offer, and I think you can do it!" That could be just what Marge needs to hear.

Concerns about Showing Feelings

In addition to sharing vulnerability, anger, or other such emotions, many supervisors have great difficulty demonstrating their underlying feelings of warmth and caring. This is most evident in the ending phase, when it is time to say good-bye because either the supervisor or a staff member is leaving. Often, as will be pointed out later, endings are dealt with too hastily, without an honest discussion of mutual feelings. We are as embarrassed by positive feelings as we are by negative ones. Yet, it is important for supervisors to let staff members know that they do care about them and, in turn, to let staff members tell them of their feelings.

The genuine concerns of supervisors about sharing their own feelings should not be dismissed lightly. They worry about disclosing personal feelings that might change the nature of the relationship. This is a valid concern if the supervisor shifts the focus of the work to examining his or her own difficulties—a form of asking the staff for counseling that is certainly inappropriate. The feelings shared should be relevant to the staff's own agenda and the purposes of supervision.

Supervisors also worry about expressing the "correct" feelings. If they were to be more spontaneous, they fear, there might be times when they would "blow up" at a staff member simply because they are having a bad day. Without doubt, spontaneous responses will be inappropriate at times, but it is always possible to apologize in such situations. An apology may be all that the staff member wants to hear. Workers do not expect supervisors to be perfect; in fact, they may be relieved if the supervisor occasionally "blows it." This makes it a little less difficult when they themselves fall short in their work with clients. The supervisor's apology also provides a model of how they can deal with such mistakes.

At any rate, if supervisors monitor every expression to make sure they never say anything wrong, it is likely that they will rarely say anything right.

Skills in Making a Demand for Work

The model of the work phase of supervision developed in this chapter stresses dealing with feelings. It starts with tuning in and focuses on the supervisory work skill factors of empathy and sharing one's feelings. The model is also based on the development of a clear contract in which the work-phase skill factor of elaboration is used to identify the staff's agenda and to reach an understanding of its concerns.

Despite efforts to ensure that both the staff and the supervisor understand the interactional nature of the supervisory relationship, and despite the attempts of both to invest the work with feelings, there is a point in the supervision process at which the staff reaction is likely to be marked by ambivalence and possible resistance. At this point, the work-phase skill factor of making a demand for work enters the model-building process.

As the work proceeds, supervisors often find that the staff is of two minds about taking direction. In part, as an expression of the need for growth, they want to move toward understanding and to risk new endeavors. But in another part, as an expression of resistance, they pull back from tackling a difficult new procedure. Effective work requires staff members to deal with troublesome subjects and feelings, to recognize their own contributions to a problem, to take responsibility for their own actions, and to lower their established defenses. In response to such difficult demands, many of them demonstrate some ambivalence.

Understanding the Change Process

Lewin (1951) described a model for change that can be applied on a number of levels—individual, group, family, or organization. His view, stated simply, is that the individual personality develops some form of balance with the environment, or a "quasi-stationary social equilibrium" (p. 224), and change requires breaking this balance. For a defensive staff member, for example, denial may work as a way of dealing with painful feelings of insecurity about practice competency; although an equilibrium can be maintained, it does not allow for growth. This comes only from facing reality.

According to Lewin (1951) the three steps in change are "un-freezing" this equilibrium, moving into a state of "disequilibrium," and then "freezing" at a new quasi-stationary equilibrium (p. 224). The process is probably familiar to anyone who has learned a second language. There is often an initial burst of learning in which words and phrases are memorized, but before they can be used in conversation, it is necessary to mentally translate each one. After an initial period of such learning, particularly in an intensive immersion situation, learners often wake up one morning and find they have apparently lost all ability to speak or understand the new language. This is experienced as a severe and painful regression. Actually, it may be the period of disequilibrium when the mind is making an important shift. After days, hours, or sometimes weeks, they discover that the language skills have come back, but now the words and phrases come naturally, without the need for a mental translation. This is the new quasi-stationary equilibrium. It is still "quasi" because it too is a stop along the way.

Because the defenses maintaining the initial equilibrium are valuable to the individual, expecting the unfreezing process to be easy is to ignore the essence of the dynamics. The more serious the issue and the more deeply an individual feels it as a challenge to the self, the more rigid will be his or her defenses, and the greater will be the ambivalence about change.

Lewin's (1951) ideas have several implications for the supervision process. The first is recognition that expressions of ambivalence, defensiveness, and resistance are normal, and they can be dealt with more easily if they are understood that way. A supervisor who is aware of this may be less threatened by the signals of resistance. To take the argument a step further, a supervisor who never encounters resistance or defensiveness may not be making strong enough demands on the staff. Most supervisors experience staff resistance, defensiveness, or evasiveness as a sign that they are doing something wrong. In fact, they may all be signals that the supervisor is doing something right.

Second, if the staff is to abandon the safety of a quasi-stationary equilibrium and accept the disruption of the disequilibrium required for change, members must feel safe and supported throughout the process. This is the reason for the emphasis on the empathic skills, honesty in sharing feelings, and the importance of relationships in the supervision model presented in this book. I suggest that a "fund" of nonjudgmental acceptance can be established by the supervisor, to be drawn on when the time comes to make demands. If the supervisor can understand a worker's feelings that lead to anger or defensiveness on the resistance side of the ambivalence, then the supervisor can reach for the growth side of the ambivalence in a way that is less threatening to the worker.

Third, the ambivalence about change may make it necessary for the supervisor to exercise more power to facilitate the process of growth. Although many changes can be made by workers on their own, those that are more difficult may require the additional energy that is transmitted when the supervisor makes a demand for work. This notion of the demand for work is one of Schwartz and Zalba's (1971) most important contributions to our understanding of the helping process. As they describe it in the context of workers' relations to clients,

> The worker also represents what might be called the demand for work, in which role he tries to enforce not only the substantive aspects of the contract—what we are here for—but the conditions of work as well. This demand is, in fact, the only one the worker makes—not for

certain perceived results, or approved attitudes, or learned behaviors, but for the work itself. That is, he is continually challenging the client to address himself resolutely and with energy to what he came to do. (p. 11)

The Demand for Work in the Supervision Process

When the notion of the demand for work is applied to the supervisor–worker relationship, the supervisor's expectations of the worker can be a key element in helping the worker to respond with strength. This is a difficult idea for supervisors to accept, particularly when they are uncertain and ambivalent about their own role. If their own self-confidence is fragile, they may back off from important supervisory work at the first sign of the staff's defensiveness or unwillingness to deal with a difficult problem. They read the subtle clues of the resistance side of the message of ambivalence from the staff, but they fail to understand or have faith in the growth side.

The staff's communication of ambivalence about a difficult area can be interpreted as indirectly asking the supervisor, "Are you really prepared to tackle this with me?" It is a situation in which a person is saying no but is hoping the other person will not really believe the message. The surface message may be "Leave me alone in this area," but the real message is, "Don't let me put you off."

The example in the preceding section about Marge, the worker about to retire, illustrates this point. The work problems may signal the area where help is needed, but simultaneously the resistance to help seems to say, "Leave me alone." Another example concerns a worker who brings up a particularly troublesome case at the beginning of a conference but who changes the subject or digresses into generalities whenever the supervisor tries to get at the specifics of the problem. Yet another example concerns Janice, the nurse who dealt with a performance problem raised by her supervisor by agreeing fully with the supervisor and by offering assurances that she would stop stalling and adopt the change in record keeping. This was a form of passive resistance because both knew, even during the interview, that the change would not occur.

In each of these examples (and the many others to follow), the supervisor must understand this process of change and his or her part in it, must develop the courage needed to deal with it, and must refuse to be put off by signs that the going will be rough. It is at these moments that the worker needs the supervisor's help the most and that the skills in making the demand for work are most effective.

The skill factor of making a demand for work is not limited to a single action or even a single group of skills. Rather, it pervades all supervisory work. The process of contracting described in chapter 3, for example, is a form of demand for work: The supervisor communicates early in the relationship that he or she means business. The attempts of the supervisor to bring the worker's feelings into the discussion are another form of demand for work. Thus, when a worker says that a client "was really being hit hard in that interview by her father's rejection," and the supervisor asks, "And how did that hit you?" this is a form of demand for work. Note that the demand can be gentle and coupled with support; it is not necessarily confrontational.

Supervisors who are able to empathize with staff members can develop a positive relationship, as noted in the preceding sections of this chapter, but they are not necessarily helpful in getting the work done. Supervisors who make only demands on the staff, while ignoring the empathy and the working relationship, often seem harsh, judgmental, and unhelpful. The most effective help is offered by supervisors who are able to synthesize caring and demand, each in her or his own way. This is not easy to do, in either helping relationships or life in general. There is a tendency to dichotomize these two aspects of a relationship. First, we may care about someone and express it through empathy. If we get nowhere, our frustration leads to anger and demand, and there is an associated lessening of empathic response. But it is precisely at this point, when crucial demands are made, that the capacity for empathy is most important.

Facilitative Confrontation

The term *facilitative confrontation*, drawn from psychoanalysis, refers to the efforts of the helping person to confront the client with reality in a supportive manner. Research has suggested that this is a crucial skill in provoking movement (Carkhuff, 1969). An example of a facilitative confrontation was the supervisor's final remarks to Marge, the staff member about to retire, as described earlier. Such a confrontation requires the supervisor to overcome social norms of behavior that he or she has internalized over the years. We have been taught that confrontation is not polite and have learned to fear its potential impact on a relationship.

In many of the examples given in the following chapters, confrontation is the key to movement in a situation. A common problem to which the skill can be applied arises in job management: dealing with a worker who is not functioning up to par. In one example, the worker was a new nurse's aide who had just completed her six-month probation period in an extended care facility for geriatric patients. Linda had begun serving at the setting as a volunteer and had then worked part time at night, under minimal supervision. She had appeared to be functioning well, but immediately after her probation period ended she began to come in late and to take extended coffee breaks. She needed to be continually prodded to handle her assignments. The supervisory staff was upset with Linda, and they were angry because they felt she had deceived them during her probation.

When this interaction was examined in a workshop, the three supervisors indicated they had not confronted Linda directly with her pattern of behavior. Each had dealt with individual incidents as they arose, but none had sat down with her and detailed the overall job management difficulties. Further exploration revealed that Linda had hoped to get into a special activity program in the setting, a job that was more interesting and stimulating than general ward care. She had been disappointed at not getting this job, but none of the supervisors had discussed the decision with her.

The supervisors suggested a number of reasons why they had not confronted her. First, they said they generally felt uncomfortable confronting a staff member about poor performance. It increased their sense of being a boss rather than a helper, and they found this uncomfortable. Second, in a setting such as an extended care hospital for geriatric patients, it can be difficult to get and to keep staff; thus, they were often willing to overlook the first signs of trouble in hopes that it would go away by itself or that the staff member would get the message through specific comments on job performance. Third, the supervisors admitted that they often felt guilty about their own job management and organization skills, and questioning their own efficiency made it difficult to demand greater efficiency from the staff. Finally, in Linda's case the supervisors felt guilty about not having given her more help in the beginning. They were as angry at themselves for having ducked the confrontation as they were at this aide for having provoked it.

It would be helpful to view this young worker, in her first full-time employment, in terms of her stage of life development. In a sense, it was unreasonable to expect her to be able to handle responsible job management without significant help from her supervisors. She was moving out of a period of life in which she was dependent and in many ways not required to be responsible, and she needed time to learn the needed skills and to develop work maturity. Helping her to do this was part of the supervisor's function. Linda's job management problems, rather then being simply provocation aimed at the supervisors, might represent her own agenda items for learning.

Understanding this young aide's life situation was as important as was tuning in to the concerns and feelings of the worker about to retire in the earlier example. In each case, the supervisor could use the understanding to help the worker deal with the job tasks related to the life tasks. Learning to take responsibility and to live with disappointments such as not getting the activity center position are normal elements in a new worker's development.

With this sense of the importance of facilitative confrontation as a normal part of supervision and of the potential help the supervisors could provide this new staff member, the workshop participants role played an interview. They pointed out Linda's poor work pattern, reached for her feelings about the job (including her disappointments), and then set clear expectations for job performance. During the role play, the supervisor admitted her part in perpetuating the problem, acknowledging that she should have dealt directly with Linda about these questions earlier.

It was clear from the workshop discussion that the supervisors would expect changes in Linda's work pattern, or she would receive a negative evaluation with consequences that could affect her employment. Her immediate supervisor thought she could make these strong demands more easily if she believed she had done the best supervisory job possible with Linda. After the supervisor's efforts, the results depended on how well the young aide could respond to the demands. That was her part in the proceedings.

Partializing the Worker's Concerns

Staff members often experience their concerns as overwhelming. A worker may present a number of complex issues, each with some impact on the others. His or her feeling of helplessness is as much related to the apparent difficulty of tackling so many problems as it is to the nature of the problems themselves. The worker may feel immobilized and not know where to begin. Furthermore, it is not unusual for such multiple problems to be presented to the supervisor at the last minute, such as 4 P.M. on a Friday afternoon, when the worker spots the supervisor and asks, "Have you got a minute?" The supervisor can quickly feel as overwhelmed as the worker.

Partializing is essentially a problem-solving skill. The only way to tackle complex problems is to break them down into their component parts and address them one at a time. The way to move past feelings of immobilization is to begin by taking one small step toward solving one part of the problem. This is where the supervisor can make a demand for work on the worker. While listening to the worker's concerns and attempting to understand and acknowledge the worker's feelings of being overwhelmed, the supervisor begins the task of helping the worker reduce the problem to smaller, more manageable portions.

The skill of partializing concerns for the worker is illustrated in the following report of a supervisor's interview with a crisis worker in a child welfare agency who was himself in crisis. Although this worker, Tad, had had some practice experience in the child welfare field, it had been in adoptions. He had recently been transferred to a downtown office to handle calls that often involved coming into contact with clients in crisis situations. This kind of work was new to him and was a bit threatening.

Tad had come into the supervisor's office out of breath, looking disheveled and upset. When the supervisor asked him what was up and acknowledged his evident distress, he began,

Tad: This new Johnson case is a doozy! I don't know what to do with it or where to go next. Maybe we should consider apprehending the child.

Supervisor: Slow down a bit and let me have the details. What has you so concerned?

Tad: When I went to visit Mrs. Johnson after that telephone call about possible abuse, she broke down and told me her husband had threatened her with a knife. She was afraid he would lose his temper and beat her up. While we were talking, the two year-old was pulling at her dress and getting into her sewing things, and she grabbed him and shook him right in front of me.

Supervisor: That must have been upsetting!

Tad: In addition to the knife-wielding husband and her shaking the kid, then she tells me she has just received an eviction notice from the landlord and she really starts to cry. She told me her sister said she would take the kid for a while, but her sister's husband hates her, and she is afraid to go there. She was really at a loss.

Supervisor: You must have felt that way, too. What did you do?

Tad: I sympathized with her and told her I would think things over and see if I can come up with an answer. What I was really feeling was that it was quite a mess, and I wondered if I should be leaving the kid there tonight.

Supervisor: You probably also wished you were back in adoption.

Tad (smiling for the first time): That's exactly what I thought!

The parallel processes of supervisor–worker and worker–client relationships are helpful in analyzing an illustration such as this one. The client feels overwhelmed by the problems and conveys this anxiety to the worker. The worker, in turn, feels overwhelmed and projects these feelings onto the supervisor. By not getting overwhelmed, the supervisor can model the skills needed for dealing with the client's concerns. He has already begun to do this by recognizing the worker's feelings about the interview. The next step is to partialize the concerns so that the worker can begin to get a handle on some next steps.

Supervisor: So you really have a number of things to deal with, just like the client. You're concerned about the possibility of violence with the husband, there is the abuse potential with mom under so much stress, and the eviction notice hanging over her head. Which one should we start with?

Tad: It's the husband who has me really scared.

Supervisor: Okay. Have you had any contact with him yet?

Although partializing does not alone solve a problem, and though each of these concerns is a bit overwhelming in itself, it at least provides the possibility of tackling them one at a time. Breaking large, over-whelming problems into their smaller components is a first step and an important beginning in the problem-solving process. In addition to helping ease the worker's obvious anxiety, the supervisor conveys the message that there is some possible next step and that, together, they will try to find out what the alternatives are.

Holding to Focus

As the worker begins to deal with each issue, its connections with other related concerns can often cause a rambling presentation, a difficulty in concentrating on one issue at a time. Asking the worker to stay focused on one question only is using a problem-solving skill incorporating a demand for work. Moving from one concern to another can be evasion of work— that is, not staying on one issue means not having to deal with the associated feelings. Holding the focus sends the message to the worker that the supervisor intends to deal with the disturbing issues and feelings.

In Tad's case, after the supervisor had partialized the issues and they had begun to focus on the knife-wielding father, Tad switched the conversation back to his concern about the child. The supervisor attempted to hold the focus by saying, "Could we stay on what to do about Mr. Johnson for a minute and then get back to your concern about the child?"

It became obvious from the discussion that Tad needed to contact the father given that up to this point he had only the mother's perception of what was going on. Even a telephone call might help to get a sense of how agitated the father actually was. The supervisor then discussed resources available to the mother and child that could provide immediate protection until Tad was clearer about how much of a threat Mr. Johnson posed. He suggested contacting a particular transition house for possible acceptance of the mother.

Checking for Underlying Ambivalence

One danger in any helping situation is that the staff may appear to go along with the supervisor and may express agreement with an idea or proposed change but all the while may feel ambivalent about it. Members may not want to upset the supervisor by voicing doubts, or they may simply be unaware of their true feelings. The supervisor may even sense this "lurking ambivalence" but fail to confirm it for fear of exposing and thus reinforcing their doubts.

As a result, both the staff and the supervisor may participate in the illusion of work. The supervisor may prefer to stress the positive aspects of the strategy or try to further convince or sell the staff on the idea in the belief that bringing the doubts to light could frustrate the required action. Actually, the reverse is often true. Only after ambivalent feelings are fully discussed and dealt with do they lose their power and leave the staff free to act. Whatever the reasons for the staff's reluctance to act, the supervisor helps most effectively by listening, understanding the ambivalence, and then making the demand that staff members act in spite of their mixed feelings.

Supervisors, therefore, need to guard against the temptation to accept a worker's facile agreement and must instead bring doubts out into the open. In the example of Tad, the child welfare worker, the supervisor discussed next steps concerning possible child abuse and how to handle the landlord and the eviction notice. Then he asked the worker to review the agreed-on strategies. Tad seemed to have forgotten the agreement to telephone the father, although when the supervisor reminded him, he quickly added that step to the list. The supervisor sensed his reluctance to call the father and brought it up directly:

> Supervisor: You don't sound too excited about calling Mr. Johnson. What is it? Are you afraid of him?
>
> Tad: Well, now that I think about it, talking to an angry father with a knife doesn't sound like my idea of a pleasant afternoon.
>
> Supervisor: I can appreciate your concern. Would it help if you made first contact by phone and then asked to see him here in the office?
>
> Tad: I think I would feel better about that. Also, I'm not sure what to say to him. Do I ask him if he really pulled a knife on his wife? He might not appreciate that.
>
> Supervisor: Let's take some time and see if you can find a way of carrying on this conversation without creating additional problems. It won't be easy under any circumstances, but with a little planning, maybe we can improve your ability to handle it. Why not start by tuning in to him to imagine what he will be feeling when you call him?

By reaching for the underlying ambivalence, the supervisor opened up an important area of work—the feelings of a worker faced with a potentially violent client and the technical aspects of how to deal with such a client. If the supervisor had not broached this and then had not tried to help through discussion and a brief role play, there was a good chance that the worker would report back that he had been unable to reach the father or that the father was resistant. If Mr. Johnson felt strongly enough in this case, both Tad and the supervisor would be hearing from him soon enough because he would really be angry at the way he was being left out.

The modeling by the supervisor of how to proceed is important because the worker is likely to be faced with the same kind of illusion of agreement from the client. Mrs. Johnson, for example, might agree to move out of her home if she feels threatened and to stay at a transition house for women and children. Tad would be surprised to find that she did not go there when she said she would or that she quickly moved back to live with her husband. If the interview with the mother were examined closely enough, he could probably find many clues signaling the mother's ambivalence about following his advice and leaving her husband. These clues might be ignored by a worker determined to get the client to implement his or her "solutions" to the problem. This tendency of workers to agree to an artificial consensus is explored further in the next section.

Challenging the Illusion of Work

One of the greatest threats to effective supervision lies in the ability of the worker to create what Schwartz (1968, 1977) termed the *illusion of work*. The capacity to engage in conversations that have no meaning is easily

developed, and the ability to talk a great deal and not say anything meaningful can quickly become a part of the supervision repertoire. For staff
members, this can often be a subtle form of resistance because by creating
the illusion that work is proceeding, they do not have to tackle the difficult
issues. The empathic skills that encourage the staff to share feelings as well
as facts in the supervision process are one way in which the supervisor
encourages work of substance. In addition, it is often necessary for the supervisor to call attention to the illusion of work. By exposing it to view, he or she
can begin the process of returning the staff to effective work.

In discussing the illusion of work in the group context, Schwartz
(1968) provided an example drawn from his work with middle-level public
welfare supervisors. When he was leading a workshop on group methods in
supervision, he detected a pattern of resistance among the participants
that in many ways paralleled the resistance they had experienced in their
own staff group meetings. Schwartz noted how this resistance affected the
workshop proceedings:

> The effect was to produce a sporadic way of working, alternating
> periods of apathy and inertia with flashes of feeling and creative work.
> But it also produced before your eyes many of the very conditions that
> troubled them, and about which they were trying to learn. About
> midway in the consultation period, I confronted each group with its
> way of working and asked them to come to grips with how they were
> using the consultation. They made a thoughtful and serious response,
> and it was at this point that they were able to crystallize many of their
> deepest feelings and ideas about their work. (p. 363)

Most supervisors fail to make this direct challenge to the illusion
partly because they fear that the problems they sense are of their own
making. Schwartz (1968) challenged this reluctance, confident that resistance is an essential part of the work and that its appearance, in fact,
signals proximity to the "deepest feelings and ideas about their work." The
challenge is difficult for a less experienced supervisor to make because the
same set of norms and taboos that cause staff members to be reluctant to
speak directly about their feelings are also operating for the supervisor.

In Schwartz's (1968) workshop, he found that the confrontation sessions in each group marked a turning point for the supervisors: "It was
thus in the context of their own groups that they could see how fuzziness
and fear could hinder creative work among people and how a direct and
honest attempt to deal with the feelings could trigger deeper work and
some hope for future possibilities" (p. 363). A number of participants
brought in examples of how they had confronted their own staffs as
Schwartz had confronted them. They realized that as a result of his confrontation, they had opened up honestly, and so they believed that the
tactic might work in the same way with their own staffs.

The role of the supervisor as a model is crucially important in presenting this skill to the staff. The supervisor who challenges the illusion of work with a staff member demonstrates its importance to the staff member's own work with clients.

Another example of challenging the illusion of work, this time in the individual supervision context, concerns how to deal with a staff member who uses a form of passive resistance in responding to the demands of the supervisor. This is the example of Janice, the nurse who always agreed with the supervisor's criticisms and suggestions but never implemented any of the changes that were described in the section on containment. After noting this pattern of resistance, the supervisor decided to challenge it:

> Janice: You're right about my problem with getting those forms in on time—and I'm really sorry. I'm going to get organized this week. I'll check those statistics and get them in to the office manager by Friday.
>
> Supervisor: You know, you have said that the last two times I have raised this issue, and nothing has happened. I get the feeling you find it easier to put me off this way than to really deal with what's going on. Am I right about this?
>
> Janice (with anger): I don't know why you have to make interpretations all the time. I've just been late, that's all.
>
> Supervisor: Look, I'm not attacking you for this. I just have the feeling you are not leveling with me about these forms. What's important to me is that we talk straight about things like this.
>
> Janice: Well, frankly, I'm so busy right now I don't have time to breathe—and even less time to fill in these ridiculous forms that no one will read anyway.
>
> Supervisor: That's better! Now let's talk about what's happening to your work load and let's look at exactly what these forms are all about.

In pointing out the pattern of resistance, the supervisor gave a signal to Janice that this evasion of work was no longer acceptable. At the same time, Janice was encouraged to start saying what she really felt, rather than what she thought the supervisor wanted to hear. If this resistant behavior recurred with another issue, the supervisor could then discuss the general pattern to be followed in handling disagreements. Such incidents could be the springboard for a discussion of the worker's way of relating to supervisors, a way she had developed over years of learning to deal with people in authority.

However, the worker's pattern of dealing with authority is not the subject of supervision. Rather, it is a way of understanding how this worker deals with this supervisor, so that a new process of relating can be developed. The theme of dealing with authority is more fully presented in the next section of this chapter. The mere identifying of the illusion of work, however, may be the critical step in helping staff members develop a new culture for work with norms of behavior that encourage rather than hinder productive, honest work.

Skills in Pointing out Obstacles

The model of the work phase of supervision presented at the beginning of this chapter (Figure 4.1) is admittedly an oversimplification. The various supervisory work-skill factors are not so well defined as to be completely independent of one another. The skill of challenging the illusion of work, for example, which was associated with the factor of making a demand for work, could also be considered part of the factor of pointing out obstacles. Certainly, identifying a pattern of passive resistance by a worker and challenging it could also be used as an example in this section.

In examining the skill factor of pointing out obstacles, however, certain impediments require specific attention. Some of these are discussed in this section in examples of staff methods for dealing with taboo subjects such as sexuality and authority.

Exploring Taboo Areas

The culture of the society in which we live imposes taboos against open discussion in certain sensitive areas. From childhood on, direct questions and discussions about sex, for instance, are frowned on. Other areas in which we are subtly encouraged not to acknowledge our true feelings include dependency, authority, money, death, and anger. Moreover, we are taught how we should feel in these sensitive areas. Boys, for example, are traditionally taught that to be a "real man" means to be independent; dependency is equated with weakness. Girls are traditionally taught to be passive and submissive. The real world is so complex, however, that everyone is interdependent. Both men and women, therefore, may feel independent or submissive, consciously or not, but think that they should feel the other way. Cultural norms include taboos that make honest discussion in these areas difficult.

Both helping professionals and their clients have difficulty in overcoming their reluctance to discuss issues in taboo areas. Staff members cannot help others feel comfortable in such discussions if they themselves are uncomfortable. If they are to be able to help clients deal with feelings, they must first examine their own feelings and learn to accept them. This skill has been identified as one of three that helps distinguish more effective workers from those who are less effective (Shulman, 1978). It also correlates strongly with clients' perceptions of workers' helpfulness.

The supervisor must create a climate for work with staff in which taboo subjects are seen as acceptable for discussion and all relevant feelings can be freely shared. One example of this comes from my work on sexuality with a group of child care workers. Jon, a handsome 22-year-old staff member, was working in a residence that included teenage girls. In the course of a workshop discussion, he made a joke about the attractiveness and seductiveness of a girl whose problems were being discussed, and the other staff members laughed. I decided to address the serious issue I felt was lurking just behind the joking. I told them I realized that they all had had some humorous experiences of this type with the youngsters, but I suggested that this whole question of sexual attraction was a serious one. They all had to work closely with young, attractive teenagers of the opposite sex, many of whom were blatantly seductive. I wondered how it made them feel.

Jon, who had introduced the subject with the joke, said he felt very uncomfortable. I asked if he found himself being aroused by the youths and then felt guilty about these feelings. He nodded vigorously, and others, male and female, gave similar examples. After some discussion of the naturalness of these feelings, I asked the group how this made it difficult for them in their work. Jon described how the teenage girl they were discussing sent him notes and made comments that made him feel she had a crush on him. He was just ignoring her. When I asked if it was harder to deal with her because he felt attracted to her, he acknowledged that it was.

I told the staff that being in touch with their own feelings was a start in dealing with this issue. The next step was to see how they could turn this interaction with the youngster into effective practice. By using the joking hint as a springboard to their practice, I signaled to the staff that I was ready to discuss this taboo area. Opening the door to this discussion simultaneously moved us into some important conversation and affected our group's culture for work. The ability of the staff to share their feelings and the comfort of finding others in the same situation are important helping factors in supervision. It would have been inappropriate to turn the session into a discussion of their sexual concerns and feelings.

I disagree strongly with approaches to helping the staff discuss such matters that are centered on an active exploration of the members' own sexuality. A staff member's fantasies, fears, or early experiences in the sexual area are not the business of the supervisor or trainer; in fact, exploration of these areas is counterproductive to work. It can easily become an invasion of privacy, a form of therapy for the staff, or a seductive distraction from the actual work of supervision. Once the staff has recognized the difficulty of talking about this subject and understands that their own feelings in relation to the work are important, the discussion must be clearly connected to their practice. The questions is this: "What is it about your feelings that makes it hard for you to deal with the clients?" When workers see that the discussions will be bounded by the working contract and that the supervisor will actively guard that contract against attempts to subvert it (if, for example, the staff asks for help with their sexual problems), they will feel more comfortable in such discussions and will be freed by the structure.

As the workshop discussion continued, we examined the practice implications of the staff member's feelings. I suggested that we could start by tuning in to the teenage girl's feelings in this area. Given her past experiences, they should consider what it must be like to be 15 years old. Could they empathize with her fears, concerns, and questions? Among the issues that emerged in this work was a concern about what made a "real woman": What qualities were needed for the gender role? Another was what qualities made a young woman attractive to men. Most of these girls had been taught that sexuality is a central tool in relating to men and that their value is related to their attractiveness as sexual objects.

Returning to the incidents Jon had described, I acknowledged the reality of the "crush" part of the message but suggested that the youngster was also saying that she needed to talk to an adult, specifically a male adult, about these concerns. Rather than just viewing her notes and comments as a come-on and ignoring them, if Jon were able to find a way of responding to them, they could become handles for work. Jon was excited about this; it offered him an opportunity to work with this girl rather than constantly trying to hide from her. We role played how we might explore this topic without crushing her feelings. Jon needed to let her know he appreciated her interest, to make it clear that he could not become involved in any way, and to indicate that he had heard the concerns she was expressing. One of the staff members got the point and said, "You mean reaching for the real message, just like you did here this morning?"

In another example of dealing with staff feelings about taboo subjects, I was impressed with how strong the taboos can be and how even the worker may be unaware of his or her own feelings. In this case, I was supervising male workers, the first group leaders for mutual aid groups being established for men who had battered their wives or women with whom they lived. Formation of these groups had been requested by staff members at the women's shelter, whose anger at these men was understandable. The male workers wanted to "straighten them out" and even suggested that films of battered women be shown to help them see the results of their behavior. It was clear that the shelter staff had great difficulty in seeing these men as clients in their own right. They were angry at them, and they wanted the service offered only because, in spite of their efforts, the battered women kept returning home.

It was agreed that it was important to hold these men accountable for their behavior toward women. It was important for the workers to make clear their feelings that violence and intimidation were unacceptable behaviors. However, it was also important for the men's groups to be seen as mutual aid groups in which members could help each other with personal issues and feelings that made it difficult for them to relate appropriately to women. While focusing on the issues of violence, the groups also had to relate to the concerns raised by their members. The male workers who were to lead these groups strongly supported the need to accept the men while rejecting their behaviors and to treat them as clients in their own right. In the early sessions, they were quick to disassociate themselves from the punitive attitudes that had been expressed by the shelter workers. As they began their pregroup interviews with these men, however, their practice began to reveal their true feelings. In subtle ways, they were communicating the attitude they had appeared to reject.

When I pointed this out to them as we reviewed the records of the interviews, I asked them to describe how they really felt in key moments of the interaction. Faced with the reality of their actions, they began to admit their genuine anger at the men. I gave them credit for their admissions and pointed out how easy it would be for them to deny, even to themselves, these "unprofessional" feelings. With the taboo challenged, the door was open for discussion of their strongest feelings in relation to the work. It went as follows:

> Consultant: Do you have any ideas about what it is about these men that makes you so angry at them [that] you have a hard time even admitting it to yourselves?
>
> Terry: You know, when I see their anger at women, it really scares me because I think I feel some of that anger as well.
>
> Frank: There have been lots of times when I felt mad enough to belt my partner—but the difference between me and them is that I don't do it.
>
> Consultant: It's a bit scarey though, isn't it, seeing how similar your feelings can be to theirs?

This discussion, and others that followed, began a process of helping the workers to be less judgmental of their own feelings and thus less judgmental of the clients' feelings. It was a difficult admission under the circumstances, but once they were able to face their own anger at the men and to identify in part the source of these feelings, they were in a much better position to provide help.

In many ways, professionals must deal with both the general societal taboos against certain feelings and a strong sense of professional taboos. The perception is that people should not have certain feelings, and a professional person certainly should not feel that way. This double burden makes it especially difficult for workers to discuss their fears, anxieties, and feelings, particularly in taboo areas, without the support and encouragement of their supervisors.

Dealing with the Authority Theme

The authority theme was described by Schwartz and Zalba (1971) in the worker–client context as "the familiar struggle to resolve the relationship with a nurturing and demanding figure who is both a personal symbol and a representative of a powerful institution" (p. 11). In a similar manner, as the worker deals with a supervisor, both positive and negative affects are generated. There are times when the supervisor appears to be a caring and supportive figure. At other times, the supervisor makes demands on the worker. Each of these processes generates some affective response. Even the most skilled supervisor operates under many pressures and cannot be "perfect." Supervisors miss signals, overreact, are not supportive enough, fail to represent staff feelings to administration, and so on in the natural course of events in the agency or other setting.

Stresses related to the authority theme should be anticipated as a normal part of the work of supervision. In fact, the energy flow caused by the affect between a supervisor and a worker can be an important part of the driving force of supervision. But because supervisors who feel inadequate often interpret problems of authority as a negative judgment of their abilities, they may be reluctant to create a setting wherein such feelings and reactions can be openly discussed and dealt with.

In my view, it is the supervisor's task to teach the staff that supervisors are to be treated as real people, not as symbols of authority. This is an ongoing, never-ending process. The goal of the work is not to create a situation in which all negative affect is resolved. Rather, it is to create a climate in which both the positive and negative feelings inherent in the work can be freely expressed. If this is not done, these feelings will go beneath the surface and will emerge later to haunt the supervisor in such forms as staff passivity, defensiveness, the illusion of work, low productivity, or even sabotage.

The authority theme includes elements of transference and countertransference that are familiar in the context of work with clients. Strean (1978) described their effects on the worker–client relationship by drawing on the psychoanalytic theory of Freud. Simply substituting *supervisor* for *worker* and *worker* for *client* makes the following discussion clearly relevant:

> This relationship has many facets: subtle and overt, conscious and unconscious, progressive and regressive, positive and negative. Both client and worker experience themselves and each other not only in terms of objective reality, but in terms of how each wishes the other to be and fears he might be. The phenomena of "transference" and "counter-transference" exists in every relationship between two or more people, professional and nonprofessional, and must be taken into account in every social worker–client encounter. By "transference" is meant the feelings, wishes, fears, and defenses of the client from reactions to significant persons in the past (parents, siblings, extended family, teachers) that influence his current perceptions of the social worker. "Counter-transference" similarly refers to aspects of the social worker's history of feelings, wishes, fears and so on, all of which influence his perceptions of the client. (p. 193)

The powerful influences of transference and countertransference make it possible that the supervisor and the staff will relate to each other as stereotypes rather than as real people. Inevitably, in such a situation, real communications break down; both parties hear what they expect to hear, misinterpret what they hear to fit their stereotype of the other, and remember selectively. The key to breaking this cycle is to build into the ongoing working relationship a mechanism for bringing differences out into the open. The supervisor must change the norms by which his or her staff have learned to relate to people in authority and must develop a new norm that rejects the commonly accepted taboo against straight talk in this sensitive and fearful area.

The process can start in the beginning phase of work if the new supervisor (or the supervisor with a new staff member) includes in the contract discussion an expectation of honesty on issues of the authority theme. One new supervisor in a residential setting issued the invitation in the form of the following statement in an early staff meeting: "I want to encourage you all to level with me about your feelings in terms of how I do my job. I'm sure there will be times you get angry with me or want something from me I'm not giving. It would help a great deal if you could level, because I need to really know what you're feeling."

Although the staff members nodded in approval of the comment, it would be naive to think they really believed this supervisor. They heard her and appreciated the invitation, but many of them had heard the same words before, only to find that the first time they gave negative feedback they were "clobbered" by the supervisor. Therefore, the staff usually waits to see whether the supervisor really means the invitation. One way of testing the supervisor is to provide a relatively safe bit of negative feedback and see how it is handled. If the supervisor accepts it without cutting down the staff member, the signal will encourage more feedback.

Make no mistake about it—all staff members watch closely how the first encounters are handled as the "internal leaders" in the staff begin the testing process. Staff members have a powerful stake in the outcome, and because they feel vulnerable, they have learned to be particularly sensitive to early cues in this area.

The testing of the child care supervisor whose introductory remarks were quoted earlier was carried out by the grapevine—the first time a decision that was resented by the staff was made, the negative reaction was voiced informally. Conversations over lunch, in the staff lounge, and at the Friday afternoon unwinding sessions in the local pub were the mediums for expression of these feelings. One staff member, acting in a crucial role, passed along the presence of the negative feelings to the supervisor. The stage was set for an important encounter, the outcome of which would set the tone for further work on the authority theme.

At the next staff meeting, the supervisor began by indicating her knowledge of the staff's negative feelings on the issue (a change in staff rotations and weekend coverage) and opened the question for discussion. It was important for the supervisor to begin with the substantive issue (the task focus) and to try to deal with that effectively. She was able to accept some of their objections and, at the same time, to clarify some of her reasons for maintaining some aspects of the change in rotation. The staff members were not fully satisfied with her position, but they agreed that a compromise was the best solution. At the end of this discussion, the supervisor turned her attention to the authority theme (the process focus) and began the work on effecting changes in the norms of the work group. The dialogue went as follows:

> Supervisor: I want to talk a bit about how this issue was raised. You know, even though I invited you to level with me if you were not happy with how things were going here, I had to find out about how mad you were through the grapevine. Let's talk about that for a minute. How come you didn't raise this directly?
>
> Ted: I can only talk for myself, but I didn't think you were going to appreciate us taking you on so early. In fact, I really wasn't sure I wanted to take you on so early.
>
> Supervisor: You weren't sure how I would handle it?
>
> Louise: Look, I have had bosses tell me to level with them before. What they really meant was, "Be honest when you agree with me."
>
> Supervisor: I'm sure you all have had experiences with supervisors and others who have invited the feedback, then acted like the king who killed the messenger. It's understandable that you are a bit wary of me and not sure I mean what I say. I can't guarantee that I will always be able to handle your feedback. There will be times when I will blow it, too—I'm only human. But I want you to know that I really mean the invitation, and I will do my best to make you feel safe when you have something to say. I can't do my job correctly unless you agree to be honest. I know it's a tough demand I'm making, but I think it's worth it. How about it?
>
> Ted: I have to admit you were open to our feedback on the rotations— even though you didn't buy all of our arguments. I sure as hell would like to be able to level. (Other staff members nod in agreement.)
>
> Supervisor: Great! I think this is a good start. I know it won't be easy to maintain this openness, so on occasion I'm going to raise it again to see how we are doing. You can raise it as well, if you think it's necessary.

By addressing the question of norms in relation to the authority theme, the supervisor was working on the structure of the work group. She also acknowledged the importance of maintaining this structure when she pointed out that they would have to return to this theme later. This is the sense in which the work on the authority theme never ends. Periodic attention is needed to make sure the structure is sound. An analogy from space technology may be helpful. When a rocket is sent to another planet, the specific orbit is preprogrammed into the computer, but scientists also recognize the need to make periodic adjustments in direction as the rocket proceeds in its flight; thus, they build in self-correcting mechanisms. Another self-correcting feedback mechanism is the home thermostat, which reads the house temperature and automatically adjusts the heating system to maintain the required temperature range.

Similar maintenance mechanisms are needed in all human relationships. In the supervisor–staff relationship, in which power can suppress real communications, it is absolutely essential not only to develop a structure for honest communications but also to maintain it systematically to ensure that it is working well.

This maintenance work is exemplified by another supervisor in a child welfare agency, one who had had a positive relationship with his workers for more than two years. Nevertheless, a number of seemingly casual comments by staff members had struck him as indirect signals of issues related to the authority theme. Determined to do some "maintenance work" on the authority theme, he invited the staff to discuss how they worked together because the comments indicated that attention was necessary. Staff members evaded his direct question in the early part of the session, probably because they were unsure that he really meant it and so were afraid to begin. When he pointed this out, they engaged in a discussion that touched on each of the major subthemes of the authority theme. These include the supervisor's (1) role, (2) position as an outsider, (3) supportive function, (4) limitations, and (5) demand function. In the course of a working relationship, all these subthemes must be considered.

Supervisor's Role

The question of role, which was discussed in some detail in chapter 2, came up with respect to how the supervisor offered help on cases. One staff member said, "When I come to you asking for advice on a case that's really giving me trouble, you usually start with a lot of good ideas about what I can do. But I can't hear any of them because I'm sitting there churning away inside with my feelings. I'm saying to myself, 'Okay, run that by me again and maybe I can hear it this time.'" The supervisor asked why the worker didn't let him know how he was feeling. The worker replied, "I know you're interested in us, and in the past few years you have given me a lot of support. But I'm not sure if these feelings really belong—like I'm not sure I'm supposed to be telling you how shook up I'm feeling. You once said supervision doesn't get into our personal lives, and I'm not sure if this isn't personal." When the supervisor checked and found others with similar concerns, he explained that these feelings were related to their work, and he needed to hear them.

Supervisor's Position as an Outsider

Even if this supervisor had been a staff member and had experienced the problems of being a worker, he is now something of an outsider. Prior experiences can help supervisors understand what the staff is experiencing, but they are no longer in the same situation. Recognition of this reality can help.

In an excerpt from the same staff meeting, another member pointed out this: "Do you remember when I had that kid I couldn't place, and I was at the end of the day, with no place to put him? I was feeling complete frustration and completely alone. You tried to tell me that other staff members were in a similar bind." The supervisor responded that he had perceived how upset the worker was and had wanted to let her know that she was not alone. The worker replied, "Well, when you said that, I figured that you just didn't understand what was happening. I mean, for you, as a supervisor, you can treat this more objectively. I mean, you're not out there with the kid." The supervisor acknowledged that his comments had not really helped. He went on to say, "You know, it's hard for me to really remember, in my gut, what it feels like to be in some of the binds you experience. I sense your discomfort and try to pick you up, but you're right—I'm not really in your shoes any more."

Supervisor's Supportive Function

I believe most workers want the support of their supervisors. They may have trouble admitting to areas of vulnerability. Their ambivalence may lead them to send mixed messages to their supervisors about their feelings. This is why it is helpful, during the course of the working relationship, to pay some direct attention to this issue.

In the example, the worker who described not being able to hear the supervisor's suggestions when he was anxious about a case expressed her need in this way: "It's not that the solutions aren't helpful. It's just that it would be better if you let me unload a bit, get all those feelings off my chest. After I clear that up, then I think I might be able to listen better to your ideas about the problem." The supervisor said, "I think I sense that you are upset, and sometimes I jump in with answers before I let you tell me what the real problem is. What you're telling me is that you need more in the way of support." Another worker quickly made a balancing comment, reassuring the supervisor that the staff felt they had received a lot of support from him, especially in the past few years. When they were in a real panic, though, they sometimes felt cut off.

Supervisor's Limitations

In addition to discussing the mutual expectations inherent in the authority theme, it is also important to recognize the limitations in the relationship. The supervisor is human, has feelings, and is often overwhelmed. Workers need to discuss and come to grips with the differences between their wishes and hopes and the supervisor's reality.

To continue with the example, the supervisor leveled in response to their feedback, "You know, to be honest, there are times when you come to me and I feel I don't have it to give you. I really sense what you're feeling, but a big part of me doesn't really want to hear it." Another worker asked, "Do you ever say that?" The supervisor answered that he probably did not;

he probably just listened and pretended to be there. The worker replied, "I can always tell when you're not with me." Another worker interjected, "Maybe he can't always be with us. Maybe we are going to have to find ways to support ourselves and not always depend on him."

Supervisor's Demand Function

This aspect of the authority theme concerns the feelings generated in the staff members by the supervisor's demands on them. Even if the demands are clearly appropriate and the workers understand them as being in their own best interest, the very process of making the demand must generate some negative feelings. Recognizing these feelings and understanding that they are part of the work process is crucial. The supervisor must acknowledge and validate these feelings and must resist the initial temptation to run from them or perhaps to share his or her "hurt" at not being liked. Running from such feelings only drives them beneath the surface where they become more powerful deterrents to effective work. Supervisors who are constantly "wounded" by them may end up generating guilt on the part of the staff, which also drives the feelings underground.

In most situations, the problem has two sides, and the supervisor has every reason for being angry at the workers as well. An open exchange of views is the healthiest way to deal with such conflict. The following example comes from another supervisory context. In a discussion of the authority theme, a nurse in a staff group said, "Even though I knew it was right, and you had to do it, I was really—and I still am—angry at you for pushing me around that way." The supervisor responded by saying, "Sure, you're angry, and I don't blame you. But, I'm not exactly happy that I have to push you on something like this. Why don't you take some responsibility so I don't always have to feel I need to be on your back?" Another staff member, speaking to the first, said, "You know, she's got a point there. We really dragged our heels on this one."

Discussion of the authority theme is a two-way process. Supervisors also have rights, can have expectations of the staff, and do not have to allow themselves to be pushed around. If a supervisor is really hiding feelings, sitting there and apparently empathizing with the staff's complaints while basically not agreeing, the artificiality will not help in the development of honest communications. Just as the staff members are free to accept the supervisor's invitation to level with their feelings, so the supervisor must have the same right. Staff members should feel free to say what they feel, but they also need to listen and be willing to take responsibility for their own part in the proceedings.

Skills in Sharing Data

In describing the skill of sharing data in the practice context, Schwartz (1961) defined data as facts, ideas, values, and beliefs that the worker makes available to the client. The skill is also central to supervision; in fact, a major part of supervision involves passing along information. The supervisor has access to agency policies, information about clients, research knowledge about practice, and a fund of practice wisdom that comes from experience in the field. It is important for supervisors to share information because of its potential in building a working relationship. But also, because the staff looks to the supervisor as a source of help in difficult areas, withholding of data, for whatever reason, can be experienced as a form of rejection.

Most supervisors identify sharing data as a central part of their function. The problems arise in relation to the way in which the information is shared. There are many misconceptions about the process. Sharing data is essentially one of the teaching skills that are examined in chapter 6. This section defines three of the skills in this supervisory skill factor: providing relevant data, monitoring the learning process, and presenting data in a way that is open to challenge.

Providing Relevant Data

The skill of providing relevant data calls for direct sharing of the supervisor's knowledge and information as they become relevant to the staff's task at hand. Workers usually will not learn something that the supervisor thinks may be needed at some future time unless they find it useful in handling their immediate concerns. Careful monitoring of what the staff is working on, so as to be ready to provide needed information as it becomes relevant, is a necessary part of the process of supervision.

Many agencies make the mistake of designing an orientation program for new workers that consists of studying the agency manual of policies and procedures. Most of these can have meaning only in the context of the practice, however. Some of the material can be learned in advance, but workers may be overwhelmed by information that is irrelevant to their immediate tasks. They may go through the motions of learning but may then need to refer to the manual to be able to apply a policy when a case requires it.

When the supervisory skill of providing relevant data is applied to the orientation program, the staff's learning needs are considered, and the program is organized to match their immediate requirements. Beginners are better off learning how to use a manual, perhaps with some common case examples, than they are attempting to learn all the information in the manual. Supervisors tend to forget how complicated the data can be. It may have taken them many years to understand the information they wish to share, and it is because of those years of effort that it now seems so simple.

Sharing data is also critical in the ongoing work. To really learn new facts or ideas—that is, to integrate them—the staff must have practice in using them. This integration takes place during the implementation of an idea. Therefore, it is wise to teach a new skill or concept close to the time when it will be needed. The tendency to present everything one knows can create merely the illusion of teaching.

As in the orientation program, the staff's ongoing learning agenda should be developed by monitoring the demands of the job. The first time questions about an area of policy are asked in a case, an opportunity is provided to explore the policy implications of that portion of the manual. Similarly, the first time a worker runs into a resistant client may be the best time to explore the meaning of resistance and to discuss those skills that help deal with it. In both cases, teaching to immediate concerns gives the staff members practical experience that provides a framework for the data.

Monitoring the Learning Process

A supervisor imparting data, in both group and individual settings, must be able to monitor the nonverbal cues of the staff members that indicate how they are responding to the presentation. Educational practice sometimes suggests that the mere statement of an idea by a teacher is enough for it to be heard, understood, and remembered by the learner. The learning process is interactional in nature, however, and requires the active involvement of the learner. A supervisor may be doing an excellent job of sharing information, but the worker may be getting none of it. This leads to the frustrating problem of the staff's asking questions about the very issue the supervisor is sure has already been "covered."

Monitoring the cues may involve simply watching the staff members' eyes and noticing when they seem to glaze over—a common response when the learning is incomplete or stops. In staff meetings, other signals that communication is breaking down are sent when members stare out the window or even fall asleep. Supervisors who read such signals as signs that they themselves are ineffective may even keep their heads down while speaking to make sure they do not see them.

Supervisors should anticipate that the teaching–learning process will break down many times during the sharing of data. Rather than ignoring the signs of this breakdown, they can use them to deepen the work. They must recognize, however, that these signals have many meanings, and the first step in using a signal is to call attention to it and determine its message.

One message may be that the supervisor has overloaded the learners or has gone too fast. Years of educational experience have trained workers to sit quietly and continue to nod in agreement, even if they have lost all threads of comprehension; thus, the supervisor has to monitor the process. In the following example, the supervisor had been presenting the organizational chart of the agency to a new worker at an early conference and had been mentioning all the names of the people with whom the worker would have to interact. The worker was nodding, but his eyes seemed slightly glazed. Noticing this reaction, the supervisor stopped and explored the reason:

> Supervisor: You look like I may have gone too fast and lost you. I am throwing an awful lot at you at one time, so I'd better check it out.
> Worker (looking relieved): I'm still not clear about the very first part of the description of our own department. I'm still trying to figure that out.
> Supervisor (laughing): Of course, you have questions about that. Here I am trying to explain the whole agency structure in five minutes when it took me months to figure it out myself. Let's go back; ask your questions. I'll take it slower. By the way, if I go too fast again, if you don't understand, feel free to stop me. That way I'll know if we are connecting or not.

Not only did this supervisor monitor the process of learning and adjust the speed of the presentation, but her comments also began to set an important norm for their working relationship. Workers sometimes refrain from interrupting or asking questions because they are afraid that they ought to understand and that it is a sign of being dumb if they do not. This supervisor indicated that she was going too fast, recognized how complicated the subject was, and gave the worker permission to not understand. She also indicated that it was important to her that the worker did understand.

Another reason for such signals may be the staff's feelings about learning. Many people are convinced that they cannot learn or understand certain data. In most cases, the real problem is with poor teaching, but they have internalized the idea that the problem is with them: They are just poor learners. When they begin to hear something they are afraid they will not understand, as if in a self-fulfilling prophecy, they do not understand. Presenting statistics is a good example of this dynamic. The minute a supervisor starts to deal with data in a research finding, a worker's eyes may glaze over in anticipation of not understanding.

Working with a computer is another technological area that can generate fear in staff members. The following example shows how a supervisor helped a staff member who was overwhelmed by her belief that she would not be able to understand a new computer case-tracking system recently installed in the agency. She was convinced she would never be able to get the knack of how to use a terminal to enter data.

> Supervisor: Let's begin by going over how you sign on with this terminal and how you would enter your data. Then we can look at the printout you will get in return. Is that okay?
> Worker (jumpy): What! What did you say?
> Supervisor: Just a minute—you look a little pale. What's wrong?
> Worker: Nothing, really, I was just off somewhere else.
> Supervisor: You really don't look happy about this whole thing. Has the computer got you worried?

Worker: Well, I have never used one of those things, and it scares the hell out of me. I'm not too mechanically inclined—I even have trouble filling out those damn cards where you have to fill in the spaces.

Supervisor: Let's talk about this for a minute. You know, it's not unusual to be a bit put off by this stuff. We weren't raised with it, and the way the computer people talk, it's enough to make you think it's a whole other language—in fact, a whole other world. I found it a bit intimidating as well, at the start. But after I got into it, I found I really only had to understand a little about the computer, not the whole thing, how it works and so on. I discovered the part I needed to know wasn't really as complicated as I thought it would be.

How about if I take it one step at a time, and I stop each step along the way to make sure I've made it clear?

Worker: That would help a great deal.

In addition to the supervisor's moving too fast, or the staff members' affective reactions to the process of learning, a third major reason for blockage in the learning process is the feelings that may be generated in the staff by the data presentation. As the supervisor is speaking, the members may have associations with data that generate strong affective reactions. Although their stares may make it appear that they have lost interest, they also can be a sign that the supervisor is really touching a sensitive spot.

A good example involves group supervision of students on an issue of practice skill. One student, Lou, made a case presentation that clearly showed he had identified with a teenage son against a rather strong, domineering father. Lou's tape recording of the interview provided ample evidence that he was not feeling with the father, and this was cutting him off from any chance of helping that client. When the supervisor suggested that the father was all alone in the family session, he noticed that some of the students in the group seemed to be withdrawing from the discussion, and their eyes were glazing over. He pointed this out:

Supervisor: There is something going on in your eyes, but I'm not sure what it means. Some of you seem to be off somewhere, not with Lou and me on this example. What happened?

Ted: Maybe it's just the heavy lunch I had before the session.

Supervisor: I'm sure that would have an impact. But, actually, I was wondering if you weren't thinking of your own cases, families you are or have been working with. Maybe you have found yourself in the same situation and did exactly the same thing.

Frank: That's what I was thinking about. My God, how many times I have blown it in that kind of situation! I get so mad at the parents I could wring their necks.

The ensuing discussion dealt with the student workers' feelings of guilt about their poor practice. The supervisor tried to reassure them by pointing out that they could give only what they had at the time, and they needed to work, as they were doing just then, at improving their ability to give more. The glazed looks were important signals of the feelings that had been evoked by the practice example. If they had been ignored, further discussion of Lou's case would have been less fruitful. With their affect acknowledged, they were able to discuss their feelings toward parents in similar situations, and the supervisor could introduce the concept of countertransference or the tendency of the students to draw on their own past experiences with people in authority and thus view the parents in stereotypical ways.

In this case, it was helpful to explore the students' nonverbal reactions because it was apparent that the discussion was hitting them hard, and if the supervisor reached for the underlying feelings, they would be related to the work. The skill of monitoring the process of work for clues while simultaneously paying attention to the content is one that must be developed over time. With practice, a supervisor can integrate attention to both. The more confident supervisors are of their own grasp of the content and their abilities to present it, the more effective they will be in monitoring the process of learning. This is a skill that comes with time and practice.

Presenting Data in a Way Open to Challenge

This skill enables the supervisor to share information in a way that makes workers feel free to dispute ideas. This is another area in which educational theory and practice have often led to misunderstanding of an important learning dynamic. New supervisors often are advised by colleagues and administrators to try to impress their staffs with their expertise, so that the staffs will be more willing to accept the supervisors' ideas. As a result, supervisors who are somewhat insecure about their positions may become defensive when staff members challenge their ideas. Evidence of this reaction can cause the staff members to accept ideas shared by the supervisor in an uncritical manner, or the way in which the ideas are presented can produce resentment and defensiveness, even a battle of wills. In neither case is learning taking place.

Supervisors must sort out the differences between subjective and objective reality. In some areas, supervisors can share facts, that is, data that are exact and indisputable. More often, however, they are sharing opinions, beliefs, or values, either their own or those of the experts in the field. A supervisor who confuses the difference between facts and opinions may present data as facts rather than as one more source of information the staff can use in developing their own sense of reality. Simple phrases such as "there are differences of opinion on this, but in my view, I believe . . ." can help workers sort out the difference. If workers sense that a supervisor is presenting a viewpoint dogmatically, then a battle of wills may ensue that prevents learning from taking place.

Supervisors also must recognize that acceptance of these viewpoints, without challenge, can constitute an illusion of work. The staff may be agreeing when they really disagree. In some situations, the staff may simply be allowing the supervisor to do their work for them by substituting the supervisor's view of reality for their own. Rather than fearing challenge and dispute of their ideas, supervisors should be worried about too quick an acceptance. Right from the start of the relationship, the supervisor should invite critical reaction with observations such as this: "I'm going to share my own views on this with you, but I want you to feel free to take on my ideas if they don't make sense in relation to your experiences."

There are some areas in which the supervisor may believe that his or her views ought to be accepted in practice, and these should be made clear at the start. Nevertheless, effective supervisors want to encourage their staff members to share their real feelings about the information being shared. If workers agree too easily with an idea, a skill described by Schwartz (personal communication, September 1979) as looking for trouble when everything is going your way, or ferreting out underlying doubts or ambivalence, should be used. If a supervisor has suggested an approach to a problem and the staff does not really agree or has unvoiced doubts or concerns, the supervisor must elicit these feelings or else they will reappear as the staff fails to implement the idea. It is a natural tendency to sell harder when we encounter doubts or resistance to our views. I think, however, that the most effective teaching takes place when we resist that tendency and instead accept and explore the reasons behind the doubt or resistance.

I also believe that the more a staff member resists or challenges an idea presented by the supervisor, the more likely it is that real learning is taking place. The meaning of resistance was explored in the section dealing with the skills of making a demand for work. If an idea is really hitting hard, perhaps at the core of many beliefs held by a staff member, then resistance to a change of thinking is natural and is a signal that the work is going well. If resistance is never encountered, it is likely that the staff member is not being challenged enough.

The supervisor's first reaction may be that the resistance is a challenge to supervisory authority. This may sometimes be the case, but more often, it is a signal that the staff is feeling challenged. The staff member who attacks the idea most strongly is often the one who is working on the question most energetically and who already has doubts and questions in the area.

In the following excerpts, both supervisors were working with staff on the issue of developing a greater capacity to empathize with clients. In the first one, the supervisor responded defensively to the staff member's angry challenge.

> Worker: That sounds good, but in reality, clients don't always appreciate being "social worked."

Supervisor (responding to the sarcastic tone of the comment): I'm afraid I have to differ with you. There is a lot of research that supports how important it is to empathize with clients.

Worker: You can get research to support whatever you believe. It's what really happens in practice that is important.

Supervisor: I think that after you have had a little more practice experience yourself, then you will be able to understand my point.

The supervisor's last comment, which was also uttered with some sarcasm, effectively cut off the negative feedback, and the worker simply sulked for the rest of the group session. If the worker had persisted in this behavior, some supervisors would see it as a signal that it was time to talk to him about his "problem with authority."

A strikingly different response was made to almost the same comment in the following example. In this case, the worker was not seen as an obstructor of learning but rather as one who could help take it further. The supervisor viewed this worker not as an enemy but as a potential ally.

Worker: I'm not sure all that feeling stuff really helps. It makes me sick to think of social work do-gooders who ask you how you feel all the time.

Supervisor: You seem to feel this very strongly. How come?

Worker: I went in for counseling once, and I felt social worked to death. Every time I said anything the guy repeated my comments, just like a machine. I caught on to what he was doing right away and started to play games with him.

Supervisor: That's what's gotten you all worked up—the idea of being mechanical, not being honest, putting the client on.

Worker: Exactly!

Supervisor: What about the rest of you (speaking to other staff members)? Have you had similar experiences?

In the ensuing discussion, many workers echoed the concerns of this worker. Would they be mechanical? Would they be seen by their clients as phony? This allowed the supervisor to discuss the differences between genuine empathy and automatic responses, a critical discussion at this stage in the workers' development. The key to opening up this discussion was trying to ascertain the meaning behind the resistant worker's comments. The supervisor experienced the challenge to her ideas as an attempt to work, rather than as an attack on her expertise and authority. To stand up to such strong indirect communications, however, she had to have some confidence in both her expertise and her authority.

Sessional Ending Skills

As with beginnings and ongoing work, endings have distinctive dynamics and special requirements for supervisory skills. This is the resolution stage, in which the supervisor concentrates on how the work of the session will be resolved. But resolution of work does not suggest that each session or encounter ends neatly, with all issues fully discussed, ambivalences cleared up, and next steps carefully planned. A sign of advanced skill is a supervisor's ability to tolerate the ambiguity and uncertainty that may accompany the end of a session dealing with difficult work. If uncertainty is present or if the supervisor and the staff group have not agreed how to resolve a conflict, then the resolution stage might consist of identifying the status of the discussion.

A number of skills are useful in this phase: summarizing, generalizing, identifying next steps, rehearsing, and identifying "doorknob" communications. Some of these have already been mentioned in this chapter.

Summarizing

In the skill of summarizing, a few minutes at the end of an individual conference or group session are spent reviewing the encounter. This might involve identifying agreements that have been reached by a staff group, reviewing understandings in relation to a case, identifying areas for further discussion, or identifying ideas that have been important to the session. Summarizing can help a worker grasp the learning more effectively, or it can identify areas in which the supervisor may have thought there was agreement when none existed. Summarizing is not required in all sessions; this is not an automatic ritual but rather a skill to be used at key moments.

Generalizing

The skill of generalizing involves moving from the specific discussion to the general principle. It is the reverse of the skill of moving from the general to the specific, which is a part of the elaboration skill. After the staff has worked on specific issues in a staff meeting or a worker has worked on how to handle a particular client problem, it is often possible for the supervisor to generalize the experience in a way that increases the learning to be derived from it. For example, the supervisor might point out the similarity between a specific case and others discussed previously. This helps the worker develop an idea about the general principles to be used in dealing with like examples.

Identifying Next Steps

If the skill of identifying next steps is omitted, much frustration can result. Suppose a staff group has agreed that an analysis of how staff time is used is crucial to make a case for more additions to the staff. Unless the supervisor addresses the question of who is going to do the analysis, it is likely that everyone will leave the meeting certain that someone else is going to do it. Asking a worker to focus on specific next steps in relation to a client can also reveal an underlying ambivalence that is essential for discussion.

Rehearsing

In the skill of rehearsing, the focus is on helping the staff members to practice handling a difficult encounter with a client or someone in the system. A worker may agree that a confrontation with a client is crucial, but the ability to find the right words is another matter. Providing a form of miniature role play, with the supervisor taking the role of the other person, gives the worker an opportunity to practice in a safe situation. The supervisor also can change roles, try his or her hand at solving the problem, and then switch back again to give the worker an opportunity to offer solutions. This is a powerful device for aiding workers to find the right words that can help them feel more confident about tackling demanding encounters.

Identifying "Doorknob" Communications

The skill of identifying "doorknob" communications refers to the phenomenon of staff members often sharing a potent concern when they already have one hand on the doorknob in preparation for leaving. When such a pattern becomes apparent, it is helpful for the supervisor to point it out and to discuss why it is difficult to bring such things up directly at the start of the session. Usually, this discussion makes the workers aware of the pattern, and this helps them to be more direct.

RESEARCH FINDINGS

A number of the skills described in this chapter were incorporated into the workers' questionnaire for the author and his colleagues' first study of supervision skill (Shulman, Robinson, & Luckyj, 1981). These skills include putting the worker's feelings into words, supporting the worker in taboo areas, understanding the worker's feelings, sharing thoughts and feelings, partializing the worker's concerns, dealing with the theme of authority, providing data, and demonstrating a knowledge of policy and procedures. The skill of putting the worker's feelings into words, considered to be one indication of the supervisor's tuning-in skill (as well as a demonstration of empathic skills), was discussed in the research section of chapter 2. The other skills are discussed in this section. In the first part, the findings of the Shulman and Buchan (1982) study are summarized, and related studies are cited. In the second part, the related findings in the author's 1991 study are shared.

Literature Review

The item measuring the skill of supporting the worker in taboo areas in the 1982 study appeared on the workers' questionnaire as follows: "My supervisor helps me talk about subjects that are not comfortable to discuss (for example, my reactions to working with clients around sexual issues)." On average, the workers said that supervisors "sometimes" demonstrated this skill. The skill was positively correlated with supervisor helpfulness $(r = .70)$.

These findings parallel those in the author's research on social work practice (Shulman, 1978, 1981, 1991, 1992). For a worker to feel free enough to discuss uncomfortable areas, a good relationship with the supervisor is crucial. Because many of the most difficult aspects of practice are associated with taboo areas (for example, sex, death, and money), and because help cannot be offered if the areas are not directly discussed, this is a crucial supervision skill.

The skill of understanding workers' feelings was phrased on the questionnaire as follows: "When I tell my supervisor how I feel, she/he understands (for example, my own frustrations with a client)." The average supervisor score indicated that supervisors understood "a good part of the time." The positive correlation of this skill with helpfulness was also one of the stronger findings $(r = .70)$. This is similar to the importance attached to this skill in a number of areas of research in the helping professions, such as social work, psychoanalysis, nursing, medicine, and teaching.

In supervision research, Kadushin (1973) found that receiving emotional support was described by 21 percent of workers surveyed as the strongest source of satisfaction with their supervision. Another study by Olmstead and Christenson (1973) used a standardized leadership opinion questionnaire to study 228 social work supervisors in three settings. Scales used in this study made it possible to rate supervisors in social work on consideration (mutual trust, respect for ideas, consideration of feelings, and warmth in the relationship). These supervisors were then compared with supervisors in other fields. Social work supervisors were among the highest rated supervisors on the consideration scale, and providing support was described as what social work supervisors did best. Another finding of the Olmstead and Christenson study was that satisfaction with supervision itself was positively associated with satisfaction with the agency, positive individual performance, less absenteeism, agency competence, and agency performance.

On the issue of keeping the supervisory function clear in relation to discussion of personnel problems, workers in Kadushin's (1973) study indicated that supervisors were not too involved in dealing with their personal problems. Supervisors, more often than workers, viewed the legitimate source of help for job-related personal problems as outside of the supervisory relationship. Among the workers, 48 percent agreed with the statement that they would want the supervisor to help them if personal problems came up in their work with clients, whereas only 30 percent of the supervisors supported that idea.

The skill of sharing thoughts and feelings was worded on the Shulman and Buchan (1982) study questionnaire as follows: "My supervisor shares his/her thoughts and feelings (for example, sharing frustrations around a work situation)." The average score indicated that supervisors were able to do this between "sometimes" and "a good part of the time." The positive correlation with helpfulness was lower on this item ($r = .53$) than on most other supervisory skills examined.

The skill of partializing the worker's concerns was worded on the questionnaire as follows: "My supervisor helps me sort out my concerns in a situation and look at them one at a time." Supervisors were rated as demonstrating this skill between "sometimes" and "a good part of the time." Its positive correlation with helpfulness was one of the highest of the study ($r = .77$).

The item on the workers' questionnaire dealing with the use of authority attempted to measure the supervisor's efforts to encourage feedback, particularly negative feedback, on the part of the worker. It was worded as follows: "When I am upset about something my supervisor says or does, he/she encourages me to talk about it." The supervisors in this study also fared well on this item; an average score was halfway between "sometimes" and "a good part of the time." The positive correlation for this skill with helpfulness was also quite high ($r = .75$).

Workers in this study made most of their comments with respect to the issue of authority. Some examples were as follows:

- My supervisor has a strong authoritarian role.
- My supervisor should feel secure enough in his self not to feel threatened by a question or a suggestion.
- My supervisor has a good sense of fair play.
- My supervisor has an excellent capacity to give workers independence yet keep track of what they are doing.
- I especially appreciate the flexibility with which he deals with different employees' needs and his responsiveness to personal work styles.
- My present supervisor is the best I've ever had . . . what has impressed me the most is the willingness to look at his own shortcomings and to work on them.

Other research on the issue of authority has suggested that it plays an important part in the supervision process. For example, Mayer and Rosenblatt (1975) found that workers who felt secure with supervisors also felt less anxious with their clients. In the Olmstead and Christianson (1973) study, when social work supervisors were rated on a scale measuring structure (exercise of control and authority), they were found to be the lowest in exercise of authority of the 36 groups examined. This conforms to Kadushin's (1973) finding that the exercise of authority is one reason for supervisors' strong dissatisfaction with the job. These findings offer evidence in support of the idea that the integration of support and demand is difficult for human services supervisors.

The Shulman et al. (1981) study attempted to get at the issue of providing data through two items. In the first, the authors asked workers to assess their supervisors' knowledge of policy and procedure with the following item: "My supervisor has a detailed and accurate grasp of policy and procedures." In the second, they asked if the supervisor shared his or her views: "My supervisor shares his/her suggestions about the subjects we discuss for my consideration." On the first question, supervisors in the study received very positive scores and were rated as being knowledgeable between "a good part of the time" and "most or all of the time." This item correlated positively with helpfulness ($r = .61$). In response to the second item, workers reported that supervisors shared their views "a good part of the time," and this item correlated positively with helpfulness ($r = .65$).

These findings were as expected. In Kadushin's (1973) study, both supervisors and workers rated "expert power" as the main source of influence of a supervisor. In the Olmstead and Christenson (1973) study, "expert power" was the first source of influence when ranked by workers, "positional power" was second, "referent (relationship) power" was third, and "reward and coercive power" was last.

Workers' comments in the Shulman et al. (1981) study dealt with the supervisors' knowledge and sharing of information. Some examples of comments were these:

- My supervisor has difficulty making decisions regarding a particular case. My supervisor has never carried a caseload and therefore is not knowledgeable.
- The supervisor should ask what a worker feels she wants to do with a case before giving his suggestion of what he would do.

The skill of encouraging the worker to raise concerns, which is crucial for the development of trust in the supervisor–worker relationship, was phrased on the workers' questionnaire as follows: "I can talk openly to my supervisor about job-related concerns." The five-point scale ranging from "none of the time" to "most or all of the time" was used. The average score was positive on this item; workers reported that they could talk openly slightly more than "a good part of the time." One characteristic positive comment described the supervisor as "open and straightforward and very approachable." In contrast, some supervisors were described as "very critical and hard to approach" or simply "too defensive."

The factor developing a supportive atmosphere was borrowed from the Kadushin (1974) study of supervisors and supervisees and was worded on the workers' questionnaire as follows: "My supervisor creates the kind of emotional atmosphere in which I feel free to discuss my mistakes and failures, as well as my successes." On average, supervisors in the study were rated positively on this factor, with a rating close to "a good part of the time." The following comments give a flavor of the reactions of those workers who thought they had a supportive supervisor, as well as those who felt that they did not:

- He backs me up!
- I get moral support in times of stress.
- My supervisor works with me, providing the help and information as I ask—gives me a real feeling of accomplishment.
- My supervisor has a genuine concern for his workers' well-being.
- I feel free to share my inadequacies and to ask for help when I need it.
- My supervisor's emotional support and praise of my efforts is really what keeps me going.
- Workers really need to feel appreciated by their supervisors.
- My supervisor is inclined to favor one worker and spend more time with that person than the rest of staff.
- I would like my supervisor to discuss my mistakes and failures more frequently than once a year at evaluation.
- There is a lack of support in all areas from my supervisor and upper management.

Finally, dealing with authority issues in the supervisor–client relationship is important to the success of supervision. Particularly difficult is working out an understanding of the worker's limits of authority, ability to take responsibility, and so on, in a way that allows the worker some freedom while still maintaining the supervisor's accountability. In another item borrowed from the Kadushin (1974) questionnaire, workers were asked to comment on the following: "My supervisor permits me to make my own mistakes (in those areas where I have discretion within the boundaries of policies and procedures)." The average supervisor in the study was rated as being able to do this "a good part of the time."

1991 Study Findings

The supervision skill component of the holistic study (Shulman, 1991) limited analysis to three central skills:[2]

---

[2]Because of the holistic nature of the study, with more than 1,200 variables under analysis, it was necessary to exclude some variables from earlier studies. The author balanced the desire to obtain data with concerns about generating respondent resistance if the questionnaires were too long.

- Articulating the supervisee's feelings. ("My supervisor can sense my feelings without my having to put them into words.")
- Communicates my views to administration. ("My supervisor effectively communicates my views about policies and procedures to the next level of the agency.")
- Encourages negative feedback. ("When I am upset about something my supervisor says or does, he/she encourages me to talk about it.")

The findings for the first skill, articulating the supervisee's feelings, were reported in chapter 3. Employees in all three levels of management (executives, managers, and supervisors) indicated some hesitancy about the use of this skill. At the same time, this skill was positively associated with rapport and the development of trust for all levels.

For the second skill, communicating the supervisee's views to administration, the executives were rated most positively (30 percent "strongly agree" and 40 percent "agree"). The managers were next (15.9 percent "strongly agree" and 52.4 percent "agree") and the supervisors last (12.1 percent "strongly agree" and 41.6 percent "agree").

The agreement responses for this skill were highest at the upper levels of administration. Apparently, the closer to power one gets in the hierarchy, the more one is perceived as effectively communicating the views of supervisees to the administration. This ability to communicate may be associated more with the position than with the person.

A further explanation may relate to a process I have observed. It can be described as a time lag in which administrations are slow to communicate back to lower levels the status of their suggestions. I have observed many examples in which worker feedback had an impact on the development of new policies or procedures; however, the lack of communications about this impact from higher levels down to the front lines often created the impression that nothing was happening.

For the third skill, encouraging negative feedback from supervisees, executives were again rated highly: One manager strongly agreed and six agreed that executives exhibited this skill. The report was less favorable on the managers' level, with 8.1 percent of the supervisors strongly agreeing and 38.7 percent only agreeing. These findings were similar to the worker–supervisor level, with 11 percent of the workers strongly agreeing that their supervisors encouraged negative feedback and 39 percent only agreeing.

Analysis of the impact of the use of these skills focused on their association with a number of relationship and outcome measures.

The supervisee's perception of rapport with the supervisor was measured by a single item: "In general, I am satisfied with my working relationship with my supervisor."

All three levels of supervisees reported generally positive working relationships with their supervisors. Combined percentages ("strongly agree" and "agree") were at or close to 70 percent. Differences were noted at the extreme, with "strongly agree" high for executives, moving lower for managers and still lower for supervisors.

The trust scale included slightly modified versions of the two variables used to describe trust between worker and client. These were as follows: "My supervisor and I can talk openly about job-related concerns" and "My supervisor creates the kind of emotional atmosphere in which I feel free to discuss my mistakes and failures."

The pattern of the findings on openness between levels of staff suggests that this variable may also be affected by position, as well as person. Both the "strongly agree" responses and the combined agreement responses show a decrease in openness as one moves down the levels. Whereas 80 percent of the managers perceived an open relationship with their executives, 74 percent of the supervisors and only 62 percent of the workers felt that way. The position explanation suggests that as one obtains more power and authority, one can relate more openly to people higher in the hierarchy.

Supervisory skill, defined by the average score on the three skill variables (articulating feelings, communicating with administration, and being open to negative feedback) demonstrated a pattern of moderate to strong correlations with a number of relationship and outcome variables. These included the social worker's trust in his or her supervisor ($r = .75$), as well as rapport ($r = .82$). Supervisory skill also was positively associated with the social worker's perception of supervisor helpfulness ($r = .76$), the worker's morale ($r = .44$), as well as a more positive job stress and manageability index for the worker ($r = .17$). When specific skills constituting the skills scale were examined, the strongest pattern of associations was with the skill of articulating the worker's feelings, followed by communicating with the administration.

A major difference between the 1991 study and the 1982 supervision project was the introduction in the latter of path analysis as a tool for exploring theoretical hypotheses about the supervision process. (A full report of the study and a description of the analysis is found in Shulman [1991].) This statistical tool allowed for a testing of a model that suggested that supervisory skill would have an impact on the working relationship that consisted of two elements—rapport and trust. The effect of supervisory skill on such outcomes as the worker's perception of the supervisor's helpfulness is through this impact on the working relationship. This parallels the process in which a social worker's skill helps develop a working relationship with the client, which in turn, is the medium through which client outcomes are influenced. The results of this initial testing supported the propositions of the model.

SUMMARY

The model of the work phase in supervision presented in this chapter is based on a number of skill factors, including the following: sessional tuning in, sessional contracting, elaborating, empathizing, sharing supervisors' own feelings, making a demand for work, pointing out obstacles, sharing data, and sessional ending. Common supervisory methods used to apply the skills within each factor are concerned with finding solutions to problems such as the poorly performing worker, the worker with personal problems, and the worker who resists supervision, actively or passively.

CHAPTER 5

SUPERVISORY ENDINGS AND TRANSITIONS

There are two general types of endings in the supervisory relationship. In the first, the staff member leaves the job (or the student ends the year), and the supervisor must pay attention to three areas of work: the ending of the supervisory relationship, the ending of the worker–client relationships, and the ending of the worker–colleague relationships. All of these are important, and they are often intertwined. In the second type of ending, it is the supervisor who is leaving and who must say good-bye to the staff while smoothing the transition to a new supervisor.

The dynamics of both types of endings are somewhat similar to those of the worker–client ending, a process discussed in some detail elsewhere (Shulman, 1992). The parallel nature of these processes can provide the supervisor with an opportunity to do some of her or his most effective work, demonstrating the very skills the worker needs to use with clients. However, many supervisors experience difficulty in endings, both their own and those of their staff members. In this phase, it is common to avoid discussing a number of powerful issues. Examples include staff members coming into work on a weekend to empty out their desks to avoid saying good-bye to colleagues. Another is the supervisor who suddenly takes advantage of accumulated vacation time to terminate early and thus avoid the ending phase altogether. Not at all uncommon is the "farewell party" for a departing staff member in which forced gaiety substitutes for serious conversation among staff members on the impact of the loss. As a result of this avoidance, instead of providing a powerful stage for effective supervision, the ending phase can deteriorate into a moratorium on work. It is also ironic and sad that often this avoidance is most pronounced in settings in which loss is most central to the work of the client (for example, child welfare, residential treatment, hospice).

This chapter explores the dynamics of the types of endings common to human services organizations. The first part focuses on the worker leaving the agency. The second part explores the process wherein the supervisor is leaving. The chapter describes and illustrates the skills that the supervisor can use to help staff effectively manage the dynamics and feelings of the ending phase. It also highlights the parallel process in which the supervisor models for the worker the skills required to terminate with clients.

THE WORKER'S ENDING EXPERIENCE

The context of the ending will, of course, vary considerably. The staff member may be leaving voluntarily or involuntarily, and the supervisor may feel a great loss or a sense of relief when a particular worker leaves. The staff member may be moving on to a new position, a promotion, or the like or may be facing unemployment as a result of cutbacks in funding for services. Although there are many variations on the theme of ending, some common themes persist. These common themes are identified first, followed by discussion of supervisor strategies for dealing with the dynamics and then by illustrative examples.

Common Ending Themes

One common dynamic is the denial by all parties concerned of the feelings associated with the staff member's leaving. As the date approaches, little discussion of the event takes place. This avoidance occurs not because staff does not care about the worker but rather often because they care too much.

A sense of urgency about unfinished business may also be characteristic of this phase. Both the staff member and the supervisor have much to say to each other as they share positive feelings, negative feelings, or both. Even if the relationship has been a poor one, a constructive discussion of the reasons why the supervisor and the worker had difficulty in dealing with each other can be helpful. Staff members may have some final thoughts—what I call "farewell bouquets"—about the experience they would like to share. The "bouquets" may be positive, or alternatively, all of the previously unstated negatives may finally emerge. Many agencies require final interviews (sometimes called exit interviews) in which staff members can share thoughts and feelings that may have been difficult to express while they were employed.

Feelings of guilt may also be present for both worker and supervisor. Could the worker have put more into the experience and derived more out of it? Should the supervisor have been more available? It is not uncommon to detect a period of mourning as the ending approaches; apathy in conferences, for example, may signal strong feelings about leaving. At the same time, there may be positive feelings about making a new beginning. Students, for example, may be starting their professional careers, ready to test themselves in the world of work.

Both the supervisor and the staff member may be inclined to be overly positive about the ending experience. If they give in to the temptation to deal only with the positives, however, they will cut off an opportunity to use the ending phase effectively. Anger and regression are also common in this phase; workers may return to patterns of work or relationships that marked their early days at the agency. If they have become close to other staff members and if the atmosphere has been supportive and intimate, their colleagues also may experience a sense of rejection, coupled with feelings of loss.

Strategies for Dealing with a Worker's Ending

One crucial reason why supervisors must devote careful attention to the worker's ending experiences is that a worker who is leaving a position needs help in ending with her or his clients. If the worker's feelings about the endings are not dealt with, they can adversely affect the effectiveness of agency services. Supervisors can use a number of procedures to make an ending a helpful experience for the worker.

First, the supervisor can call attention to the approach of an ending by noting the date at a conference or a staff meeting. This sets the ending phase process in motion.

Second, the supervisor can identify the dynamics of the ending phase as they emerge. If the supervisor notices apathy in conferences, for example, a direct question can be used to examine whether it has something to do with the worker's ending experiences.

Third (and most important), the supervisor can acknowledge his or her own feelings about the worker's departure. Because it is hard to express feelings of warmth and closeness, as well as negative feelings in any situation, the supervisor must take the first step in this. When these feelings are shared honestly, they often provide the catalyst for helping the worker discuss similar emotions.

Fourth, the supervisor can structure an ending evaluation period that includes systematic attention to the supervision experience. The strengths of the relationship, as well as the weaknesses, should be specifically identified. A summary of the learning that has occurred and identification of a future learning agenda can help. Because of the tendency to be overly positive about the experience, the supervisor will have to balance that by encouraging the worker to share negatives as well.

Fifth, attention to the ending between the worker and other staff members is often appreciated. It is as important for the supervisor to pay attention to the separation process when a staff member leaves as it is to deal with the engagement process when a member joins the staff. Making announcements at staff meetings, briefly discussing the worker's contributions, asking staff members to express their feelings, and sharing one's own feelings can all go far in helping the staff deal directly with the loss of a colleague. If the members are not assisted in this way, the ending is often no more than a "farewell party" wherein the talk is merely superficial, and the staff is left with the feeling of unfinished business.

Although personal good-byes are the responsibility of each staff member, the ending of the relationship with the formal staff group should be addressed by the supervisor. In some settings, such as residential treatment centers, attention to this process is particularly important because personal loss (for example, family, childhood) is at the center of the practice, and staff members who avoid saying good-bye to each other may not be as effective in helping residents with their own peer group endings.

Finally, the supervisor can use the experience to help the worker focus on the specific skills of dealing with client endings. By identifying what is happening in their own relationship, as well as in the parallel process with the client, the supervisor can contribute to the worker's ability to deal with the often neglected termination phase of practice.

Illustrations of Ending-Phase Work

The first example illustrates the ending process wherein a positive relationship had been developed between the supervisor and a student. The second example focuses on the equally important work involved in ending a difficult relationship. The third example focuses on helping a staff member end with colleagues.

Ending a Positive Relationship

The following student supervisor's report of how he dealt with a student's ending of her experience at a family agency illustrates a number of the dynamics of workers' endings. The supervisor and the student had been together for one year, and the beginning of their work on endings was intermingled with his efforts to help her terminate with clients. The supervisor's report began:

> Preparatory work: In working with Fran [the student] on her practice with Terry [the client], it was apparent that she was most concerned about the coming ending. Fran had only three weeks left on her placement, and I felt it was time to focus on her ending work with Terry. Fran had been working with Terry for five months, and it was not certain whether Terry would want to continue counseling with another worker or whether she would terminate with the agency when Fran left.
>
> In a conference during which we discussed Terry, we did not go into great detail in discussing the skills needed to make the endings a useful piece of work. Fran, on her own, had made a list of the issues that she and

Terry had tackled together that she wanted to review with her. I mentioned that she and Terry had developed a relationship over time and that there would be some feelings about the coming ending. I suggested that perhaps Terry might feel mad or sad about the ending and that Fran should try to pull for these feelings in the session. Fran agreed that this would be important. I also stated that endings can be difficult work, because the worker often has strong feelings about the endings as well. I pointed out that you are in a session dealing with your own feelings as well as the client's. Fran thought this might be true. She agreed to audiotape the next interview for our discussion at our next conference.

In this case, as often happens, the supervisor discussed the ending in relation to the client but ignored it in relation to the worker. The discussion of the dynamics of the worker–client process will remain lifeless as long as the dynamics of the supervisor–worker relationship are ignored. After studying endings, Fran could agree intellectually about what needed to be done, but emotionally she was not in touch with what was happening. Even though the supervisor described what it would be like for the worker to deal with her own feelings and the client's, unless he modeled how to do this in their session, the worker would respond to his actions, not his words. This is another case in which more would be "caught" than "taught" as the worker observed the supervisor's behavior. In the supervision conference that followed, the supervisor caught this mistake nicely and moved into a discussion of the parallel endings.

> Supervision session: I asked her how it went. Fran said that it was OK, and then, immediately, that it was terrible. She was obviously upset. Fran then proceeded to summarize her session with Terry. They had talked about the various areas of Terry's life that had improved since coming for counseling. Terry summed up the improvement by saying that she felt a lot more confident and under a lot less pressure. She attributed this to the fact that she and Fran had done a lot of work on her self-esteem, and it had really improved. Terry said she was able to break her high–low cycle and live a more even life.
> Fran said it was at this point that she raised the issue of ending the counseling with Terry, because Terry was doing so well. Fran said she tried to reach for Terry's feelings about the ending but simply could not do it. She found it to be very hard and pulled back. Fran began to cry when describing the process. The end result had been an agreement for Terry to call Fran when she returned from a short trip to discuss whether she needed another session.
> I empathized with Fran, saying this was the hard part of the work, especially because she was feeling sad about ending, as sad as Terry. Fran said that she did not want to cry with Terry. I asked her what held her back. She said that she did not like people seeing her cry. I asked if she felt that being a worker made it more difficult for her to cry. Fran felt there was some of that happening, but mostly, it was that she did not like to cry in front of people. I then talked about a theme we had discussed before, that a social

worker was both a worker and a real person when working with a client, and at times it was very appropriate to react from one's feelings about the work and the person. I continued that with Terry it would have been fine to tell her how much she would miss her and that she was feeling sad and that the two of them could have cried together. Fran agreed that it would not have been so terrible.

At this point, the supervisor addressed the issues involved in the student's own endings. By focusing on the process of the student's ending with the agency, with him, and others, the supervisor modeled the skills required for the student to end with the client:

I picked up the theme of endings for Fran. I said that she was not only ending with her clients, which was hard, but also that she was ending her stay at the agency. She had made a lot of friends here, and soon she would be ending with each of them. I told her I thought that must be hard for her. She agreed and began to cry. I then said that our relationship was also ending soon and that I would miss her. She agreed and said that she had had a fine time here. At this point, there was a lovely, quiet pause.

We then returned to talk about Terry. Fran wondered if she could do something more, like call her back, because she would have liked to have said more to her. She said she regretted not saying some of the things we talked about. I asked some more questions about how close she felt to Terry and suggested that she could say some of what she felt about the endings when Terry called her. She agreed.

I suggested we listen to the tape. Fran resisted a bit, saying it was painful to listen to the session. What emerged from the tape was that Fran did a fine job with summarizing her work, and it was clear that Terry was ready to end the counseling relationship. It was also clear that Fran had had many openings to talk about their feelings in relation to ending but had passed them up.

I talked about some of the endings skills, suggesting that one way to pull for feelings was to talk about her own first. We also discussed Fran's other clients who may feel somewhat differently about ending. For Terry, it was a natural ending of counseling, but others might want to continue and feel a bit angry at Fran's leaving in the middle. We did some tuning in about her other cases.

Fran felt that Jake [another client] was mad, and in fact, had been coming late to their appointments. Jake and his wife had been more aggressive in the past few sessions, for example, questioning closely what happened when I listened to Fran's audiotapes of their sessions with her. I suggested that perhaps Fran's hunch was right and that some of their behavior was related to the ending dynamics. She thought she should confront them directly. I agreed, and we role played a number of ways she might get into this discussion. I suggested that there would be some sadness as well as anger, and Fran asked if I had any ideas about how to reach for it. I role played as follows: "I know you're feeling kind of frustrated with this situation about me leaving and your having to be transferred, but you know, I'm also feeling sad about it. I'll miss you both, and I was wondering if you might be feeling some of the same." I asked how it sounded to her, and she said fine. I said it was going to be hard. She agreed but felt it would probably be easier than ending with Terry.

We then went on to discuss our coming evaluation and how we would handle supervision in the next few weeks.

Ending a Negative Relationship

Not all supervisory relationships work out well. Perhaps the supervisor was hesitant about openly raising the negative quality of the relationship and allowed the problems to remain submerged and ignored. The supervisor may have avoided confronting the staff member with her or his work problems, unwilling to face the negative feelings that might result. On the other hand, the supervisor may have made an honest and skilled effort to deal with the problems, but the worker may not have been able to respond. Whatever the reasons, as the relationship comes to a close, as when the worker takes another job, there is usually a reluctance to deal with the endings honestly. As one supervisor said, "What good would it do to raise all of this now? Isn't it better to just let it alone?"

This attitude is a mistake because an honest ending and transition is just as important, perhaps even more important, when ending a poor supervisory relationship as when ending a good one. In fact, in this phase of work the supervisor may be able to do the best work. An honest conversation about what went wrong can be helpful to the supervisor and to the worker who may otherwise repeat his or her mistakes on the next job. The supervisor may be more helpful in this phase of supervision than in their entire relationship. The ending phase offers an opportunity for the supervisor to salvage a sense of professionalism about what has been done with this worker. In addition, because the worker is also ending with clients, there may be negative relationships between the worker and some of these clients. Thus, in handling the supervisory ending well, the supervisor is modeling how to end a stressful relationship. The following was the opening statement of a supervisor who was beginning a process of ending with a worker who was leaving the agency in four weeks.

> Supervisor: I wanted to discuss how we were going to handle the ending and evaluation process over the next few weeks. Frankly, given how we have been not getting along, I suspect it's tempting to not continue to work together. I feel, however, that it is important for us to have some conversation about our work together, where it went wrong, how I might have been more helpful to you, and what I perceive was your part in the problem. I was concerned about raising this discussion with you, and almost decided to pass it up, but I think I owe this to you and I genuinely want to hear your views. It may be helpful to me with future supervisees, and I might be able to help you in terms of your future supervisors.
>
> Worker: I don't think it would be helpful at all. To be honest, I never

liked you from the beginning, and I believe you had it out for me right from the start.

The supervisor's next response is crucial. Without some prior tuning-in preparation, it would have been easy to understand if the supervisor had continued the battle by responding to the anger and had counterblamed the worker or had dropped the conversation in response to the comment "I don't think it would be helpful at all." Either response would be a signal to the worker that the supervisor had not really meant the offer. It would also be an indicator that the supervisor was still too angry at this worker and was not really prepared for the conversation. In a preparatory role play in a workshop before this session, the supervisor had responded defensively to a similar role-played comment that led to an exploration of the depth of anger and hurt feelings that the supervisor had about the failed relationship. In particular, it had become clear that the supervisor felt guilty about not establishing rapport with the worker and had taken too much responsibility for the problem. Workshop participants were supportive and helpful to the supervisor in putting the conflict in perspective. With this insight and the ability to manage his feelings, the supervisor was better prepared to ignore the comment about the process being useless and instead respond to the second half of the worker's statement, which was actually the beginning of a discussion. The supervisor practiced the skill of containment by not jumping in and refuting the charges; instead, he encouraged an elaboration of the worker's perceptions.

Supervisor: What do you mean that I had it in for you from the beginning?

Worker: You were always on my back and always critical of my work. Frankly, I couldn't do anything right as far as you were concerned.

Supervisor: When I think back to my start here, I think we were all under a lot of pressure. The firing of Ted [the previous supervisor] and my being brought in and told to "straighten out this unit" probably made it tough for me to connect up to how staff was feeling. In retrospect, I think I came on too strong and probably made you feel more defensive. I could have been more supportive, but the reality was that the unit was not in very good shape.

Worker: We all knew there were problems, but you didn't help with your critical attitude.

Supervisor: Granted, but when I got this out on the table in my second month here, everyone else agreed to start over except you. I feel I was able to overcome my start and make good connections with the rest of the staff, but I never felt I was able to get past your initial anger. Even when I asked you about it, you told me I was mistaken and kept your wall up. I finally decided to let it go and work out a relationship in which we could get along at a tolerable level, but that was a mistake. I should have confronted you earlier on this, and I think you could have been a little more open with me.

Worker: You are the supervisor—it was your job to straighten things out.

Supervisor: I can accept responsibility for my part in this process, but frankly, I'm not hearing you taking any responsibility for yours. Even when I tried to open up this conversation, your first response was to be put off—to tell me it wouldn't do any good at all to talk about it. I know it's too late for us to resolve this, and I don't expect you to leave here feeling too good about our work together—I know I'm not happy about it either—but I think I at least owe you some honesty. I may have made some mistakes, but you're not that easy to supervise either. To be honest, I was so mad at your attitude, I almost decided to pass up this conversation.

Worker: Well, maybe you should have done just that.

Supervisor: The issue for me now is that you are ending with your clients and the agency in the next few weeks, and I want to discuss your wrapping up your caseload and transferring your clients to their new workers without it becoming a battle between us. Believe it or not, I would like to try to help you with this ending if you will let me. I know you care about your clients and would want to end well with them. I think you need some time to think about this conversation and that's why I'm raising it today. I will give you a chance to respond at our next conference, and then I would like to begin a review of your caseload and a discussion of the steps we need to take to ease the transition.

A balanced response was needed and provided by the supervisor in this conversation. The supervisor listened and acknowledged some of the problems in his start with the unit. In effect, he was taking responsibility for his part in the problem. Just as important was his confrontation asking the worker to take some responsibility for his part. Also important was the supervisor's recognition that although he had had some time to prepare for this discussion and to explore his own feelings, the worker had not. Thus, the supervisor did not rise to the bait when the worker said, "Well, maybe you should have just done that," referring to the supervisor's temptation to pass up the conversation. Instead, the supervisor made an appropriate demand for work by focusing on the professional tasks that needed to be carried out over the next few weeks. The worker might not accept any responsibility for the relationship problem, and he might recreate in other jobs the struggle with authority so evident in this relationship. The important point is that the supervisor is implementing his role professionally and responsibly. The honesty in this conversation and the supervisor's nondefensive acceptance of a part in the problem may at least clear the air for effective supervisory work concerning the worker's ending with clients.

THE SUPERVISOR'S ENDING EXPERIENCE

In large part, the dynamics and processes involved in the worker's endings that have been described in the preceding section are equally relevant to a supervisor's departure from a staff, an agency, or another institutional setting. Again, the particulars will vary depending on the situation. In some cases, both staff and supervisor will be pleased to say good-bye; in others, the departure of a supervisor will have a profound, perhaps surprising, impact on all concerned. The processes of transference and countertransference can lead to the development of relationships of unexpected intensity. Supervisors are as likely as workers to underplay their impact and the intensity of the feelings associated with leaving.

All the skills described earlier—announcing the ending early, sharing feelings about endings, evaluating the working relationship—are useful when the supervisor leaves a setting. In the interests of agency effectiveness, special attention should be paid to the issues of transition: What are the staff members' thoughts and feelings about the new supervisor? How can the staff work to expedite a positive relationship with the new supervisor? If there are angry feelings about the supervisor's leaving, can they be openly expressed so they will not be transferred to the new supervisor? If the new supervisor is known, can he or she sit in on the last staff meetings to get a feel for the ending?

In all working relationships, a new beginning is inherent in each ending. Supervisors who approach endings as a learning experience can use them to enhance their own personal and professional development. By focusing on the content of their work with the staff, as well as on the process of ending, they can use feedback from the staff to discover their own strengths and weaknesses, examine their behavior under pressure, and evaluate their ability to handle problems. Such an assessment can provide invaluable guidelines for future relationships.

Illustration of a Supervisor's Ending

In the following example, a supervisor of a hospital social services department invited her replacement to her last staff meeting to participate in her ending as a way of easing the new supervisor's beginning.

> After introducing Karen [the new supervisor] to the staff group, I explained that I had felt it would be helpful to her and to them if she could sit in on our last session together. I told them that even though we had talked about my leaving before, now that I was at the last day, it was really hitting me. I had enjoyed my four years as their supervisor and had gotten a great deal from them. I told them I would miss them in my new job and hoped that we could keep some of our contacts alive. I had the sense from the looks on their faces that they were both pleased to hear what I had to say, as well as a bit embarrassed to talk about it. I asked if we could use the time to talk about what went well with my supervision, as well as how I could have been more helpful. I said this would help me on my new job, as well as help Karen to connect up with them. Karen told the staff that she appreciated being in on this last session and would find the discussion helpful.
>
> Ron began by saying that he had always appreciated how I had been there for them, how I had kept my door open for them, and the support they could get from me. He said the job was often tough, like the time he felt overwhelmed when he had to deal with the family of dying child. It had been helpful to unload and to have me listen. I told him I had also gotten a great deal from that incident, understanding better how to help staff when

the going got rough. Sandy said she appreciated my respecting their autonomy and professionalism. When I asked her what she meant, she went on to describe the way I offered supervision of her case—providing help where needed but also allowing her to develop the agenda.

I said it felt really good to hear the positives, because I cared what they thought about me. I went on to point out that it was also important to discuss the negatives. Ted said, "Well, that's what I do most of the time anyway, so I might as well offer some of them today." I joined in the laughter and said that I did not always enjoy hearing what Ted said but that I very much appreciated his honesty and took it as a sign of caring about me and how we worked together. Ted described my tendency to keep my own problems to myself, always open to their concerns but rarely sharing my own. I asked if others felt that way, and they did, indicating they could often sense when I was in trouble or upset, but had the message that they should not deal with that. I told them it was something I needed to work on, because I carried the image of a good supervisor having things worked out and always being available for the workers. Ted said that was the opposite of what I suggested they do with clients. I agreed it was probably easier to preach than to practice. I would try to keep that in mind in my new job.

There was further discussion about the specific ways we handled supervision sessions, our staff meetings, and the problems in the hospital. In each case, I had them expand on the specifics of what they found helpful and what was not so helpful. As we reached the end of the meeting time, I asked Karen for her reactions to the discussion. She said that she was impressed with the relationship between the staff and myself, but a bit awed by it. She thought it would be a tough act to follow. She said she hoped that the staff would grow to trust her and to be just as honest with her. It was clear from the reactions on their faces that the staff group appreciated her remarks.

As she was speaking I found myself trying to hold back my tears—feeling very choked up. I finally blurted out that they had all been special to me and that I would really miss them. Ron said the feeling was quite mutual. We sat silent for a while, and then Ted suggested it was time for our farewell lunch. We left quietly, had a nice lunch, and I saved my individual good-byes for the afternoon.

A Supervisor's Ending Resulting from Promotion within the Organization

One variation on the theme of a supervisor's ending results when the supervisor is promoted to the next level of administration within the system and is still physically available to his or her former staff. If the relationship has been a good one, it is not unusual for former supervisees to try to keep some form of consultation going. For example, in the absence of the new supervisor attending a workshop, staff may bring case issues to the former supervisor even though they might easily have waited until the new supervisor returned. This pattern of holding onto the old supervisor and resisting supervision from the new supervisor may occur if the ending and transition has not been dealt with effectively.

This problem is most often raised in my workshops by the new supervisor who may feel undercut by the former supervisor. As one put it, "How am I ever going to develop a good relationship with my staff if they keep on going to Lou for advice?" Tuning in to the former supervisor's feelings usually helps the new supervisor sensitize himself or herself to the difficulty the old supervisor is having in saying good-bye and abandoning the direct supervision role. A role play can help prepare the new supervisor to raise the issue directly with the former supervisor in a nonthreatening manner. An example follows:

> I wanted to talk to you about my first few months here. It is apparent to me that your former unit still misses you. I am experiencing a pattern in which they use every opportunity to seek out help directly from you, which often leaves me feeling out in the cold. To be honest, I have sensed that it's probably been tough for you to let go of them as well. I wanted to discuss this with you and to enlist your help.
>
> Tom responded by apologizing for putting me in the spot and said he would send staff back to me if they came to him again. I told him I appreciated the offer but wondered if some direct conversation with the unit might also help. I thought if we could discuss this at the next meeting, perhaps acknowledging that the change has been difficult for him and for them, I might help to resolve the unfinished business of his leaving the unit. I said I thought he had meant a lot to them and it was no surprise that they wanted to stay connected. As part of the discussion, I thought it would help if we could work out with staff under what conditions it would be appropriate for them to come to him because I felt it would be a mistake to simply say that they should never talk to him about their work. There were times when it could be most appropriate and helpful. He agreed, and we discussed what we would both feel comfortable with as directions on the issue, as well as when he could come to a staff meeting and how we would handle the discussion.

The resulting staff meeting led to a good conversation about mutual feelings of loss and a delineation of the guidelines for future contacts. The new supervisor shared her feelings as well, including her acknowledgment of the strength of the relationship that had existed with the former supervisor. She indicated that she wanted a chance to build a positive relationship as well. She reported that the result of the meeting was a significant decrease in staff members asking for help from the former supervisor and an increase in their bringing issues to her for assistance.

SUMMARY

In the ending phase, there are similarities between supervisor–worker endings and worker–client endings. The dynamics of the ending process suggest procedures that the supervisor can use to help the worker end relationships with the supervisor, with clients, and with colleagues. Supervisors also must deal with their own leaving and with the transition to a new supervisor.

PART III

EDUCATION AND EVALUATION FUNCTIONS

CHAPTER 6

EDUCATIONAL FUNCTION OF SUPERVISION

The focus in this chapter is on the educational function of supervision. Kadushin (1976) described educational supervision as a specific staff development, in which "training is directed to the needs of a particular worker carrying a particular case load, encountering particular problems and needing some individualized program of education" (p. 126). His research (1974, 1976) suggests that educational supervision provides two of the main sources of satisfaction for both supervisors and staff members.

To explore the educational function of supervision, this chapter first sets out some assumptions about the teaching–learning process. It then examines how the teaching function is implemented in supervision. The main body of the chapter consists of a section on teaching core practice skills. These skills parallel those that have been identified and described in the chapters on the preliminary, beginning, and work phases of supervision. In the *Parallel Processes* sections, each skill is illustrated with process recording excerpts from practice with clients. In each, different methods that supervisors can use to help workers develop the skill are discussed and illustrated with process recording excerpts from supervision practice. This gives a clear picture of the parallel process in which the supervisor models the same skills that the worker needs to develop. The chapter also provides a standard for skill development for beginners in the field that supervisors can use to evaluate their workers' progress. Finally, there is a discussion about the variant elements introduced when experienced workers are supervised.

The focus in this chapter is on social work interactional skills. These represent only a part of the total educational agenda for staff. Supervision can include work on human growth and behavior theory, research findings of importance to practice, assessment skills, job management skills, and other such areas. Interactional skills are given a priority in this chapter because they are the least often addressed in the supervision literature yet are the most likely to cause supervisors difficulty. Even highly skilled supervisors find it hard to articulate what they do with clients and to develop techniques for teaching their views on method. Many supervisors experience this area as threatening and prefer instead to discuss management issues, the client, or the underlying knowledge base of practice. These discussions are important, but when they become a substitute for dealing with the development of specific practice skills, they leave an important gap in the educational process.

An additional factor that leads to the deemphasis of practice skills teaching is the diagnostic paradigm guiding our professional practice. This model, borrowed from medicine, describes practice as a three-stage, linear process involving, first, study, followed by diagnosis and then treatment. This paradigm focuses our attention on the client, and it heavily emphasizes our ability to obtain data in the study process and then to use those data to make an accurate diagnosis or assessment. Relatively little attention is paid to the specifics of the treatment interaction itself. When I have participated in case consultations, I have noted how much of the discussion centers on the worker's information about and observation of the client and how little attention is paid to the interaction between the two. When I intervene and ask the worker to describe his or her actual conversation with the client, for example, when the client is experienced as resistant, then a different picture of the client emerges. Often, the team can see the client's behavior as, in part, a reaction to the worker's interventions. I have discussed elsewhere, in detail, the interactional model of social work practice (Shulman, 1991, 1992). Elements of this model are shared in the practice discussion in the balance of this chapter. For now, I simply emphasize that supervisors who ignore the specifics of the interactions between their workers and their clients have been, in part, influenced by the general paradigm guiding the helping professions.

ASSUMPTIONS ABOUT TEACHING AND LEARNING

The teaching and learning process in supervision has been influenced by the myth that teaching essentially involves transmitting existing ideas to learners who somehow absorb them and make the ideas their own. This myth suggests that all that is necessary for teaching is to have a good grasp of the knowledge and to transmit it clearly by organizing ideas well and articulating them systematically.

As with most myths, there is an element of truth in this one. In my study of college teaching (Shulman, 1972), I found that these two attributes—having knowledge and the ability to transmit it—were positively associated with student perception of effective instruction. The next most important variable, however, was the instructor's ability to empathize with students. The fourth most important variable was the instructor's ability to present ideas so that they are open to challenge. The notion behind this idea is that it is through the process of challenge, *real* understanding and acceptance can take place. These findings suggest that there may be more to teaching than just knowing a subject and putting it across. In fact, they support what we usually experience as consumers of teaching: We have had teachers who were very knowledgeable and clear presenters from whom we learned little and other teachers who were less certain of their grasp of the subject and more hesitant in their presentation from whom we learned much.

In short, experience should suggest that the complex process of teaching and learning is affected by many variables in the subject, the context of learning, the teacher, and the learner, as well as the interaction among them. The learner is not simply a passive object onto which the teacher can project already developed ideas. Rather, the learner is actively involved in the learning process. This view, elaborated by Dewey (1916), maintains that "the organism is not simply receiving impressions and then answering them. The organism is doing something; it is actively seeking and selecting certain stimuli" (p. 46).

Schwartz (1979), in discussing education in the classroom, also commented on the importance of the active involvement of the learner. Citing the contribution of 18th-century historian and philosopher Biambiattista Vico, he argued that "this is the true process by which students learn: they cannot own their knowledge until they have 'made' it, worked it over, put their mark on the data, imposed their own order upon it, and altered it to fit with what they already have" (p. 14). Of course, the more factual the knowledge, the less it is open to being "altered."

This is the central assumption of this chapter on the educational function of supervision. The staff members are active participants in the learning process. The supervisor's job is to present ideas and to monitor the way in which the worker relates to these ideas. This may range from simply monitoring the worker's eyes to make sure he or she is understanding the directions for filling out a complex form to having regard for the worker's feelings while trying to help him or her tackle a difficult practice issue. It can also mean being sensitive to the subtle interplay taking place between the supervisor and the worker that has been described as the authority theme; the affect resulting from this relationship can enhance the learning or can generate major obstacles to the integration of new ideas.

Knowing the subject and transmitting the ideas clearly is an important precondition to teaching, but these skills should not be confused with the entire process. Schwartz (1979) put it as follows:

> In this light, the problem of the transmitting function is not that it is "unprogressive" or even unproductive, but simply that it does not go far enough into the educational process. When the facts are told, the notes taken down, the "truth" laid out, the work is only just begun. The hardest part remains. (p. 9)

REQUIREMENTS FOR EFFECTIVE LEARNING

A first requirement for effective learning is that the learner must have a stake in the outcome. A worker who is to learn new skills or procedures must be willing to invest some affect or feeling in the process. In effect, workers should become copartners with supervisors so that by engaging in the activity together, they can have the same interest in its accomplishment and share in the ideas and emotions that result.

This may seem a rather obvious idea, but its implications for teaching are often ignored. The supervisor must be clear about the usefulness of the content for the staff, or the connection will not be made. Orientation programs with extensive content on the organizational structure of the agency or the policy manual, for example, may have little immediate meaning for the worker. As a result, little learning occurs.

In many situations, the connection between the content to be learned and the staff member's sense of urgency may be hard to perceive without extensive experience. Initial supervisory efforts must search out this connection and must help the members understand clearly why the information is important. This is a form of contracting at the start of a supervision session: The supervisor concentrates on helping the staff members connect the data to be learned with their own sense of need.

A second key requirement for effective learning is that the staff members be actively involved in the investigation of ideas and in building their own models of reality. No matter how much the supervisor may want to impart understanding to a worker or to share quickly the results of his or her own years of learning, it cannot be done. Holt (1969) put it well:

> We teachers—perhaps all human beings—are in the grip of an astonishing delusion. We think that we can take a picture, a structure, a working model of something, constructed in our own minds out of long experience and familiarity, and by turning that model into a string of words, transplant it whole into the mind of someone else. (p. 39)

Many educators seem to persist in believing that by speaking the words they can transmit an idea, even though their own educational experience has taught them differently. The myth that words are magic—and that if they are spoken they are heard, understood, and remembered by the learner—is still widely believed. If we think back to how we learned something new, we know that the ideas did not exist until we created them for ourselves. Real learning requires the active creation of knowledge by the learner, using all the resources available. The teacher can be one central resource among others, but the construction of the idea, fact, or theory must be undertaken by the learner.

Comprehension of the idea that knowledge does not exist for the learner until he or she creates it leads to major changes in thinking about the teaching–learning process. Teaching cannot be conceived of as simply handing over knowledge or covering the agenda. Instead, the teacher must concentrate on the interaction between the learner and the ideas to be learned, placing a priority on continuous monitoring of the learning interaction and keeping in touch with the learner's progress in constructing the ideas.

This emphasis is especially important in teaching complex skills that may have taken years to develop. Supervisors are apt to forget the steps they followed to deepen their own insights into the content. Ideas that have become obvious to them in their current practice may not be simple or obvious to their staffs. For example, learning to contract with clients (by clarifying purpose, clarifying role, and reaching for client feedback) may have been learned in their first semester as social work students. In their second semester of practicum, as they became bogged down in the work phase, they realized that they had only a superficial understanding of the power of the idea. As they moved to a new setting, in their second year of practicum, or as they started practice with a different category of clients or began using a new modality such as group or family work, these new experiences deepened their grasp of the contracting notion.

Unless supervisors work at it, they can forget how they had to construct, element by element, their understanding of a complex construct such as contracting. They believe they can hand over the years of learning and are surprised to discover that a student or staff member is having great difficulty constructing even a simple version of the idea. As learners who themselves have ventured into this subject area, have discovered some of the shortcuts, and are aware of some of the pitfalls, supervisors can guide their staff members and make their journey more certain and quicker, but they cannot take the journey for them.

Another requirement for effective learning is that the learners must have structured opportunities for using the information presented. A theory about social behavior, for example, will become meaningful when a worker uses the ideas to understand a client on his or her caseload. The doing part, the application of theory, strengthens the worker's understanding of its elements.

Practice skills development is another area in which this is most obvious. A social worker learning a new skill is more likely to learn it if he or she can practice it while it is being taught. Practitioners developing group leadership skills can go only so far in their understanding of group skills before they are blocked in their learning by a lack of practical experience. When actual practice experiences are not easily available, laboratory simulations may be useful, but they lack the reality of trying skills out with actual clients.

In summary, the three essential requirements for effective learning are perceiving an investment in the knowledge, being actively involved in creating the ideas, and having an opportunity to practice the use of the information. Even with these requirements present, many obstacles can emerge to block the learning effort. The supervisor helps overcome these obstacles by mediating the learner's mastery of the skills needed for effective work in the helping professions.

SKILLS OF PROFESSIONAL PERFORMANCE

In an article on classroom teaching of social work practice, Schwartz (1964, p. 5) identified four categories of professional performance: (1) professional practice, (2) professional impact, (3) job management, and (4) professional learning.

Professional practice refers to the work of helping professionals with clients, which calls for skills in communication, relationships, and assessment. *Professional impact* is defined as the skills required to implement a course of action designed to make one's professional contribution to the processes of social change—in the agency, in the neighborhood, and in the profession itself. *Job management* includes the skills required to organize a practice such as meeting agency recording requirements, collecting data, and monitoring outcomes. And *professional learning* includes the skills required to work on professional problems and to incorporate resources such as supervision, the literature, colleagues, and specialists in a personal approach to professional problem solving.

This structure is useful in conceptualizing the broad learning areas involved in the educational element of supervision for social work. Some of the issues related to job management have been dealt with in preceding chapters. This chapter focuses on the teaching of skills for professional practice and professional learning. The category of professional impact is considered in Part V, wherein supervision is examined in relation to helping workers deal with the system.

In teaching the skills required in these categories of professional performance, the supervisor's role is that of a mediator between the learner (the subject of the learning process) and the ideas to be learned (the objects). Dewey (1916) was one of the first to recognize the possibilities of such a functional role, noting that "the teacher should be occupied not with the subject matter itself but with its interaction with the pupils' present needs and capacities" (p. 74).

The role of mediator is an essential one in the interactional concept of supervision that is presented in this book. It also is suggested as a useful statement of function for the helping person in Shulman's (1992) text on practice skills. This practice theory, derived from Schwartz's work, is useful in explaining how the worker tries to help clients work within the various systems of demand they encounter, such as school, work, peer groups, or family. In this book, the idea of a mediating function has been applied to the practice of supervision, and the supervisor's role is seen as intermediate, between the workers and the systems with which they must deal—the agency, the client, colleagues, the community, and so on (see Figure 2.1).

TEACHING CORE PRACTICE SKILLS

The mediating character of the teaching function can be used by supervisors to help staff members develop core communication, relationship, and problem-solving skills. Many of these skills have been discussed in earlier chapters in relation to supervision. Here, the focus is on the same skills as they are applied by the worker in direct practice. Implications for the educational function of supervision are noted. Each skill is illustrated by an account describing how a worker has used it with a client, followed by a section on the parallel process, suggesting how supervisors can teach the skill by modeling. These supervisory suggestions are also illustrated with reports, and the ways in which supervisors can model use of the skill for workers are pointed out.

The skills discussed include tuning in, contracting, dealing with authority, and those that make up the skill factors of empathy, elaboration, the demand for work, sharing one's feelings, and sharing data. These are the key skills required by beginning workers in most helping relationships. They are also the skills most adaptable to teaching through modeling by supervisors. (A more complete discussion and illustrations of these skills and others can be found in Shulman's text on practice, *The Skills of Helping Individuals, Families and Groups*, 3rd ed., 1992.)

Tuning in and Responding Directly to Indirect Cues

Many important communications shared by clients, particularly in taboo areas such as authority and sex, are expressed indirectly. Clients often hint at a concern that they are afraid to express openly. The tuning-in skill helps workers put themselves in the place of the client as a way of developing preliminary empathy.

A key question clients often have when first meeting a worker is "What kind of worker will this person be?" They may be concerned that workers will judge them harshly and will not understand their feelings. Parents, for example, may ask workers they have just met whether they are married and have children, as an indirect way of finding out if the worker can understand their concerns. Workers who respond by providing a detailed description of their training can alienate these clients in the first interview. If, however, they are tuned in to the possible meaning of this question, they can use the skill of responding directly to an indirect cue. A worker could say, for example "No, I'm not married. Why do you ask? Are you worried that I might not understand what it's like for you to raise kids?" Such an invitation encourages the clients to be more direct about their concerns, and it gives the worker an opportunity to demonstrate an understanding of the difficulty the clients are experiencing in the encounter. This can help develop a more positive relationship between them.

Workers can tune in to a range of possible feelings and concerns on the client's part and can prepare to deal with them. Tuning in is tentative, however, as was noted in chapter 3 in relation to supervision, and the worker must be prepared to abandon preconceived ideas about what the client might feel and must instead respond to the reality of the interview. The preparation of tuning in gives the worker a better chance of responding to the real meaning of indirect communications rather than reacting defensively.

Parallel Processes

Supervisors can teach the skill of tuning in by providing an exercise to prepare workers for a first interview. The workers should be encouraged to sense the feelings of the clients by remembering a similar instance in their own experience when they sought help from some professional. The exercise becomes a form of role play in which the workers try to become attuned to the clients' underlying feelings by tuning in to their own feelings, like nervousness at being new to the job or concern about not having enough professional or life experience to be able to help a client.

The supervisor can help by understanding and empathizing with the workers' feelings as beginners. If supervisors can remember what it was like at the start of their own practice, they are more likely to be supportive of workers. Supervisors who are themselves tuned in and who respond directly to the feelings of new workers will thus demonstrate the importance of these two skills for workers. The supervisor's modeling of these skills is an effective way of teaching them, as was noted in chapter 2.

In the following example, a supervisor tries to respond to a young student's feelings of panic when called by a new client who is herself in a panic. The client, Mrs. Cline, was extremely upset and had called the student to demand that she find an immediate placement for John, her six-year-old child. Mrs. Cline claimed that she was no longer able to handle the child and did not know what to do if social services could not get John off her hands. The student, Susan, was so upset herself that she panicked and told the client she would call her back after she called her supervisor.

The supervisor's account of how she tried to tune in to the student's feelings during the telephone conversation and help her develop a strategy for handling the client included the following notes:

> Susan said she felt overwhelmed by Mrs. Cline's [the client's] demands and didn't know how she should respond. I went on to explain that it was not Susan's role to provide solutions, rather that she should work to explore Mrs. Cline's feelings, the options she could envisage, their possible consequences, and so forth.
>
> I stopped talking, and there was silence on the other end. I told her I was quiet to allow her to raise concerns I might not yet have addressed. She said she was thinking how she would say this to Mrs. Cline. She told me she

had copied down everything I was saying. I acknowledged her problem in that she had my words but that it is hard to feel good about using someone else's words.

Student: I'd like to be able to tell her something. Mrs. Cline feels that the psych. assessment unit and our work with her hasn't done any good because she's still got the problem. I really feel terrible.

Supervisor: Mrs. Cline seems to have misunderstood what you, the assessment team, or any other helping person is able to do, and you're feeling bad in recognizing how limited we as helping persons are. We can only help Mrs. Cline work out ways of coping with her problems; we can't come up with her answers.

Student: I'll try to think about all these things and get all my "social working" notions put together before I call her this evening.

Supervisor: That's good, but don't let your concerns get in the way of being able to hear her concerns.

Student: But what if she still wants to put John in a foster home like she did this morning?

Supervisor: Mrs. Cline was in a panic and was proposing a panic solution, and it sounds like you're getting caught in her panic.

Student: That's exactly where I am!

Supervisor: I figured that. Let's look at what panic does. It crowds your mind so you can't think, and there's one idea that gets stuck in your head, and you can't think your way past it.

Student: Yes, that's how I feel.

Supervisor: So now we need to figure out a way to help Mrs. Cline past her panic thought of foster placement.

I proceeded to talk about what Susan could do to lower Mrs. Cline's anxiety level and her own until they were both calm enough to consider a whole range of options and critically explore their respective advantages and disadvantages. She said, "That sounds good."

I went on to suggest that going through this exercise with Mrs. Cline and exploring this process with her is more helpful to Mrs. Cline than trying to solve her problem for her. Learning how to cope with and overcome panic so that she can deal with the issues in a reasonable way will, in the long run, be much more beneficial to Mrs. Cline than her frantic pursuit of answers.

My impression was that she was beginning at this point to overcome her own panic and was starting to think constructively about how she would deal with this evening's interview or phone contact. I told Susan to contact me at home in the evening.

This supervision report provides a good example of two aspects of the parallel process in action. First, the student felt the client's panic and reproduced it in the conversation with the supervisor by acting out her own confusion. One could almost consider the student as saying to the supervisor, "Let me show you what Mrs. Cline's panic feels like, and then you can show me how to handle it." This is not a conscious process; however, supervisees often appear to act out in the conference the very behavior they are experiencing from the clients. Second, as the supervisor helped the student begin to manage her own feelings so that she could better manage her problems in dealing with a panicked client, the supervisor modeled the required skills of helping. Of course, to be able to demonstrate these skills, the supervisor first had to manage her own feelings when faced with the stress of a panicky client.

Contracting

In the beginning phase of work the client is probably wondering: "What's this all about?" An important part of the worker's preparation includes planning to clarify the potential working contract with the client during the first interview. As in supervision (see chapter 2), four critical skills of the worker in contracting are clarifying purpose, clarifying role, reaching for feedback regarding purpose, and dealing with the authority theme. The first three of these skills are discussed in this section, and the authority of the worker is the topic of the following section.

Helping professionals often have difficulty clarifying the purpose of their work and their role. Our use of jargon and global, overly general statements can obstruct our ability to define precisely what the social worker can do. In the case of a family support worker, the example used to illustrate these skills, it is not unusual for workers to be unclear about what they can offer a family. A first interview will be uncomfortable under the best of circumstances for both the worker and the members of the family, but this discomfort will be increased if there is doubt about the worker's role. To set the client quickly at ease, it is helpful for the worker to prepare a brief opening statement describing the reason for the referral and the services that can be offered.

The following interview illustrates the skills of clarifying purpose and role. It is an example of a first contact with Mrs. Hubert, a 28-year-old mother of three children. After being introduced by Mrs. Hubert's social worker, the family worker attempted to explain her purpose in these words:

> I thought it would help if I took a moment to explain why I have been asked to work with your family. John [the social worker] has told me that things are rough right now for you, with a lot of concerns on your mind. I understand it has been upsetting for you since your husband left, and with your oldest boy having trouble at school, it is easy to understand how these things can pile up. John felt that if I could spend some time with your family, there might be some ways I could take some of the load off of you. For example, I would be glad to talk with you if the going gets rough some days with the kids. I could listen and maybe help you figure out what to do about some of the problems the kids are making for you. If you thought it would be helpful, I would be glad to go down to the school and see what is going on with your boy, Frank. Maybe if I talked to the counselor, the teacher, and then Frank, I could help get him back in. Does any of this sound like it might be helpful from your point of view?

By beginning this way the worker has been direct about her purpose and has provided some "handles" for work—suggestions of ways she might help. These handles partialize the problems and provide some concrete indications of what the worker means by her offer to help. This directness helps the client quickly sort out how the worker might help, and it decreases the client's concern that the worker is there to do something to her. Workers are often embarrassed at being direct with clients; they fear alienating the client by being too forthright, or they begin with a notion of their role as "changing" the client. They have a hidden agenda that explains their reluctance to be direct. Because clients do not lend themselves to being "changed," the sooner the worker gives up this hidden agenda, the quicker a more honest working relationship can develop.

Reaching for feedback is important because the client has to accept the offer of service. In this example, Mrs. Hubert may respond to only one part of the contract: the part she feels urgency about or is willing to risk, often a "near problem," one close to the more difficult concerns. Alternatively, she may be ready to trust the worker and deal with more serious problems instead of near problems. It is important to recognize that the worker can help only in those areas where the client feels some sense of investment and a freedom to risk. Mrs. Hubert began to take the family worker up on the offer, as the worker reported:

> Mrs. Hubert said that things had been rough and that the school problem just was the last straw. Frank had been suspended for not doing homework and fighting in the classroom. I told her that I thought that must have come as quite a blow. She said she just didn't know what to do. She was at her wit's end. She found herself getting angry at her son when he hung around the house.

With the feedback from the client the work has begun. Because the worker is willing to listen and to respond with some empathy, an important start is being made on the working relationship, the medium through which the worker can provide help. I have described the elements of the working relationship as including a client's sense of trust in the worker, the client's belief that the worker is concerned about him or her (for example, not just concerned about the children), and a sense of positive rapport (Shulman, 1991, 1992). The contracting skills described in this section, when used in the beginning phase of practice, were found to contribute positively to the development of this working relationship (Shulman, 1991, 1992).

Although the specifics of the purpose and the role may differ according to the situations in which help is provided, contracting skills are crucial to all helping situations. In the following example of a first session between a social worker and a foster adolescent, the worker attempts to spell out his role:

> Because I'm going to be your new worker, I wanted to meet you to find

out how things were going with you, and to see if there was anything I might be able to help with. I know you have been moving around a lot this past year, and that starting in a new foster home, at a new school, and with new friends can be difficult. How about it, how has it been?

The client may not immediately respond to this offer, because there is no working relationship yet, and the client may not trust the worker. In addition, the client may not feel there are any difficulties to discuss. Nevertheless, the worker has made the offer and the client has heard it. If problems emerge later, or as the relationship develops, the client may be more ready to use the worker's help. Conversely, if the worker had not articulated "handles for work," the client would not be clear about the contract even if he or she wished to accept the offer.

Clarifying purpose and role is also essential in a brief, limited-focus interview. An example is the following offer by a worker in a medical setting meeting with a patient about to be discharged:

Your doctor has told me that you are about to be discharged. He was concerned that it might be difficult for you when you return home, because you have been through a tough time here at the hospital. I wanted to see if I might be helpful in any way—perhaps by sending a homemaker or someone to help out with the kids until you get settled back in. Is there anything you are concerned about?

As the client describes the situation, it is often possible to identify other areas where services may be helpful. A worker might perceive, for example, that a single parent is having difficulty dealing with her children and might suggest a referral to a family agency.

This discussion is not meant to suggest that contracting is a mechanical process for the worker. Each one approaches first sessions differently, and each must respond to the individual nature of her or his client's responses. A worker might find that the client is eager to talk, and the worker needs to listen first, before stating what he or she has to offer. The important point is that at some time in the first interview, the discussion should focus on the connections between the felt needs of the clients and the service that the agency or other setting can provide.

Parallel Processes

One of the best ways for the supervisor to help a new worker get ready to make a first contact with a client is to suggest a role play in which the worker tries out an opening statement of purpose and role. The supervisor can then respond in a number of ways, preparing the worker for possible reactions. The worker's effort at making an opening statement often reveals a lack of clarity about purpose and role. This gives the supervisor an opportunity to help the worker rethink her or his purpose and role. The use of jargon instead of precise terms and meaningful expressions can be pointed out, and the worker can be helped to think of alternatives. The role play often reveals many of the worker's fears about the encounter and gives the supervisor an opportunity to discuss them.

This exercise can provide workers with the confidence to be more relaxed in the first session and thus less defensive. It may also reveal the worker's feelings in the situation, feelings that can influence his or her willingness to offer help to a client. For example, in child welfare practice, workers may be reluctant to contract with the client in this way if they believe that the legal removal of a child at risk is a distinct possibility. In a role play with a supervisor, a worker may stress the protection and investigatory purpose of a first interview but offer little help to the parent as a client in his or her own right. When the supervisor inquires about the worker's hesitation at making an offer to the parent, it may turn out that the worker is afraid of "feeling like a rat" if she or he encourages the client to be candid and then has to suggest the removal of the child. With these feelings and fears on the table, the supervisor can help the worker explore the importance of integrating the "helping" and "protection" roles inherent in child welfare practice.

Another way of helping workers with their contracting is to follow up after an interview and discuss the details of the encounter. The worker could write up notes describing the discussion, or, if time does not permit, recall the dialogue from memory (memory work). The supervisor must get some of the details to be helpful. If the worker comments on the client's defensiveness, for example, the supervisor should request an account of what both client and worker said. Often even a few moments of analysis of a dialogue will help a worker understand the interaction in a new way. As the worker begins to see the client's actions as responses to his or her interventions, the focus can shift from discussion of the case to discussion of the interaction and the worker's skills.

There is an interesting parallel between this form of supervision and the work done with clients. For example, when a parent discusses a problem with a teenage child, the worker, like the supervisor, should ask for the details of the encounter—what the client actually said and how the child responded. The worker can be most helpful by examining the specifics of the interaction, and the same is true for the supervisor.

A process recording can be a useful teaching device. The worker writes a brief description of the conversation at the start of the session, including some verbatim dialogue. A summary describes what followed, with expanded detailed descriptions of crucial aspects of the middle of the session. The ending is also written verbatim, for a total process recording of two pages (see the Coda for a discussion of process recording).

Another important way the supervisor teaches the contracting skills is by demonstrating them in the supervision context. In early interviews with a new worker, the supervisor should clarify the purpose of supervision and the role of a supervisor and should reach for worker feedback, as noted in chapter 3. The supervisor can also prepare an opening statement to begin the contracting with the worker. The contract will inevitably be broad, because the supervisor has many responsibilities. But the part of the contract concerning the development of practice skills might be stated like this:

> Part of what I will be doing with you is helping you look at the way you work with clients. When you are getting ready to go out on first interviews, I can help you prepare by thinking through what you might say. After an interview, particularly one you feel you had trouble with, I will be glad to listen to what went on and try to help you figure out what you did right and what you might have done differently. In addition, there will be some days when the work gets rough and you're feeling low. If you want someone to talk to, I'll try to be available to listen.

There are a number of reasons why supervisors often ignore the specifics of workers' interactions with their clients. Some may not have experienced this kind of work themselves, or they may have had bad experiences with punitive discussions of their practice. They were not allowed to make mistakes. Others refrain from this work because they sense resistance from the worker. Still others are afraid to make this offer because they feel they will not be able to respond adequately if the worker asks for help. But it is not really necessary for supervisors to have all the answers. What supervisors can provide are ways of working on the questions, some insights from their own experiences, and some support for the worker in the struggle. In a parallel way, this is exactly what the workers will be offering the client.

The problem of limited time is often appropriately cited by supervisors who have many demands placed on them. In reality, however, they may have to spend a great deal of time dealing with the problems created by lack of worker skill. For example, a placement breakdown of a teenager in care may have been indirectly hinted at by the client but not picked up by the worker who had contracted poorly with the client. This problem may then demand many hours of time and much energy, all of which could have been avoided. Removing an abused child from a family (a situation that might never have arisen had the worker developed more skillfully the initial working relationship with the frightened mother) also takes its toll on both time and emotions.

In the reality of agency demands and time pressures, supervisors have to pick and choose the appropriate levels of intervention. Some workers may require more time and others less. Workers may need more detailed help at the start of their practice, but a consultative form of supervision is more appropriate as they gain experience and confidence. Choices may need to be made about which clients are discussed in a summary fashion and which ones need more detailed analysis—either because of the demands of the client's situation or the learning agenda of the worker. The only argument made here is that some level of detailed analysis must be included in educational supervision if workers are to be helped to grow. This process also provides the fuel for the supervisor's growth as well.

A final note on this issue relates to the sources of support available to the supervisor. When I work with administrators on their supervision of front-line supervisors, I most often find a parallel in the general nature of the supervision discussion. For example, a supervisor presenting a problem with a "difficult" worker will rarely be asked to share any of the conversation with that worker. Thus, the administrator models the same lack of attention to the interactional detail in his or her supervision of the supervisor that the worker may be experiencing in conferences. Once again, the most powerful forms of help will come in an analysis of the moment-to-moment interactions of the supervision interview or group meeting rather than in a general discussion of the problem worker. If such help is not available from a supervisor's administrator, then alternative sources of consultation or peer support can be used to take its place. The key point is that a supervisor will also need support if he or she is to provide it to a worker, who in turn, needs support to provide it to the client, and so on.

Dealing with the Authority of the Worker

Whenever a client first comes into contact with a helping person, the tendency is to perceive that person as an authority figure. This is true even in situations in which the client is a voluntary one or does not fear the worker's legal authority. The client transfers to the new encounter feelings and perceptions derived from past experiences with people in authority (for example, parents, teachers, and other workers). The worker must be sensitive to how authority affects the client and must be prepared to discuss it directly if it blocks the working relationship. Because authority is a taboo subject, the worker may have to help the client feel comfortable enough to discuss it. The necessity of discussing this relationship periodically should be anticipated. In this sense, the authority theme may represent an obstacle to work, as it was described in chapter 4.

In addition to the possibility of transference of feelings by clients, workers should guard against countertransference of their own feelings and perceptions from their past personal and professional experiences. It is not uncommon for young workers to identify with children in a family conflict situation, for example, because they perceive the parents in a stereotyped fashion. Loss of their sense of function may lead them to take sides, which cuts them off as helpers to the parents.

In cases in which the agency does carry clear authority over the life of the client, as in child abuse situations, wherein it has statutory responsibility for the child, it is essential to deal with the authority theme early in the worker–client relationship. Defensive or hostile clients often have a stereotyped idea of workers because of past experiences or what they have heard from other clients. A client's underlying fear of a worker as, for example, a "baby snatcher" may be expressed through hostile and defensive behavior.

A worker meeting this kind of response should deal with it directly, as a start to contracting. The following report illustrates this process:

> I told her I had come because we had had a call from one of her neighbors who was concerned that she was neglecting her kids. I told her I was here to see if this was true, to determine if her kids were safe, and to see if there was any way I could help her. The client responded angrily and defensively, saying her neighbors were lying and out to get her. She told me that what went on with her kids was none of my business and that she would rather not talk to me about it.

> I told her it was obvious that she was upset that I was there. I went on to say that it wasn't easy for me, either, but that our agency was required by law to investigate all such complaints. I told her it was important for me to hear her side of the story as well. I asked her if she was worried that we might be thinking of taking her kids from her. She told me in a very angry voice that she wouldn't let me if I tried. I told her that we often get calls from neighbors, and just getting a call did not mean we would remove children from their families. I told her we were more interested in helping kids stay in families and that it was only under serious circumstances when children were being beaten or neglected and their parents were having problems with the kids that we could not help with that we considered removing children—it was only under those serious circumstances. We would much rather help parents out with their problems so that the kids could stay at home.

> I asked her if she had had experiences with social workers before. She said she had not, but a neighbor of hers had. She went on to describe an incident in which the worker had removed a child. I told her I could understand why she had been so upset and worried when I arrived. I asked her if we could start all over. I told her that we had lots of parents who came to us because the going was rough with their kids. When you're alone with three kids, and they are after you all day, and you can't get out because you have no help, it's easy to understand how you could get overwhelmed and angry and even lose your temper. That did not mean you were a bad parent. There was a long silence. I waited. She was staring at my face, probably trying to decide whether to believe me. She finally said it was rough sometimes. I asked if she would like to tell me a bit about what made it rough.

Many clients will not accept the worker's offer of help, particularly in a stressful situation such as fearing the removal of a child. In such cases, wherein the worker believes a child is at risk, further legal intervention to protect the child (and in the long run the parent) may be necessary in spite of the parent's denial. My research has indicated that even in those cases in which removal of a child and court involvement is needed, it may still be possible for the worker to develop a positive working relationship with the parent (Shulman, 1991). The use of effective contracting and empathy skills, even in adversarial situations, can buffer the relationship.

In other cases, it may take a long time for some clients to believe the worker; however, it is important for the worker to make the offer. Unless direct statements of purpose and role are made in the beginning stage of work, the sessions will be constantly hindered by lack of clarity of contract.

Parallel Processes

The parallels between the supervisor–worker and worker–client relationships are most direct in the authority theme. The authority of the supervisor can have a powerful impact on the working relationship. By monitoring this issue and encouraging their workers to be open with them, supervisors can effectively demonstrate this skill. Early in the working supervisory relationship, they should encourage discussion of how comfortable the workers feel in "taking on" the supervisor, being honest, and so on. After such a discussion, it is often helpful to point out to the workers that their clients probably feel the same way about them. Supervisors also need to consider the possibility of countertransference of their own feelings to their relationships with their workers.

This is illustrated in an excerpt from a first interview between a white supervisor and a Native Canadian student who was a mature woman but was new to training. The student described with much feeling a court case she had sat in on in which, she felt, a white lawyer had made racist remarks while supposedly defending a Native Canadian mother who wanted her child returned. The lawyer had asked a witness if she had ever heard of "native time," implying that it was common for Native Canadians to be late. The student described how she had confronted the lawyer during a recess and had told him how she felt about the comment. After some discussion about her anger at white professionals who did not "understand," the supervisor addressed the authority theme in their relationship in this way:

> Supervisor: Can I just stop for a minute? I'm just wondering, going back to what you were saying about what we should be sensitive to. Let's not leave what you're talking about now, but I'm wondering how that applies to me. How can you help me be sensitive to yourself and Native culture so that I can be helpful to you in this situation and also grow myself? Because I have to be helpful to you in this, and obviously you're Native and I'm white. You have something to teach me about this. Let's do a tuning-in exercise for me. You're talking about "white people"—well, I'm a white social worker, so I'm wondering maybe I should also be addressing that.
>
> Student: I think perhaps you could. These issues aren't raised for me until I see a Native in such a situation. I would be more apt to stick up for

myself than my clients would, so I don't think you have to be as conscious in dealing with it with me.

Supervisor: I'm not sure that I'm saying that. I'm just saying, help me tune in to what I should be aware of—not necessarily with you, but with the Native clients I deal with. Also, the people who I supervise, who by and large are going to be white, I need to help them to tune in to their Native clients. I'm probably not going to be supervising that many Native social workers, because there's not that many of you around. There's not many in the school, and more's the tragedy for that. What should I be aware of? I think I see racism, and when I see it, I pick it up, obviously. But how can I be sensitive to . . .

Student: I have an excellent book that you might like to look at, Sue. I'll bring it in next Wednesday. But, I think, more than that—realize that a Native, especially an older one—say, from 30 on—is not too apt to disagree with you, even if you're not respecting their rights.

Supervisor: Would you disagree with me?

Student: Yeah, I would. But, very likely, it would be like that Native client when she came up and talked to the family support worker in court, and said, "I don't want you to worry about . . . feeling bad about testifying against me." Later, that worker said to me, "Now isn't that terrific! I mean, she's a real trooper; she knows that the truth is the truth." Actually, in my view, that client was saying, "Please don't be mad at me, and don't think I'm mad at you and react badly to me." I'm making an awful lot of assumptions, and perhaps I'm completely off base.

Supervisor: You're making your assumptions from your perspective, from your cultural perspective and your personal perspective. And maybe they're right. Most likely, they are right.

Student: My idea is that the Native client wouldn't have had the self-confidence to go up and say, "Look, you bitch, I let you in my home every day and. . . ."

Supervisor: I'm asking you to be sensitive to your assumptions. Let's say you were the client's family worker; you're a Native social worker dealing with a client. Being sensitive to your assumptions, and to the cultural similarities that you have, how is that going to affect the way you work with her?

Student: I would not take her first comment as being her true feelings.

Supervisor: Okay.

Student: Like, if I said, "How do you feel about me coming in every morning?" and she said, "That's really nice of you to do something for me," I would look at that more closely.

Supervisor: Would that be any different for a white client?

Student: I think I would look at it that way if it was anybody that I felt was feeling in a one-down position, like badly in a one-down position.

Supervisor: I think that I would ask you to be sensitive to the fact that it's a function of maybe being a Native but it's also a function of being one-down anyway. And if you were dealing with a white client, by and large that white client would say back to you, "Oh, I'm feeling fine about you being here," when actually they want to say, "You bitch, get out of my house." I think it's really important for you to remember the client is one-down, more than the client is Native. Maybe they feel they are two-down if they're Native. We still have to deal with an authority thing going on in there, whether the authority is Native or white and whether the client is Native or white. I think part of your learning is to really be aware that the client is one-down anyway and that, by and large, a white client would say the same thing back.

Student: That is quite possible, but I think a Native might be better at hiding their true feelings.

Supervisor: Right! And that's probably where your sensitivity to what's going on is really good.

Although the worker did not take up the supervisor's offer to explore their own relationship further, perhaps feeling hesitant in an early supervisory session, the supervisor did make it clear that this could be an agenda item. The supervisor might also have dropped the issue, feeling it was too threatening to the worker (and herself) in a first conference. However, the supervisor did highlight the authority theme in terms of the worker's relationship with clients, as a Native Canadian working with Native Canadian or white clients. Thus, the sensitive and taboo subject of race was brought out in the open for future work. The Native Canadian student's suggestion that a white worker should not too quickly take the Native Canadian client's reassurance as a signal that everything is fine in the worker–client relationship is an interesting comment. Once again, relying on the notion of the parallel process, this may be an indirect cue to the white supervisor that their relationship will need close attention as well.

Empathic Skills

A central assumption about empathy is that the way people feel affects how they act and that the way people act affects how they feel. For example, a single-parent mother who is feeling lonely and unhappy, perhaps judging herself harshly and blaming herself for the marital breakup, may express these feelings in the way she acts toward her children. The mother's tensions can lead the children to act out their feelings through negative behavior, which, in turn, causes the mother to be less tolerant. A vicious cycle develops. If the mother is also a member of an oppressed and vulnerable population, years of experiencing the oppression of racism, classism, and sexism may lead to an internalizing of the "oppressor without" and a resulting alienation from her self and her children.

In another example, a mother on welfare whose children have grown up may decide she would like to go back to work and consults an employment counselor about available opportunities. If she feels inadequate about reentering the work force after so many years at home, she may act this out by missing job interviews. Such a client is ambivalent: On the one hand, she wants independence and self-respect; on the other, she is afraid of risking herself. In a similar way, an adolescent who has been rejected by his family and has moved through a number of foster homes no longer believes he can have a stable, close relationship with adults. Because he has been hurt so often, he refuses to take any more risks. He then begins new contacts in a residential treatment home with acting-out behavior, which brings about the rejection he fears. A hospital patient who is anxious about an impending medical procedure also may express the feeling through demanding or hostile behavior. In each of these cases, the clients' feelings affect their actions, and their actions further affect their feelings in a reciprocal manner.

Because of this connection between feeling and doing, there is a need for workers to be sensitive to the affective portion of a client's message. Unfortunately, in our society the open expression of feelings is somewhat taboo. The norms under which most people operate forbid direct expression of some of our most private feelings. Workers need to develop skills that will help clients become more aware of their real feelings and be willing to share them. As the worker helps clients manage these feelings, clients will be better able to manage their problems. The worker's efforts to understand a client's feelings will also strengthen the worker–client relationship. The empathic skills discussed in this section are the same as those that were described in the work-phase model of supervision in chapter 4: reaching for feelings, acknowledging feelings, and articulating the client's feelings (or putting them into words).

Reaching for feelings involves listening to the client's description of a problem and asking about the associated feelings. For example, a mother describes a conflict situation with a daughter who had come home at 2 A.M. without having let the mother know where she was. The worker might inquire, "What did you feel when your daughter arrived?" The intent is to encourage the client to express her feelings at the time of the encounter. It is important to be genuinely empathic; the worker must be interested in understanding the feelings and not just ask about them in a mechanical manner. For these skills to be effective, workers must attempt to actually feel, as best as they can, the emotions of the clients. To do this in a meaningful way, they need to become tuned in to their own affective responses during interviews.

Acknowledging feelings calls for the worker to communicate acceptance and appreciation of the client's affect. This skill is demonstrated in an interview with a client who was fearful during the first interview and responded defensively. Later, the worker reported:

> Mrs. Frank told me that she had been fearful of me in the first interview. She didn't feel she could trust me and tell me what was really on her mind. I told her I could easily understand that if I had been in her shoes, I would have been just as scared and upset.

A more sophisticated skill is articulating the client's feelings before they are expressed by the client. In any relationship, particularly at the beginning, people are reluctant to share their true feelings. Workers who are listening to clients and are tuned in may be able to sense how the clients feel, even before the clients say anything about it. When the worker articulates these feelings, two objectives are accomplished: Clients are, in effect, given permission to discuss their feelings, and they perceive the worker as someone who understands. Even if clients do not acknowledge a feeling, hearing it expressed may be enough. Here is an example of this skill in action:

> Mr. Gregory asked me how long his youngsters would be in care. I told him for six months, or longer, if he or his wife wanted to extend the agreement [a voluntary placement]. He said it was a long time for the kids. I said, "And for you too." He went on to tell me that his son John was confused and sad. I said, "That must make it hard on you to see him." He said it was, because he was not sure of what to say to him. I said, "You mean when he asks you when he is coming home?" He said, "Well, yeah."

This worker was tuned in to the feelings of the parent, particularly the guilt involved when a child is placed in care. She understood that parents often feel so bad about the placement that they cannot face the question in the eyes of a child wanting to know when it will be possible to come home. Natural parents often avoid that question by not coming to visit their children who have been placed in care, by appearing to be cold and indifferent, or even by getting drunk before a visit. In this case, the worker was so tuned in to the client's feelings that she was able to state her affective hunches slightly ahead of him. She did this when she said, "That must make it hard on you to see him" and "You mean when he asks you when he is coming home?" The value of the skill is that the worker's empathic reaction encourages the client to risk sharing these feelings. It also strengthens the working relationship because it demonstrates the worker's caring for the client.

In another example, a nurse spoke in these terms to a mother in a hospital emergency waiting room about her child, who had had an eye injury:

> Mother: How long will it take to find out what's wrong? I've been here for almost an hour.
> Nurse: I'm sorry it is taking so long. The doctor is examining your daughter right now [pause]. It's really hard waiting when you're frightened about your daughter's sight.
> Mother (starting to cry): Oh God, if I had been watching her, it wouldn't have happened.
> Nurse (after a few moments, putting her hand on the mother's shoulder): It's okay to cry—it's very tough for parents to see their own child hurt and not know how badly. I can't give you any real information, but for what it's worth, she didn't look too bad to me when I took her in. I'll try to find out what's up, and I'll let you know as soon as I can.

In any expression of empathy, the feelings must be genuine. Many workers have had training that has taught them to deal with feelings routinely. When the workers themselves are not actually feeling anything, the clients quickly see these efforts as false. Workers who simply echo a client's response in an effort to use the reflection skill, for example, are not helping. If the client says, "I'm angry at the agency," and the worker responds, "You're angry at the agency," the client has every right to say that he has just told the worker that and cannot understand why it is being repeated. On the other hand, if the worker uses reflection in a genuine and feeling manner, it can be a helpful skill.

A ritualistically asked question such as "How do you feel about that?" may also be perceived as artificial. Mechanical responses such as "I hear you saying that . . ." often repel clients rather than help them discuss their feelings. Many students indicate that they feel awkward and unskilled in dealing openly with clients' feelings and that these expressions help them make a start. I support the use of such expressions but insist that they can be effective only if the student actually feels the emotions. With experience and practice, I assure the students that they will eventually find their own voice and will no longer need these expressions. Workers must develop their own personal styles of empathizing, but the key to the effectiveness of the skill is a sincere response to the feelings of the client.

My research on practice has found that the worker's ability to acknowledge the client's feelings contributes to the development of the working relationship, which in turn, is the medium through which help is provided to the client (Shulman, 1978, 1991, 1992). In addition, the ability to articulate the client's feelings before they are expressed, when used in the beginning phase of practice, appears to contribute to the establishment of a good working relationship (Shulman, 1991, 1992). These results support the notion that workers would do better to err on the side of risking expressing their affective hunches and committing the error of commission rather than withholding and making the error of omission.

Parallel Processes

With the empathic skills, supervisors can model the helping process most effectively. It does little good for supervisors to tell workers that they are not empathic with their clients if at the same time they are not empathic with their workers. In the beginning phase of supervisory work, the supervisor can demonstrate the importance of empathic responses by tuning in to an inexperienced worker's feelings and starting to articulate them when the two first meet. Before a worker's first interview, the supervisor might ask, "Are you worried about seeing your first client?" and later might say something to the effect that "It must be scary wondering if you have anything to offer that client." Workers will appreciate a supervisor's genuine efforts to understand the experience and to support them during the difficult times. The supervisor's articulation of these feelings can also free workers to express their doubts and concerns.

Discussion of interviews is another instance in which the supervisor's use of the empathic skills is helpful. As a worker reports a client's comments, the supervisor might say, for example, "Do you remember what you were feeling at that moment?" By reaching for feelings, the supervisor indicates an interest in the worker's affect during interviews. It is also helpful to explain that how the worker feels during an interview is important to the supervisor. Feelings affect what workers do and say, just as they influence clients' behaviors. Often, what a worker says to a client may be unrelated to what the worker feels. The client, sensing this incongruence, mistrusts the worker. Workers need to be encouraged to trust their own feelings and to allow themselves to make "active" mistakes from which they can grow.

Such supervisory discussions can lead to consideration of what makes it hard for workers to articulate their own feelings. Because workers are affected by the norms and taboos of our society, they may feel uncomfortable and embarrassed about discussing people's feelings. Even though the worker is empathic with the client, expression of this empathy may be blocked. This is a normal response, and acknowledging the reasonableness of the workers' feelings may free them to deal with their clients affect more effectively.

Another helpful device is to ask workers how they might deal with an incident if it should recur. Sometimes simply attempting to express empathy in a role play can assist a worker to find the right words to deal with a situation in practice.

The supervisor can also support workers by pointing out that the ability to empathize develops slowly and is influenced by age and experience, but it does eventually emerge. A worker's capacity to empathize with clients will grow with practice. As the supervisor examines cases when the worker was not empathic or seemed distant, it may become apparent that another feeling was interfering with the worker's capacity for empathy. Workers who judge clients harshly because of their actions (for example, child abuse) must learn to consider the clients as people with needs and problems of their own while still holding them accountable for their behavior. In effect, workers learn from their mistakes, and the supervisor's support and understanding can help them risk their feelings and feel more comfortable about learning in this way. The supervisor has to acknowledge that there will be times when the worker will be too tired, too rushed, or too upset to empathize. All these can also be problems for supervisors who need support from their own administrators and peers if they are to help their workers.

The following excerpt shows how a supervisor helped a beginning worker to examine her feelings about working with a father who had been accused of sexually abusing his child. Dealing with perpetrators of traumatic violence, such as sexual abuse, is one of the more difficult areas for workers (Shulman, 1991). New workers naturally bring to the relationship a host of reactions to clients, and supervisors must show them that they can admit to these feelings and begin to understand them more deeply. Workers must learn to see past the possible pathological behavior of clients and must tune in to their real feelings and concerns. The supervisor's report noted:

> Theresa began by presenting me with a case. She went into detail about the case, which involved sexual abuse. She said "That guy was really icky." I asked her what she meant by "icky." She said, "Well, when Mr. Brown was standing near Jean, he put his hand on her head and she cringed." I observed that she really had some feelings about Mr. Brown. She said emphatically, "I sure do hate him, the son of a bitch." I looked at her—silence. She said, "Whew! That was pretty strong!" I said "Yeah, you sound really angry." She said, "I have angry feelings about abuse. I've seen too much of it. . . ."
> I asked her to tune into Mr. Brown and what he might be feeling. She said, "Mad." I asked, "How come?" She said, "Because we social workers were in his house." I asked what else; she said, "Maybe he feels icky, too." We talked about why he would feel icky. Later she said, "I really forgot to tune in to him and see him in the system. Next time I'll be more aware."

Each new type of client will generate new reactions in the worker, and the supervisor can help even experienced workers to become more aware of these diverse feelings. Workers need to be helped to develop professional methods for sharing their feelings and reactions with such clients rather than simply trying to suppress them. For example, this is what one worker in a first session with a perpetrator of sexual abuse said:

> I have to honest with you. When I think of what you did to your daughter it makes me very angry and upset. In spite of these feelings, I want to reach out to you because I think you must be in some pain as well. I'd like to try to help you, because I think you need some help right now— and that's important—but it is also a way of helping your daughter.

In another example, experienced male workers who were preparing to work with men who battered their wives or the women they live with had to look deeply into their own feelings about women and violence before they could honestly tune in to these clients. When audiotapes of interviews preparing clients for a first group meeting were examined in a group supervision, I pointed out that a worker had been lacking in empathy for the potential group member and had seemed judgmental in a subtle way. The consultation continued as follows:

> I asked Frank why he had seemed so angry at the client—if he could put his finger on what he was feeling at the time. He indicated that he really hadn't realized he was feeling angry. I acknowledged that this was some-

times the hardest part—dealing with real feelings that are just beneath the surface. I asked if anyone else had any ideas.

Terry responded that Frank was probably really feeling angry at this guy for having beaten his wife and that he knew he felt that way as well, even though we were trying to be nonjudgmental. I said, "Good, that's a start." Frank continued, "It's easy to say we shouldn't judge these guys, and I feel funny feeling this way, but I do get furious at them." I asked if they had any idea why this type of client hit them so hard. I told them I knew they were experienced workers and had learned to handle tough problems, such as parental abuse of children. I wanted to know what was different with these men.

After a long pause, Frank said, "I think they remind me of my own anger toward women." I asked what he meant, and he explained that there were often times when he had felt so angry at his wife that he could have hit her—and that the difference between him and these clients was that he could control his anger, and they couldn't. I said, "So when you see your own feelings in these men, it's very tough to face them—because they hit you so hard, and because it's tough to admit you have them." Terry said I had hit the nail on the head. I replied that I thought we were now starting to make a real start on tuning in to these men, because they were being so honest in tuning in to their own feelings.

Continued work with these social workers explored the issue of how to provide support for these clients while still making sure they were held accountable for their behavior and not allowed to minimize it or deny it. Additional work was done in understanding the subtle and not so subtle forms of sexism that male workers need to explore in their own attitudes and behaviors toward women if they were to be helpful to these clients who represented more extreme examples of structural sexism issues in our society. As these issues emerged, the contract governing the consultation continually turned the discussion toward the issue of the impact of a worker's sexist attitudes on his ability to practice effectively with the male batterers.

The concern of supervisors about responding emphatically to workers and exploring personal feelings and attitudes was described in chapter 4. Even those supervisors who have strong practice skills and little hesitation about being empathic with clients may be afraid that this could amount to "social working" their workers. They recognize that workers are not clients, and they feel it would be inappropriate to bring up areas of personal concern. Nevertheless, the feelings workers have about their practice are directly related to how they deal with clients, and these feelings must be discussed. As long as the supervisor's sense of function is clear and the work stays within the boundaries of the supervision contract, workers appreciate evidence that the supervisor understands their dilemmas, concerns, and feelings. Supervisors appreciate the same sort of understanding from their administrators.

Sessional Contracting

In direct practice, as in supervision, sessional contracting involves an attempt at the beginning of each session to determine the central areas of concern. The assumption is that clients will invest themselves only in matters about which they feel a sense of urgency. The skill involves asking clients at the beginning of each session what they would like to discuss. Even if the worker has an agenda that must be dealt with during the session, this negotiating process reassures clients that their concerns will also be heard. In addition, because clients often use indirect communications at the beginning of an interview, it is helpful to be tentative about the agenda so that their real concerns can be explored.

In the following example, a teenage girl had approached the worker for help in finding a foster home. The worker began the session by discussing the working contract but remained tentative about it. Rather than dealing with the first issue raised by the client, the worker used the sessional contracting skill to give the client an opportunity to get to a more difficult issue. The worker noted the following:

> Jean had opened the interview by telling me she had heard from friends that I would be able to help her get a foster home. She said that she wanted to leave home right away. I told her that we often did help youngsters find foster homes, but first we had to be pretty clear that they were unable to live at home. I asked if she could tell me why she wanted to move out.
>
> She presented a long description of a fight she'd been having with her mom, not being able to get enough clothing, hassles over the time she needs to get home in the evening, describing a generally difficult relationship. Although it sounded stressful, it didn't sound serious enough for Jean's sense of urgency. I told her that it sounded like she was having a hard time with her mom, but what she was describing didn't seem to be way out of line with the problems that happen in most families. I wondered if there was something else that was also troubling her. There was a silence, and then she said she didn't like the men that hang around the house. I asked her if she could tell me a bit more about that. I noticed as she talked that she looked down and seemed embarrassed. She told me there was a lot of activity with men at night in the room next to her. It was a small apartment, and she was very uncomfortable.
>
> I told her I realized it wasn't easy to talk about these matters, but it would be important for me to know what was happening if I was to be able to help her. Acting on a hunch caused by her embarrassment, I asked if any of the men had been bothering her. She looked up quickly, seemed relieved, and said that her mom's latest boyfriend had been making passes at her.

Had the worker simply responded to the first issue, she might have explored the concern simply as a problem between Jean and her mother. The real concern, an embarrassing one in a taboo area, might not have surfaced for a number of interviews. By being tentative at the beginning of the interview, the worker was able to get at the problem behind the problem.

Parallel Processes

Supervisors can help workers become more conscious of the importance of sessional contracting by concentrating on the tentative beginnings of their contacts as they discuss their practice. Asking "What was the client working on?" can help workers see that particular interviews or sessions with clients moved on too quickly, without adequate exploration. Often, real concerns emerge near the end of the session, in what has been described earlier, in the supervision context, as the "doorknob therapy" phenomenon. By examining the conversation at the beginning of a session, it is often possible to pick up the cues to concerns that will emerge later.

The supervision process can be an important demonstration of the skill of sessional contracting. Workers often bring partial or incomplete concerns to the attention of their supervisors, who can use the same tentativeness in their discussions with the workers. The following excerpt is an example:

> Fred came into my office appearing agitated and somewhat upset. He asked if I had a minute for an interpretation of a policy question. I said, "Sure, what is it?" He described the problem, which was related to agency policy and eligibility for service in an example of a specific client. I interpreted the policy as I understood it, and he nodded his head vigorously, agreeing with me. I said he seemed upset about this issue and I wondered why. He then went on to describe an interview he had just had with a client where the client had been abusive when he had made his interpretation of the policy and had attacked him and the agency. I said I thought that was upsetting and wondered if he wanted to spend a minute talking about it. He said he did because he hadn't really known how to handle it and wasn't feeling too good about what had happened.

Supervisors who are themselves busy and under pressure may find it easier to deal with only the first issue presented, even though they sense that there might be more behind it. Some, as has been noted, are concerned that if they invite workers to explore an issue more deeply, the workers might accept the invitation. Certainly, there are times when it is necessary to put off discussion until both the worker and the supervisor can devote adequate attention to a problem. Often, it is not possible to pick up details on every issue. In any case, if an issue is not dealt with the first time it comes up, it could emerge again and thus provide a second opportunity to deal with it.

Elaborating

As in supervision, workers' skills that are helpful in encouraging clients to tell their stories include containment, questioning, focused listening, reaching inside silences, and moving from the general to the specific. In direct practice, containment helps the worker resist the tendency to provide a solution or an answer to a client's problem before the client has elaborated it in some detail. The feeling of many workers that they are effective only if they can "solve" their clients' problems can lead them to propose answers before they really understand the questions.

As clients describe their concerns, they should be helped to provide details with questions like "Could you tell me a little more about that?" Often, the worker has a hard time understanding why a client has brought up a particular issue; it may seem to be idle chatter, irrelevant to their meeting. Focused listening encourages the worker to listen with purpose in mind, to discover clues to the real meaning of a conversation.

Although silences are key moments in practice, it may be difficult for workers to understand their meaning. They could experience discomfort during silence and try to change the subject. Observation of videotapes of the practice of 11 workers in individual and group practice indicated that more than 60 percent of the time, the discussion following a silence moved away from the client's concern (Shulman, 1978) because the worker changed the topic. If workers understand that silences are a form of conversation, they can wait the silences out and ask why clients have become silent, or if they have a hunch, they can reach inside the silences and try to articulate the feelings. This often frees the client to make a next move. This skill was found to be an important one in this author's first study of practice (Shulman, 1978). In the most recent study (Shulman, 1991), it was particularly important in developing the working relationship when used in the beginning phase of practice—a time when a client might be less likely to take risks.

The skill of moving from the general to the specific is important in practice in the helping professions. The client may begin an interview by raising a general problem such as, "It's getting awfully tough these days to raise teenage kids, what with drugs and the way morals are changing." But if the worker begins a general discussion of the problems of raising teenagers, the client's real concern may be missed. Underlying most general comments by clients is a specific concern. Workers have a better chance of getting at the concern by probing for the specifics with a question such as, "Have you had trouble with your daughter this week?" The general problem of raising teenagers may quickly become a specific problem a client is having with her daughter.

Requesting elaboration of the specifics of the problem is also helpful. Note in the following example how the worker helped the client to provide details of the concern:

> Mrs. Fredericks told me she found it very hard dealing with her teenage foster daughter. I asked if there had been a specific example recently. She said there was and described how the daughter had come in at 3:00 A.M. earlier that week and Mrs. Fredericks had had no idea where she

was. I said I thought that must have been pretty upsetting for her. She said it was. I asked what happened when the daughter came in. She told me that she had gotten very angry and ended up getting into a big fight with her. I asked if she could tell me a bit of the conversation with her daughter. I said we could take a look at what happened, and I might be able to help her think through what to do when it happens again.

Parallel Processes

In modeling the skills of elaboration, supervisors can help workers understand their functional role, as well as how to deal with their feelings about the work. The tendency of workers to try to offer solutions because they believe that that is how a worker helps has been noted; often, they see the worker as someone who "has the answers." The model of practice in their minds is that the clients tell them their problems, and they come up with the solutions. Because life is not that simple and solutions are often hard to find, workers are frequently disappointed at not being able to help enough. After warning of the temptation to intervene precipitately, the supervisor can open up a discussion of the worker's sense of the helping role with a question such as, "Exactly how do you see yourself giving help?"

When workers feel less responsible for providing instant solutions, they can allow clients more time to elaborate. To help workers develop the skill of dealing with silences, the supervisor can ask about their feelings during a silence. Often, workers seem to regard a silence as negative feedback on their work. This is true in some cases, and supervisors need to help workers develop the confidence to reach for such feedback from clients. More often, however, silence is not negative feedback at all. The supervisor can ask workers to speculate on what a silence might mean. As they become more aware of how silences affect them, they develop self-confidence and begin to reach inside the silences.

The supervisory relationship is a perfect one for demonstrating the skills of elaboration to workers, particularly the skill of moving from the general to the specific. As in client relationships, the most common problem in supervision is the tendency to deal with generalities (see chapter 3). Behind a general question raised by a worker is often a specific troubling incident. It takes only a few minutes of the supervisor's time to ask the worker to describe what happened and, when the worker reports what the client said, to ask, "How did you feel when she said that, and what did you say back?" I call this *memory work*, as the worker recalls from memory the details of the process including his or her affective responses at the time. The supervisor must let the worker know that the details of the interaction are needed to think through the problem. A case conference in which the discussion centers only on the client, focusing on the diagnosis and treatment plan, can leave the worker at a loss. Instead, the discussion should center on the interaction between the worker and the client. An understanding of the situation and a plan for action will emerge from the specifics of the interaction.

The following example is a report of a supervisor's discussion with a worker of her first interviews with a client. The discussion remained at a general level and was of limited help. The worker, Nancy, raised concerns about her interview with a young woman client in a hospital who was considering an abortion. She was also concerned about how to handle procedures with other professionals with whom she had consulted on the case. In this first worker–supervisor conference, the discussion went as follows:

> Nancy (Worker): As I was saying, I don't have any great things to say today.
>
> Supervisor: Oh, everything you say is great, Nancy.
>
> Nancy (laughing): Right. I had two sessions with this young girl named Fran in the clinic last week. One each day. And I consulted—is that how you say it?
>
> Supervisor: Consulted.
>
> Nancy (laughs): Consulted with Risa and Frank both, about this girl, in between the sessions. She was having an abortion. It was sort of abortion counseling, I suppose you might call it, and seeing if that's what she really wanted.
>
> There were some problems with her family. Her mother was supposedly very much against it. She's living in the home. Her parents are taking on a lot of stuff. Anyway, I guess the only thing I did about that is I went back the next day. I came back here, and I was thinking that it was all quite clear. What I had tried to do—although it just kind of emerged out of the interview—was just to try to get it all out and look at it with her and get her to look at what each issue was.
>
> Supervisor: Uh-huh.
>
> Nancy: You know, the abortion and what it meant and what was happening at home, I guess. When I came back, I asked Risa a little bit about why the parents were upset, and then Risa got into it about the seriousness of the whole thing and how important it was and what a big deal it was in a way. It just seemed that that's what she was saying, that this was a very huge thing for somebody to be doing. And it struck me that I didn't . . . think it was so big, and then I talked to Frank [the other worker], and he said the same thing. I'm beginning to think that there's something wrong with my conception [laughs] of how I see problems. And he was saying there's a lot of dynamics there, and you have to sort out all of these different things.
>
> Supervisor: I guess I'm wondering, what stage was she at?
>
> Nancy: I think I sort of look at it quite simply, like I don't want to go into all that stuff right away. She was quite clear about what she wanted to do.
>
> Supervisor: I mean, how far along was she?
>
> Nancy: Oh, seven weeks. She'd been in for an operation and they found out that she was pregnant, too. . . . So there was a . . . there were an awful lot of complications.

Supervisor: Why do you think that their views are so different—Risa's and Frank's and yours?

Nancy: Well, I guess, the negative part of me thinks, "These workers, they just have to be so professional that they really need something to do" [laughing].

Supervisor: You mean, Risa and Frank are creating a mountain out of a molehill?

Nancy: Yeah, exactly. And then the other part of me thinks, "Gee, you know, there must be something I'm missing." I can see that there are some things that have to be ironed out and looked at, but it just didn't strike me as being so . . . such a big deal.

Supervisor: I've worked with some people in this area, and it can be a big thing and it cannot be a big thing. I guess my sense of it is, how does the girl view the abortion? Does she see it as a murder? Which is what some people who are very anti-abortion might feel.

Nancy: No, no.

Supervisor: Or does she see it as a birth control kind of a measure, almost?

Nancy: Well, as more like a birth control thing. She just felt that she just wasn't ready to have a child.

The conversation continued in a general vein, moving back and forth between the client's perception of the problem and Nancy's continued concern about the other professionals' opinions. At no point, however, did the supervisor ask her to describe, in some detail, how the interviews with the client had proceeded. Nancy persisted during the conference in emphasizing her inability to see why the abortion would be such a "big deal."

Note the differences between this general discussion and the following excerpts from a conference between the same worker and supervisor about another client just one week later. In this situation, Nancy feels that the client, who is in a hospital, is avoiding talking about a number of real issues related to when she returns home. For the worker, the issue is similar to the one with her previous client: What is my role, and how do I bring to the surface possible underlying issues and feelings? This time, quickly moving to reconstruct the interview by using role play, the supervisor helped Nancy explore the question more productively.

Supervisor: Okay, anything else about Louise?

Nancy: Well, I guess I kind of know what to do with that, but I wonder, because her [the client] thing is that everything's got to be okay, because she can't face pain very well. And when I'm there, often she'll say, "Everything was really terrible a week ago or a few days ago, but everything's just fine now, I'm just living blissed out. . . . Everything's just great, and it's going to be good when I go home; it's just going to be fine."

Supervisor: And this happens every time you come?

Nancy: Yeah, yeah.

Supervisor: Maybe you ought to talk about that.

Nancy: I said to her this morning, "You probably feel okay now, right at the moment, but there must be a lot of hurt and a lot of pain, or you wouldn't have gone through all that stuff." I was trying to get back to the pain, but I'm just not sure where to go with that.

Supervisor: How does she answer when you say that?

Nancy: She won't get into it.

Supervisor: What are you feeling at the time, when that's happening?

Nancy: I'm feeling like this is getting into a social visit, and I'm just not sure what my role is here. It seems like a nice, cutesy little visit, where you go in and visit somebody that's sick in the hospital. And I just don't know how much I should try to therapize [sic] or just listen or . . . I don't want to interfere, but I don't want to be completely useless, either.

Supervisor: Your feeling, your gut feeling is that she tried to turn it into a social visit. And I'm wondering what your sense is, going on that feeling, what she might be trying to accomplish.

Nancy: She's just avoiding, I think, and trying to make it all seem nice, when . . . and afraid of the real feelings. Afraid of putting it out, afraid of the pain. Breaking down, or whatever. And feeling that she's on the verge of tears.

Supervisor: She has a good pattern of avoidance. Her whole family does that. Do you want to try that interview again with me? I'll play the part.

Nancy: And you're saying how nice it is now, everything's just fine.

Supervisor (role playing client's part): I really had a bad time, but I'm feeling really good now, and it's going to be okay when I get home.

Nancy: How do you know it's going to be okay when you get home?

Supervisor: Well, I can really feel it's going to be okay. I just know, 'cause it was really bad before, and I think I know what to do now. It's really going to be good now.

Nancy: Well, I kind of . . .

Supervisor: But I still want to see you.

Nancy: Yeah. I feel, I guess I should just say, "I don't think we're getting anywhere the way we're talking. Because it's all just surface niceties, and I can feel that there's a lot of pain in you—you're almost crying right now, and you're saying everything's just great. And I just don't believe it. How are you really feeling?"

Supervisor: You know what that does for me. I feel really scared.

Nancy: How?

Supervisor: Like I really feel, wham, you hit me.

Nancy: Oh dear, oh dear!

Supervisor: No, it's good.

Nancy: Is it?

Supervisor: Yeah.

Nancy: I thought it was too heavy.

Supervisor: No, I mean, it was heavy, but I'm not sure what I'm going to do with it, being Louise. I don't know Louise that well, but I feel you really connected with me. Have you talked to Louise that way?

Nancy: I came close to it today, and I just didn't think . . . I wanted to talk to you about it because I just didn't know what my role was there.

Supervisor: I felt really good. You saw my tears, you acknowledged them, you read behind my tears to my pain, and you refused to believe me. You called it the way it was. Part of me was scared to death, but part of me really liked it. I guess, up to now, you have also been avoiding.

Nancy: I think I have been.

Supervisor: You're avoiding like she's avoiding.

Nancy: I think I was, and I don't know what my role is, because I'm afraid I won't know what to do. I think I'd better clarify exactly what my role is, and then I'll feel more comfortable.

Supervisor: That avoidance thing is deadly.

Nancy: Yeah, I really let it go this morning.

Supervisor: So, how did that feel, trying that out?

Nancy: It felt a lot better. It felt a lot more real to me, because I was beginning to feel like, like a visitor [laughs].

Supervisor: I've been in that spot before; it's an easy spot to get into. When we're working with people and we're confronted with their problems, because their problems seem so overwhelming, it's easy for us to avoid them because we feel inadequate. I don't know where to go with this girl. You know, obviously, she has really deep problems. All these psychiatrists have been poking around at her, and nobody knows the answer.

This brief excerpt shows how Nancy began to face the issues of clarity of role, denial on the part of the client, and some of her own feelings that made it difficult for her to penetrate behind the facade of denial and to demand real work (see the following section). In a sense, the supervisor modeled the demand by reaching behind the general discussion of the client's and the worker's own denial ("everything seems to be going all right") and getting into the specific details of the work. Thus, effective teaching by supervisors involves a continuous moving between specific analysis of the worker's practice and the generalizations that emerge from that practice.

If a supervisor senses resistance to such a discussion, the worker's feelings should be explored. The worker may be unsure of the supervisor's intent or may have had poor experiences with supervisors in the past who were punitive in their comments. As the purpose of the discussion becomes clear and as the supervisor is supportive rather than judgmental or harsh, the worker may be more open to this kind of help. If resistance is still present, the supervisor must make a demand for work, because discussion of the specifics of the interview is critical if help is to be offered. A supervisor who feels comfortable about offering this kind of help will find it easier to make this demand.

Making a Demand for Work

Schwartz and Zalba's (1971) notion of the demand for work (described in the supervisory context in chapter 4) is based on the assumption that clients feel some ambivalence about the work to be done. In part, the client is trying to solve problems, deal with life, and take responsibility for actions; simultaneously, another part of the client wants to avoid this necessity. A client may want to discuss painful feelings, for example, but at the same time may be afraid of them. This ambivalence results in both a willingness to work, as well as a resistance to work.

There are many forms of resistance. Clients may not return to the agency or may miss an appointment following a particularly difficult session, refuse to be serious about the work, or avoid dealing with difficult areas and feelings. Workers may report sessions that appear to be an illusion of work, lacking in substance and feeling. Apathy, acting out, and passive resistance are other ways that clients resist moving into difficult areas. The important point for workers to understand is that resistance is often a sign that the work is going well, rather than a sign that it is going badly. When ambivalence is understood more clearly and resistance is seen as part of the work, workers can recognize the importance of being prepared to make a demand for work on the client, rather than becoming discouraged and easing up.

When a positive relationship has been established within a clear contract and the worker has demonstrated a capacity for empathy and an understanding of a client's feelings, then it is possible for the worker to make clear demands on the client to act in his or her own interests. The client may initially get angry at the worker's demand, but that is exactly what is needed from the worker. In all life situations, people who care about each other are willing to take risks by making demands on each other.

Specific skills that workers can use in making a demand for work include partializing, holding to focus, challenging the illusion of work, and engaging in facilitative confrontation. Partializing is used to help clients who present numerous problems with which they are having difficulty. It is often a way of saying, "Look, there's nothing I can do without your help." By breaking overwhelming problems into more manageable parts, the worker is, in effect, demanding work from the client. Although partializing has consistently emerged as an important skill in developing a working relationship and being helpful to clients (Shulman, 1978, 1991), in the latter study, its use in the beginning phase of practice appeared to contribute directly to a client's perception of a worker's helpfulness.

When clients begin to work on one part of a problem, it is not unusual for them to switch from one concern to another as soon as the work gets close. The skill of holding to focus entails asking clients to stay on a particular issue until it is resolved. The following example shows how a worker partialized a client's multiple problems and held the client to focus:

> It was our first session together. Mrs. Carter told me that her son (age 16) had been suspended from school and had gotten into a fight with a neighbor. The neighbor had complained to the landlord, and now he was threatening to evict her. The neighbor had also come to see her and had been abusive and threatening. When she had talked to her son to try to get

him to apologize, he had gotten angry and had stormed out of the house. She wasn't sure what to do about anything. I told her I could see it was an upsetting time for her. I pointed out that she had to deal with the school, her landlord, her neighbor, and, most difficult of all, her son. I said I thought it would help if we could take things one at a time. Where would she like to start? She said the landlord's threats were most frightening to her. I asked her to tell me about the conversation with the landlord.

By partializing this problem, the worker made it more manageable. As the conversation continued, however, the client shifted back to the school suspension, and the worker needed to hold to focus:

> Mrs. Carter said she couldn't promise the landlord her son would behave, because he was suspended from school, and hanging around the house all the time led to trouble. She went on to talk about the call from the school principal. I asked if we could stick to the landlord for a moment and then discuss the call with the principal. I could see they were connected problems, but it would help if we stayed with one at a time.

Another form of making a demand for work is the skill of challenging the illusion of work. A worker who finds sessions with a client boring and lacking in substance and feeling and who believes that the client feels the same way, may sense that they are getting nowhere. By challenging the illusion of work, the worker can call attention to the pattern. It is important to make it clear that the client is not being accused of having created the illusion of work—the worker is merely pointing it out to help both of them explore its meaning. The worker might say, for example, "I've been thinking about our past few sessions. It seems to me that the discussion has been superficial. We haven't gotten our teeth into anything important. I wonder if you have any ideas why that's so." Opening up the discussion in this way can encourage the client to suggest a reason why the discussion is difficult; the work may have entered a taboo area, such as sexual relations. As the client discusses the difficulty of talking to the worker about sex, the conversation will change from illusion to substance. The underlying concept is that the resistance is always a signal—a form of communication to the worker. It is a part of the work. Exploring the resistance is the key to deepening practice.

The skill of facilitative confrontation is illustrated in an example in the next section that shows how a worker shared her anger in confronting Mark, a teenage client who was making no effort on his own behalf at school. This was done effectively and in a facilitative manner because a good working relationship had been developed over time. The client knew that the worker cared about him, and he trusted the worker. Used prematurely, the skill could be experienced by the client as evidence of the worker's harshness and lack of understanding. The proper blend of caring and demand is subtle and difficult to achieve, as was noted in the supervision context in chapter 3. Workers are often either demanding or empathic;

usually, they find it difficult to integrate the two and to make an empathic demand. Because this is a problem in all human relationships, it is no wonder that it is difficult in the helping professions. Workers who are empathic and understanding can develop a good relationship with clients but are not necessarily helpful. Workers who are merely demanding are rejected by clients as being harsh. Workers who put the two together appear to be most effective.

Parallel Processes

Analysis of worker practice often reveals moments when workers felt like confronting a client but did not because of their own discomfort. Workers describe being bored in an interview or being upset because a client keeps making commitments but never follows through on them. They have moments when they feel angry at a client but are afraid to let the client know because, they say, they fear taking too much responsibility for their clients' lives or "losing" the client.

By examining these moments and helping workers understand the interplay between confrontation and caring, the supervisor can help them to trust their own instincts in most situations. It is not unprofessional to care whether a client makes it, and the client needs to know that the worker cares. One does not take away the right to self-determination by confronting people to act in their own self-interest. In fact, the client often desperately needs just such a demand for work to take the next step.

In discussions of the demand for work, workers often reflect on the general difficulty of confronting friends, children, spouses, colleagues, and others. Such discussions can be helpful if they focus on how this difficulty affects their practice with clients. One reason workers may avoid making a demand is that they lack confidence in their ability to help. Workers have said, "If I make a demand on a client and he takes me up on it, then what will I do?" This is an indication to the supervisor of a need for help in developing and deepening the worker's own work-phase skills. It is also often a cue that the worker is concerned about dealing with the client's feelings (for example, anger at the worker or pain related to the problem).

As with the other practice skills, the supervisor's demonstration of the power of making a demand for work is helpful. Workers may be very resistant, for example, about sharing their material with supervisors and other colleagues through the use of process recordings or videotapes. Their negative reactions to being asked to use these techniques often serve as covers for their fears about self-disclosure or inadequacy. Their resistance may be a signal that they are waiting to see if the supervisor will relent. The supervisor who recognizes this will empathize with the worker's concerns while still making clear his or her expectations about the work.

Another way supervisors can model the demand for work is in relation to job management issues. Supervisors who set clear expectations about how workers are to manage their agency responsibilities and who also are open to consideration of the realities of the job situation help workers become more responsible. Making a demand for work is also especially helpful when a worker is in personal trouble. Supervisors must be empathic about the strains faced by workers experiencing marital difficulties or other personal problems and the effects these can have on their work, and they can often be helpful in referring workers for outside help. However, it is not helpful to stop making expectations of workers or to try to cover for a worker who is having a hard time. It is better for the supervisor to maintain reasonable expectations about the work and thus help troubled workers to function effectively in the work place, which can, in turn, help them deal with their personal problems.

The following example, in which a supervisor requests a worker to share the details of his practice with process recordings, illustrates the demand for work coupled with empathy:

> I told Frank that I was expecting to get some of his material on his first interview so we could discuss how he began. I hadn't received it and wondered why. Frank said he'd been very busy that week. I told him I realized the load was heavy, but I thought he would have had time to dictate some notes on that interview. He paused and then said that he wasn't sure why it was necessary to do that. Frank had stiffened and looked defensive at that point.
>
> I told him that I had sensed that there might be some reluctance on his part to do it, and perhaps this would be a good time to discuss it. I asked why he felt it wasn't necessary. He said he couldn't see the purpose, and anyway he didn't think he could remember what went on at the sessions. I said that developing the skill of recall was a difficult one. I asked if he had ever written anything like this before. He said he had not. I told him perhaps part of the problem was that I could have been more helpful in describing what it was I was asking for. I asked if he understood. He said he wasn't clear, so I explained that I did not want the whole interview but rather just some brief comments about the conversation in the beginning, a summary of how the interview went, some more detail about any parts he was interested in discussing, and how it ended. I told him I thought it wasn't easy as a new worker to share his work with me, but I wanted to reassure him that I wasn't asking to just snoop or to be critical. I felt that if I had some of the detail of what he was saying and doing with his clients, I might be more helpful to him.
>
> I asked him if it was true that he had been concerned about what I would do with the records. He said he was and that he felt that the first interview hadn't gone well at all. He was embarrassed to present it. I told him that I didn't expect these interviews to go perfectly and that I thought by going over some of his work with clients I might be able to help him identify what he did that went well, as well as what he could do better. I then asked if he could recreate from memory some of the details of this first

interview. I would try to show what I meant. I said I was willing to work from his memory of the experience this time but that the next time I would be expecting a written record.

It was important for the supervisor to explore the worker's feelings about using the record material, while at the same time making it clear that the material was expected. There would be a slightly different problem in encouraging use of process recordings by experienced workers, who may not have had such experiences or training in their previous practice. Such workers may feel that they are expected to know more than they really do, and they may be embarrassed about sharing their uncertainties with their supervisors. A problem also arises if recordings have been used in a punitive manner. If they are used to focus only on mistakes and if the supervisor conveys displeasure rather than acceptance and support, workers will understandably be reluctant to use them. One worker described how her field instructor in her first year of placement had written in bold red letters in the margin of their recording comments such as "How could you have missed this?" and "You're all off base here!" When I asked the worker how she had responded to such consistently negative feedback, she answered, "I started to make up process and to give my supervisor the recordings I thought she wanted."

If workers are told that they are expected to be perfect, this can become a block to any future use of the technique. A supervisor who uses recordings to explore with the workers past experiences and then tries to help them sort out how they could have done better frees the workers to take chances. In any case, they should be expected to meet the demand for work, in spite of their past experiences.

An important element in making the demand for work is that the helping person—worker or supervisor—is assuring the other person—client or worker—of faith in their ability to take the next step. People, in general, do not want others to give up on them. Even if workers appear to be asking a supervisor to back off, they are often disappointed if the supervisor does so.

Some supervisors fear that if they ask workers to provide details or evidence of their work, they will then be expected to provide help. Because most supervisors are still learning about practice with their right hand while they are teaching with their left, some uncertainty should be expected. When the supervisor's uncertainty is matched by the worker's, however, the result can be an illusion of work.

Sharing Own Feelings

In their interactions with clients, workers experience many normal emotions. In more traditional theories of practice, expression of the worker's own feelings while working with clients is considered unprofessional. This split between the personal and professional selves is conceived of as a defense against the many problems that can result from inappropriate self-disclosure. As one worker put it, "On work days, I am supposed to take my professional self to the office and leave my personal self at home." There are many genuine concerns related to the improper expression of a worker's emotion. For example, countertransferance on the worker's part can lead to inept comments that represent an acting out of the worker on personal issues. The inherent sexism, racism, classism, homophobia, and so forth that all workers must examine throughout their professional (and personal) lives can lead to mistakes. Stress on the job may lead workers to act out their frustrations on clients or to self-disclose information that turns the interview into a session dealing with the worker's problems rather than those of the client. All of these concerns about a worker's expression of feelings are real; however, the solution of splitting personal and professional selves turns out to be worse than the original problems.

According to the practice theory developed by Schwartz and Zalba (1971), however, this split is a false dualism. It suggests an artificial dichotomy between the personal and the professional selves. Rather, he maintains, feelings can be used professionally, as long as they are related to the worker's function and the purpose of the encounter. A worker can learn to share feelings of frustration, anger, and caring for clients in a professional manner. Appropriate self-disclosure of personal experiences or reactions, when used to enhance the work or the client, can make an important contribution to the client's work. Clients also find it easier to trust such a worker, whom they describe as being "a real person."

Workers must seek to develop the same capacity to express feelings that they expect of their clients, as well as the ability to express their feelings spontaneously. They will make active mistakes along the way that they may need to acknowledge to their clients and for which, at times, they may need to apologize. Clients are more accepting of workers who are honest and who apologize when they make a mistake than they are of those who appear to be paragons of virtue, always cool, objective, and composed. As workers deepen their understanding of their function and their insight into their personal selves, they will learn from these mistakes and grow from the process. If a client is belligerent, for example, and expresses concerns by making an angry attack on the worker, the worker needs to respond honestly at the moment, with real feelings. With experience, however, workers develop the ability to see past the anger and try to understand the hurt that is underneath. This ability will never be acquired, however, if workers are constantly monitoring their own feelings and are afraid to take risks.

In the following example, the worker's expression of feeling was critical. The example is drawn from the ending phase of work with an adolescent teenager about to leave the care of the agency. Mary had known the worker for two years, and a close relationship had developed. During the conversation, the worker revealed her feelings about Mary:

> "I was beginning to think about the fact that we only have a couple of more sessions together. To be honest with you, although I'm glad you're going to be able to move out on your own now and start to be independent, I'm going to miss you." There was a long silence, and I could sense that Mary was struggling for composure. She said, "You were the best worker I've ever had. I could always talk to you when I had things on my mind. I'm a little afraid about who I'm going to talk to now." I said, "Can you say some more about what it was about me that you thought made me the best worker?"

By asking the client for the specific qualities she found helpful, the worker can help her begin to think about the transition she will need to make to other support systems such as family or friends. If the client is aware of the qualities she had found helpful in the worker, she may be able to find people with the same characteristics. An important conversation was taking place between the worker and the client about their parting; it might not have occurred if the worker had not honestly expressed her own feelings.

Being honest about feelings includes a willingness to share the anger and frustration workers often feel when they think a client is not trying. For example, after months of helping a client through a difficult school situation, a worker found out that Mark, the client, was again avoiding doing homework and was about to be suspended. The worker felt frustrated and angry at the waste of all of her efforts. She told Mark,

> I want you to know I'm really mad that you are just ready to blow everything at school. We've put a lot of time and effort into this, getting you back in, sorting out the problems you had with your teacher. Things were starting to straighten out, but now, you seem willing to just let your life get screwed up. That makes me frustrated and mad.

Mark responded with anger and said that it was not any of the worker's business. It was his own life, and he would do with it as he wished. The interview ended on a note of tension. At the next session, however, Mark reported that he had seen the teacher, had gone over the missed assignments, and had worked out a plan for what he had to do to catch up. The confrontation, anger, and frustration, all of which represented real caring on the part of the worker, were critical in helping this client take a next step on his own behalf. Once again, this confrontation was supported by the two years of work during which had built up a fund of positive relationship. Confrontation might have had a totally different impact early in the relationship.

A final example concerns the importance of appropriate self-disclosure. A student was working with a group of institutionalized, mentally challenged young adult males who were dealing with problems associated with the recent death of someone close to them, usually a family member. The group was set up to help them with the grieving process that many of the members had avoided through denial. The clients' behaviors, including ongoing depression, apathy, and acting out, were interpreted by staff as signals of their unfinished business related to their losses. After a few weeks of sessions in which barriers to the expression of emotion remained strong, the worker received word that her own father had died. She was absent from work for two weeks while she went home to deal with the funeral and other family issues. The group members were aware of why she was away.

At the start of her first group meeting back, she acknowledged having been away and then quickly turned to inquiring how the clients had been coping. She had decided in advance of the session to set her own issues aside and focus on their work. In response, one member said, "Barbara, your father just died, didn't he?" The worker reported later that she was filled with emotion but struggled to maintain her "professional composure." She answered his question factually, but her appearance revealed that she was emotionally affected. After a pause, another member said, "That's OK, Barbara, you can cry—God loves you too." At this point she did cry, and a number of group members did as well. (In the class in which she shared this incident, her recounting of the event led to her own tears, as well as matching emotions from many of her fellow students and this author as well). Returning to the group session, she indicated that after her expression of emotion, she said to the clients, "Here I have been encouraging all of you to face your own pain at your losses, to get it out of your system, and I have been sitting there covering up my own. It's not so easy to face it, is it?" The group members moved immediately into a discussion of the difficulty they were having, and as if a dam had broken, they began to share with each other, with emotion, their pain at their losses.

The worker in this example helped the clients to share their own feelings by her willingness to share her own. It was important that they moved immediately to the implications for their work because her own issues around her grieving did not belong in this group. She needed to deal with these in her own social support system. In addition, she needed to explore with her supervisor a way of monitoring her work with these clients because she was so close to her own loss and pain.

Parallel Processes

A review of client interviews provides a helpful medium for teaching about professional use of self and sharing of the worker's feelings. Inquiring what workers felt at particular moments when the supervisor thinks they might have been upset or angry, for example, can encourage them to share these feelings. They may also share their thoughts about spontaneity and sharing feelings, not just in practice but in life in general. This provides an opportunity for the supervisor to empathize with the difficulty of sharing feelings, while pointing out how it might have helped in a particular instance. The supervisor might say, for example, "If you had leveled with the client right at that moment, how do you think she might have reacted?" In thinking about how the client would have responded, it often becomes clear that leveling could have brought a positive reaction.

Workers often respond to an exercise such as this with a comment like this: "It seems so simple; I don't know why I don't do it." This stimulates a discussion of the difficulties of sharing feelings in our society and provides an opportunity for the supervisor to point out how the worker can be professional and personal simultaneously. Most important, the supervisor can use the exercise to give the worker permission to make mistakes. I often suggest to a worker who has made a mistake when being spontaneous with a client that it was "a good mistake." It was good because the worker was honest, and it was a mistake because it was not directly related to the current concerns of the client or there was a better way of dealing with the client's problem. When the supervisor believes in the importance of spontaneity, learning is seen as a process in which the worker makes mistakes, analyzes them, learns from the analysis, goes back and corrects the mistake, and then makes more sophisticated mistakes. This provides a sense of freedom that allows workers to explore their own skills in this area.

The skills in sharing one's own feelings are easiest to teach when they are actively modeled. Anger, a common reaction in human relationships, is one of the feelings we are usually taught to suppress. When supervisors are angry with workers, it is a mistake to get angry "professionally" instead of being honest about it. Professional anger is usually less direct, colder, and more hurtful than is real anger. For example, one supervisor was furious at a worker for constantly challenging her authority. Rather than openly expressing the anger, which the supervisor felt might be inappropriate, she expressed it indirectly by asking the worker, "How long have you had this problem with authority?" This psychological interpretation was in reality an expression of the supervisor's anger. But expressed in this way, it further increased the gulf in the working relationship and made it harder for the worker to respond honestly.

Workers who find, perhaps after some time, that they can have a positive relationship with their supervisors that includes caring, as well as anger, and that getting angry does not destroy a relationship are freed to experiment in the same way with clients.

Sharing Data

Another important skills factor for workers is the ability to share data with clients in a meaningful way. Data includes information, facts, values, and beliefs held by the worker that may be relevant and helpful to the client in a particular instance. This is an area of much confusion in the helping professions. Social workers may consider it improper to provide data to clients because they believe that clients should "figure things out for themselves." Workers are also concerned about not imposing their own values and views onto clients. Clients, in turn, may want access to the worker's data but not want it presented dogmatically, as the "revealed truth." Workers who realize that their knowledge, beliefs, and values are only one part of reality are able to make them available to clients without feeling the need to convince them of their accuracy. In fact, workers can develop strategies for sharing data that allow for challenge and disagreement.

The notion of presenting ideas as open to challenge runs contrary to many views about how people help. Workers have become so used to being "sold" on ideas that they may believe they are effective only if they can sell their ideas to their clients. The opposite is true; they are more effective when they make their ideas available than when they try to impose them. Clients will use information or values or beliefs only when they perceive their importance. In fact, they may reject ideas they feel are being forced on them by the worker. If information is shared at a time when it is not relevant to the client, it will not be useful. Workers who suggest that a client "needs to know" something in an area that is unrelated to the client's sense of urgency will be perceived as pursuing and imposing their own agenda.

Workers should feel free to share their ideas directly. Trying to lead the client to an answer the worker has in his or her head, for example, or asking questions that will get the client to give the answer the worker wants often shifts the work away from the client's task. Instead of working on the problem, the client attempts to figure out what the worker wants. This is called playing the game of "educational hide and seek." Workers, therefore, should make their data available directly, making sure they are related to the client's urgency and leaving the client free to use the ideas or reject them.

The following excerpt is from the records of a worker who was asked for her opinion by a young unmarried mother faced with a decision of whether to keep her child:

> I explained to Dora that she was asking a tough question. In the last analysis, she was going to have to make that decision, and only she really knew whether she could keep the baby or not. I asked her why she was asking me at this point, what was troubling her. She went on to tell me that a part of her wanted to keep the baby, but she was afraid that she was so young she would have nothing left of her life if she did. On the other hand, she kept thinking of what it would be like if she gave the baby up and felt guilty for not being more responsible.
>
> I acknowledged some of those feelings, telling her it was not unusual to feel both at exactly the same time. I told her it was a tough decision, because no matter which way she went, it was going to hurt. I then went on

to say that, from the agency's point of view, there was no indication that she would be an unfit mother. Therefore, the choice was really up to her. From getting to know her over these weeks, however, I had the sense that the biggest part of her really wanted to have more time to experience life. If this was true, she probably would be better off in the long run if she placed the child than if she tried to keep it because she felt guilty.

I paused and there was silence. I said, "I've just told you how I felt, but I don't think that really helps very much. In the end, it still has to be your decision because you have to live with it." She nodded and said she knew that was true. She then went on to say it helped for her to take in other points of view and that she really had wanted to know how I saw things.

Parallel Processes

By exploring workers' feelings of responsibility for providing information, the supervisor can be helpful in sorting out the differences between their opinions and reality. When the supervisor sees that workers are trying to impose their ideas on clients, it is often possible to identify the clients' resistance and to demonstrate that clients cannot be easily "changed." When the supervisor senses that workers are holding back, it is helpful to explore their mixed feelings about giving advice and sharing their own views.

Practice research findings have indicated that better working relationships may be developed by workers who freely offer their own ideas to clients and leave the clients free to reject them (Shulman, 1978). Workers can be helped to understand this from their own experience with the supervisor. Asking how workers would feel if the supervisor had some information they needed but held it back so that they might learn it for themselves, for example, can help them understand clients' similar feelings.

Skills in sharing data are most closely related to the educational function. The supervisor has to recognize that workers, like clients, must learn by themselves; they have to develop their own ideas and insights as they go along. Even ideas that most supervisors are very clear about have to be learned anew by workers, and time must be allowed for them to assimilate ideas that supervisors have developed over a period of years. Supervisors can be helpful as guides along the way, and if their views are qualified and shared in an undogmatic way, workers will find them helpful.

Sometimes a supervisor suspects that a worker accepts too easily whatever the supervisor says. The worker is sending signals of dependency on the supervisor rather than seeing the supervisor as a resource in his or her own educational struggle. In such a situation, a discussion of the authority theme is in order. In effect, the supervisor needs to teach the worker how to question the supervisor's statements. Helping workers to keep the supervisor in perspective and to use her or him as a resource for the worker's own learning is a part of the supervision process. It also models for the worker the strategies needed for the worker to encourage the client not to accept too quickly everything the worker says.

MONITORING SKILLS DEVELOPMENT

Supervisors are most directly involved in monitoring the skills development of beginning workers; however, some ongoing supervision must also be provided for those with experience. The process of examining skills development contributes to effective practice at any level of the worker's experience.

Beginning Skills Development

This section discusses the order and timing of skills development for beginning workers to give supervisors a general standard against which workers' progress can be measured and evaluated. The description is based on workers' professional development during the first six months of practice. It assumes they have had a varied caseload, a chance to discuss the work with a supervisor, and other training opportunities.

The following pattern can be expected in developing practice skills. At the end of six months, workers should have some beginning skills at making clear statements of their purpose and role, and they should be making efforts to reach for client feedback. They should be somewhat tuned in to the client's feelings and concerns in first interviews. They should be beginning to define the authority theme as it emerges in the first sessions. It is likely that they will have difficulty with strong negative feelings from clients. They will need more experience to develop the confidence to handle really tough clients and to make demands for work in the face of strong client resistance.

Workers at this stage should be listening for indirect cues, but they will find it hard to discern them in the first sessions. In the first months, workers should be able to show their interest and concern for clients. They should be listening and trying to understand the client's problems and points of view, as well as learning to contain themselves until they are clear about the sessional contract. Their efforts at dealing with feelings will be apparent in tentative steps to reach for the client's affect or feelings and to articulate them. These skills should be strengthened during the first year. Efforts to deal with affect will often seem artificial as workers struggle to develop ways of putting feelings into their own words. Imitation of the supervisor may be a first step in this process.

The skill of reaching for negative feedback will not be evident until the worker develops greater confidence in his or her practice. This often comes later in the first year of practice. The ability to share feelings spontaneously is a difficult skill to develop, but there should be evidence that it is being used with greater freedom during the later part of the first year. The skill of sharing relevant data should be evidenced, as well as a willingness to leave the client free to accept or reject the worker's ideas.

As this summary suggests, there should be limited expectations for skill development by beginning workers. Actual progress will vary depending on what the worker brings to the situation in terms of personal and professional experience. In addition, the nature of the supervisory relationship will affect the pace of learning. The supervisor must not forget how difficult the development of core skills can be and must not be too easily frustrated by the time required for workers to develop these skills. If contracting, listening, empathizing, and expressing feelings honestly emerge in the first six months, the worker should be considered to be learning the skills satisfactorily.

Supervision of Experienced Workers

Close practice supervision is most critical for inexperienced, new workers. Professional development continues throughout one's practice, and workers who have had experience also need supervisory help. With very experienced workers, this may take the form of consultation with the supervisor or group discussion in which colleagues can provide mutual aid.

Limitations of time and other resources often make it difficult for supervisors to provide detailed help to workers on a regular basis. Some monitoring of skill development is important, however, because if workers do not continue to examine their own practices, they will lose the skills they have already developed. Tools that can help workers analyze their own work include tape recordings, client feedback instruments, and videotapes. Experienced workers need to be encouraged to use these techniques on an ongoing basis, even though supervisors may not be as intensively involved.

With experienced workers, supervisors must be sensitive to possible defensiveness caused by guilty feelings about past cases. Being asked to discuss a particular piece of work with a supervisor often recalls associations with other clients. In such a session, the worker's eyes may take on a dazed expression as the worker appears to withdraw. The supervisor who recognizes that the worker may be associating to past clients has an opportunity to explore the worker's feelings about unsatisfactory experiences. Experienced workers who appear defensive on a particular issue are often sending a signal to the supervisor that they have touched on an area of self-doubt. They need a great deal of support at this point to help them moderate their harsh views of themselves. The supervisor should point out that they have been able to offer clients only what they had at the time they worked with them, and they should not hold themselves responsible for more than that. Workers need to focus instead on what they will do for their present and future clients. Helping workers be less judgmental of themselves is often the most important way a supervisor can help them to make their practice a continuous process of learning from their experiences.

RESEARCH FINDINGS

In an early supervision study (Shulman, Robinson, & Luckyj, 1981), workers were asked to identify what they would like to have discussed in their supervision contacts, as compared with the actual content of these contacts. Their first preference was that supervisors should devote more time to teaching practice skills, followed by more time on discussing research information and providing feedback on performance. Such supervision–consulting roles also were the favored tasks of supervisors queried in the study.

These findings were replicated in another study (Shulman, 1991). The specific findings were reported earlier in chapter 2 in the section dealing with the role of the supervisor.

Other research has supported the idea that both supervisors and supervisees regard the educational function of supervision as important and as a source of satisfaction. In the Kadushin (1973) study, two of the three strongest sources of supervisor satisfaction were found to be related to helping the supervisee grow and develop professionally and to sharing social work knowledge and skill. In the same study, workers indicated that two of the three main sources of their satisfaction with supervision were receiving help in dealing with clients and in developing as professionals. In a study by Scott (1969), professionally oriented workers expressed a preference for supervisors who knew their theoretical fundamentals, were skilled in teaching, and were capable of offering professional assistance.

The idea of the parallel processes of work with clients and supervision of staff, which provides the basis for relating the skills of supervision to the skills of workers in this chapter, is based on the similarity between supervisor–worker and worker–client dynamics. Doehrman's (1972) study of eight sets of concurrent supervisor–supervisee relationships over a 20-week period indicated that patterns in the supervisor–worker interaction are similar to those in the worker–client interaction. A study by Arlow (1963) also supported this position.

The parallel processes idea also suggests that supervisors themselves need help and support if they are to provide these for their workers. The Shulman et al. (1981) supervision study found that stress, for example, was not as strongly associated with being an effective supervisor as was access to ongoing emotional support.

SUMMARY

The dynamics and skills of the educational function of supervision discussed in this chapter are based on assumptions about teaching and learning. The supervisor's knowledge of the subject area and ability to transmit ideas clearly are central to teaching, but they are only part of the process. The task for supervisors is to mediate between the learner and the subject areas to be learned. In teaching core practice skills to workers, supervisors must demonstrate the same skills they teach. Modeling the use of these skills in supervision practice is an effective way of teaching their use in the worker–client context.

A basis for monitoring and evaluating the development of these skills can be found in a profile of the skill development pattern of the average new worker (or student) and in the suggestions provided for dealing with the special problems of educational supervision of experienced workers.

CHAPTER 7

EVALUATION FUNCTION OF SUPERVISION

An evaluation is an objective appraisal of a worker's performance. It is one of the most important elements of the supervisor's role, and when handled well, it makes a major contribution to the worker's development and to client services. One formative type of evaluation provides ongoing feedback to workers on their activity to help form or shape their job performance. Such evaluations may be made on a continuing basis in supervision contacts, as the supervisor provides immediate assessments of the work of the staff. Occasionally, there may also be more formal evaluations when performance in a wide range of areas, such as job management and direct practice skills, is assessed. Another type of evaluation procedure combines formative purposes with agency assessment functions. In addition to providing feedback for the staff's development, this evaluation process may be used as a basis for career decisions about an employee, such as passing a probation period, promotion, merit salary increases, or firing. Formative evaluation, as a process, was explored in chapter 6 dealing with the educational function of supervision. This chapter focuses on the structure and skills of the formal evaluation process.

OBSTACLES TO EFFECTIVE EVALUATIONS: THE SUPERVISOR'S VIEWPOINT

Most supervisors report some discomfort with the evaluation process, but most workers want more feedback on their work, although they may be somewhat uncertain and fearful of the outcomes. As Kadushin (1976) pointed out, evaluations call attention to the status differences between supervisor and worker and provide a sharp reminder that they are not peers. When the power of the supervisor has been muted during the supervisory process, both parties may feel discomfort at its sudden reassertion.

He also pointed out that a negative assessment of a worker may cause the supervisor to feel guilty because he or she "has not taught the worker what he [or she] needs to know, has not given the worker the help he [or she] had the right to expect" (p. 277). One participant in a supervision workshop who had to provide a negative evaluation of a staff member on areas she had not discussed with him during his three-month probation period expressed this concern: "It was easy to avoid each of the individual problems because they were not by themselves serious enough to force me to respond. Every time I thought about doing something, he seemed to sense it and improve. So I took the easy way out, and now when I add it all up and see what has to be said in the evaluation, I feel sick about what I didn't do."

Another difficulty from the supervisor's viewpoint is the possibility that the worker may react angrily to an evaluation. Supervisors are not sure they want to face all the feelings that may be directed at them even if they feel justified in their judgments. If the relationship is generally good, they are afraid that a negative evaluation may strain it. This is especially true for a new supervisor who has moved into an established unit or has been promoted from the ranks. One supervisor found herself in a difficult position: "I was shocked when I realized that every member of the unit had received all 'superb' on their evaluations for the past three years. My predecessor had treated it as a joke, and now I was stuck having to be honest."

When she brought this up at a supervision workshop, the members reassured her that even though there might be criticisms initially, the staff would appreciate some honest feedback because they must know that their past evaluations had been meaningless. We all need critical feedback to improve our performance, as well as credit for what we are doing well. If the only feedback we receive is uniformly positive, it is perceived as useless and valueless.

Another major problem is posed by the need for a negative evaluation that may threaten a worker's career. The power of being able to recommend whether a worker becomes a permanent staff member, gets a raise or promotion, or is fired can weigh heavily on a supervisor. One supervisor described how bad he felt when he had to give a negative evaluation to a probationary worker who was pleasant but incompetent. The young man had a family to support, and jobs in this field were in short supply. The supervisor said he lost sleep over the problem until finally he decided that it would be unethical not to be honest, both for the sake of the clients and the long-term interest of the worker, who, he felt, should seriously consider another line of work. Even then, knowing that he had provided as much help as possible, the supervisor still said he felt like a "louse."

There is also the possibility that a negative evaluation will be contested. With the growth of public employee unions among social and health services, supervisors must be prepared to defend their opinions and actions at appeal hearings, under extreme pressure. Workers do need protection for their basic rights so that they need not fear losing their jobs because of vague or arbitrary charges against them or because of a confrontation with the supervisor or the administration. Safety measures such as appeal procedures are necessary to protect against such abuses.

Although such procedures are necessary, they also place a premium on the ability of supervisors to justify an evaluation. In a job management issue, even though the supervisor may have had to deal with a host of complaints from colleagues of a worker, the other workers may all suddenly lose their memories of the incidents if they are asked to testify against a colleague. With direct practice problems, the supervisor may have documented complaints from consumers of the service, but even these can be interpreted away. Most difficult to prove without documentation is a charge of lack of skill. Because most case recording does not include process descriptions of the practice and because most supervisors do not use audiotape or videotape recordings of interviews in supervision conferences, this charge is particularly hard to document.

A supervisor who expects a problem to develop and foresees the need for a negative evaluation would be wise to document all communications and contacts with the staff member on the matter, starting as soon as possible. The material must be explicit, with a minimum of euphemisms or fudged statements. For example, take the case of a probationary worker who repeatedly ignores a supervisor's complaints about lateness and absenteeism and disregards all efforts to help. A memorandum from the supervisor that states, "If this pattern is continued, I shall have to recommend that you not be kept on at the end of your probation" will have a much better chance of standing up at an appeal hearing than will one that states, "Your continued pattern of lateness and absence causes great concern on my part."

If the recorded material is not needed, all the better. If it is, the supervisor will be ready to make a case and stick to it, even under great pressure. There is no easy way for a supervisor to take part in such grievance procedures; when under attack, even the most competent supervisors feel tremendous strain. However, the supervisor can be secure in the knowledge that he or she is doing the right thing for clients, the worker involved, other workers, and his or her own personal integrity. At times such as these, the supervisor needs all the emotional support possible from administrators, colleagues, workers, friends, and family. It is one of the moments they may wish they had not taken the job, and, at the same time, it is one of the opportunities to do their most effective work.

EVALUATION CONTENT AND PROCESS

The importance and difficulty of evaluation for supervisors were indicated in a report based on a study of fieldwork instruction in a school of social work (Gitterman & Gitterman, 1979). The supervisors who were surveyed reported various sources of strain inherent in the process, including "defining criteria, writing the formal document, assessing student practice, and engaging the student in the evaluation process" (p. 106). Similar procedures can cause difficulties for supervisors evaluating the performance of staff members.

The evaluation process has been made more difficult in the helping professions by vagueness about the skills to be evaluated. For example, getting statistics in on time is easy to assess, but "providing support to clients" is a different matter. Gitterman and Gitterman (1979) described the general content areas of evaluation in terms similar to the four subject matter areas identified in chapter 6: (1) professional practice skill, (2) use of learning opportunities, (3) work management, and (4) professional influence.

Kadushin (1976) provided a sample of an evaluation form and scales that can be used in the process (pp. 297–311). The content of evaluation is also explored in the Appendix, which provides a sample of an evaluation guide from the University of British Columbia School of Social Work. This guide, developed in 1976 by a number of contributors whose work was coordinated by the director of field instruction, Kloh-ann Amacher, specifies practice skills and indicates the desired level of performance on each one for the various levels of students. Supervisors concerned about how their students rate in comparison with others have found it particularly useful.

Steps in the Evaluation Process

The process of evaluation in the helping professions varies according to the situation, but a number of general principles can be incorporated in seven specific steps. First, whenever possible, an evaluation guide should be presented to staff members at the beginning of the working relationship. They should know what areas will be assessed and from where the evidence of work will be drawn. For a new worker, in particular, such reassurance is helpful so that the amount of work to be mastered does not seem overwhelming.

Second, items in the guide should be referred to periodically in the supervision process. They should become a natural part of the content of supervision.

Third, periods of assessment before the formal evaluation should be built into the supervision process so that both supervisor and worker are aware of progress or lack of it and of areas that need concentration. One of the most positive uses of an evaluation guide is in continually helping identify the learning agenda. In addition, periodic assessments (or checklists) help ensure that important areas are not being missed and that the worker is systematically informed of progress. The general goal is to avoid surprises in the final evaluation. There may be differences of opinion, and these should be clearly identified and noted, but there should be no surprises.

Fourth, both the supervisor and the worker should take some responsibility for reviewing the evaluation guide and preparing a preliminary assessment. A supervisor who asks the worker to fill in the form and then simply starts from there will seem to be lazy and not serious about the process. But a supervisor who takes the whole responsibility, without asking the worker also to make a first assessment, is letting the worker off the hook. If a worker shows resistance to filling out the form, the supervisor should explore the reason in some detail. The worker may have had some bad prior experiences with such evaluations, may be afraid to commit his or her ideas to paper, or may be unsure of the standards or unaware of the process involved. Time spent in this way will be worthwhile in ensuring that the evaluation is experienced as a joint process and not simply as something the supervisor does to the supervisee.

Fifth, in preparing the draft versions of the evaluations, both the supervisor and the worker should provide some documentation of their views. For example, a supervisor who suggests that a worker "has developed appropriate skills for dealing with client feelings but is having some difficulty in reaching for negative client reactions, particularly with hostile clients" should try to mention particular cases that demonstrate both the skills gained and the need for more skill. The same is true of comments regarding job management; particular details should be provided to illustrate strengths and weaknesses. This task of documenting the evaluation can be onerous if left until it is time to write the evaluation. If the supervisor has kept some records of the supervision with the evaluation in mind, the writing is much simpler.

Many supervisors think that agency evaluation forms stifle their ability to express meaningful opinions, especially when they use standardized checklists that ask for overall or global ratings to produce a computerized score. When pressed, however, supervisors often admit that there is really nothing to keep them from expanding the evaluation into any format they wish—except their own discomfort with the process and the hard work it requires.

Sixth, a joint meeting to discuss the two versions of the preliminary evaluation (which both supervisor and worker have had an opportunity to review) is the crucial working time in the evaluation process. This provides the opportunity for both to expand on their comments, make their cases if there are differences, identify areas of agreement, and so on. It is often helpful to go through the form section by section and then devote some time to areas in which differences are evident. These areas should be identified early in the conference. If negatives are saved for the end, the interaction can take on a tone of suspense, as happens in the commonly used procedure wherein the supervisor identifies all the workers' strengths as a means of "massaging" the workers and then reviews their weaknesses.

In reality, the workers probably hear very little of the positive points while waiting to get to the trouble spots. A brief introduction that identifies both strengths and weaknesses for discussion often relieves the pressure of waiting. A supervisee can be asked, "Where would you like to start?" Most supervisees want to begin with the problem areas. In reality, it is usually the supervisors who feel more comfortable in starting with all of the positives.

Finally, when agreements have been reached or disagreements identified, it is up to the supervisor to make a final decision about the content of the evaluation. If persuaded by the worker's arguments, the supervisor should change the tone or content of some passages. If not, it is important to note the worker's disagreement in the final form.

Considering the difficulties involved in these seven steps, it is little wonder that supervisors experience evaluations as hard work. Although there are many variations in the content and process and although agencies and supervisors must develop their own styles, proper attention at these critical times in the supervisory process will pay important dividends to the worker, the supervisor, and, ultimately, the service.

RESEARCH FINDINGS

In the Shulman, Robinson, and Luckyj (1981) study of supervision skill, an item on the workers' questionnaire dealing with evaluation asked the worker to indicate the percentage of time actually spent discussing ongoing job performance in supervisory conferences, compared with the percentage of time the worker would like this topic to be discussed. The responses indicated that 11.5 percent of the total time in supervisory conferences was devoted to ongoing job performance, whereas workers would have preferred it to take 13.6 percent of the total.

Correlations between these variables and other items on the supervisors' and workers' questionnaires provide interesting insights into factors that may affect the actual and desired proportion of time devoted to evaluation. Supervisors in child welfare were less active in evaluating ongoing job performance than were those in residential treatment and nursing. This fit another finding that indicated an association between supervising large numbers of staff other than front-line professionals (for example, clerical and administrative workers) and a lessened involvement in evaluation activities. One interpretation is that the larger supervisory load for many of the supervisors in child welfare, particularly supervision of non–social work staff, substantially cuts into the time available for evaluation feedback. This confirms many of the comments of the supervisors and workers.

Items on the workers' questionnaire that were associated with percentage of time spent on evaluative activities were the following: the worker's field of work ($r = .38$), actual time spent on individual case planning ($r = -.60$), and preference for social work skill training ($r = .27$). Area of work reflected the impact of less evaluation feedback by the child welfare supervisors. The negative correlation with case planning provides some idea of what is discussed in place of ongoing feedback (case planning). The preference for social work skill training is also logically associated with a desire for more feedback. Of additional interest was the strong association between the actual time spent on such feedback and the worker's desire for such feedback ($r = .64$). It is understandable that it is easier for a supervisor to provide continual evaluation to a worker who is eager to receive it.

Findings from the Kadushin (1973) study indicated that for workers, supervisors who were not sufficiently critical of their work were the second strongest source of their dissatisfaction with supervision (26 percent). Conversely, supervisors who provided constructive feedback so that workers knew how they were doing were a strong source of satisfaction for 24 percent of the sample. The dilemma experienced by supervisors in this respect was reflected in the findings that for 26 percent of the supervisors, conflict between the educational aspects of their work and the evaluative aspects was a strong source of dissatisfaction. Moreover, 21 percent of the supervisors identified the evaluation responsibility as a strong source of dissatisfaction for them.

SUMMARY

An evaluation is an objective appraisal of a worker's performance. It is one of the most important elements of the supervisor's role, and when handled well, it makes a major contribution to the worker's development and client services. One type of evaluation, called *formative evaluation*, provides ongoing feedback to workers on their activity to help form or shape their job performance. Another type of evaluation procedure combines formative purposes with agency assessment functions. In addition to providing feedback for the staff's development, this evaluation process may be used as a basis for career decisions about an employee, such as passing a probation period, promotion, merit salary increases, or firing.

Many supervisors report some discomfort with the evaluation function because it forces them to use their authority, but most workers indicate a preference for honest feedback.

The evaluation process comprises seven elements. These include a discussion of the evaluation instrument early in the relationship, inclusion of items from the instrument in ongoing supervision discussions, provision of formative feedback during supervision to eliminate surprises at the evaluation conference, involvement of both the supervisor and supervisee in preparing preliminary assessments, identification by both illustrations of strengths and weaknesses, a joint meeting to identify areas of agreement and disagreement and to negotiate modifications if appropriate, and, finally, the supervisor's taking responsibility for final evaluative decisions, including areas of worker disagreement.

PART IV

WORKING WITH STAFF GROUPS

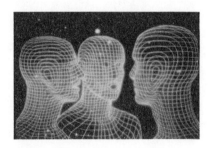

CHAPTER 8

SUPERVISION OF STAFF GROUPS

Supervisors are constantly working with both formal and informal staff groups. The formal groups are easiest to conceptualize: staff meetings, group supervision, committee meetings, and other groups in which staff members come together on a more or less formal basis. A good share of a supervisor's time, however, is devoted to dealing with the dynamics of the informal group, the unstructured collective of staff members that is in operation continually, not only during scheduled sessions. This informal group consists of all staff members who interact with one another as they carry out their tasks. Even though the professional staff may be the only group represented at staff meetings, for example, its informal group inter-actions with the clerical staff can powerfully affect the delivery of services. Indeed, in many settings the most important interactions take place in the informal group, whereas the formal staff meetings may take on the char-acter of a charade in which the staff members and the supervisor merely go through the motions, creating an illusion of work.

This chapter will look at how the supervisor can intervene to make formal group occasions such as meetings more effective, as well as how to deal with issues arising in the informal system. Because a single chapter cannot do justice to a subject as potentially rich as this one, this chapter considers only those problems, dynamics, and examples that have been raised most often in the author's supervisors' workshops. The group work aspects of the interactional model are explored in more detail in the author's text on social work practice (Shulman, 1992), in which a major part describes group leadership skills. The parallels between worker–client and supervisor–worker relationships that have been drawn in preceding chapters are evident again in the parallels between client groups and staff groups formed to work on the business of the agency or other institu-tional setting.

The focus of the chapter has also been limited to front-line supervision work, even though much of the content can easily be applied to middle- and upper-level administration. The dynamics and skills involved in leading effective groups are the same whether the participants are front-line workers or a management team made up of department administrators. In workshops I have conducted for administrators, many of their themes and concerns have proved to be similar to those of supervisors, only one or more levels removed from front-line practice. Whereas a social work supervisor might struggle to deal with the conflict between clerical and professional staff, an agency administrator might have to tackle a conflict between the heads of different departments.

One area of group supervision discussed in this chapter focuses on the supervisory tasks involved in helping the staff deal with the work environment—for example, dealing with conflict when an administrative decision creates an angry backlash by workers. Supervisors report meetings in which their staff members demand to know which side the supervisor is on, followed by management team meetings at which the administrator asks the same question. The dilemma of feeling "caught in the middle" is an important one in supervision work.

The chapter begins with some general comments about the dynamics of supervisory work with staff groups and the potential advantages of mutual aid in staff groups. This is followed by a section on the beginning phase of work with a staff group that examines questions of group purpose and the supervisor's role. The section on work-phase issues describes the development of a group culture, various roles of individuals in groups, and managing group conflict. The authority theme as related to group–supervisor relationships is examined in a separate section. Examples in these sections deal with both formal and informal groups. The section on endings and transitions focuses on the dynamics involved when a supervisor or staff member leaves a staff group; some of the skills that can turn endings into productive experiences are discussed. In chapter 9, the use of the staff group as a social support system for helping staff cope with traumatic events such as the sudden death of a client or staff member or the impact of cutbacks in funding is examined in detail.

DYNAMICS OF SUPERVISORY WORK WITH STAFF GROUPS

Staff groups can be a potent force for carrying on the work of the agency or other setting. They cannot be positive forces, however, if they are simply left to themselves. Effective leadership is needed to help staff members release the potential for mutual aid and constructive work existing within each staff group, both formal and informal, and to learn to work together effectively. The obstacles that emerge in the normal course of events are not signals of the impossibility of working effectively as a group; rather, they are agenda items for the group leader and the staff members to address.

Unfortunately, most supervisors are even less prepared for their group leadership responsibilities than they are for their individual supervision tasks. Individual supervision can at least seem close to the work they are comfortable with, such as individual counseling, but supervisors often bring to their tasks a dread of group leadership because of their own unsatisfactory experiences. Perhaps groups they have led in the past went badly, leaving them feeling responsible and less than competent. Everyone has participated in groups of some sort, and because there are many ways groups can go wrong without effective leadership (and even at times with effective leadership), negative experiences are not uncommon. No wonder new supervisors face their first staff groups with less than total enthusiasm, sometimes, as one supervisor told me, feeling "scared spitless."

Because only minimal training in group leadership skills is usually available and little can be expected in the way of regular assistance, some supervisors try to avoid group sessions completely or try to have as few as possible. When they have group meetings, they adopt procedures derived from their experience as participants, because that is all they have to go on. All too often they use ineffective or boring practices that they know are unhelpful. A worker may have experienced staff meetings in which a supervisor read administrative directives with his or her face buried in the paper, looking up occasionally to ask if there were any questions. The supervisor may have quickly moved on to the next item on the agenda when the group responded with silence. Without additional training or better examples to follow, this worker may do the same in a supervisory capacity, despite knowing exactly what the group participants are thinking and feeling about the meeting.

The strength in numbers represented by the staff group makes it a potent force for supervisors to deal with. If a supervisor senses negative feedback in the workers' comments or nonverbal expressions, it is easy to understand why he or she might not reach for these feelings. Supervisors who feel overly responsible for a group's session often have difficulty tolerating silences and immediately assume that they are doing something wrong. Interestingly enough, often these same supervisors understand the meaning of silences in their work with clients and recognize the need to deal with the underlying communications.

Because of their own powerful feelings of inadequacy and their fears of being disliked or being judged incompetent, many supervisors seem to find that even their most elementary skills escape them when they must face a staff group. Their lack of confidence in themselves can lead them to adopt the strategy of leaving the difficult or most contentious items to last on the agenda, knowing that they may not be reached or that there will be so little time left to deal with them that the discussion will be superficial.

If supervisors simply see a staff meeting as a convenient way of communicating directly to all staff members simultaneously, they might as well save their time and circulate a memorandum. They may fear that the staff will not read the memorandum, but what makes them think they will listen at a meeting? Whenever the staff is brought together for a committee meeting or an administrative session or for group supervision, the supervisor must understand and facilitate the active role of all the participants. If group supervision is to be meaningful, for example, it is important to establish what other staff members are expected to do as a worker shares practice examples. Rather than sitting quietly as observers, patiently waiting their turn, they can be actively involved in the process if they are shown specifically how they can be helpful. It is naive to assume that workers know how to participate, particularly in the beginning phase of a group's development, or to assume that they will do so easily if they know how to get involved. They need some instruction and support as they try to get engaged, and regular demands for work must be placed on them by the supervisor. To play this active group leadership role, the supervisor needs to believe in the potential of mutual aid.

MUTUAL AID PROCESSES

If the supervisor is willing to take risks and to invest time, feeling, and energy in an effort to make the staff group effective instead of an illusion, the benefits can be immense. Positive group morale and a supportive atmosphere may be developed. Staff apathy, often the signal of underlying problems in the formal and informal systems, can be relieved; thus, the workers' potential to contribute to the service can be released.

An effective staff group can provide help to workers in a number of specific ways. One way is through the mutual sharing of data. The supervisor is not the only source of information; staff members can draw on their own life and work experiences and can share facts, values, ideas, or beliefs that may be valuable to others.

A second form of mutual aid comes from the clash of ideas during debates as members share their views on a question under discussion. Group members can risk their tentative ideas and use the group as a sounding board—a place for their views to be challenged and possibly changed. In this kind of group culture, the argument between two or more members is dialectical: Group members listen as one member presents the thesis and the other the antithesis. Then each member can use the discussion to develop a synthesis. It is not always easy to challenge ideas in a group, however, and a later section will describe how such a culture for work can be developed.

The section on developing a culture for work in the work phase in groups also describes the third way in which mutual aid can operate: opening up discussion in a taboo area. Each staff member brings to the group the norms of behavior and implied taboos of our society's culture.

The staff group, a microcosm of the larger society, quickly recreates the rules of the culture. Workers thus may experience direct talk about certain subject areas—authority, sex, loss, or dependency—as taboo. Each worker will feel the power of the taboo differently. Some may be more ready than others to take a risk and move into the area of discussion. If staff members are upset with a supervisory decision, for example, they may act it out in the form of passive resistance. A staff member who either directly or indirectly expresses the real feeling, which has been blocked by the taboo against challenging authority, can help to lead the group into a vital area of discussion. The group will watch what happens when the member ventures into threatening territory, and if the supervisor handles it well by encouraging rather than discouraging honest feedback, he or she will be giving the staff permission to enter a formerly taboo area. If the supervisor does not feel comfortable enough to hear what the staff has to say, intervening to block the conversation will reinforce the taboo. Unfortunately, negative feelings never just go away: They come back to haunt the supervisor in significant ways.

A fourth form of mutual aid comes from the "all in the same boat" feeling. As staff members listen to others and discover emotions of their own, some of which they were aware and others which surprise them, they can experience the relief of knowing that others feel the same way. Their feelings are less frightening and overwhelming if shared by others. For example, workers who find it difficult to deal with the sexuality of clients who make seductive overtures, particularly those whom they find sexually attractive, will be relieved to know that others share this difficulty. Child welfare workers who fear the potential violence of some of their clients are helped by knowing that their fear is a natural one and is not a sign of inadequacy. Staff members may joke about sexuality and violence, a use of macabre humor that is often a form of flight from emotional pain, but they find it hard to discuss these feelings seriously.

Mutual support is another way that group members help one another. In a supportive group culture, the capacity of staff members to empathize with one another is evident. The empathy must be genuine, however; workers must not feel they are being "social worked" (in the negative sense of the expression) by their colleagues. Because staff members experience issues in individual ways, often differently from the way the supervisor understands them, they may be in the best position to provide meaningful support in times of stress.

Mutual demand is also important in a staff group. Mutual aid can be provided by expectation, as well as by caring (that is, group members can confront each other within a context of support). If the supervisor helps develop the proper conditions, workers may be able to make demands on each other better than the supervisor can. When a worker is presenting case material defensively, for example, it may be most effective for another worker to suggest that the presenter lower the barriers and let them all in.

Other sources of help in groups are individual problem solving and rehearsal. Staff members can present a particular issue to the staff group for advice. When colleagues offer suggestions, they are actually helping themselves with similar concerns while providing help to the individual. This is one of the most important dynamics in mutual aid groups: Participants are getting help for themselves when they provide it to a colleague.

Finally, when faced with a difficult task, like a troublesome encounter with a client or an important person in the system such as a judge or doctor, group members may welcome the opportunity to rehearse and get feedback from their peers. The opportunity to practice a conversation through brief role playing can provide important preparatory help for the coming encounter.

The following sections examine how group dynamics and these mutual aid processes may operate in supervisory work with staff groups. They illustrate how knowledgeable (and courageous) interventions of the supervisor and the hard work of the staff can contribute to effective work in both formal and informal groups.

BEGINNING PHASE IN GROUPS: THE CONTRACTING PROCESS

The beginning, or contracting, phase of work with the staff group will lay the foundation for effective work. Unfinished business in this phase will come back to haunt the supervisor and the group throughout its life. This discussion focuses on the beginning phase of work when the staff group is new or when a new supervisor joins an established staff group. The constructs discussed are also relevant to ongoing groups and supervisory relationships. In many cases, it is necessary for a supervisor to return to the work of the beginning phase through a recontracting process in which an attempt is made to redefine issues of group purpose, the role of the supervisor, and the nature of the work expected.

A formal staff group generally consists of staff members who come together specifically to work on the business of the agency. It is neither a social nor a therapeutic group, although the staff may have experienced other staff groups in these ways.

It is not a social group because there is always work to be done. Working together effectively can have a positive impact on social relationships among staff, one of the additional benefits of an effective working group, but it is not the reason for the group to meet.

A staff meeting is not a therapeutic group because it would be inappropriate to deal with individual personal problems or general discussions of interpersonal relationships, as in an "encounter" or "T group" (training group). Just as the supervisor must guard the working contract to prevent supervision from becoming personal counseling, even when the supervisee asks for it, the same clarity of purpose is necessary in the group context.

If a serious personal problem, perhaps illness or marital discord, is shared in a staff meeting, the support of the staff should be focused on how the problems will affect the work and on what staff members can do to help in the work context. A discussion among staff members about a conflict in the informal system, such as a social worker refusing to deal with a particular colleague on a case, should be focused on the problems of delivery of services to the patient, not the social worker's or the colleague's personalities.

The proliferation of "sensitivity" or "growth" groups in our culture may cause some confusion about the purposes of staff work groups. It is important to discuss how effectively a group is working and to deal with patterns of interaction, such as defensiveness, that are blocking the work. The purpose of such a discussion, however, is simply to free the group for more effective work or to uncover what the pattern of interactions may indicate as a form of indirect communication. For example, a staff member who presents a case defensively may be signaling his or her insecurity about the practice and a lack of trust in the staff group. These concerns may be felt by other staff members as well. The problem of defensiveness needs to be discussed as a group issue, not in terms of the personality problem of the particular staff member.

The discussion, therefore, should not be focused on helping the individual members "grow." In fact, it is essential for staff members to feel free to share their thoughts and feelings spontaneously, knowing that they will be protected by a supervisor who is clear about purpose and function and who will respect their right to privacy. There are those who claim that personal therapy is needed for workers to function effectively with clients. I argue that such help should be sought in appropriate places such as other agencies or with private practitioners. If the staff group takes on such tasks, I have found, it soon ceases to deal with other tasks that are appropriate and necessary. Some more appropriate and more essential purposes for staff groups are described in the following section.

Purposes of Staff Groups

There are four major purposes for formal staff groups: (1) staff meetings, (2) case consultation, (3) group supervision, and (4) in-service training. Separate groups may exist for each purpose, or a single group may incorporate one or more of them. There could be a staff meeting one week followed by case consultation the next, for example, or different purposes can be served during a single meeting. Because the content and dynamics of the group and the focus of the group leader differ for each purpose, clarity about group objectives can make a major difference to the group's productivity for both the leader and the members.

Staff Meetings

Staff meetings focus on the job management aspect of the work and issues of policy and program. For example, when work must be done to provide a service, an appropriate discussion for a staff meeting might be the division of labor—who is to cover what shifts or handle which aspects of the case-load. Other appropriate group activities are evaluating overall performance of the unit, interpreting administration policies, eliciting reactions to policies and formulating feedback, and discussing innovative programs or special needs.

Although it is important for the supervisor to develop an agenda for discussion, the staff also must have some input into the agenda-building process. This corresponds to the sessional contracting process described for individual supervision in chapter 4. One way to accomplish this is for the supervisor to circulate a preliminary agenda and for staff members to add their own items. Another way to incorporate staff input is for the supervisor to begin each staff meeting by reviewing the set agenda and inquiring if staff have additional items to add. Finally, even when an agenda is agreed on, the supervisor needs to proceed tentatively, alert to the possibility of the existence of hidden agenda items.

The following example is a hospital social work supervisor's report of how she opened a session by describing the agenda and soliciting other items:

> I told them I needed to discuss the new admissions policy and what it would mean to our staff. In particular, I was interested in their views as to the impact so I could share these at the next department directors' meetings. I also had a few brief announcements, which I would share at the beginning, but that was all on my agenda. I asked if they had anything they wanted on. There was no response, so I continued with the announcements. I felt I was getting very little reaction and that I was essentially speaking to blank faces. I decided to proceed with outlining the admissions policy.

In addition to sharing her own agenda, the supervisor described why she was raising the new policy. All too often there is little clarity as to the purpose of a group discussion. Is it for information only? Is there need for a response, and what will the supervisor do with the response? Supervisors need to be clear about what they expect from the staff and must guard against the temptation of creating an illusion of democracy. In this fairly common error, the supervisor raises an issue that has already been decided on by the supervisor or the administration under the guise of gaining staff input into the decision-making process. When the staff does not provide the "right" input, the supervisor is stuck, and the staff soon recognizes the attempt at manipulation. It is much better to be honest about the limits of the discussion, letting the staff know whether it is input or just reaction to an already firm decision that is desired. The supervisor must clarify which decisions the staff can make on its own and over which ones he or she must retain a final veto.

In the excerpt cited earlier, the supervisor invited additional agenda items from the staff and received none. It would have been a mistake simply to assume there were indeed none and to proceed to cover the agenda. However, as the session proceeded, the supervisor sensed the apathy and dispirited involvement of the staff. This represented a group example of the illusion of work. Conversation was taking place, but nothing of substance was happening. Although she passed over the first cues, she could not ignore their lack of enthusiasm for the discussion of the new admissions policy. Her second effort at sessional contracting involved directly confronting the illusion as follows:

> I stopped my recitation of the new policy and asked if there were any questions or reactions. Frank asked for an interpretation on one point, and after I provided the answer, the group lapsed into silence. I pointed out their lack of enthusiasm and their apparent lethargy and asked what was really going on. More silence followed. I asked if they really had something else on their minds, because they were not getting into this question of the intake policy. I had thought they had a stake in it and was very surprised.
>
> Beth said, "It's hard to worry about intake of patients if you're not sure you're going to be around to deal with them." It suddenly hit me that they were probably still upset about my comments at the end of our last meeting that indicated budget cutbacks were possible that could affect our staff complement. I asked if that was what was on all their minds. There was much nodding of heads. I said, "Perhaps we can spend some time on what I know about the cutbacks, even though I don't have any real facts yet, and then we can discuss how this is hitting you and affecting your work. I know it has me worried as well, and perhaps that's why I ended up ignoring it this week. After that we can get back to the admissions issue." The staff agreed, and their involvement picked up noticeably.

There are always important issues to be discussed at staff meetings. The reason so many meetings seem boring, even to the supervisor who is leading them, is that the real agenda often stays hidden just beneath the surface. It is not uncommon for staff to describe the "real meeting" as taking place over lunch or in the coffee room after the staff meeting. For a staff meeting to be effective, staff members have to have a stake in the work, and they need some opportunity to express their sense of urgency. Once they realize that the agenda item is out in the open, they are often content to wait until later in the meeting to deal with it or even to put it off until another meeting if necessary.

The supervisor in this example used the skills of monitoring the process of the meeting and examining the obstacle when she sensed that the work was not real. The attention to process led directly to work on the task. If the supervisor had simply accepted the tone of the meeting as "the way staff meetings usually go," she would have missed an important cue to an urgent issue affecting everyone's performance. Her comments to staff indicated a keen insight into her own ambivalence about facing a discussion of a painful and anxiety-producing topic. As is often the case, staff can sense when a supervisor is ready to face an issue or would rather avoid it. The next chapter includes an example of how a supervisor can go further in helping workers provide services in a time of cutbacks.

Case Consultation

Case consultation is a type of staff meeting that is often confused with both group supervision and in-service training. The confusion stems from the fact that practice is the central subject in each type of session. In all three types of meetings, workers may be discussing issues related to their work with clients. In each, however, the organizing principle of the discussion is different. Another way to think of it is to ask which elements of the discussion are in the foreground and which elements are in the background.

In case consultation, the focus of the discussion is the case itself. A worker presents a case to tap fellow workers and the supervisor as sources of help in thinking through his or her work with the case and developing strategies for intervention. In contrast, group supervision has in the foreground the development of the worker's practice skill. Even though the same case may be presented as in case consultation, in group supervision the focus is on using fellow workers and the supervisor to consider the worker's skill development and to provide help in strengthening it. The same case could be discussed in both situations, but the way the group members and the supervisor respond would differ significantly. In case consultation, the focus remains on the case, so that discussion of the worker's interventions is designed to facilitate service delivery. In group supervision, the focus remains on the worker while the case is more in the background. To illustrate this difference, a case consultation session on work with a family in the child welfare context is presented in this section; how a similar situation would be handled in group supervision is considered in the next section.

Louise, a young, inexperienced worker, had returned from a first home visit with a young mother of two children who had been the subject of a neglect complaint. At a group session, she began her presentation of the case with some facts on the family situation and then indicated that she was concerned over the mother's handling of the child while she was there. The house was not clean, there were dirty dishes in the sink, and she felt the mother was defensive during the interview. She wanted help on the case because she was not sure that this mother was doing an adequate job, and she felt the mother might not be "workable." The supervisor's summary of the case consultation process noted:

I told Louise that it sounded like a tough case for her to be starting with. She acknowledged she was really concerned about what to do next. I asked if anyone could get us started. Fran asked some questions about the ex-spouse and family, trying to see if there were other resources available. I commented on that being a helpful start. Louise described what she already knew and indicated that she could have explored that a bit more with the client. Ted wanted to know if any other agencies were involved. Louise indicated that a public health nurse had made some contact after the client had visited a community health team. She said she intended to contact her but was not having much luck.

At this point in the discussion, the supervisor made an extremely important demand for work. As other workers began to intervene with suggestions, comments about similar clients, and so on, the supervisor asked Louise to move the discussion into some of the details of the home interview. Thus far, the staff group had little to go on regarding what had happened during the interview. Often, case consultation merely involves using the group members' opinions to come up with a group assessment of the client and a specific treatment plan. Behind this process is the traditional medical model in which the worker provides the facts (the study), the group makes an assessment (the diagnosis), and then the group and the worker develop an idea for next steps (the treatment plan). The disadvantage in this process is that the staff group finds itself trying to assess the client as if he or she were a static entity, rather than seeing him or her in dynamic interaction with the worker. In the interactional model of social work practice, the client must be seen in a reciprocal relationship with the worker. The client's behavior is understood as reacting, in part, to the worker's interventions. The same reciprocal influence affects the worker's responses.

This is a crucial distinction because it is impossible to understand the behavior of the client unless it is considered in the context of the worker's behavior: The client is continually acting and reacting, and the worker's input may have an important impact on the proceedings. The danger is that if the staff group decides that the client is "resistant" and develops a treatment plan (which may involve eventual removal of the child from the home), it will be doing so with insufficient information.

The next excerpt reports what happened when the supervisor asked Louise to do some memory work to recall a bit of the detail of the interaction. What did she say to the client, and what did the client say back to her? This process makes the client seem less one-dimensional; in fact, it begins to open up possibilities for her to be very workable indeed, if the worker handles the interview differently. The supervisor's report continued:

I asked Louise if she could take us back a bit to the interview and share how it began. What did she say to the client, and how did the client respond? She provided some of the details, indicating she had followed through on some of the preparatory work we had done and had begun with an honest statement of why she was there, which included both her role in investigating and protecting the children, as well as offering help to the mother. I complimented her on her opening and asked at what point in the interview she really started to worry. She described how the mother had been sitting tensely during the discussion and had shaken her four-year-old and scolded her when the child hit the two-year-old. I asked how Louise felt when that happened, and she replied, "I felt tense myself, because I began to think this might not be a good mother and I could end up in court."

Phil said he could understand that, because you know it will not be pleasant down the line. Carol said it's really tough with a young mother who looks so vulnerable herself. I agreed and asked if Louise could return to the interview. What had she said to the mother? Louise described how she had suggested that the client might handle her four-year-old differently, perhaps explaining to her why she shouldn't hit the two-year-old. I asked what the client's response was, and Louise said she seemed to freeze up. According to Louise, that was when she began to feel she would not get anywhere with this client.

I asked the other workers to put themselves in the client's shoes and try to tune in to how she must have been feeling. I thought this might help Louise. There was nice work on how defensive the client must have felt and afraid of the worker's judgment of her; she must have worried that her children would be taken away. Phil pointed out how oppressed she must feel being at home with those two kids, no husband, no family—in fact, not much of anything for herself. I wondered if this could explain part of the defensiveness that had led Louise to feel it might be hopeless to try to work with her. Louise said she had not seen the mother that way because she was too upset herself. She was mostly thinking about the children.

I asked if we could consider what Louise might say to this mother at her next interview that might start to help the client lower her defenses and begin to trust Louise a bit more. Perhaps nothing would help, because the client has a part in this, but was there any way Louise could try to engage her more? The workers began to try out some opening lines, most of which focused on how uncomfortable the client must have felt when the worker last visited and how the worker was concerned for the mother as well as the children.

Clearly, those few minutes of effort on the supervisor's part to obtain some of the details of the interaction deepened the case consultation process in important ways. It is the lack of moving from the general to the specific that often results in group discussions based on the worker's subjective feelings rather than on the actual details of the interaction. The worker wanted some help on next steps (the treatment plan) that might allow work with this client. It would not have been helpful to simply agree on the client's lack of motivation and then begin to devise structural plans for handling the problem, such as arranging temporary foster care. These steps may be necessary at some point in the future but certainly were not at this time.

The key difference between this process (in which the worker presented details of her practice and the discussion dealt with her skills) and group supervision is the focus on the case rather than the worker. As case consultation, the process called for the supervisor to keep the group focused on the case and on the next steps involved. In group supervision, the same discussion might move more deeply into the worker's struggle to find a way to establish a working relationship, while simultaneously carrying a mandated responsibility for the protection of the children. Group members would be expected to harness their efforts to help the worker think through this common skill development problem for new workers. It would be quite possible, and in fact often helpful, for the supervisor and the group to consider other cases that might help the worker see her pattern across clients. As is seen in the next section on group supervision, the worker is in the foreground, and the specific case is in the background.

Group Supervision

Group supervision is a variation of individual supervision that is often used as a supplement to work with individual staff members. A central consideration is the professional development of the workers being supervised. All of the learning subject areas of supervision specified earlier—job management skills, professional practice skills, impact skills, and continued learning skills—may be appropriately addressed in group supervision. The supervisor uses the group to serve this purpose because of a judgment that the other staff members can make important contributions to the worker's development, not because it saves time to approach all the workers together in a group. It is important for group members to understand their role in the proceedings and to know that they will be actively involved in providing support and making demands when appropriate.

In the following example of the process, the setting is a hospital social services department. As in the previous excerpt, the worker was fairly new and inexperienced. The worker, Lou, had presented the case of a family with whom he felt he was not getting anywhere. A teenage daughter had been committed to the psychiatric ward of the hospital, and he was attempting to engage the parents but was running into resistance. The supervisor made a demand for work and encouraged Lou to present some of the details of the interaction. At the point at which he reported feeling the resistance from the father, it was obvious that Lou was identifying with the daughter and was missing the father's feelings. The supervisor's report of the group supervision process notes how the discussion was moved away from the case to focus on the worker. The case example was used to provide an illustration to explore the worker's learning agenda:

Lou described how he had reached for the daughter's feelings when her father told her he had given up and didn't care if she didn't come home when she left the hospital. He described how the daughter had lowered her head and started to cry softly at this point. I said I thought it must have hit Lou very hard. I asked where his feelings were at that moment and he said, "I was really with Lois [the daughter]." I asked what he did, and he described how he tried to get the father to understand his daughter's hurt at this comment, but that he didn't feel he had gotten too far. I said I thought that must have been very frustrating for him. I asked if anyone had any ideas that might help.

Phyllis said it was tough when you saw a father hurting his daughter that way. It would make her very angry. Jane wondered whether Lou had been so mad at the father, and so identified with the daughter, that he couldn't sense the father's hurt. I noticed Lou's reflective expression and asked if he understood what Jane was saying. He said a bit. I asked Jane if she could elaborate. She went on to describe how upset the father must have been and that he was probably hiding his hurt behind a mask of indifference. He probably wouldn't want to admit he was so vulnerable. John said that it's tougher for a man, who thinks he should have these things under control.

I asked if we could focus on Lou here. I enquired if Lou or anyone else had any idea why it was so hard to stay with the father. Lou said it was probably the same thing that happened when he identified with the husband last week and ended up putting the wife down—and she didn't return to the interview. I said we should stay with this: "What goes on in your feelings, Lou? What makes it so tough?" Lou said that he gets lost when people act in ways that make him mad. I said that it seemed he wanted the father to feel for the daughter, and the wife to feel for the husband, at precisely the same time he was having trouble empathizing with them.

John said, "Don't feel too bad, Lou; we are describing my problem exactly. It's so hard to identify with these people." I asked Lou if this could be described as an issue of countertransference, the placing of feelings onto clients that don't necessarily belong there. He asked what I meant, and we discussed this for a while.

Some important work was taking place as the group helped Lou examine the problem of countertransference in his work—not just his work with the original family members but his practice in general. Before the session was over, the supervisor returned to the original case to ask the group to help Lou think through how to handle the next interview with the father, and they role played some examples. Clearly, although the content of the work was similar to that in the example of case consultation, it was the worker's development that was the central and organizing factor.

In-service Training

Just as the case is central in case consultation and the worker is central in group supervision, ideas are central in in-service training. Countertransference, for example, might be a subject for discussion by an in-service training group. The worker just discussed, Lou, might even present the same case example, but if this were an in-service training session on the concept of countertransference, his example would be used as an illustration of the practice construct under discussion, not as a means of furthering his personal skill development. Other staff members would be encouraged to share their own experiences and examples in the discussion, rather than having to set aside their sense of urgency about their own cases and concentrate instead on the work of the presenter. In addition, the supervisor or some of the workers might be prepared to present some background on the subject under discussion, or outside resource people might contribute ideas. The purpose of such in-service training is to deepen everyone's understanding of the subject.

Fulfilling Staff Group Purposes

Whichever purposes are adopted for a staff group and in whatever format they are presented, the supervisor needs to clarify for the staff the general purposes of group sessions, as well as to obtain feedback on the staff's investment in those purposes. When mutual agreement on purpose has been reached and the supervisor's role has been defined (the subject of the next section), the group will have a tentative working contract. The supervisor's work will then focus on carrying out that contract and helping staff members work effectively together to serve the group's purposes. This includes maintaining the focus by guarding the working contract. Keeping purpose in mind, the supervisor carefully pursues the discussion in relation to purpose. In the illustration of case consultation, the supervisor made certain that the group returned to the particular case under discussion when their conversation moved into broader areas. An effective group leader would, for example, ensure that a case presentation for consultation by a worker did not turn into group supervision for which neither the worker nor the group had bargained. This protection of the contract will enhance trust in the group and thus encourage participants to risk discussing their work.

If a supervisor has neglected to clarify the group purpose or the supervisor's role, it is always possible to recontract, even in groups that have met for years. The supervisor can suggest this possibility with a comment such as this: "I was thinking about our understanding of the purpose of these sessions and my role in them, and I don't think I ever made clear what my ideas were about those two issues. Perhaps, because I don't think I was always clear myself, we should start again. . . ."

Later sections in this chapter focus on a number of the problems that make it difficult for staff groups to work together. It is not unusual for members to resist fulfilling the various purposes for staff meetings. The reasons for this resistance often have a great deal to do with the group's culture for work, which is examined in some detail in the section on the work phase in groups.

Supervisor's Role

Because there is confusion about the role of the supervisor in group practice, defining and clarifying this role should be undertaken directly in an early session with the staff. Nevertheless, it will take time for the role to be clearly understood and tested by staff members. The first meetings will be the testing ground, in which the staff will watch to see if the supervisor really means the role definition that has been worked out. When negative feedback on the first session is offered, often very tentatively and cautiously, the staff will watch to see how it is handled. The supervisor's true leadership style will emerge in the day-to-day operations of the staff group.

Leadership Styles

Most people have had many conflicting models of group leaders in their experiences. They may have known autocratic leaders, who attempt to dominate the work by using their authority; laissez-faire leaders, who often pretend they have no authority while dominating the work in more subtle ways; and democratic leaders, whose authority emerges from the group. None of these models corresponds exactly to leadership in the supervision context, but they are characteristic of the major modes of group leadership practice.

The autocratic leader who takes responsibility for the group may turn staff members into submissive group participants who act out their feelings through passive resistance (long silences) or who sabotage group decisions by such techniques as failing to implement policies. This type of leadership often provides such a tight structure that there is no freedom for innovation, no provision for group members to play constructive roles, and no room on the agenda for issues of concern to the staff. Workers clearly perceive this type of group as "owned" by the supervisor. They will take little or no responsibility for making it work effectively.

The laissez-faire approach, in contrast, makes it seem that the leader is taking no responsibility for the group. Sessions often begin with the classic query: "So what do you want to talk about?" Because no structure is provided, group members may be overwhelmed and, in fact, may have as little freedom as their colleagues in groups with autocratic leaders. The laissez-faire leader allows discussion to ramble, provides little direction, and rarely, if ever, makes a demand for work. In practice, although appearing to relinquish control, a leader who operates in this manner often exercises control in more subtle ways. If a staff group does not work effectively, it seems, the supervisor must make all the decisions. When the structure is so loose that group productivity is low, the real decisions on important issues will be made away from the group. Such groups may suffer from depression or else express anger toward their passive leaders. If they demand that their leaders become more autocratic, they merely substitute a different leadership problem.

The laissez-faire approach has even been institutionalized in some settings. Certain agencies, for example, have established "team approaches" in which "collegiality" is the key word and in which each participant, including the supervisor, has an equal say in the operation. These "leaderless" groups often try to solve the problem of autocratic leadership by doing away with the idea of a leader. This ultimate overthrow of authority arises from a misunderstanding of the nature of group leadership and the key functional role of the leader, without whom most groups cannot operate effectively.

Another variation on this theme of diminishing the supervisor's authority is to assign staff members the responsibility for chairing meetings in rotation. Under certain circumstances, individual staff members can effectively chair a meeting or segments of meetings. However, when the chair is seen as simply rotating each week, this structure can frustrate group members. When challenging problems arise, members naturally turn to the supervisor and thereby indicate that they have never really lost sight of where the authority is vested. Staff members who are asked to take on the role of leader for a session report that they can do a number of things well in leading a group discussion, but when it comes to making some forms of the demand for work, an ability that is rooted in a clear sense of authority and role, they find themselves unable to act. Colleagues cannot make the same demands on each other as can a supervisor who carries external authority granted by the agency.

Democratic leadership comes closest to the functioning of the supervisor–group leader role, but it lacks the element of external authority. In any group, an internal leader may be elected or assigned the role of group leader (that is, one of the members may be asked to take on the role of helping the group operate effectively). This member's authority is derived from the group members, and when the members no longer support this leader, effective operation in the role comes to an end.

Practical experiences, as well as the research on group leadership, have indicated that when the democratic leadership role is well implemented, it offers the best possibilities for involving group members actively in the work of the group. It provides members with a sense of achievement, enhances group morale, and even, in the long run, gets things done effectively. I say in the long run, because more efficient short-term effectiveness is often possible with other forms of leadership.

The major difficulty with this type of leadership for supervision is that supervisors do not derive their central authority from their workers. Rather, their authority comes from the agency or institution that hires them, fires them, and holds them accountable. Supervisors are not internal leaders; they are external leaders with external authority that can both help and hinder their effectiveness. In fact, in every supervisory group an internal leader or leaders, with functions slightly different from those of the supervisor, will emerge. Thus, although in the last analysis, the ability of supervisors to lead staff is derived from their workers' acceptance of their leadership, their authority to lead is externally sanctioned.

It is important to recognize this difference openly with the staff and to clarify the role boundaries as quickly as possible. On some issues, the supervisor may be responsible only for helping the staff come to a decision that concerns them. On other questions, the staff may only provide input into the deliberation process, which eventually must be resolved by the supervisor. The staff should know which situation is the case before they undertake consideration of a problem. Supervisors who cloud this issue, in the name of democratic leadership, will pay for it when the staff comes up with the "wrong" decision.

Mediation Role

In the following simple statement of role, a new social work supervisor attempted to clarify how he saw his part of the proceedings. He had already described the staff meeting and case consultation purposes for the social work staff group and had received positive responses from its members.

> Let me take a minute and spell out how I see my role in these meetings. I see myself as bringing issues to your attention that come from the administration or my own observations of what we are doing, as well as helping you to raise things on your mind. Once we decide on our agenda, I'm going to try to hold us to the discussion, as well as help you all talk to and listen to each other. In effect, I'm going to try to help us have an effective staff group. I can't do it alone, so I'm going to ask all of you to take some responsibility for making things work well. That's why, if you don't like what's happening at a meeting, let me hear about it right away— not a couple of days later. I think you all have a lot to contribute to these meetings. I think you can give each other a lot of good ideas, as well as some real support when you need it. I'm going to try to help you do that. Any questions?

In part, the role described by this supervisor could be conceptualized as mediating between each staff member and the group as a whole. This is a special case of the general mediation function of the supervision model described in chapter 2.

The similarity to the mediating roles described in preceding chapters is apparent. Individual supervision was described as mediating between the worker and his or her clients, colleagues, the agency, and the like. The staff group is viewed as a special case of the more general worker–system interaction, and the supervisor mediates the engagement. Many of the

Interactional Supervision

same principles apply in the implementation of this role in the group. In addition, as discussed later in chapter 9, the supervisor also implements this function between the staff group and the agency or institution.

WORK PHASE IN GROUPS

Work-phase tasks for staff groups include dealing with the authority of the supervisor, developing a positive group culture, dealing with individual–group issues, handling conflict among members, and working within the environment. The first four of these tasks will be explored and illustrated in the following sections. The task of relating to the environment (for example, agency, host setting) is examined in chapter 10.

Various forms of formal staff groups were described earlier in relation to group purpose: staff meetings, case consultation, group supervision, and in-service training. Some of the most significant encounters among staff members, however—encounters that can profoundly affect the delivery of services to clients—take place in the informal groups consisting of the staff members whose normal activities cause them to interact with one another regularly. The informal group or system on a hospital ward may consist of the social worker, the nurses, aides, and clerical staff who work together on regular shifts. The interactions of these staff members may be a source of great aid and emotional support to the staff, or conversely, they can generate serious obstacles that make it difficult for an interdependent staff to offer sound services to clients.

The examples in this section, drawn from both formal and informal groups, highlight the similarities in the dynamics involved, the functional role of the supervisor, and the skills required for effective leadership. The boundaries between the informal and formal groups are not sharply defined because the activities of one often affect those of the other. Day-to-day interactions among staff members may generate feelings and attitudes that are then brought into the formal staff meetings. In turn, the activities of the meeting may influence the informal staff group interaction. The supervisor consistently needs to pay attention to both groups.

Developing a Group Culture

When a group of staff members comes together, formally or informally, an entity is created that is greater than the simple sum of the parts. This entity can be thought of as an organism with a life of its own. The organism called the group has a number of properties that are not related to any individual member—but rather, are properties of the group as a whole. For example, a staff group is either cohesive—operating with feelings of closeness and bonding among members—or it is not cohesive. The property "cohesiveness" is a group property. The difficulty in perceiving this organism called the group is that its properties are not immediately visible. When a staff meeting begins, an observer cannot see cohesion itself. Rather, as the interaction develops, an observer can infer the level of group cohesiveness from the nature of the group members' interactions.

Another group characteristic is its norms of behavior. If group members share a stated or unstated belief that certain subjects are taboo and should not be discussed, the observer may infer the existence of this norm by the members' behavior of avoiding the issue or only hinting at its existence. These group properties are often interactive. As group cohesion develops, the norms of the group may change and may thus allow for discussion of formerly taboo areas. Honest discussion of these issues may lead to an increase in a sense of group cohesion.

One of the stronger norms of behavior in our society (as noted in preceding chapters) is the requirement that anger is not expressed directly. It can be dangerous to express anger openly. Also, rules of politeness requires that it be suppressed, or if it is expressed, that this be done indirectly and according to certain generally acceptable rules. As staff members join a staff group, they bring with them a number of cultural ideas, such as this norm against the strong expression of anger. In effect, there is a social prohibition, resulting from convention or tradition, that forbids direct expression of anger.

The existence of this norm of behavior and of the associated taboo must, once again, be inferred from the behavior of group members. If expression of anger is suppressed, group members who violate the norm may find themselves subject to group sanctions or punishments that are used to enforce the group's rules of behavior. For example, the silent treatment, in which colleagues ignore a staff member, can send a powerful message. Although the rules are not formally codified (that is, written down for all to see), these informal norms of behavior can nonetheless be immensely powerful, and they can cause potent problems. In any close relationship, it must be expected that frictions will generate anger. If the anger is suppressed, so will be other important emotions such as caring. It is not possible to select which feelings will be experienced. Unexpressed negative feelings will go under the surface and emerge in indirect forms of all kinds, including apathy, competitiveness, lack of cooperation, and the burnout syndrome.

One function of a group culture is to provide some certainty about how people will behave. For example, the norm that our personal concerns should not be shared with every acquaintance, but rather reserved for more intimate friends, protects us from inappropriate intimacy. The norm against unhindered expression of negative feelings helps keep the social interaction reasonably lubricated. Group norms may be positive and supportive, such as those that rally support for colleagues experiencing traumatic personal difficulties.

The difficulty with group norms occurs when they block productive cooperation. In such a situation, the norm does not contribute to the development of a culture for work; rather, it generates obstacles to oppose effective collaboration. All staff groups have group norms that reflect the general societal norms, and problems will inevitably occur. It is the supervisor's job to identify these obstacles, bring them to the attention of staff members, and then help them develop new norms or rules that are more conducive to effective work.

When a group leader becomes more knowledgeable about the properties of his or her informal and formal staff groups and is able to interpret behavior as evidence of these properties, then a striking change in perception takes place. The staff group leader is able to observe individual members of the group while simultaneously noting the group as a whole. In the model of social work practice with groups described elsewhere (Shulman, 1992), this group organism is called the "second client." Although the staff group is not literally a client of the supervisor, group leadership involves helping the staff to build and strengthen this group as a whole.

Thus, as has been noted, the supervisor is responsible for monitoring not only the content of the work in the group but also the process—the group's way of working. This task of the supervisor involves a constant attempt to train the staff group to help it develop a more functional group culture. Supervisors often find this a difficult role. Their first line of defense is to point out that it is time consuming and that they are always hard pressed simply to get through the day's business. Closer examination of this rationale indicates that even though most of them really are hard pressed, some of the pressures they undergo result from work that they have to do in response to the strains created by a poor group culture. They spend a good deal of their time intervening to straighten out conflicts between staff members, each of whom may have come to the supervisor upset and angry but refusing to speak about the problem with the other member. Instead of moving into conflict after conflict, the supervisor can save time by trying to change the group culture that causes all conflicts to end up on his or her desk. (This process will be illustrated later in the section on conflicts.)

Most supervisors agree that much of their energy goes into dealing with problems that might not occur or that could be handled by the staff members themselves if the group culture were different. The real reason why this work is difficult for them may be that they are also products of the general societal culture, and the norms and taboos are just as powerful for them as for their staff members. It is not that they cannot see the negative impact of the culture on their staff's work; rather, they are afraid of what might happen if they tackle the question. The current problems and the illusion of work, although frustrating, are safe. Once supervisors recognize that they have a stake in maintaining the status quo of the current culture, they make a first step in preparing themselves to take a risk to improve the effectiveness of the group. The following example illustrates how a supervisor challenged the illusion of work to improve the work group culture.

Boring Staff Meeting

One of the most common complaints of supervisors is that they get bored at staff meetings, even meetings they are chairing. They can see that the workers are bored, too, so they may simply lower their heads and try to plough through their agendas quickly. A boring staff meeting is always an indirect signal of an issue or problem. It may be that the topic for discussion is not relevant to the workers, or the topic may be so relevant that it is strongly affecting staff members in an area they find difficult to discuss.

In the following excerpt from a record of a staff meeting in a residential setting, the apparently simple discussion of time tables and division of labor took too long and kept getting interrupted:

> Sue felt the evening shift should not have to pull so many weekend duties. Jill disagreed and felt they should all pull equal weekend duty. I pointed out that was the fourth time we had gone around this, and we didn't seem to be getting any closer to consensus. I asked if anyone had any ideas. Chris said we should really tie down the training program for next week, because there was not much time left. A number of the group members nodded in agreement. Alice started to make a long, rambling statement about training philosophy and goals, and I could see people looking as if they were thinking "Here she goes again." After a few minutes of this, I felt as bored and frustrated as they looked.
>
> I finally decided to challenge them. I said, "This meeting is getting boring, and I don't think we are getting anywhere!" People looked up at my comment and a number of heads were shaking. I continued: "It started to get boring when we were going around in circles on the weekend issue, and then the subject was changed. Can we get back to the weekend issue? How come we weren't getting anywhere and no one seemed ready to budge?"
>
> There was a silence, and Jill said, with feeling, that she was sick and tired of evening staff asking for more privileges. As far as she was concerned, they had it cushy as it was. There was a stunned silence. I said (feeling considerably less confident than I projected): "Good! Now it's out in the open; let's deal with it." The argument began with Jill leading one side and Sue the other. Each group of staff members thought the other had it easier. Evening staff felt the day staff had time when the residents were at school or attending other programs and could therefore take care of things that they often left for the evening staff to pick up on. The reverse feeling was true, with day staff figuring it was a breeze to handle residents at night—they just watched TV and then went to sleep. These feelings had been festering for a while without being openly revealed. As I thought back, there had been hints at meetings, sarcastic cracks or jokes, and certain important tasks consistently falling between the cracks, with neither side doing a thing.

I listened for a while, intervening if it got too hot, to say things like, "I know you're angry, but can you say it in a way the others can hear?" After some ventilation, I pointed out that there were two distinct camps in the group and that each seemed to feel the other did not understand how tough their part of the work was. I wondered if we might break the log jam by talking about this a bit: Could the evening and the day staff educate each other a bit? Each group began to identify their special problems as I tried to help the others listen.

I pointed out after it was over that they all appeared to have a tough job, and that might be why they end up getting mad at the others. There was some agreement with this. I asked if there were any reasonable steps we could take to make everyone's job a bit easier. I recognized that I had my work to do as well, in getting administration to understand their pressures more clearly. A number of staff members started to come up with suggestions for minor yet important changes.

The evasion of work evident in the boredom that characterized this group was a signal to the supervisor that a difficult issue was at hand. The norm against direct confrontation between people who had to work together was strong for these members. They could not make progress on the scheduling question because the real issue was lurking just beneath the surface.

When group members are close to an important issue, they may choose to avoid discussing it by using the mechanisms described in psychoanalytic terms as *fight/flight* (Bion, 1961). In this example, flight behavior involved a group member's taking the role of leading the group into flight from the real, but frightening, discussion. In other situations, discussion of emotional matters may lead a group to avoid the pain through the mechanism of fight: Two or more group members will confront each other and argue rather than face the strong emotions they have in common.

By challenging the illusion of work, the supervisor signaled that she wanted "real talk." When one of the members accepted the invitation, the supervisor quickly credited her, sending a reinforcing message to the rest of the group. The culture of work underwent a change here by the very process of ignoring the taboo and entering the formerly prohibited area. After the discussion was over, the supervisor moved to deal directly with the question of the culture of work.

I asked them if we could spend a few minutes talking about what had happened at this meeting. I pointed out that we were afraid to deal with an issue that involved angry feelings and that, as a result, we were going around in circles. When we finally had the courage to get it out in the open, it turned out to be very helpful, and we made some good steps.

I asked them what they thought about what I had just said. Leslie said she had had these feelings for a long time and was afraid to say anything. I asked why, and she told us she didn't want to make things worse between the two shifts; it was bad enough already. I asked if others felt the same way, and there was some discussion of fear of confrontation. I told them I could understand their fears, because I had them as well. In addition, I did not think we needed to confront each other all the time—I wasn't sure I could take it. They all laughed in agreement.

I went on to say that this was a good example of something that had to be dealt with, and I hoped that next time they had an issue like this, they would raise it directly. I would be glad to help them if they felt uncertain about bringing it out in the open themselves. I thought we could handle it, and it was the responsibility of all of them to get these issues on the table where we could handle them, rather than simply complaining in the coffee room all the time. There was general agreement with my comments.

Throughout the life of this staff group there would be many times when they could not be honest. Although feelings of anger were one taboo, an even stronger taboo prevented sharing of some of the stronger feelings of sadness and pain related to their work. When the supervisor pointed this out, another discussion was necessary.

In effect, the supervisor helps the staff group learn how it operates in its milieu. Both the general group themes, such as the difficulties of confronting members or of sticking to the topic, as well as the specific group themes, or problems related to their particular work, are explored. The example described here is only the beginning of the educational process as staff members are taught how to take responsibility for their group activities.

Individual in the Group

Although the group culture affects the functioning of particular work groups, the individual members also bring their personalities to bear in their group interactions. The concept of role describes how individual personality is translated into group interaction. Various individuals in the group may take the roles of deviant member, internal leader, quiet member, or scapegoat, for example. This section examines the roles of these individual members, while stressing that it is usually impossible to understand individual behavior without considering it in the dynamic context of group interaction.

The concept of role in a dynamic system that is presented in this section draws from the work of Ackerman (1958) for a definition of role and from Lewin (1935) for a conception of the group as a dynamic system. Ackerman defined social role as "synonymous with the operations of the 'social self' or social identity of the person in the context of a defined life situation" (p. 53). He suggested that individuals have a private inner self and a social outer self that emphasizes the externally oriented aspects of their personalities. For this discussion, the crucial idea is that each individual brings to the staff group a particular pattern of social activity, the outer self, that may differ in part from his or her real inner self.

Lewin, often referred to as the Father of Group Dynamics, established the need to consider the activities of each member of a dynamic group in terms of his or her reactions to the activities of other members. It is not possible to understand the activity of a part of a group without seeing it in the context of the activity of the whole.

In summary, the behavior of any member of a dynamic group must be seen, at least in part, as the expression of the individual's social role in relation to the activities of others. This principle applies in the following examples of a deviant group member, an internal leader, a quiet member, and a scapegoat.

Deviant Member

The term *deviant* is not used here in a narrow, pathological sense but refers to any group member who exhibits a pattern of deviating sharply from the normal group behavior. The example cited most often in workshops for supervisors is the staff member who is always griping and complaining, who constantly takes pot shots at the supervisor, and who seems to lack enthusiasm and commitment. The supervisor may lament, "If only I didn't have Jim in my staff group, it would be very cooperative." This deviant member is experienced as an "enemy."

If such staff members were not seen as entities separate from the interactive process in the group, they would be regarded in a different light. When staff members feel negatively about issues in the system, for example, but do not feel completely free to share their feelings, they may "elect" a deviant member to play the role of expressing the feelings of the group as a whole. The election is not formal: More often than not, after a session in which a member has pressed a point that the supervisor may not have wanted to hear or deal with, another staff member privately expresses support, perhaps by saying, "Nice going; it needed to be said." In a subtle, even unconscious way, the group is cultivating one of its members to play an important functional role.

The staff member who accepts the assignment of deviant member is usually one who plays this role in other situations as well and thus fits Ackerman's (1935) notion of a social role. For a number of reasons, the deviant member feels the urgency of the concern strongly. Thus, the deviant member's behavior is partly a function of his or her social role and partly a response to the dynamics of the group.

Deviant behavior can be considered a communication in which the deviant member is speaking to the supervisor for the staff group. If the supervisor really wants honest communications from the group, therefore, the deviant member can be considered the supervisor's ally instead of the enemy. Striking evidence of this dynamic process may be observed if the deviant staff member leaves the group (quits or is fired). Almost instantly, a formerly more quiet and apparently cooperative member will assume the role of deviant member. The role is thus a functional necessity for the group, and someone must fill it. If the supervisor could allow the staff to raise all issues directly, even controversial ones, the group would have no more need for the deviant member.

The following report illustrates a common response to a deviant group member. The supervisor reacted defensively and attempted to use the group to suppress the deviant:

> I had explained the meaning of the cutbacks, why our department had to take its share, and had asked the staff if they could come up with some ideas of how to make do with less and still maintain our service. I pointed out I knew it would not be easy. During my explanation, Frank had sat with a smirk on his face, as if to say, "Here it comes." I knew he was angry, so I just avoided his look.
>
> A few people asked some questions, there was some silence, then Lou made a suggestion for a minor cutback in his area. I said I thought that was a helpful start. Frank jumped in and said he thought the discussion was a waste of time. I was angry at his cutting off what I thought was a beginning at a hard job. I said, "I'm sorry you feel that way, Frank. It's not a very constructive attitude. I don't think you are being helpful, and I am sure the others in the department feel the same way." Lou said, "I don't like this either, Frank, but we are just going to have to live with it." Frank was quiet for the remainder of the discussion, which, although lethargic, did produce some suggestions.

By cutting off the discussion in response to Frank's comment, the supervisor prevented the staff group from expressing their real feelings about the cutback. They would have to wait until they were in the coffee room, when the supervisor was not present, to let Frank know that they really agreed with him. Contrast this with a follow-up meeting in which the supervisor tried to catch his mistake and pick up on the meaning of Frank's outburst:

> I began by saying, "I don't think we really leveled at the last meeting. When Frank said the discussion was a waste of time, I felt on the spot, so I put him off. I didn't admit how uncomfortable the whole idea of talking to you about the cuts had made me. I suspect many of you probably agreed with Frank. Is that true?"
>
> Loraine said she thought across-the-board cuts were unfair. The fact is, many other departments had fat in them, we all knew it, and yet each department was being treated equally in the cuts. I was surprised by how strongly she said this, obviously very upset.
>
> Joan jumped in and said she thought they were being penalized for having done a good job of cutting to the bone last year. There was no recognition of the particular impact that across-the-board cuts would have on us, as compared with other departments. If the administrator had any guts, he would set a procedure for evaluating exactly where the cuts should go, instead of this across-the-board bull.
>
> As Joan was speaking, I was beginning to wonder what I had opened up and how I was going to deal with it. I shared that with staff, and Lou suggested that we might be able to make a case, if given the chance, that

this cut was unfair. He asked if I would consider setting up a meeting with the administrator. I told him I could do that, although I didn't know if it would help. After all, we had to realize he was also under pressure from other departments. Frank said, "That's what he gets paid for!" We all laughed, and I said, "And I guess that goes for me too."

This second session not only allowed the staff members to vent their feelings, but it also let them see that there was something they could do about the problem. The strength of the staff members strengthened the supervisor to pursue this issue further, particularly because he fully agreed with them. Chapter 10 discusses the strategies and skills involved in attempting to negotiate between a staff and the administration.

Another common example of the deviant as an ally is given in the following excerpt. The supervisor tried to make sense of the indirect cues of a staff member who had missed staff meetings, usually came late, and often sat in the corner, staring out the window or pointedly reading his mail. The supervisor's first reaction was to want to give the staff member a boot in the derriere. Instead, he attempted to address the message behind the behavior by using a staff meeting to start to deal with it:

About halfway through the meeting, I said I wanted to talk about Terry's participation in the meeting. I did not want to put him on the spot, but I did feel his continual lateness, lack of interest, and lack of involvement was probably saying something to me about his feelings about the meeting. I asked if I was right. He paused, then said he frankly found the meetings a waste of his time. I told him that as the person responsible for our staff meetings, I did not like to hear that—but that I could see how it might be a waste for him and others as well. There were times I didn't find it useful and felt like I would read my mail too, only I had to chair the damn thing. The group members laughed. I asked if others felt the same as Terry, because then maybe we should discuss what's wrong with the meetings and how to improve them.

The rest of the discussion revolved around their lack of interest in many of the agenda items, their feeling that the discussion was often superficial, and their opinion that they did not get into their practice enough. Terry, who was very much involved in this discussion, revealed that he was having problems with a particular case and needed some help. As is often the case, the group member who seems most unhappy about the meetings may be sitting there with an urgent problem to be addressed. Rather than wanting the meetings eliminated, this member desperately needed to have them enhanced.

Another common example of a deviant member raising issues for the group comes from the context of a nursing group on a ward. The staff complement was short, the beds were full, and the pressure on all staff members was heavy. One fairly recent nursing school graduate was having tremendous difficulty handling her responsibilities and was beginning to disappear for a time when things got hectic on the ward. This made the other staff members angry, and a staff discussion resulted. The supervisor was able to help the new nurse share how overwhelmed she was (she cried as she spoke) and then to help the other members express their sense of being overly burdened. In addition to providing a catharsis for all staff members, the discussion turned to how they could help each other in times of stress, as well as how to communicate the problems to administration. The deviant member in the informal system was playing a functional role for the group as a whole.

In large, complex systems such as hospitals, entire departments may play the deviant role for the system as a whole. For example, staffs in surgery, emergency, and intensive care, because of the special stresses of their jobs, often become the first departments to signal to the whole hospital the extent of a stress-related problem. In a child welfare agency, it may be the emergency services or investigations unit that plays this role. This notion of a department, agency, and the like as playing the deviant member role is explored in more detail in chapter 9, which deals with the impact of trauma on staff.

Internal Leader

The supervisor is the external leader of the group because he or she carries the authority that comes with the role and is granted by the system. In contrast, the internal leader is a staff member (or several members) who emerges through the group process and who helps the group tackle important developmental tasks, as well as deal with its business. As seen in the previous section, when the internal leader confronts the supervisor or raises issues that the supervisor may want to avoid, the internal leader may be perceived by the supervisor as a deviant member. This internal leader can be an important ally for the supervisor.

When supervisors feel insecure in their role, they often see the internal leader as challenging their leadership. This is a misunderstanding of the ways in which groups work. All groups develop internal leaders, regardless of how effective the external leader may be. They are functionally necessary; they help develop the emotional function of the group (for example, expressions of group caring for members under stress), as well as the task completion functions (for example, getting jobs organized). Although the supervisor may provide an external demand and may be a source of real support, in a well-functioning staff group, peer support and peer demand are also indispensable elements. Rather than seeing internal leaders as competitors, supervisors should be grateful for all the help they can get.

Quiet Group Member

Supervisors often express concern about members who never or rarely speak in group meetings, even if it is obvious that such a member is listening and is involved in the transactions. The usual techniques for involving quiet members often end up making things worse. Examples include going around the table, asking everyone for opinions, just to get the quiet member to speak; turning to the quiet member and directly asking for his or her opinion; or, even worse, asking the quiet member to chair a portion of the meeting. Most of the procedures are easily recognized by both the quiet member and the rest of the staff, and they often result in acute embarrassment. As one quiet member said, "When I'm put on the spot that way, even if I do have something to say, it flies right out of my mind."

It is important to recognize that there is nothing wrong with some staff members participating more than others in group discussions. A member can be actively involved without saying much at all. On the other hand, those who are always silent, and perhaps have been silent in group meetings all their lives, may begin to feel embarrassed about not contributing. In addition, those who speak a great deal may begin to wonder if they are being judged for what they say or if the others would like them to simply keep quiet.

A supervisor can be helpful to both groups, but the help has to be direct and supportive. An example is the following discussion between a supervisor and a new staff member who had not said anything at all while attending four staff meetings in a row. The supervisor stopped this member, Mary, in the hall after the fourth meeting, and this private discussion took place:

> Supervisor: I just wanted to check to see how you have been finding the staff meetings. I noticed you haven't said very much, but you are obviously interested. I thought I'd see how it was going.
> Mary: I know I should be speaking up more, but, frankly, I feel a bit intimidated because I'm so new.
> Supervisor: I think we all know how that feels.
> Worker: Actually, I don't speak too much in groups anyway. I just finished two years at social work school, and I don't think I said a word in class unless I was asked a question. By the time I was in my second year, I was afraid to say anything. I thought all of the other students would fall out of their seats if they heard my voice.
> Supervisor (laughing): Seriously, though, are you feeling a bit of that here, too? [Worker nods.] Look, you can take your time getting into the discussion, but obviously, after a while, if you don't speak at all it will make others uncomfortable. They may feel they are risking their ideas while you're just sitting back in judgment. If you like, I can help by watching for you, and if you want to get into the discussion but the action is going too fast, or you're a bit unsure, just give me a signal and I'll help you in. I won't do it, unless you give me the signal. How does that sound?
> Mary: Thanks, I may take you up on that.

During the next staff meeting, the worker sat absolutely still, obviously taking great pains to make sure she did not accidentally give a signal. At the next session, midway through a heated discussion on an issue of which Mary had some special knowledge, she nodded to the supervisor, who interrupted the flow of discussion and said, "Did you have something to say, Mary?", and the ice was broken. Although Mary did not become the most vocal member of the discussion, she did enter it more frequently, sometimes using the supervisor's help, at other times on her own.

In situations in which those who speak a great deal are concerned about talking too much, the supervisor can be helpful by opening up a discussion of how the staff group operates. In the following example, the supervisor picked up on the hint and reached for the real feelings behind it:

> Louise: Well, I've been talking enough about this; let someone else speak for a while.
>
> Supervisor: Louise, are you really feeling you talk too much in this group? Because if you are, let's talk about that for a moment. [Louise nods.] What are you worried about?
>
> Louise: Well, a lot of people sit around saying nothing at these meetings, and I figure they must be thinking, "Why doesn't she shut up?" or maybe they are thinking I'm just running off at the mouth and sounding dumb. Last week I decided to just keep quiet for a whole meeting, but I couldn't make it.
>
> Supervisor: How about it, you quieter members, how do you feel about Louise's participation. [Silence.]
>
> Terry: Frankly, Louise, I'm glad you have the guts to get into the discussion. I'm often sitting here thinking similar things, but I'm afraid to say them. I kind of figure it's easier to keep quiet.
>
> Supervisor: . . . and let Louise say it? [Terry nods.]
>
> Sam: I'm one of the quiet ones. It's not that I'm not interested or think you guys are saying dumb things—actually, you're often right on. I have always had a hard time speaking in groups, since I was a kid, and this one is no different.
>
> Supervisor: Even speaking right now was tough for you? [Sam nods.] Look, I think people participate differently in groups, depending on their own patterns. I don't believe others resent your participation, Louise; I think most envy you. On the other hand, if the same people always have to carry the ball, then we get input from only a part of the group, and I think that deprives us of a source of help. After a while, I bet people like Louise will feel a bit used by the group and want something in return. [Louise nods vigorously.] Can we agree to allow some to speak more than others but that everyone takes some responsibility to contribute in some way? [All group members nod at this comment.] Actually, I think you have all made a great start by being so honest about your feelings.

Scapegoat

To understand the dynamics of the scapegoating process, it is helpful to consider the origin of the idea. The scapegoat is derived from an ancient

Hebrew ritual each year, when on the Day of Atonement the chief priest would symbolically lay the sins of the people on the back of a goat (the scape) and then drive the goat into the wilderness. This symbolized the ritual cleansing of the sins of the people. In a like manner, when a group scapegoats one of its members, the members usually attack the aspect of the scapegoat—the sins—that they most dislike in themselves. The supervisor can consider this a form of communication of the group members' feelings about themselves.

This process is familiar to those who work with families (Shulman, 1967). The child in the family who is in the most trouble often turns out to be a family scapegoat, signaling to the community a problem in the family. If this child is seen as the problem and perhaps placed in a residence or foster home, another child may assume the role. This will continue until the real problems in the family dynamics are addressed.

Understanding scapegoating as a dynamic process can help supervisors avoid a common mistake—identifying either with the staff against the scapegoat or with the scapegoat against the staff. Either position cuts the supervisor off from being able to help in the dynamic interaction between the two. If the mediating function is truly integrated by the supervisor, it is possible to identify with both the scapegoated individual and the group at the same time. Then the supervisor can pay attention to what Schwartz (1979) called, in the practice context, the two clients—the individual and the group.

In the following example from my own teaching practice, a group discussion was taking place on a sensitive topic. This particular student group had been together during the previous year in a two-year program. As the students explored their feelings, Len began to theorize about practice in an abstract manner; he appeared to be trying to impress the group with his understanding of different points of view. This group had been meeting under other leadership for a time, and this pattern was a long-standing one. Whenever Len began to intellectualize and theorize, the group members sent out all sorts of nonverbal cues of displeasure, as if to say, "Here he goes again." I had noticed the pattern in my first few weeks with the group and had simply ignored it, but I decided that this week, if it happened again, I would challenge it. My recording noted the following:

> I stopped the discussion and pointed out what had just happened—Len started to theorize just as we got to the emotions, and the group was obviously displeased by this but was not saying so directly. I said it seemed to be a pattern in this group, and I felt we should get it out in the open. I asked what was going on. There was a long silence, which I waited out. Then Ian said, with much feeling, that Len always did this, all last year; he always intellectualized instead of dealing with feelings. Len looked taken aback by the comment, so I offered some support. I said, "I know it's tough to hear this, Len, but try to stay with it for a minute or two; I think it can be important." Others joined the discussion, starting to list all of Len's

faults. He was intellectual, cold, clinical, and so forth, a typical "professional." The affect was anger, and the word *professional* was uttered almost as a curse.

After listening for a while, monitoring Len, who seemed to be painfully taking things in, I asked the group members why they were so angry at Len. I said, "So he intellectualizes, theorizes, seems to be cold, and so on. Why are you so mad at him for that? Maybe that's just Len." There was a period of silence, and then Theresa said, "You know, all those things you just described, that's what I'm worried my training here at school is doing to me. I'm beginning to worry if I'm also becoming too professional."

I said that was honest, and hard to say, and asked if anyone else worried about that at times. A dam seemed to burst loose as they entered the discussion about their previous experiences, how they had come to school feeling good about some of their natural talents and then had started to wonder, as they read all the theories, if they had just been naive. Others commented how they were finding themselves analyzing everyone, their clients, their friends, even their families. They were getting the feeling other people were not really enjoying hearing all of their insights. The core of the discussion was that they were troubled about how to integrate personal self and professional self, especially when so many of the theories seemed to split the two.

I enquired how Len was doing during the discussion, and he nodded and indicated they should continue. I tried to take some time to put their concerns into perspective, to normalize them as appropriate for this stage in their educational development. After further discussion, I complimented them on what I thought was a crucial piece of work which, if they noticed, we would never have discussed if we kept simply being angry at Len for the very qualities we didn't like in ourselves.

In this part of the discussion, I had uncovered the group's real feelings communicated to me through the attacks on Len. I was not sure what they might mean when I started the process, which is why I was nervous about opening things up, but, with my help, the strength of the group came through beautifully. There was more work to do, however, because we still had Len sitting there through all of this. The group needed a scapegoat because they had trouble handling difficult feelings directly. But why had Len volunteered to play the role? I turned to Len at this point.

I asked Len how all of this discussion had been hitting him. I said it probably was not easy to hear some of the things they said about him, even though they admitted they had the same problems. Len sighed, and then he said they were right in accusing him of being intellectual and not dealing with emotion. He said he had discovered that being too emotional wasn't always such a good idea.

I asked if he could share why that was so with the class. After another long pause, he described a 16-year-old boy he had been working with during his last practicum, a boy who had been on the street for a while after being kicked out of his own home and every residential center in town. Len described how he had befriended the boy, gotten really close to him, and even thought he was getting somewhere. He continued, with some bitterness in his voice: "Sure, I dealt with his feelings, I helped him to open up, he even cried one night with me. But two weeks later he killed himself."

The group and I sat in shocked silence as Len started to cry. I said I thought they probably wanted to reach out to Len. Rose crossed the room and sat next to Len, putting her arm around him. Others in the room, including myself, were showing the emotions we felt at the moment. After a while I said I thought Len had just shared a big hurt with us, one he had kept inside all of last year. It would help a lot to understand why it might be easier for him to equate professional with intellectual. I wondered if there was any help they could give Len on this, in addition to the obvious support they were expressing.

A number of students revealed similar experiences with clients, describing how they felt as Len did, responsible and guilty, and how they had to work those feelings through to get things into perspective. The theme of the discussion was that one always wonders if one could have done more but that one tends to be too hard on oneself. As they were talking to Len, I felt they were all talking to themselves as well, and I said this to them. I pointed out how easy it would be to close up our feelings when faced with such hard emotions.

The session was over by that time, and I congratulated the group and Len on some very hard work. I suggested we continue on this discussion of professional and personal and their sense of responsibility next time.

The key to helping effectively in all of the individual–group situations described here—with the deviant, quiet, or scapegoated member or the internal leader—is in searching out the connection between the individual (the one) and the group (the many). This is what Schwartz (1979) described in his theory as searching out the common ground. In the earlier example, although the differences between Len and the group appeared obvious, with a little faith (perhaps I should say a lot of faith) and some willingness to take a risk, I was able to identify the more powerful areas of common ground. This is not so different from the practice skill of learning to find areas of mutuality when clients often see only the obstacles that keep them apart. This same task for the supervisor, to search out the common ground, is crucial in dealing with conflicts, which is the topic of the next section, and in negotiating the system, the topic chapter 10.

Conflict in the Group

One of the most difficult issues for supervisors to handle in the formal or informal group is conflict. In the typical example, one worker approaches the supervisor with a complaint about another: "He doesn't pull his share of the load" or "She just sits and drinks coffee all the time" or "I know my staff are only clerical workers and he's professional staff, but that doesn't give him the right to treat us like dirt!" These are the moments that most supervisors dread, particularly when their suggestion that the staff member talk directly to the other person meets with a response like "I couldn't do that" or "I've already tried, but he just won't listen" or "That's what you get paid for!" The problem is compounded when the supervisor agrees to talk to the offender to see what can be done, and the worker says, "But don't tell him I said anything." When the supervisor inquires why not, the response is often "I have to have coffee with her every day." The supervisor is thus being asked to accept the task of speaking to an offending staff member without divulging where the information was obtained and then to "straighten out" that member.

It is not so surprising that staff members ask supervisors to do this; what is surprising is the fact that so many supervisors agree to try. In terms of the functional role of the supervisor as a mediator, which has been developed in this book, it is possible to redefine the supervisor's tasks at a point of conflict and make them more manageable. In addition, the supervisor can place responsibility for helping to deal with problems more firmly on the staff members themselves. In implementing this role, however, a number of principles must be followed.

First, the personal relationships between staff members are their own business. Whether members of a staff group choose to become friends is completely up to them, although working near people who share problems, tasks, and feelings often leads to the deepest friendships. Many workers look forward to Friday afternoon sessions with coworkers at the pub when they wrap up their week and prepare for the weekend. However, it is not necessary to be friends to work effectively together. Constructive communal work can be done by people whose relationships to one another range on a continuum from strong friendship to antipathy. It is not the supervisor's business to deal with the staff's friendship patterns, but it is very much the supervisor's role to deal with interpersonal relationships as they affect the delivery of services to clients. Thus, dealing with staff conflict in the informal system is an essential part of the job.

Second, the supervisor makes a mistake by taking on the role of judge, arbitrator, confidant, or ally in conflicts between staff. There are times when a supervisor may have to play such roles, as when there is no way for the staff to resolve strong differences and, for the sake of continuity of service, the supervisor must take a stand. But if the supervisor accepts responsibility for "solving" all the group's problems, even if the staff asks for this, so much of the supervisor's energies will be spent in this area of work that little time will be left for other vital tasks.

Instead of defining their role as solving problems, supervisors should define it as helping staff members develop the abilities to solve their own problems. Thus, they will be building into the group culture valuable self-correcting mechanisms that will help the staff to work effectively together, particularly at points of conflict, in mature and responsible ways. In this sense, each conflict becomes not only an instance of substantive work but also an opportunity to develop staff skills and a sense of personal responsibility for effective working relationships. When supervisors invest time in this role, it can significantly decrease the number of problems that are dumped in their laps.

A third principle is that the supervisor should not get sidetracked in dealing with the content of a complaint (although it may be important in its own right) and instead should pay close attention to the process of the encounter. All efforts should be made to bring the conflicting parties together, eventually at least, so they can work on the problems themselves.

The following example suggests a technique for implementing these principles. The setting is the emergency room in a medium-size hospital in a rural area. A new nurse was needed for a particular role in the emergency room, and Marie was hired from outside the hospital. She had strong general training, but although she had recently taken a refresher course in emergency room work, she had little actual experience there. Two current staff members had coveted the job and had more experience, but because of their level of training, they had lost out. They had feelings about the matter. In addition, Marie was French Canadian, and she was coming to an area of Canada where everyone did not welcome people from Quebec. After her arrival it was also clear that she had a language problem and spoke only halting English.

The first weeks were predictably difficult, and many of the staff came to the supervisor with complaints. After a number of these, the supervisor spoke to Marie:

> Supervisor: I was wondering how things were going now that you have been here for a while.
> Nurse (Marie): There are no problems. I still have a lot to learn, but I'll get there.
> Supervisor: Don't you think that being so new to the job, and having so little experience, there might be some ways I could help you—some techniques you could brush up on—you know what I mean?
> Marie: Why are you asking? Have I made some mistakes? I thought I was doing okay.
> Supervisor: Well, there are a few things we can work on when I get some time. [The nurse nods in agreement and the conversation is over.]

When this supervisor brought up this example at a supervisory workshop, she admitted she had not been direct about the problems the staff were bringing her because she was too embarrassed. In the discussion it became clear that she was trying to lead Marie to accept that there were problems. The supervisor had not addressed the issues, brought up the feelings of the other staff, or mentioned the language problem. When the consultant noted that Marie must have been feeling unhappy about how things had gone, the supervisor said she had sensed that but had not acknowledged Marie's feelings because, she said, "I guess I'm really angry at her myself." Her honesty was credited when she pointed out she had really preferred one of the other staff members who had been turned down for the job. When the consultant pointed out that in part she would probably be just as happy if Marie failed, she agreed and then said, "But I would feel lousy if she did, because I know it's my job to try to help."

The fact that this supervisor brought up the example probably meant she really wanted to help. It was a good example of a supervisor identifying with one side in a problem and not being able to help with the interaction. If Marie was going to make it in the job, given her inexperience and language problems, she would need all the help she could get from the supervisor and the other nurses. The task might be too great, and she might not be able to meet the requirements, but at least all of them would know that she had had a fair chance. The supervisor agreed that, in spite of her feelings, she wanted to do her job properly

The workshop group then did some preparation on how to deal first with the staff and then with the nurse in this conflict. They began by role playing how the supervisor would handle the staff members' next complaint. The focus was on being supportive to the staff but at the same time making a demand for them to take some responsibility in the process. In the role play, Lillian took the part of the next nurse to voice a complaint:

Nurse (Lillian): Look, something has to be done about Marie. We had a man in this morning, and when I tried to get her to help she just froze. [Fran, another nurse, agrees.]

Supervisor: Can you describe what happened?

Lillian: Well, I shouted to her to get some things I needed immediately, and she hesitated and seemed to go blank.

Supervisor: What did you do then?

Lillian: Well, I blew my top and told her she was next to useless.

Supervisor: You must have been feeling under pressure to get so upset. Probably, when you shouted at her that way, she got more frozen.

Lillian: That's what happened! I'm afraid it could lead to a serious problem if she stays around here.

Supervisor: Look, we know she may not be up to snuff, and perhaps she will have to leave eventually, but frankly, we probably haven't given her a fair chance. We were really against her from the start, and she must have sensed that. Most of us didn't want her, and I'm sure she has gotten that message from us. No wonder she freezes up.

Fran: Maybe that's true, but now we can't do anything about that— and she is just not working out.

Supervisor: I think it's time we had this out in the open. All of you come to me with your complaints and won't share them directly with Marie. She knows you're upset with her, but it's all under the surface. Maybe if we could discuss it honestly, it might clear the air. I could try to be more helpful in getting you to level with her about your expectations, and perhaps she could let us know what it's been like for her starting here. Maybe it won't help, but at least it's worth a try.

When a supervisor begins to make demands on the staff to play an honest and responsible role, as in this example, he or she must stay sensitive to the feelings of the staff. Precisely at this point resistance to the idea will emerge. Instead of ignoring the resistance, it is important for the supervisor to explore why it would be hard for the staff members to confront the isolated nurse.

In the supervisory workshop, the role play continued:

> Lillian: Maybe you're right about her tough start here, but I think because you're the supervisor, you should talk to her.
> Supervisor: Sounds like you're not too anxious to talk to her directly. Why not? Are you feeling uncomfortable about it?
> Fran: Of course, we are. I don't know about you, but that kind of directness scares me. If I say what's on my mind, I might get angry at her; she could get angry back, and who needs a blowup? You talk to her!
> Supervisor: I'm going to have to speak to her, to get things started, because I think I have to clear the air with how I started with her. But after that, I'm going to get us all together and ask all of you to start leveling. I think that's part of our responsibility, as hard as it is, as professional nurses, and I can't do it alone.

Lillian and Fran, who were role playing the other two nurses, did not look too happy about the decision, but they agreed they would have to follow up if the supervisor insisted. If a supervisor wants to help a staff member to talk directly to another, it sometimes helps to role play, asking what the staff member might say. A little practice, some support, and a push often make staff members more willing to take the next step of being honest. The key idea is that staff members should receive support and help when they are asked to do something that is admittedly difficult, such as handling a confrontation with a person in authority.

In this example, preparatory work also needed to be done in the workshop sessions to help the supervisor work with Marie, the outcast. In the role-playing preparation, the supervisor practiced confessing to Marie her feelings at the start, how she had felt she had not really been as helpful as she should have been, and how she wanted to try to make it up now. She role played, listening to Marie's side of the story, trying to understand and to express her empathy, and then making a demand on Marie to deal openly with the staff conflict.

When the workshop group tried to prepare for the eventual meeting between Marie and the staff group, it became apparent how fearful all the supervisors were about confrontation. They were afraid that anger might be unleashed, that people would say hurtful things they might later regret, and, most important, that they would not know what to do. As one put it, "It's really opening a can of worms!" Another responded, "I wonder what's more painful for everyone involved—having the can of worms open or just leaving the lid on. I don't know how much worse things could get."

The group speculated on how to introduce the session. Perhaps the supervisor could say something like this:

We know there have been many strains between Marie and the rest of you, and these first few weeks have been uncomfortable for everyone, myself included. However, I thought if we could get some of the problems out in the open, in a constructive manner, maybe we could find ways we can be supportive of each other and make this place easier to work in for all of us. We all know it's no picnic in the best of times, and with these added pressures, it's even rougher. I'm going to try to help you talk to—and, most important—listen to each other. I'll put my own two cents in as we go along. Who wants to start?

The group agreed there would be a silence, and the supervisor would need to wait for some moments, perhaps acknowledging that it was awkward, but then continue the demand. As the discussion began, it would be important not to stifle it (for example, "I wish you could say that without sounding so angry") because the feelings were real and would be part of the work. The supervisor would concentrate on the process (for example, "How are you doing, Marie? Is this getting tough to hear?" or "It seems all of you are feeling the emergency room pressure so much yourselves [that] you hardly have room for anyone else's feelings of pressure").

It would be important for the supervisor to help Marie convey the hurt, fear, and loneliness she must have felt as she started, an outsider in the hospital and probably also in the community. The other staff members needed to convey their real sense of disappointment at having been passed over for the job and perhaps their anger at the administration for not appreciating them. The supervisor agreed it was helpful to think it through in advance, but she admitted there were going to be times when she just did not know what to do. If she told the group members at that point that she did not know what to do, perhaps one of them could help.

The workshop group also anticipated that all might not work out well, particularly in this first session. In fact, the real impact of such a session might take some days as the thoughts and feelings were assimilated. The supervisor had to prepare for some ambiguity at the end of the session. Even if a sense of unfinished business prevailed, a start would have been made. The supervisor would also have to be alert to the impact of the language issue, a subject generally taboo in Canada.

The general model is the same, although the particular examples may differ: helping the night shift at a residential treatment center begin to deal frankly with the day shift, opening up communications between the clerical staff and professional social workers, helping those who crossed the picket lines and worked during a strike talk to those who did not, helping the registered nurses talk to the licensed practical nurses, and so on. A considerable amount of a supervisor's energy must be invested in helping staff members relate to each other effectively. Needed are courage to take the risk, skills to help it work well, and most of all, faith in the capacity of the staff to deal with hard problems if given enough support and demand. In any staff system, the supervisor will find that as in any intimate relationship (like marriage or parenting), conflict and caring go hand in hand.

AUTHORITY THEME: GROUP–SUPERVISOR RELATIONSHIPS

Although much of the preceding discussion has dealt with group member interactions, there is another major dynamic in staff groups. This involves the sensitive relationship between the supervisor and the group as a whole. Supervisors are conscious of being judged by their staff groups, although much of the communication in this area is indirect. Most supervisors have themselves been members of supervisory groups, and they are keenly aware that their strengths and weaknesses are common topics of informal group discussion.

A myth persists that good supervisors always have a positive relationship with their staff groups. Supervisors are told, "If you are effective, you will have no problems; if you have problems, you are ineffective." When the taboo on open communications by staff to the supervisor is combined with the myth of the perfect supervisor, powerful forces are at work that can easily block honest communications.

In essence, effective supervision, like effective practice, involves catching one's mistakes as quickly as possible. The skillful supervisor is not the one who has no problems but the one who can get the inevitable problems out in the open. The relationship between the supervisor and the staff, what Schwartz and Zalba (1971) referred to as the *authority theme*, is one that requires constant attention. This theme has a number of sub-themes, as was noted in earlier examples in chapter 3. These subthemes are (1) the question of control and power, (2) the supervisor as an outsider, (3) the supervisor as a source of support, (4) limitations of the supervisor, and (5) the supervisor as a source of demand. The examples selected to illustrate a number of these subthemes in this section use excerpts from group discussions between supervisors and staff groups.

Control and Power

The authority theme in supervision can be discussed in terms of specific issues of group leadership. One of the foremost questions on the minds of staff members is who "owns" the staff group. Most of their experiences with group leaders have led them to see the staff group as an instrument for the use of the supervisor. The selection of agenda items, the group discussion, and the conclusions all appear to be in the hands of the supervisor. As a result, staff participation is often reactive, with staff members taking little responsibility for the effectiveness of the meetings. It is as if the staff were saying, "If the supervisor owns the group, she or he can be responsible for how it works."

A number of ways that the supervisor can help the staff make the group their own have been suggested in preceding chapters. Sessional contracting at the start of each session is a skill that allows meetings to be used to explore the staff's sense of urgency, as well as the supervisor's agenda. The supervisor also can indicate a willingness to change the agenda and move into new areas if the needs of the staff shift during a session, or the supervisor can ask the staff to take responsibility for the way the members work together.

The following excerpt shows how a supervisor directly addressed the issue of responsibility for the group process:

> I explained that I had been unhappy at the way our last meeting had gone. I said that we were often getting off the track and that I, and everyone else, just let it happen. I told them I thought that this had happened a lot in meetings and wondered if they felt the same way.
>
> Chris agreed that we rambled a lot, and at times it was boring. I asked if others felt the same way, and they nodded. I asked why they didn't say anything when it happened. Terry said that I was leading the group, so why didn't I speak up? I admitted that it was my responsibility, and I guessed I just felt uncomfortable about interrupting, or at times I felt that we might finally get back to our discussion. By the time I realized we were getting nowhere, the meeting was almost over.
>
> Terry said that I should say something when this happened. I agreed, but asked why it had to be just me. I asked why they couldn't say something as well. I continued that I could use all the help I could get because sometimes I was confused and lost as well. Jean said she always thought that was the leader's job. She said she would usually sit there wondering if I were ever going to intervene. I said that I could understand that because I too had always said, "Let the leader do it." I told them that now that I was the leader, I realized it was important to have everyone take some responsibility for our sessions, not just me.
>
> I asked them if they could agree to be more active and responsible for how things went in the group sessions and that I would try as well. The group members nodded in agreement. Terry smiled and said, "Don't you think we have discussed this long enough and should move on?" We all laughed in acknowledgment of his quick acceptance of the new role.

Supervisor as an Outsider

Some of the most difficult feelings a supervisor must come to grips with are associated with the role as an outsider. Having come up through the ranks, perhaps in the same agency, and having experienced what the staff has gone through in his or her own practice, the supervisor may feel like a part of the team. In reality, however, a supervisor will never be an insider again. Once the supervisor moves one step beyond direct practice, the workers perceive him or her as different. A supervisor can partially overcome that feeling by using past experiences to tune in to the staff and to demonstrate a capacity for empathy. In the end, however, the supervisor remains the perpetual outsider.

The following excerpt is a segment of dialogue from a videotaped recording of a supervisor's staff group meeting that he had called to ask the staff to discuss his role. At the start of the meeting, he contracted clearly, pointing out he had been hearing many hints about his way of relating to them. After giving examples of what made this discussion necessary, he sat back to listen. The first staff responses evaded his question and instead focused on the practice issues embedded in his examples. After a few moments of listening, he made a demand for work by acknowledging their concerns on the practice issues but stressing that what he wanted to talk about was how he related to them when they brought those concerns to him. Because he repeated his request, the staff then understood that he really meant his invitation to talk directly about him and began to respond:

> Supervisor: For example, John, you came to me with a kid you couldn't place after you had tried all the resources, and I tried to come up with other resources and, failing that, told you not to feel so bad because others were having the same problem. I didn't get the feeling I really helped.
>
> John: You know, you're sitting there at the end of the day with this kid in your hands and no place to go. People say have you tried specialized resources, but you've already done that. The fact is, it's 5 P.M., you have the kid, there is no place to put him, and you're really all alone.
>
> Supervisor: And my trying to tell you not to feel so bad really doesn't help.
>
> John: You try hard to understand, and I know you were a worker too, but nobody, not even the supervisor, can understand what it feels like when you're stuck like that and all alone.
>
> Supervisor: I think I do sense your pain, but instead of just sharing it with you, I probably try to cheer you up, which is next to useless.

In this illustration, the supervisor effectively set the stage for the work. This conversation is continued in the next section on the supportive role of the supervisor.

Supervisor as a Source of Support

Even though the supervisor is an outsider, the staff wants and needs him or her to be a source of support when necessary. The ability of the supervisor to feel and express empathy is a crucial variable in determining whether supervision will be effective. The supervisor who genuinely empathizes with the worker provides a helping model of how to relate to clients. The following excerpt is from the same group:

> James: Sometimes, when I come to you with a big problem, I really

don't want to hear solutions; I just want to get the stuff cleared up in my head.

Supervisor: And that's when I usually start to try and give you answers to the problem—ideas, things you should try.

James: I'm going to need those ideas, and they are probably good ones, but right then I can't hear them. I know as you're talking I'm thinking, "Run those by me once again; maybe I'll understand this time." But it doesn't work, because I'm sitting there too upset. Maybe it's my fault, because if I come to you and ask for a solution, that's what I'll get.

Supervisor: It sure doesn't help if all you hear are answers when you're sitting there all upset with your feelings.

James: Don't get me wrong, you have changed a lot over the past three years—you're much better now on letting us know you feel for us. I guess I don't come right out and ask for your support because I'm not sure that's what supervision is all about. I mean, somewhere back there I heard you say that you weren't our counselor for personal problems, so when I'm feeling overwhelmed I'm not sure if that's personal and if I should bring it to you. I think that I should have that all together before I come to see you, that it's my job to work that stuff out and come in ready to work.

The discussion of the supervisor as a source of support leads indirectly into unresolved contract issues and provides the supervisor with an opportunity to clarify for the whole group that their feelings are part of the work. Although their feelings are personal, they are relevant to the supervision process when they are related to their work. It is interesting that the worker, James, was struggling with the problem of a split between what he thought he should feel (in control) and what he actually felt (overwhelmed). This discussion continues in the next section.

Supervisor's Limitations

The next excerpt, dealing with the supervisor's limitations, shows how the unresolved issue raised by James—the dichotomy between how we really feel and how we think we should feel—parallels the difficulty faced by the supervisor. So often, when staff members are having trouble doing something, it is the supervisor's problem as well:

Louise (speaking to the supervisor): How must you be feeling about all this? We seem to be putting a lot of responsibility on you to be there for us. Maybe there are times you wish we would just go away.

Supervisor: To be honest, there are times at the end of the day when I'm sitting there listening to you and feeling that I really don't have anything to offer you.

James: Do you ever say that?

Supervisor: Probably not.

John: But I can always tell. [Group members laugh.]

Louise: I guess we always expect you to have everything together, because you're the supervisor. You're not supposed to feel as overwhelmed as we do. You're supposed to come in always ready for work. We really do put a lot on you.

Supervisor: And I think I haven't been honest enough with you. I should just level when I don't have it for you; it would be better than just pretending.

John: I think we could appreciate that.

Simply discussing this problem in a nondefensive way can make a profound change in the culture of the group. The supervisor and the workers find that they can talk about a formerly taboo subject, be honest with each other, and thereby strengthen the relationship. The discussion is not over yet, however, because the supervisor will have to build in continued structures for maintaining the relationship. Staff members never "work through" the authority theme, never resolve it; they simply learn how to address a subject that will be with them, in one form or another, throughout their relationships.

This conversation between the supervisor and his staff went well because he already had a good relationship with the workers. It would have sounded very different if they did not trust him. However, his being "pretty good the past three years" had built up a fund of positive relationships on which he could draw. Fortunately, it does not take three years to do this.

Supervisor as a Source of Demand

All through this chapter the need for supervisors to make demands on their staff groups has been emphasized. They must push them to talk about uncomfortable subjects. They must dig for lurking negatives when the entire group conspires to evade honest discussion. They must insist that staff members take an active responsibility for group operations. After a while, all this pushing, digging, and insisting is bound to generate some hostility. Even if the supervisor has combined these demands with the kind of caring and support that builds a sound relationship and if the staff members understand that the demands are in their own interests, they naturally respond angrily. In fact, as has been noted, if staff groups never get angry at a supervisor, it is usually because that supervisor has not made enough demands.

This anger is hard for a supervisor, particularly a new supervisor, to take because the myth calls for a perpetually positive relationship: Anger seems a sign of poor supervision. Although it can be that in some situations, in other cases it may simply be a reaction to effective supervision. The supervisor thus has to guard against letting staff reaction touch his or her own understandable self-doubts too deeply, so as not to be put off. In tough situations such as these, it helps to have colleagues or other supervisors to talk with as a source of emotional support, as well as a sounding board for one's perceptions. As the supervisor's confidence increases, it is a bit easier to maintain his or her position, and, in the end, the staff will appreciate it. They may also gain the confidence to do the same with their own clients.

ENDING PHASE IN GROUPS

The departure of a supervisor or a worker from a staff group is an ending, as was noted with respect to sessional ending skills in chapter 4. General ending issues and evaluations were discussed in some detail in chapter 5, which described endings when a worker leaves a job and when a supervisor terminates a staff relationship.

There are stories of staff members or supervisors quietly cleaning out their desks a week before their last day and then taking vacation days to avoid the last week and the need to say good-bye. The dynamics of endings with clients (Shulman, 1992) parallel the ending processes with a staff, but staff members often have an even greater reluctance to discuss them. Still, a close observer can see the various stages of the ending process: denial, anger, mourning, learning to live with the idea, and the farewell party syndrome.

It is helpful if the supervisor calls the ending process to everyone's attention early enough so that some discussion can take place. If a staff member is leaving, allowing some group time to discuss his or her involvement, perhaps to provide some feedback for the agency, and, most important, to examine the feelings associated with the leaving, can turn the ending into one of the most productive phases of work. And after all the work has been done, everyone can go to the farewell party.

RESEARCH FINDINGS

The findings of two supervision studies (Shulman, 1991; Shulman, Robinson, & Luckyj, 1981) were summarized in relation to group sessions in chapter 2, in the discussion of the context of supervision. In the latter study, when workers were asked if their supervisors set regularly scheduled time for group supervision, the average response was "sometimes." When asked to approximate how often these sessions were held, the average score indicated twice a month.

Holding regularly scheduled group sessions correlated positively with a number of variables: good working relationship ($r = .34$), the supervisor playing the role of teacher ($r = .36$), the supervisor helping the worker to deal with taboo subjects ($r = .29$), and the ability of the supervisor to clarify his or her role ($r = .30$). The frequency of group supervision also correlated positively with the supervisor's role as teacher ($r = .30$).

In another study of group supervision, Sales and Navarre (1970) compared students who experienced group supervision with ones who received individual supervision. When their instructors' ratings of them were compared, both groups of students performed equally well in the fieldwork.

However, supervisors reported saving time when they used group supervision. In additional support of the "strength in numbers" phenomenon, students in group supervision indicated they felt a greater freedom to disagree with the instructor and to express dissatisfaction with the agency. They also indicated that they liked the varying ideas and experiences to which they were exposed as they listened to cases presented by other students. Students receiving individual supervision especially liked the specific help they received.

SUMMARY

Supervision in the helping professions is concerned with the dynamics of both formal and informal staff groups. There are different purposes and procedures for the different types of formal staff groups: staff meetings, group consultation, group supervision, and in-service training. In addition, informal staff groups consisting of all staff members who interact together can powerfully affect the delivery of services.

Supervisory work with groups can be examined in relation to the phases of work. In the beginning phase, the role of the group leader and the contract process are highlighted. The work phase focuses on helping a staff group develop a culture for work, the individual in the staff group, and conflict in the group. In addition, the authority theme is related to the leader–member group relationship. The importance of dealing with the dynamics of endings was also stressed.

CHAPTER 9

HELPING STAFF COPE WITH TRAUMA

As social workers in a state child welfare office arrive for work on a Monday morning, they can immediately sense an atmosphere of crisis. They quickly learn that a young child on the caseload, who had recently been returned to his parents after months in foster care, was killed over the weekend. The local manager is attempting to keep up with the urgent demands on her from the central office staff requesting the immediate faxing of all documentation on the case. There are telephone calls from the local press requesting interviews, and a local politician has also called. The worker who carried the case is sitting at his desk looking distressed as he attempts to review his case records in preparation for a visit from the central office investigation unit—whom staff often refer to as the "death squad." His supervisor is busy on the phone dealing with the supervisor from an associated contracted agency reminding her that they had documented problems with the family and therefore were not at fault. Social workers talk to each other in hushed tones but carefully avoid the worker whose client has been killed. They get busy reviewing their own records to make sure they are up to date and that they have not missed taking the appropriate steps or completing the mandated visits. A hectic, hyperactive atmosphere pervades the office as everyone seems intent on determining "who's at fault" just at the time when all of the staff most need someone to ask, "How are you doing?"

This is not an atypical response to the crisis of a traumatic event. Unless the system at all levels can respond in a more supportive manner and can recognize the impact of the trauma on all staff, the practice behavior of all of the workers in the office—perhaps even in the region or the state—may be affected for months after the incident. This chapter examines the influence of traumatic events and discusses the skills and interventions required on the part of managers and supervisors to buffer their impact.

There are many different kinds of trauma that may hit a staff group. These can include the natural death, suicide, or murder of a client on a caseload; the death or serious illness of a staff member; a physical attack on a staff member by a client; the public revelation of issues related to questionable agency practices—through a newspaper story or court action; or the stress associated with cutbacks in funding and the associated limitation of resources, freezing of hiring for new positions, firing of employees, and bumping of junior staff by those with seniority. Traumatic events can have a profound and lasting impact on staff members and the effectiveness of the agency service. The argument is made in this chapter that social services and health systems are often the least effective at dealing with such traumas in a manner that protects staff from their impact. In fact, because of the stress on the larger system, intervention by administration often adds to the problem rather than helps staff members cope with it. In contrast, support for staff during traumatic times can pay off in the long run with positive staff morale and more effective services to clients.

In the following sections, illustrations of some of the most common examples are used to develop a protocol for effective administration and supervision in response to trauma.

DEATH OF A WORKER'S CLIENT

The term *burnout* has been used to describe a syndrome exhibited by workers dealing with intense stress over a period of time and lacking support. Although most used in the child welfare literature, it is also seen in reference to workers in any high-stress field of practice and, in particular, in large government agencies (see Copans, Krell, Gundy, Rogan, & Field, 1979; Daley, 1979; Falconer, 1983; Freudenberger, 1974; Riggar, Godley, & Hafer, 1984) and in other fields of practice as well (Borland, 1981).

One source of stress common to all fields in which workers experience high levels of burnout is the powerful nature of the events and the emotions in the life of the client. The impact of the death of a child on one's caseload, the emotions associated with sexual and physical abuse, counseling a grieving family in a hospital or a suicidal client, and working with people with acquired immune deficiency syndrome (AIDS) are all examples of work that can take an emotional toll on the caring professional. A particularly traumatic incident, for example, a suicide on a psychiatric ward, may have effects that are felt by the specific worker involved, as well as by all colleagues. In those systems in which the initial agency response is to investigate to determine blame rather than to provide support to the helpers, the impact of trauma can be exacerbated.

I have referred elsewhere (Shulman, 1991) to the "spread effect," a process by which a traumatic event for one case influences a worker's practice across a caseload. A worker's traumatic incident can also be spread to influence the work of his or her colleagues. For example, other workers may be less inclined to take risks with their caseloads.

When the stress gets too high, I have often observed a form of hyperactivity on the part of workers and supervisors, administrators, support staff, and others. The hyperactivity is both a reaction to the demands of the job (for example, 10 unanswered telephone message slips sitting on one's desk, all marked urgent), as well as a means for the worker to defend against his or her emotional reactions. If one keeps going fast enough, one does not have to feel the client's or one's own pain.

In my experience, I have found that using denial as an adaptive mechanism is actually maladaptive and contributes to burnout. A helping professional needs to face his or her feelings and must learn to use them in pursuit of the professional function. This is difficult to do without sources of support. To illustrate the impact of trauma on workers and the importance of support, the following example, also shared in my text on empirical practice (Shulman, 1991), is provided. It serves as a model for a discussion that could be held in any social work setting after a traumatic incident.

I had the opportunity to work with a group of administrators, supervisors, and front-line workers who had just experienced a traumatic case in which a young child was apparently killed by his own mother. The client was seen once by the worker, who made many efforts to follow-up on the case but could not find the mother or the child. The case received wide coverage in the local press, which compounded everyone's stress. I was asked to meet with the staff group to help them to cope with their reactions to the incident. I stated my purpose to them as follows:

"You have all been going through a very rough time recently. The purpose of this session is to help you share your grief with each other, to consider ways you can be supportive during what will be a stressful time, to explore the impact this tragedy may have on your practice, and to discuss the implications for your other clients." I invited the staff to start by sharing some of their reactions.

One worker responded, "I can't feel it yet. I have wanted to cry all week, but I just can't." Another said, "I haven't stopped crying at home—but I try to pull myself together when I come into work." A third commented, "I know it's crazy, but somehow I feel guilty—almost as if we were the perpetrators."

Another staff member commented on how angry they felt when on the first day they were besieged with requests for documentation. The worker at the center of the storm, who had dealt with the mother, said, "I know it's important to have my documentation—and I had it up to date in this case. I received a lot of support. But what if it wasn't up to date? There are times we all get overwhelmed and fall behind. You shouldn't be able to turn it on or turn it off—I need help no matter how I may have handled the case."

A supervisor described a telephone call from an administrator at another, related agency. The other agency shared some responsibility for the case. The first question by the administrator inquired as to how the worker involved was doing. All the staff agreed that the call, and the other agency administrator's concern for the worker, had meant a lot to them. It would become an important positive factor in the future work of the two agencies. A local administrator described how easy it was to get caught up in the hectic activity around documentation and that now, in retrospect, it was clear that it was partly a way of avoiding the pain. I pointed out how it seems that each level was reacting from deep emotion in response to the case. Another worker said it would have been helpful if we had just all sat in a room together on that first day—"We didn't even have to talk—just to be there for each other." Still another worker said, "I haven't really faced it yet. . . ." After a few moments of silence, she began to cry and was joined by a number of staff members and myself.

One worker talked about the anger she was getting from neighbors about the case. She described holding back her feelings and now realizing that was wrong. She needed to let people know that they were not faceless civil servants and that these incidents affected them deeply. "People needed to be educated, and we have to do the job."

In response to my request, they started to explore what steps each one of them could take to respond to this stress, how they could be helpful to the worker involved, and what they needed in the way of help from each other and their agency. A number of specific suggestions emerged, ranging from a worker who offered to interview the child's other family members so that the involved worker would not have to do it, to secretaries (who were part of the group) talking about how they could provide a buffer for the worker over the next number of weeks. He replied, "That would help a lot. I find myself getting lost at times. I'm sitting at my desk and writing out a note, but after 15 minutes I realize I haven't written more than one sentence." I pointed out that it would take some time to get back to normal on this one, and probably some of the feelings would not simply go away.

Discussion moved to attempting a realistic assessment of what workers could and could not do in cases such as this. One worker said, "We have to get really clear about the limits of our abilities—we are simply not gong to be able to stop children dying no matter how well we do our job." Another pointed out how helpful the supervisor had been through all of this—to all of the workers, not just the one involved. They felt she was with them, taking responsibility for the case, not just trying to "cover her ass." The worker said to her, "When you told me not to worry, that you would stand with me on this one and wouldn't let me face it alone, it was extremely important to me."

As we came to the last part of the morning, I asked them if they had the energy to discuss the implications for their current work with their clients. I pointed out that clients read the papers and watch television.

They would know about this case, and it might have some impact on them. Some workers said they did not have the energy for discussing their clients—they were not ready. Others responded to my invitation and observed that some of their clients had commented to them about the case, but they had been too upset to notice. They said they wanted to discuss what they could do. The group agreed, and at my request one worker described her conversation with a young mother of about the same age and in a similar situation to the mother in the case. I asked the workers to consider what she might be worried about. They quickly saw the indirect cues in her comments raising concern about her own situation. Could she get angry enough to hurt her own child? The worker role played how she could explore these concerns during her next contact. Others provided similar examples of cues they were hearing but ignoring because of their own feelings. As the discussion turned the corner and began to focus on their professional responsibilities, a noticeable change was evident in the atmosphere in the room. The sadness was still there, but energy seemed to be returning and hopefulness along with it.

The last part of the discussion turned to agency and community policy issues related to the increase in drug use (crack cocaine) and how overwhelmed the child welfare, police, courts, and lawyers were by the severe changes taking place in their caseloads. Cocaine had apparently been involved in the case under discussion. Some ideas emerged for a community meeting to bring the involved groups together and to use this case as a catalyst.

The group was positive about the discussion during the evaluation. They asked the worker if he knew how upset they had been, and he replied that he did now. It helped to have their support. He went on to say that he did not feel "out of the woods yet." He was afraid of what might happen if a scapegoat was needed. One worker said, "I kept thinking that you are such a good worker, and it still happened to you. My God, it could happen to me." Another worker broke the tension by pointing out how they were all rapidly catching up on their overdue case notes. I credited them with the support they provided to the worker and to each other and hoped that they could keep providing it over the next few months.

This discussion reveals just how important support from the agency administration can be at a time of stress related to a traumatic event such as the death of a client. In an illustration from a large, statewide child welfare agency, a letter from the senior administrator to a front-line worker, which arrived on the day I was providing a workshop on the impact of trauma, offers one example of such support.[3]

---

[3]The letter is being reprinted with the permission of the administrator and the worker. Names have been changed to protect confidentiality.

Dear Ms. Smith:

I am aware of the recent traumatic death of a child in your caseload and wanted you to know of my sadness at this tragedy and my empathy for you as Steven's caseworker.

I am very appreciative of the important work you and your coworkers carry out on a daily basis under incredibly difficult circumstances. Of all of our challenges, certainly supporting you, as you in turn support Steven's family, is of utmost importance to me.

Please accept my thanks for your caring and commitment and my sympathy to you at this difficult time.

Sincerely yours,
Fred Jones,
Director

When this letter was shared in the workshop, one long-time employee stated the general reaction: "A part of me wonders if this letter isn't only a political move by the director. Another part of me wants to believe that he really cares. I think we are all hurting so much right now [that] I'm going to go along with the part that wants to believe he really meant it." The comment was followed by a long silence broken by the recipient of the letter, who indicated in an emotional manner that the letter meant a great deal to her. Others expressed hope that this might be part of a general move to be more supportive of staff.

DEATH OF A STAFF MEMBER

The dynamics of denial described in the previous section can also be noted when a traumatic illness or death strikes a staff member. In one example, a staff member in a residential institution for adolescents contracted AIDS and was at the stage at which his physical symptoms were extreme enough for him to request medical leave. The supervisor was dealing directly with him on the issue as a personal matter although all staff (and residents) were aware of his progressive deterioration. The subject of his illness had not been discussed openly at any of the staff meetings and had remained a taboo subject. Within weeks after the staff member began his medical leave, he died. The supervisor presented this example at a workshop, recognizing that the issue had been ignored with staff and residents and seeking help in how to deal with it at the next meeting.

Using the help offered by fellow workshop participants, the supervisor tuned in to the impact of the loss on herself, on staff, and on residents and developed a strategy for dealing with the issue. She announced the news at her next weekly staff meeting and was greeted by a stunned silence. She acknowledged that they had been avoiding the subject, in particular, because she had felt the staff member's illness was a personal problem. She acknowledged that she had been hit very hard by the loss and probably had also avoided mentioning it because it was so painful. She continued that in retrospect she realized he should have explored with the staff member his feelings about how to handle the issue with colleagues and residents. By not doing so, she realized now that they had not had an opportunity to end with the staff member before his leave began, and therefore a great deal of unfinished business remained. She pointed out that she was raising it now not only because she wanted to give the staff an opportunity to discuss their reactions but also because she felt it was not too late to consider the impact on the residents and how they might help them with their feelings. Because loss was so central to all of the teenagers in the center, she realized now that it would be a major mistake to ignore this wrenching loss of a valued friend and colleague for them and an important worker for the residents.

Staff members reacted to her opening statement and her expression of her own loss with a sharing of the grief that they felt at the staff member's death. The first part of the meeting was the beginning of a mourning process that would continue right through and even after the staff member's funeral. During the second half of the meeting, the supervisor called on the staff to consider how the residents might react to the news when it was announced later that day. She asked them to discuss some strategies for helping the residents deal with their grief over the loss in a supportive manner. Staff members prepared for the possibility that the teenagers would resort to their usual methods of fight and flight to run from their pain. They considered how this loss might trigger memories of other losses in their client's lives and that there would be a need for both group and individual work on the problems.

In dealing openly and supportively with staff about this death, the supervisor was able to help them by modeling the very work they needed to do with the residents: providing an opportunity to grieve and then connecting the loss to other areas of loss where appropriate. Also, the staff could focus on helping the clients make positive use of their peers as a source of support—the mutual aid process. The staff members were better able to do this after having just experienced the process themselves. At the end of the meeting, the supervisor asked them to reflect on how they had avoided the illness up to this meeting and to consider how they might handle such traumatic events more effectively and supportively in the future.

This discussion not only helped to bring the staff closer together at a time of crisis, but it also helped them to generalize their experience to their practice issues with the residents. If the staff had avoided the pain through denial, the same denial would probably have been evidenced and supported by staff with the teenagers. This could easily have resulted in a reinforcement of the taboos against dealing with loss and an acting out of the grief through fight and flight. The death of the staff member provided an opportunity for significant work on experiences of loss for staff and clients.

PHYSICAL ATTACK BY A CLIENT ON A WORKER

One of the major taboo subject areas in the social services is the violence against workers. Although increased violence resulting from a changing caseload (for example, crack cocaine addiction in child welfare) has resulted in a growing attention to helping workers protect themselves, the issue is usually still dealt with indirectly in most settings. This is one area in which use of macabre humor is most evident—workers tell war stories and joke about apparently serious and threatening situations. When this humor is confronted directly, it quickly becomes clear that it is a form of flight and that just beneath the surface is the real fear that can immobilize a worker who must face potential violence in dangerous situations. Child welfare workers report making home visits in response to a report of domestic violence wherein the accompanying police officer says, "After you, social worker."

Although humor can be an important form of escape and an adaptive response to stressful situations, it becomes a maladaptive response if it takes the place of a real conversation about the underlying feelings and an associated discussion of steps that might be taken to increase the worker's sense of security.

In one workshop, a social worker reported having made a visit with a police officer in response to a report of family violence. As she and the officer approached the porch of the house, the father in the family stepped out of the door and began to fire a gun at both of them. They both ran for cover, and a report was called in for additional police help. The father was eventually subdued, and the worker returned to her office. She reported how strange it felt when none of her colleagues spoke to her about her frightening experience. In my view, they were not uncaring. Actually, her scare had moved them greatly and had heightened their own fears, which they had long suppressed to help them get through each day. Her supervisor briefly stopped into her office and suggested that she might want to take the afternoon off—that was the best he could do in his effort to provide support.

The worker reported that she was in a state of shock for weeks. She also revealed that she could not respond to the police request to come down to the station and identify the assailant. She confessed to the workshop group that she felt inadequate as a worker because she had not been able to maintain her composure and respond professionally. As she reached this part of the story, she began to cry. After a moment, she said that the incident had occurred over two years ago, but this was the first time she had cried about it. She said she realized that she had "bottled up" her feelings.

The participants in the workshop immediately moved to offer her support. Others who recounted similar incidents and similar reactions suggested that she not be so hard on herself. One participant told her that he felt she had great courage in sharing such a personal example and that it turned out to be one to which they could all relate. As the other workers responded, one could see the presenting worker getting the help in dealing with her feelings that should have been available two years before. It was clear to her, and others, that her practice in the past two years in potentially violent situations had been profoundly affected by this incident. All of the workshop participants could identify how they had modified their work, not always in a positive manner, when they or colleagues they knew had experienced a violent trauma. Most participants, and there were more than 200 of them, indicated that they had not had this kind of discussion in their own settings when these frightening events had taken place.

The conversation turned to some of the ways workers and the agency could build in some protection even though they recognized that the possibility of danger was always present—for example, telephone call-back procedures on a home visit when the client had a telephone. If the call was not received after a certain time, an alarm would be passed along for the police to check. One worker described how such a system had been crucial to her when she had been held at knife point by a distraught and psychotic mother. The worker at least knew someone would be coming if she did not call in. Another worker described how her office had developed a protocol for handling potentially dangerous situations so that they would be certain to make such visits with a coworker or have a colleague or supervisor available if the visit was at the office. One worker described how in her office she could always ask a male worker to accompany her in threatening situations. A male participant in the workshop pointed out that just because he was male did not mean he might not be just as frightened and vulnerable in such situations. He did not think it was fair or accurate to assume that his gender would necessarily prepare him to deal with a threatening and violent situation.

The important point is that the very conversation about the impact of violence and the fear of violence on practice; the development of procedures to protect workers and, if necessary, provide support after violent incidents; and the ensuing discussion of strategies for reacting to threatening situations would not have taken place if the culture of the group did not encourage the open discussion of the realities of fear on the job.

PUBLIC QUESTIONING OF AGENCY POLICIES

An agency itself can be the focus of a traumatic event. For example, in one case, a public social services organization was accused by an advocacy group of systematically placing foster children of color in white homes, without attempting to first locate appropriate alternative care resources in the extended family or the community of color. The accusations emerged from a court case that made the headlines by charging that the specific case was the result of a long-term, racist policy. The judgment of the court was that the pattern of placements supported the argument that a problem existed, and it ordered the social services agency to make major changes in its policies and procedures. The case and the judgment, together with the associated court order, hit the community like a bombshell. Many staff in management and on the front lines agreed that a problem existed and that the agency had not paid appropriate attention to issues of race. They were stung by the charge of racism and believed that the outcomes were more a result of a lack of appropriate resources for recruiting foster homes in communities of color rather than the specific intent of workers. They could recognize, however, that an agency policy that historically did not emphasize same-race placements and did not provide the appropriate resources was de facto racist in nature.

The agency's response to this court-mandated change in policy could be viewed as an example of how efforts to alleviate the oppression of clients may be experienced by staff as oppressive themselves. Instead of implementing a program of involving all staff in educational discussions on the importance of race and ethnicity and mobilizing staff at all levels to address how this now-exposed problem could be resolved, the administration responded to the pressure of the press and the political system by instituting what amounted to a tribunal in which each social worker had to defend his or her placement decisions over the past years. The social workers felt that they were being asked to be the scapegoats for a system that had neither declared this issue a priority nor had offered enough resources for the workers to accomplish these goals. As a result, many workers who supported the court order and the new policy direction found themselves the targets of attacks because of their placement decisions. Instead of mobilizing the workers' efforts on behalf of children of color, the specific procedure caused many to turn inward and become defensive.

Further complications occurred whenever efforts were made to discuss the issue, because staff from management to the front lines were polarized along racial lines and fearful of engaging in any conversation that might lead to confrontation and charges of racism. As long as the subject was informally declared taboo, all of the meaningful discussion took place outside the formal meeting structure. I had been prepared for the issue by workers from a front-line workshop I had offered the same week who confided in me about the devastating effect of the problem on them and their colleagues. Because the established norm was not to discuss the issue directly, no structure existed for staff to deal with the impact or to contribute to a discussion of how to implement a more effective policy and heal the agency's wounds. Thus, the very intent of the court order and the policy change was being frustrated by the conspiracy of silence. When the issue was indirectly raised at a training workshop of mine for agency managers, I zeroed in on their unspoken concerns. My notes from the session describe the process:

It was clear that discussion was difficult in the mixed racial management group, with many participants uncomfortable and hesitant to speak. I pointed out how hard it seemed for us to discuss the example and that this probably replicated the problem they were experiencing at all levels of the agency. There was much head nodding in response to my drawing the parallel. I adopted the strategy of exploring the reason for the taboo as a means of freeing the group from its power. While a group's culture might not be well enough developed to immediately tackle a tough issue, often the simple request to discuss the obstacles to discussion is a way to begin. As group members begin to talk about why "it" is hard to talk, they are actually talking about "it."

I said, "I realize that race is a difficult issue to discuss. I wondered if it might help us if we first discuss what made it difficult to talk openly about this issue." One white manager said she was scared stiff that she might say something that would be offensive and that she would then be accused of racism. So, instead, she said nothing at all. Another white manager said whenever he tried to open up the subject, he felt he was walking on eggshells. This was true at management meetings he attended, as well as at his own staff meeting. A third white manager, with an all-white staff group, indicated that when her staff raised their feelings and fears about the "tribunal," she closed off the discussion with Pollyanna-like comments and reassurance. As a result, when one of her workers came back and reported feeling devastated at the process, her staff members were angry at her. She was feeling caught in the middle and without a clue as to how to help.

I pointed out that many of the white participants had expressed concern about saying something that might be interpreted as racist. I wondered if they experienced the same fears which I had—that in the course of such a discussion we might make a comment or observation that, in reality, reflected the racism that was a part of all us—the deeply hidden racism, or sexism, or homophobia that all of us in the majority populations carried with us from years of living in a society filled with "ism" messages from family, friends, the media, and so forth. I told them I had tuned in to my own fears as a workshop leader as I prepared for this session, having been alerted that the issue was a hot one. Many participants were nodding in agreement with my personal observation.

At this point in the discussion, an African American manager spoke up, indicating that he thought there was significant mutual mistrust and fear on both sides of the racial barrier. He was sure that after having experienced so much subtle and not so subtle racism in his lifetime, his "antenna" was up and perhaps, at times, was overly sensitive to the existence of racist undertones. I told him that, given his life experience and the reality of the need for defenses, I'm not sure he could ever be overly sensitive. However, if white managers were fearful of speaking up and if African American managers were hesitant as well, this crucial and long overdue policy modification might fail simply because of lack of open communications. I pointed out that unless the managers could find a way of talking about this with each other and challenging the taboo, there was little hope that they could help their staff members.

I suggested that now that we had at least identified the barriers, maybe we could do some joint work on how they could deal with the issue in their staff groups and with each other. The woman who felt immobilized about her angry group of white workers said she would appreciate all the help she could get. With that request, the white managers and those of color began to analyze her dilemma and to strategize about how she could go back and reopen the conversation with her staff. She role played how to begin the next meeting by owning up to her own fears and to how she had cut off their discussion. Group members strategized how she could reach for the hurt under the social workers' anger and how she could mobilize them to begin to deal with the next level of administration on the issue. Other examples soon followed, and the management team, at first with some evident mutual wariness, began the work of examining how each of them could begin to help their staffs cope with the impact of the trauma.

As is often the case, the workshop group was using the process to raise the substantive issue of dealing with a taboo and frightening subject. My effort was to model a manner in which a group leader might confront the illusion of work by using his or her own feelings to lead the way and then helping staff overcome the barriers to effective work. The workshop was a beginning; the hardest part was still to come. For some managers, the experience led to more confident exploration of the explosive event. For others, their fears of opening "Pandora's box" in a highly charged and political situation led to continued avoidance. In the last analysis, it would be up to senior administrators to create the atmosphere in which managers, supervisors, and workers would feel free to take risks.

SERVICE REDUCTIONS, STAFF CUTBACKS, AND REORGANIZATION

Cost containment programs go under many different titles including "restraint," "retrenchment," "reorganization," "cutbacks," and "reduction in force [RIF]". New expressions have entered our social services vocabulary, as workers discuss their anxiety over the possibility of being "riffed." Medical and mental health settings find themselves increasingly modifying their practices because of judgments made over the telephone by an auditor for a third-party payer who refuses to cover specific services or length of time in care for a patient. Whatever these programs are called, they all involve reductions in funding that can result in fewer programs or resources, more restrictive service policies, closing and reorganization of physical offices, and loss of jobs by attrition or firing. The severe impact of these efforts often results in diminished services and increased stress for staff and clients.

In one example, services that are considered to be "marginal" to the agency's central mission, such as preventive work in a child protection agency, may be eliminated with resulting loss in positions for workers, supervisors, and administrators. A slower erosion of services can take place when a budget "freeze" is implemented that prevents agencies from hiring replacement staff when someone quits or retires, from filling existing empty positions, or even providing auxiliary staff to cover caseloads during summer vacations. I have reported in detail elsewhere an analysis of a major cutback in child welfare services in the province of British Columbia in Canada (Shulman, 1991). This cutback in funding occurred during a study that was designed to provide an empirical base to the development of a theory of social work practice. In an opportunistic effort, the study was expanded to include as a contextual variable the impact of massive cutbacks on social work practice.

One finding of the study, using qualitative and quantitative data analysis, was that the supervisor and the staff group could provide a buffer for workers under stress and thus help them cope with the demands of the cost containment efforts. Staff were helped to develop strategies for continuing to provide some services for some clients, to document the impact of the cuts as a means of attempting to restore services, and to support each other during the period of intense stress and anxiety. Although supervision and the staff group might mediate the effect of the trauma, it must be kept in mind that the impact was still profound on staff members and clients. In the last analysis, only the restoration of funding and the associated services could appropriately solve the problems.

The balance of this section explores how supervisors and managers can help staff members cope with stress and maintain professionalism under difficult circumstances. Three examples are examined. In the first, staff are helped to become proactive in attempting to manage the reduction in level of services. In the second, the emphasis is on helping staff deal with the loss of jobs by members of the team. The final example focuses on helping staff cope with reorganization of the administrative structure that resulted in the closing of some smaller branch offices and the integration of staff into a larger, regional office.

Reduction in Level of Services

The cost containment program analyzed in the author's child welfare study (Shulman, 1991) will be used to illustrate the reduction-in-level-of-service model. The reader is referred to the full study for a complete report. Although each situation will differ significantly, some generalizations may be inferred from this specific illustration. Retrospective analysis noted three distinct stages in the cutback process, each with different degrees of impact on staff. These stages were (1) the freeze, (2) the "bloodless" cutbacks, and (3) the full-scale cutbacks.

The first stage consisted of a "restraint" program implemented through a freeze. This involved cutting costs through staff attrition and nonreplacement of staff. Funding for new projects was also frozen. A number of freezes during the period preceding the study had led staff to see these actions as a normal part of the funding cycle. This stage of restraint was disturbing to staff but was not immediately threatening to their jobs. In most settings, a form of denial caused staff and supervisors to ignore these early signals.

The second and more threatening stage of the process involved reduction in staff positions. It is referred to as "bloodless" because in most cases, the people in these positions were reassigned to different jobs. A first effort was made to reduce administrative rather than front-line positions. In most cases, the actual staff holding these positions continued to be employed in new roles. Disruptions caused by staff being "bumped" out of a job by someone with more seniority or staff having to take on an unfamiliar role were not uncommon. The fact that supervisors paid little attention to the moderate impact caused by these disruptions suggested that denial was still the dominant theme. Workers later reported feeling threatened and angry as staff from central office were bumping their colleagues. These feelings were often beneath the surface and emerged only in indirect ways such as the poor reception that transferred staff received from continuing team members.

Staff facing new responsibilities or the return to old positions were often left to cope with their feelings on their own. These feelings could have a profound impact on how well they moved into their new roles. For example, when taking over caseloads from bumped workers, the transferred staff might avoid discussing the client's anger and feelings of loss because they were still too full of their own emotions. Supervisory interventions that might have been useful in these situations are discussed in the next two sections. In summary, the impact of this stage of the cutbacks on services to clients was both direct and indirect; some effects were felt immediately, and others were not.

The emotional impact on staff of this second stage of cutbacks was much stronger than that of the first but was still manageable. Study findings noted that stress on staff increased dramatically in this stage just before the announcement of the more drastic cuts affecting hundreds of staff. As staff sensed the degree of seriousness of the cutbacks and realized that this was not just another freeze cycle designed to balance a budget, they became more deeply concerned.

The third and most dramatic stage of the process began with the announcement of a full-scale and drastic cutback program. This was part of a provincewide program designed to eliminate 25 percent of the civil service positions and many social programs. The immediate impact on the ministry responsible for child welfare included the phasing out of hundreds of family support workers whose contracts would not be renewed on termination. Although this step had differential impact on regions and offices because contracts ended on different dates, the effect on the entire system (and province) was immediate and dramatic. Increased personal anxiety and lowered morale were evident in most contacts with ministry staff. The data also suggest that staff anxiety was at its highest just before the actual announcements, a fact suggesting that the rumor mill was working overtime. Many staff reported weeks of immobilization as services ground to a halt and as everyone seemed to be "waiting for the other shoe to drop." It was precisely during this period of time, when hard facts were not available, that supervisors and managers tended to avoid discussions with staff. The opinion was that they did not want to cause anxiety until the facts were known. Retrospective analysis indicated that meetings to discuss the distress of the uncertainty itself were helpful to some units in softening the impact of this high-anxiety stage. In all likelihood, many supervisors avoided holding such sessions because of their own parallel concerns.

Analysis of data from the study indicated that with fewer staff under more pressure, more restrictive intake policies designed to reduce services demand took hold across the system. Workers described turning away cases they believed would be back in a short time with problems serious enough to qualify for service. A survey of supervisors conducted approximately every three months yielded results suggesting that as the impact of the cutbacks increased, the seriousness of new cases increased, along with the incidence of traumatic client events (for example, death of a child). In addition, more children were starting to enter care, stay in care longer, and were less likely to be returned home to their families. Qualitative and quantitative data from the study indicated that services to clients were affected by these cutbacks, and worker morale declined significantly. As one worker put it, "During the past few years we had begun to take real pride in the increasingly professional nature of our work with these families. Now, it feels like we are completely reactive and losing the fight."

One set of data suggests that those offices with strong social support systems were able to somewhat shield workers, and possibly clients, from the worst of the impact of the heavy cutbacks. The following excerpt illustrates how a supervisor attempted to deal with the effects of the second stage. The example is taken from a report of a meeting called by the supervisor with front-line workers after the announcements of the second stage, the bloodless cuts.

> I began the meeting by sharing the information we had received at the regional supervisors' meetings. All regions were losing their training coordinators and their family and children's services coordinators. I explained that staff in these positions, as well as some others in central office, were going to be reassigned to district offices in front-line staff positions. I wanted to discuss what this would mean for us because we were likely to have some bumping going on. John said, "I guess that means me, because I am the person with least seniority." I told him that could be true, and I was sorry

about that since I felt he had fit in well with the unit. I said I felt he would be a real loss. Louise was angry and wanted to know why they weren't cutting back on senior administrators rather than the staff who really did the work. She felt mad that John would have to move and be replaced by someone who probably didn't even want to do the job.

Frank said he thought we might be able to survive without the training coordinator if we took more responsibility for organizing our training ourselves. He went on to say that the loss of the resources coordinator was going to be a real blow. Theresa [the coordinator] had just implemented an effective tracking system that was making a difference in how we monitored our kids in care. She also was doing a terrific job in finding placements for our more difficult kids. He felt this was going to set us back to where we were two years ago. Jules said, "The people in the Tremont building [central office] didn't give a damn about the services. They just wanted to protect their own asses with the politicians."

It was important for the supervisor to allow his staff to ventilate their feelings and to identify the issues for work. The supervisor had used a workshop to prepare for this meeting and was therefore ready for the fact that he would also be angry and resentful at the cutbacks; his feelings would be mirroring those of the staff. He understood that it would not be helpful to leave matters at the complaining and angry stage. He tried to identify issues that might arise in the meeting and to prepare to challenge staff to become proactive in response to them no matter how angry they felt.

I told them I understood how angry and distressed they were because I felt some of this as well. I was hoping we could use this meeting to think about this impact on us and to try to see if there was anything we could do to soften the blow. I said, "I have done some thinking about this and feel we need to address a number of areas. First, if John is bumped to another office, we need to help him with how he is going to handle his endings with clients. I know he is angry right now, but I think he would want to handle the changeover in a professional manner. Second, if we get someone transferred into our office, we should give some thought about how to help that person get connected. I don't want us to take out all of our anger on him or her. The issue of tracking and resources is an important one, and although I don't think we can replace the coordinator's role, I want us to do some thinking about how we might be able to cope." I also felt it was important for us to develop some means of monitoring the impact of the cuts so that we might be able to use the data with the regional office to provide ammunition to halt or at least slow down the erosion of services. Jules angrily asked, "What good would documenting do? They don't give a damn anyway." I told them all that Jules might be right and it might be a waste of time. I said I could even understand their wanting to say "the hell with it" because a part of me felt that way as well. However, if we didn't bear witness to what was happening, I felt we would be ducking our responsibility. Even if it doesn't help right now, the data would be important for when the funding turns around and we want to restore essential services.

This combination of support and a demand for work was important because it was directed at the part of staff that was professional and responsible in the face of administrative and governmental decisions that were neither. It also offered a way for staff to take some action in those areas within their control—it provided an alternative to feeling totally impotent. It was a modeling of the principle that "there is always a next step." This was exactly the demand that these workers needed to make for the clients who might also feel angry and distressed over the loss of services. In the sections that follow, illustrative examples explore in more detail some of the topics that were raised.

After discussion on each of the issues, the supervisor raised another underlying concern that he had perceived in his preparatory work, namely, the possibility of further cuts. Although no staff member had raised the question, the supervisor's assumption was that some of the anger might be related to their anxiety about their own jobs. In the next excerpt, the supervisor brings up this concern and discusses how they will cope for the next few months.

> Before we ended the meeting I indicated that I wanted to raise another concern that might be on their minds. I wondered if they were worried about what might happen next. It wouldn't surprise me if there were some anxiety about our own jobs. After a brief silence, Jane asked me if there was more bad news that I was holding back. I told the staff that I had shared everything I knew at this session. However, we all knew that there were rumors that there might be more cutbacks down the road. I wondered how they would want me to deal with information I received. In situations like this, things could change almost day to day. Would they prefer if I waited until I knew things with certainty, or should I share the tentative information as I got it? They all insisted they wanted to know as much as I could give them as soon as I knew anything at all. I agreed to do this but also told them that I didn't want a lot of complaints later about changes if I shared stuff that was only tentative or still evolving. Most staff felt that not knowing anything at all was more anxiety producing. I thanked them for their hard work and suggested that we carefully monitor how we took care of ourselves during this difficult time.

By involving the staff in a discussion about how to handle the flow of information, the supervisor was asking them to join him in taking some responsibility for coping with the stress. An example of dealing with the impact of the third stage of the cutbacks, when jobs were lost, is provided in the next section.

Loss of Jobs by Team Members

The loss of jobs by team members, associated with the third stage of cutbacks, has a profound impact on the workers involved, the "survivors" who do not lose their jobs, the clients, and the supervisor. A supervisor or manager has a responsibility to provide an opportunity for work that is designed to be helpful to all concerned. Because endings and loss are difficult to discuss under any circumstances, the supervisor will have to work hard to create a supportive culture for addressing the professional issues involved at every level.

This work is illustrated by an example from my consultation practice with the staff of a private contract agency that was facing the loss of positions because of a change in policy of a state child welfare agency, as it responded to governmental demands for budget cuts. Child welfare support services were to be withdrawn, and many of the clients were to be transferred to the state agency. Some workers were simply losing their jobs. Other workers were offered the opportunity to transfer with their clients to the state agency. Still other workers were transferring to the state agency without their clients. The stress of the transition was intensified by conflicting reports about how many staff would be involved and the timing of the changes. After being reassured that there would be a number of months for the transition, staff was jolted by the announcement that the changes would have to take place within two weeks. Staff members were angry, demoralized, and depressed at what was happening to them and their clients. I was asked to spend a morning working with administrators, supervisors, and front-line staff on the impact of the announcement and how to cope with it. The following excerpts are from my written recording of the session.

> I began the session by indicating that I understood this was a tremendously stressful time for all of them. The purpose of the session was to give them an opportunity to discuss the impact of this traumatic event on them and their clients and to find ways, if possible, to buffer its impact. I suggested we consider three areas of work. First, the impact of the cutbacks on them needed to be discussed. Then, I thought we could explore what administration, supervisors, and each of them could do to try to be helpful. Finally, I thought we needed to discuss the impact on their clients—both those they needed to end with and those whom they would be taking with them to the state agency. I asked where they would like to start.
>
> The first comments were angry and directed at the administration of their own agency and the state agency for constantly changing the timetable. They had just received notice that they had less than a week to end. The general attitude, expressed with much bitterness, was that it would take that much time just to deal with all of their paperwork. As they discussed their anger, I acknowledged it and commented that there must also be a lot of pain under that anger—pain over what they felt was being done to them but also pain over what was happening to their clients. Pam, who had been the internal leader in expression of the anger, started to cry. Other workers offered her some support.
>
> It became apparent that some of the workers were taking some of their clients with them whereas others had to tell some clients that there would be no one to work with them. I told them there was not much we could do

immediately to remedy the situation; however, I felt how they handled the endings and transitions with these clients would be important. I pointed out that the client might also feel anxious, angry, and depressed about what was happening to them. I suggested that the workers needed to deal with their own feelings if they were to be able to help the clients with theirs. Louise asked how she could end in one week with many of her clients whom she would not be able to see. I asked the rest of the group for suggestions. They began to work on the use of the phone and a mailed letter to make sure to reach every client with some form of a contact. The group began to strategize on what to say to clients on the phone, in the letter, and, for those whom they could see directly, during the last interviews. They discussed ways to share their feelings honestly, without turning the sessions or the letters into angry diatribes that might help the workers with their feelings but do little to help the clients deal with their own. The administrators and supervisors offered suggestions as to how they could facilitate this work by using the help of the clerical support staff and volunteering to help themselves. Workers who were not leaving also offered to help.

It was important to acknowledge the pain without ignoring the reality of their anger. The demands on them for an immediate termination of working relationships contradicted sound, professional practice. They and their clients had every right to be upset. It was also important to acknowledge their pain because it would be useless to ask them to tune in to their clients if at the same moment I was missing their feelings. The discussion continued as one worker, Terry, asked how was she to end professionally with those clients with whom she was glad to end.

I asked Terry to give us an example, and she described a client with whom she felt she never developed a working relationship. They had not gotten along from the beginning. When I pushed her to describe what turned her off about this client and what she would really like to say to her, she replied, "You never gave me a chance. You treated me as the enemy right from the start, and we never got a relationship going." When I asked for the group's reaction, they all agreed this might be a great way to start the conversation and to look at why this had happened. I pointed out that Terry's best work with this client might come in the ending if she could be honest about her own part in the problem, as well as confront the client about her contribution. I suggested that Terry might help set up the conditions in which this client might be more open to the next worker. I encouraged the staff to consider the ending with clients they did not get along with as important, if not even more important, than ending with those they felt good about.

Pam continued to provide internal leadership to the staff group by raising her feelings about her move to the state agency. As with most large, government child welfare agencies, it had a reputation in the community as rigid, bureaucratic, uncaring, and unprofessional. Most of this reputation was undeserved and was the result of a scapegoating process in which some agencies that are under great stress are scapegoated by staff in other agencies. I pointed this out and then asked Pam to describe her concern. She indicated that she felt she had been degraded in this process. She was left out of the communication process, had been strung along, and now she was going to accept a job with the state, bringing a great deal of resentment and anger with her. When I reached further, she said she was also concerned that the staff group there might not accept her. Others echoed her concern. I asked the group to examine how Pam and the others could avoid creating a self-fulfilling prophecy by not starting with her new colleagues in such a way as to encourage the rejection she was worried about. Some thoughtful work and role playing about how to begin in a new system without stereo-typing the staff already there was carried out. It was clear that unless she and the others did some tuning in to themselves and the staff at the state agency, her start there could make things more difficult for her clients.

During the first part of the meeting, I had noticed that most of the people talking were those who were losing their jobs. In preparing for the session, I had tuned in to the possibility of "survivor's guilt" existing in the office; that is, those who did not lose their jobs might be unclear about what they could do or say to be helpful to the others. They also might not see this session as an offer of help to them as they played their role in the process; thus, I decided to turn my attention to the quiet members.

I pointed out that I had noticed most of the conversation was coming from those who had lost their jobs. I wondered if the other workers were feeling a form of survivor's guilt—and if that was causing them to keep quiet. Sara said she just didn't know what to say to her colleagues who were losing their jobs. She had just transferred to a program in the agency that was protected, and so she was going to continue. She had felt guilty over the fact that they were going and she was staying. She was keeping quiet because she wanted the session to be for them because she was feeling their hurt. I pointed out that the session was for them as well and that there might be ways they could be helpful to those who had lost their jobs. Others commented that they had wanted to speak to those who had lost their jobs to tell them how sorry they felt about losing them as friends and colleagues, but they had not been sure what to say or if it would be appreciated. Terry said she appreciated hearing their concern for her now.

Serina said she had wanted to reach out to them but was afraid to look them in the eye because she had kept her job. She felt she had something to share with them that might be helpful because she was in their shoes last year when she lost a job in the same way. I encouraged her to try to help. In a moving and eloquent manner, she described her shock and pain when she found out she was fired. She went on to describe how she had tried to hide her hurt and put on a brave front to her colleagues and family members, but it just didn't work. She was fired just before Thanksgiving, which made it even worse to think about the coming holiday period. She described how her efforts to pretend she was coping broke down on Thanksgiving day, when she realized she had forgotten to stuff the turkey. She had cried that day and finally was able to accept support from her family, who knew she was distressed but felt put off by her barriers. She said the most important thing was to let herself have some time to feel sorry for herself. After that, she picked herself up and started sending out resumes. She pointed out that the depression finally passes and that this year she remembered the to stuff the turkey. A number of the other workers thanked her for sharing the experience.

The final phase of the discussion focused on how the administrators and supervisors had handled the flow of information and what they could do in the future. It was clear that administrators were feeling guilty about what was happening but were also unable to discuss this with their workers. The staff talked about what how the administrators could be helpful in such a situation. They thought it was important for all information to be shared as they went along even if the situation might change almost daily. The staff who were moving to the state agency also asked for the administrators to take a more proactive stand on their behalf regarding some disturbing personal transition issues. For example, in one way they were being treated like new workers—a delay in obtaining health insurance caused a potential gap in converge unless they paid a large premium. At the same time, they were treated like experienced workers and were not given the same lower caseloads provided to new workers. This, they felt, was unfair, and the administrators agreed to raise it in their discussions with the state staff, although they were not sure they could get anywhere.

> As we summarized the discussion, Pam, who had been so angry and also so upset at the start of the session, said that I had come up with some very helpful ideas. She went on to say that she was also angry at me because I had forced her to think about these things when a part of her wanted to just say "to hell with it." I thanked her for her honesty throughout the session, and in particular, for articulating with some force what other members of the staff group were feeling. I told her it took professional commitment to be willing to work at all when she had a right to feel so angry and bitter. After a review of the ideas that had been important to them, I thanked all of them for working so hard this morning. An out-of-town colleague was visiting me and was attending the session as an observer; with the group's permission he told them that he had been struck by their courage and love for each other and had been very moved to be a part of the session.

It is important that a supervisor or manager help staff move past their anger and the hurt that is just below it. Staff want to be supported and understood, but they also want to be respected for their professionalism. By tapping the strength of staff members, even at the most difficult times, a supervisor affirms staff members at a time when they need it the most.

In a coincidence, I had the opportunity to work soon after this workshop with administrators from the state child welfare agency to which these workers were going. I was able to use this experience to help these administrators to begin to inquire how they could help these workers make an effective transition to their staff groups. Some of the principles that help in this process are elaborated in the next section by an unrelated example.

Reorganization and Combining of Offices

Reorganization and restructuring of a large system is one method used to attempt cost containment. It usually involves the closing of some offices and the integrating of staff into other areas or regions. Sometimes it may entail closing a small office that has functioned independently and incorporating it within a larger region. It may be associated with a new building designed to combine staff for economic reasons. Administrative positions may be lost as smaller offices are combined with larger ones. Although reorganization often seems simple on paper, in reality it may create a complex minefield of human emotions and reactions to be negotiated very carefully.

In one example, a new county office building was built with the goal of taking widespread units of a social services system and bringing them all together for increased communications among professionals. The planning for allocation of office space was conducted from the top down, as the administrative staff from the larger units participated in the decision-making process. When the date for moving in arrived, the staff in other units found that the most desirable offices (for example, best windows, largest rooms) were all assigned to the unit with more power and higher status. The unit with lower status found itself located in basement offices without windows. The short-changed staff reacted with anger and resentment. As a result, staff members went out of their way to avoid any contact between units and thus defeated the stated purpose of sharing the new building.

In a contrasting example, a more astute administration established a planning committee from all units of the organization to meet with the architect to discuss initial planning for the building. The goal was to find the best way, within the limits of the funds available, to incorporate into the design the goal of better communications among units. For example, some units could share two floors, with functionally related subunits on each floor. The chair of the planning committee recognized at the first meeting that the issue of fairness in allocation of prime space and offices would be important, and that was considered as part of the planning process. Committee members were able to keep their own staff groups informed of the progress and the problems faced by the architects so that when the building was completed, staff felt they had been able to have some input into its development. Although there were still problems and limitations to the design, there was a sense that these had been distributed fairly, not arbitrarily. The communication to staff inherent in this attention to process was that their thoughts and feelings were valued. In reality, staff input into the process provided the architects with important suggestions for how to design the building so that it met the functional needs of its occupants.

Attention to process and tuning in can also prove helpful when reorganization leads to the absorption of a smaller unit into a larger one. In one case in which this was ignored, a cost-saving consolidation effort involved the closing of a small, rural office and the moving of staff and services into the larger regional office. The smaller unit had a long history of independent operation and had thought of itself as offering a strong professional service. Morale of staff members was high. The regional office was located in a medium-size town with a more problem-filled caseload and a more stressed staff with lower morale. The change also meant that the smaller unit would lose its well-liked administrator and would now answer to the senior administrator in the regional office.

As this step was contemplated, it would have been helpful if senior administrators had given some forethought to the implications of this move for all staff members. A direct discussion with staff might have led to efforts to try to deal with the many concerns that staff in both offices expressed. For example, the staff in the smaller office were concerned about increased commuting time, the stress they would face in dealing with an unfamiliar and more threatening caseload, their fear of being lost in the larger regional office—becoming second-class agency citizens, and the loss of their administrator. They were also concerned with how they would be accepted by the front-line staff in the regional office. Staff in the regional office were also concerned about how the balance in the office might be upset by the influx of new staff from an office that they had perceived as "looking down on regional." Although the change was inevitable because of cost factors, and not all of the concerns could be dealt with, staff members in both offices would have benefited if the management team consisting of administrators and supervisors had invested some time in developing strategies for dealing with these very human elements involved in a major restructuring.

The ignoring of these issues was a mistake that came back to haunt the administration in a number of ways. First, the staff in the smaller office resisted the move and were supported by a local community board that had also been left out of the process. A public fight erupted; there were threats of legal action and an effort to split the office off from the agency. These efforts were not successful; however, they left a residue of bitter feelings. The local administrator resigned his position suddenly in protest over his change of status from administrator to supervisor. This left the staff and the community without leadership to deal with the transition. The staff was openly hostile to the administrator appointed by the agency to effect the move. When the move was finally completed, the staff group from the smaller office rejected the offer of integrated offices in the regional office; instead, they chose to stay together as a group in a less desirable block of offices. Staff in the regional office were angry at the new members for their attitude toward the integration, and a polite but clearly evident hostility marked their early interactions.

A full-day retreat, led by myself with the involvement of all levels of staff, consisted of a retrospective analysis of the divisive events associated with the integration. Staff groups from both units were surprised to hear that some of the feelings associated with the move challenged the stereotypes each held of the other. Front-line staff's anger over the process needed to be expressed, and administrators had to take responsibility for their part in ignoring the stress. Front-line staff were also asked to examine the part they played in aggravating the conflict. It required considerable work, after the fact, to reopen the wounds of the mishandled integration and to repair the bruised feelings. Although the integration would never have been easy, early attention to the process would have required staff to take some responsibility for managing the transition in a less destructive manner.

The second part of the retreat discussion focused on what steps staff could take, at all levels, to begin the reunification process and to decrease the sense of mutual alienation. As a first step in the healing, the staff from the integrated office agreed to move out of their enclave and to begin a physical integration. A protocol for handling potential conflicts in the future was also discussed so that the staff group as a whole could better manage its inevitable stresses.

IMPACT OF A SOCIAL TRAUMA

A social trauma is an event that affects a whole community in general and a human services organization in particular. It can be a natural disaster, such as an earthquake or hurricane, or a large-scale social unrest such as the riots that followed the Rodney King court decision in Los Angeles. I had the opportunity to lead workshops on supervision for Los Angeles supervisors and managers, as well as for school of social work field instructors, just a few weeks after the crisis. Because the aftershocks of the societal quake were still being strongly felt in the community and having a profound impact on the delivery of services, the issue was included as an example in the training sessions.

All supervisors reported that the events had hit everyone hard no matter what the location of the agency or host setting. For those in affected areas, immediate questions of staff safety had to be addressed. Many agencies closed down and instructed staff not to return to work until notified. In one agency, however, front-line staff members received a memorandum from an administrator instructing them to continue to make home visits, even in areas that were clearly dangerous. Staff resentment and anger were strong, but the impact of the order was nullified as middle-range managers intervened to work out alternative procedures. Lack of sensitivity to staff issues, however, was further demonstrated by a management suggestion that only minority group staff members should continue to work in the community. This proposal was also quickly withdrawn when staff from the minority groups angrily pointed out that they were also at risk. Although the initial orders were withdrawn, it would take some time and hard work to counteract the negative effect of these actions on staff morale. It was clear that a protocol for helping staff deal with such a crisis would have been helpful and should be developed as soon as possible.

In many cases, management involved staff members in considering how best to deal with the crisis. Because the problem was shared by all staff members, solutions needed to be developed jointly. For example, in those cases in which staff members were prepared to offer emergency services, special arrangements were made such as the borrowing of cellular telephones and the establishment of command centers to maintain contact with staff. Often, strategies were discussed to determine whether it might be more or less dangerous to ask the police to accompany staff. In some cases, staff members were moved to other offices in areas not involved in the disturbances so that they could begin to telephone clients and help them deal with the impact of the events.

The workshop discussions revealed that many dormant and often ignored issues surfaced under the stress of the social trauma. The fear of physical violence, always present in some settings such as child welfare, was brought to the forefront by the events. One could no longer hide behind macabre humor. In some places, racial tensions between staff surfaced directly; one manager reported how one white and one African American staff member came to blows in the office. Where racial harmony existed or where tensions had been openly dealt with before the crisis, the impact of the trauma brought staff members closer together.

Social work students in field placements, or about to enter them, also felt the impact. In some settings that were not located in the immediately affected areas, agency staff seemed gripped by denial as they went about their work, apparently ignoring the events. Students in such settings were more stressed than were those who had formal and informal support groups. Obviously, front-line workers and students who were not helped to deal with their own emotional reactions to their fears and to the graphic pictures of violence would be ill-prepared to help clients with their fears. Many supervisors saw the crisis as an opportunity to help their students understand the alienating effect of long-term racism and economic and social oppression on communities of color.

The impact persisted after the immediate crisis as directors of field-work for schools of social work reported a surge in requests for changes in the already-determined new field work settings for the coming summer term. Because the events had awakened students' fears, schools were considering sponsoring group meetings to help students discuss the impact of the trauma and their assessment of where they wished to be placed.

As with all examples of trauma in this chapter, an important part of the recovery process for staff was the help they received to take a proactive role as a way of dealing with the feelings of being overwhelmed and helpless. Involvement in developing creative strategies for managing the crisis was empowering for staff. On a community level, the establishment of a crisis telephone hot-line for the community by school of social work faculty and the staff of a local television station was one such creative step. Human services volunteers and students from all over the city participated in a brief training session followed by shifts during which they answered questions and tried to deal with community anxiety. This became another example of receiving help by providing help.

The impression of all involved was that the community in general and human services in particular would never be and should never be the same after this community trauma. Although the riots were discouraging and at times overwhelming, most professionals still viewed them as an opportunity for positive change. As I pointed out in my workshops, the Chinese characters for "crisis" are represented by a combination of the characters for "danger" and "opportunity"—a clearly fitting way to describe what faced the Los Angeles community, as well as the rest of the country.

The examples in this section illustrate a fundamental principle in management. As is often the case, efforts to ignore conflict simply drive it underground and increase its inevitable negative impact. Supervisors are much better off dealing with a problem as it arises rather than hoping that if they "leave it alone, it will go away." It rarely does.

SUMMARY

This chapter reviewed a number of different types of traumatic events that can have a powerful impact on staff and the delivery of services to clients. These include the death of a client or a staff member; a physical assault on a worker; public challenging of agency practices; and the impact of cost containment efforts on service reductions, staff cutbacks, and agency reorganization.

In each example, it was suggested that helping staff members face the stress, rather than allowing them to use fight or flight as maladaptive means of avoiding pain, would help them to develop the social support system needed to cope with these traumatic events.

PART V

MEDIATING CONFLICT BETWEEN STAFF AND THE SYSTEM

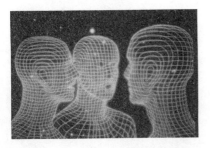

CHAPTER 10

WORKING WITH THE SYSTEM

The feeling of being caught in the middle is one of the most difficult problems faced by supervisors. On the one side is the staff, with whom the supervisor often identifies strongly. On the other side is the administration, with whom the supervisor may feel some sense of shared identity. In all settings—large or small—a pervasive "we versus them" attitude is common. This one problem, which is raised most often in my workshops for supervisors, is explored in this chapter from the perspective of the interactional model. It is suggested that "in the middle" is exactly where the supervisor or manager should be. The role is described as acting like a "third force," a buffer against the complexity of any complex and bureaucratic system. It is argued that the supervisor, rather than taking sides with staff or administration, must find a way of being simultaneously with both in times of conflict. In effect, the social work supervisor is seen as having two "clients"—the staff and the system.

SUPERVISOR'S ROLE IN MEDIATING CONFLICT WITH THE SYSTEM

Conflicts between staff members and the administration are the rule rather than the exception, and they make up a large part of the interaction in the formal and informal systems. Unworkable policies are sometimes set by administrators who may be too far removed from the realities of practice to understand their effect on services. New programs or procedures may be developed by study groups or outside consultants with little understanding of the actual nature of the practice. Competition for funds is always fierce, particularly in times of cutbacks, when too many services must fight for a share of inadequate resources.

At the same time, staff members may resist changes that are threatening to the status quo or that require sacrifices such as weekend or evening work. They may be unwilling to consider the requirements of the entire institutional setting and instead stubbornly dig in their heels, remaining untouched by pleas for flexibility or consideration.

The causes of staff–administration friction vary, but in numerous situations wherein friction exists, it poses a difficult dilemma for supervisors. From the administration's point of view, a supervisor who identifies with the staff becomes a "traitor"; from the staff's point of view, a supervisor who sides with the administration becomes one of "them." As a result, many supervisors respond with apathy and echo their staffs' position that "You can't fight city hall." This acceptance of the impossibility of change causes negative feelings to go underground, to emerge in many indirect ways that affect ongoing services. A staff that feels oppressed and helpless in the agency system cannot easily help clients who feel the same way to deal with their problems.

The mediation role for the supervisor provides a framework in which the supervisor does not chose between identifying with either the staff or the administration. In most cases, rather than taking sides with one over the other, the supervisor can take a stand on the side of the process. In fact, being "caught in the middle" can be a most effective position for stimulating change.

Playing this role, however, does not mean that the supervisor never takes a position or is neutral on every issue. On the contrary, honest expression of his or her own point of view is an important part of the supervision process. The argument here is that a supervisor's personal point of view on an issue does not determine the part he or she must play. If the role of supervisor is dictated by personal views, a supervisor who agrees with an administrative change might try to mollify the staff members so that they will accept it more easily, despite their reservations. Alternatively, a supervisor who disagrees with a policy might identify with staff in an attempt to subvert or sabotage the administration. In the mediation role, however, the supervisor is a third force, or buffer, in the complex hierarchy of bureaucratic systems. Agreement or disagreement with a policy does not determine the supervisor's actions. Rather, the job requires him or her to open up areas of differences so that both parties in a conflict—staff and administration—can deal with them honestly.

The mediation role does not mean the supervisor will shy away from conflict in attempts to smooth over real differences of interest between social workers and the administration. Just the opposite is true. Effective implementation of this role requires that conflicts smoldering beneath the surface be brought to light. There will be times when advocacy of a staff position and confrontation of the administration are essential tools for the supervisor, although careful thought must be given to how these tools are used. Even in the role of advocate, the supervisor must not lose sight of the essential common ground between the staff and the administration.

To implement the mediation role, the supervisor must maintain a vision of this common ground even when all others—workers and administrators—have lost sight of it. Schwartz (1968) addressed this issue in a report of his work with supervisors and middle-level administrators in a large child welfare system:

> one had to believe that staff and administration could find some common ground on which to develop strategies of service that both could own and act upon. Was there a real relationship between the stake of the agency and that of its workers? Was it always a "versus," or could the administrator find the common interest between them— not in broad, philosophical terms, but on a given problem of service? Much of the we–they feeling is certainly inevitable in any worker– employer relationship, and particularly in a large bureaucracy. But in every meeting record we examined, on every specific practice question, the motives of staff and administration could be harnessed so that the job that brought them together could be done more effectively. Both had a stake in solving the problem—because it would make their jobs easier and more enjoyable, because they wanted a better service to people and because their own performance would look better in the process. And the administrator's skill lay in finding the way—often tangled and obscure—to this common ground. Where he could not find it, all the exhorting, persuading and cajoling he could muster would not produce the action he needed on any important problem. But where he could, he was able to precipitate an open and dignified problem-solving process that had at least the ring of reality, however difficult the issue. (p. 360)

In my own efforts to help supervisors examine ways to play this mediating role—by searching out and implementing the common ground, by challenging obstacles that make it difficult for both staff and administration to see their mutual interests, and by demanding strength in both their staff and their administrators—one of the most serious barriers has been their despair about the possibility of change. They may have tried, sometimes skillfully, other times crudely, and met with resistance. Or they may have developed a stereotype of administrators that made it difficult for them to deal effectively with resistance and ambivalence that can occur in administrators as easily as in workers. Their attitude is "These administrators—they should be different."

HELPING STAFF NEGOTIATE THE SYSTEM

Professional impact skills are used by staff members in their day-to-day interactions with other professionals within their own agency, with professionals in other agencies, and with their own agency administration. Some problems of collegial interaction were described in the discussion of staff groups in chapter 8. Here the focus is on the particular problems involved in staff members' relations with others in their own system who have either implied or direct authority. The first example describes a supervisor's efforts to help a staff member who had to work with a rude doctor. The second concerns a supervisor's work with a staff member's conflicts with an agency administrator over her career development.

Staff–Authority Conflict

Nurse–doctor conflict, which is common in hospital settings, provides a good illustration of the dynamics involved when the staff must deal with those who have authority in the system. In a supervisors' workshop, an experienced nursing supervisor who was new to the service described the doctor serving as the chief of service as one who frequently spoke harshly to nursing staff members about patient care that failed to meet his expectations. The relationship between this doctor and the nurses on the ward was strained, as was the relationship between the nursing supervisor and the doctor. The supervisor described in detail a conversation with a nurse who had reported a particularly upsetting incident. The record of my consultation work with the nursing supervisor follows.

> I asked the supervisor how she had felt when the nurse was describing the incident. She replied that she had been upset and angry and had felt that this problem had to be dealt with. I asked her what she said to the nurse, and she replied that she had comforted her and told her she would speak to the doctor. I told her it would be interesting to see how she handled the conversation with the doctor, but before that I wondered whether there might have been some ways she could help the nurse figure out what to do in such situations.
>
> The other workshop participants joined in as we discussed some strategies for dealing with the nurse. I pointed out that the supervisor did not want to be always called in to deal with these conflicts, and some time invested when a conflict arose might be worthwhile in the long run. In this way, the staff might feel more comfortable dealing with such problems, wherever they came from. We role played some alternatives, and I (playing the supervisor's role) encouraged the supervisor (role playing the nurse) to describe her feelings in the encounter and what she had said back to the doctor. As the role play proceeded, it became clear that the nurse had not said a thing, feeling too embarrassed and afraid. The problem involved had not really been her fault, but she had failed to share that with the doctor.
>
> As the role play proceeded, I (as the supervisor) explored the nurse's feelings and why it was hard for her to confront the doctor and to be honest with how she felt when he dealt with her that way. I pointed out that if everyone simply rolled over and took it, how would the doctor ever get an idea of his effect on staff nurses? I suggested we role play how she might have handled the confrontation differently and could still handle it if it came

up again. At the end of the conversation, I then said that I, as supervisor, would also be speaking to the doctor about the impact he had on the staff, and that that might make him more receptive to her. I said I would suggest that he speak to her about the incident, to clear the air, and she agreed that would help.

In the discussion, the supervisors revealed how hard it was for them to help their staffs be more honest and assertive, partly because they themselves were not. One long-term nursing administrator, about to retire, brought gales of laughter to the group when she commented that she had been trained to "wear her little white hat, sit on a pink cushion, be lady-like, and take whatever crap was handed to her." It became clear that there was much confusion and mixed feeling about authority issues and how to deal with them. Most of the participants admitted that they had trouble dealing with people with authority in the system, even other nursing administrators.

When I explored the conversation the nursing supervisor in this example had with the doctor, it became clear that she had burst in on him and exploded. All of her pent-up feelings came out as she unloaded her frustrations with the way he was relating to her staff. His response, she said, was to listen impassively and then say, "I guess it's true, what they say about you; what you need is a good man!" When she reported his comment, the consultation group exploded in expressions of anger and recognition. I asked the supervisor how she had felt, and she replied "speechless with anger." When I asked what she had said, she replied, "Nothing! I just stood there and started to cry."

As the supervisor reported this incident in the workshop, she began to cry again. I pointed out how embarrassed she must have felt about her response and asked others in the workshop if they could offer some support. They were quick to do so—one supervisor put her arm around her, and others agreed how hard it was to deal with both the implied and direct examples of sexism they experienced. They reported numerous incidents of a similar nature, in which male authority figures had made such comments as, "Must be that time of the month again" or "Does menopause really have to be that stressful?" It quickly became apparent that in this field, authority and gender issues are closely related because most administrators and doctors are male and most nursing supervisors are female.

As the workshop continued, it became obvious that before the supervisors could help their own staff members learn ways of being more direct with this system's representatives with authority, they needed to be able to do the same themselves. The workshop group went back to the original presenter and tuned in to what might have been influencing the doctor, why he reacted the way he did, and how the supervisor might go back and reopen the question directly in such a way that he could not simply dismiss it with a sexist stereotype. I pointed out that although being honest about her feelings might make the supervisor feel vulnerable, it might also be the way to break a vicious cycle. Some participants were skeptical about the doctor's ability to change, and although I agreed that they might be right, I said that simply giving up without some direct attempt at dealing with the problem could be an illustration of sexist stereotyping on their part: "He's a man, so what can you expect?" I felt it would be important to confront him with his behavior and its impact on the supervisor. I pointed out that there would still be time to lodge a formal complaint with the hospital administration if the supervisor could not get a satisfactory response from him.

In case after case, I have observed that direct and honest confrontation, if handled constructively, can force the person in authority to respond differently and become less one-dimensional. In one case, direct discussion between a nurse on a neurosurgery ward and the chief surgeon over her anger at his implied orders to withhold life support systems to a dying patient led to a remarkable discussion of the anxieties faced by a surgeon who finds himself unable to help a patient. In that example, all the staff, doctors, and nurses were operating under considerable stress, but rarely did they share their similar feelings. Lack of openness led to abruptness and apparent lack of caring, a perception that was far from the truth.

In another case, a supervisor confronting an administrator with her unhappiness over a budget decision was able to listen to his problems with some genuine empathy, and she soon discovered how much pressure he was experiencing. She reported obtaining a greater understanding of the demands and the loneliness of his job. It was still necessary for her to press for her own department's budgetary needs, but at least she could do so with an understanding of some of the constraints he was experiencing, a fact not lost on the administrator.

The examples in this chapter demonstrate that the combination of empathy and confrontation, so crucial to every supervision process described thus far, is equally important when dealing with the system's representatives of authority. Nevertheless, supervisors or staff members who have developed skill in tolerating and understanding deviant behavior by workers or clients appear to have little ability to understand the same behavior when it is demonstrated by people with authority in the system. When workshop participants say, "They [the administrators and the like] should be different," I can only respond, "But they're not! Now, do you want to deal with the way they should be or the way they are?" This comment usually meets with a reflective silence.

Career Planning

A second example of helping staff members deal with the system involves a problem experienced by a staff member who had been following a particular career line in the agency, and it had led her to a dead end. She was interested in receiving agency support for training that would allow her to move into another career line with more room for development and promotion. Although training opportunities did exist in the agency, policy had excluded staff members in her particular category from access to such support. As a result, she felt frustrated and hopeless about her future at the agency. When this particular staff member's concern was presented in a supervision workshop, it became clear it was a problem throughout the system. At the time the policy had been set, the administration had failed to consider its full effects on the morale of the staff.

The supervisor in this case arranged to meet with the regional administrator, the area administrator (a member of the administrative group that set policy), and the worker. His plan was to bring the matter directly to their attention, rather than using a memorandum that could get lost in the system. This bold step had been a waste of time, however, because the area administrator simply commiserated with the worker but indicated that there was nothing he could do about the policy. The supervisor thought that the meeting had simply increased both his and the worker's frustration.

When asked for details of this meeting, the supervisor made it clear that once the issue had been stated, his approach had been passive. He described how he felt and how the staff member looked as the area administrator spelled out the policy, but, as I pointed out, he did not help the staff member share her real feelings about the situation, and he did not share his. The group decided to role play the conference, with the supervisor taking the role of mediator between the staff member and the administrator and concentrating on trying to keep the communications honest and supportive of both parties. After a brief silence following the explanation by the administrator, who was role played by an actual administrator on this level who was attending the workshop, the supervisor turned to the worker and said,

> Supervisor: I have a feeling Sam's explanation hasn't helped. Am I right?
> Worker: I already know the policy. What I don't understand is why they stick to it when it makes so many problems.
> Supervisor: Perhaps you could explain to Sam what it means to you, in particular—how it feels to you.
> Worker: I feel I'm in a dead end with no place to go. I'm only 30, and it already looks like I have no future at this agency. I like working with the agency, but frankly, I don't see staying on if I'm not challenged by my work—and yet I can't seem to get anywhere within the system. It feels like the agency just doesn't care a damn about staff, and this is supposed to be a helping profession.
> Supervisor: I know that sounds a bit strong, Sam, but I have heard it from others in the system as well—and I think it's important for you to hear it directly. I know you do give a damn.
> Administrator: Look, I don't agree with the policy, either. You think

we are all the same at the central office, but the fact is we have many differences of opinion up there as well. There were pressures on us from a number of regional administrators and the civil service people to set the policy up that way.

Supervisor: I can understand how it came about, but now that we have had two years' experience with it, is it possible that the central office might reconsider? Perhaps you can use this example, or if it would help, I would be glad to document the problem. I could probably get other supervisors to provide documentation as well.

Administrator: I guess we have to face this sometime or another. You are not the only one we have been hearing from. Why don't you put together some documentation? I will get it on the agenda at the central office.

Calling the meeting was just the start of the process; the supervisor had to be prepared for the hard part: making the meeting meaningful. By concentrating on bringing out the real feelings, he was able to turn an illusion of work into a meaningful discussion. In addition, by treating the administrator as someone who did care, he refused to accept the stereotype of an unfeeling bureaucrat, even when the administrator appeared to be acting like one. He appealed to the strength in the administrator, in the worker, and in himself.

As an interesting side note, the participant who role played the administrator and who was actually part of the central office planning group used the experience as a basis for raising the issue, with some success, at a policy meeting held later that month. All such interventions will not be so successful because, obviously, other factors will be involved. Nonetheless, the supervisor who plays his or her part effectively may help others be more effective in their own roles.

THIRD-FORCE FUNCTION

Three areas of work are involved in implementing the third-force function of the supervisor: working with the staff group, working with the administration, and working with the two together.

Work with the staff group involves helping staff members to be honest about their thoughts and feelings on agency policies and procedures. They need help in developing a sense of responsibility for the impact that they may have on the system and the skill required to have such an impact. In addition, they need support in overcoming the apathy and sense of hopelessness that are common in complicated systems. At times, it may also be necessary to help staff members identify elements of their reactions to policy and procedures that may be signs of their fears and insecurity. An example is a negative reaction to a policy change that would require the staff to develop new skills.

Work with the administration requires the supervisor to communicate the staff's thoughts and feelings accurately in a way that minimizes an administration response of defensiveness or evasive tactics. Developing a working relationship with the administrator also involves many of the supervisory skills identified in previous chapters. In general, the goal is to turn the administrator toward the staff by helping identify and strengthen the areas of common ground, even when the differences are strong. I have seen effective work done in preparing an administrator for a meeting with staff, for example, by anticipating some of the anger and helping the administrator develop a strategy for dealing with it.

At times, work in this area requires confrontation and advocacy as a staff representative when the system does not respond to the supervisor's efforts to "speak softly." Such confrontations must be handled skillfully, and supervisors are well advised to develop skills in mobilizing the informal group system in support of their efforts. The development of allies in the system, such as other supervisors or department heads, can significantly strengthen a presentation and can prevent a supervisor from being isolated as the deviant member. Consistent work by a supervisor in building up credits in the system—by offering support, cooperation, and so on—is important when it is time to "call in the tabs" and ask others in key positions to provide needed support.

At a large residential institution where I worked, there was a daily lunchtime Ping-Pong game in the staff recreation room in which many of the key department heads were avid players. As a fan of the game, I joined in and was pleased to discover that I quickly developed working relationships with key actors in the system. These relationships were extremely helpful to me later when I became involved in a major effort at systems impact (for a discussion of this process, see Shulman, 1969a, 1969b, 1969c, 1970). And I developed an effective backhand as well.

When administrators and staff members are brought directly together, the supervisor needs to help them talk to and listen to each other, keep the talk honest and invested with genuine feelings, and overcome the barriers on both sides that may be obscuring their common ground. In some cases, it is necessary to help both sides find ways to keep their working relationship going when understanding or agreement in some specific area continues to elude them.

The following sections present examples from my records of supervision workshops dealing with the three areas in which the supervisor implements this third-force function.

Work with the Staff Group

One workshop example concerned a change in governmental policy that required child welfare social workers to explore the possibility of financial support by natural parents when children were placed in alternative care facilities. A sliding scale was developed, and parents who could not afford to make payments did not have to do so. The argument advanced by the government officials was that making support payments was one important way for natural parents to continue their connection with their children. The change would also help save money, which could be available for other children.

Many of the workers and supervisors believed, however, that this was a return to a means test and was a disguised way of cutting services. They were furious, worried that their relationship with clients, already tenuous at best, would be destroyed. They did not want to become financial investigators. At the workshop, the supervisor revealed that he had heard out their complaints, had agreed with them, but then had said, "We can't fight city hall." The staff had reluctantly accepted the new policy, but the supervisor knew they were not happy.

In the discussion, there was some disagreement among the supervisors. Some accepted that there might indeed be an advantage in involving natural parents in supporting their children. Some had experiences in other agencies at which a sliding scale was used for services, and they thought clients appreciated being able to pay something for what they were getting. When I asked these supervisors how they had handled the reaction of staff members, they indicated that they had tried to advocate the idea by pointing out all the possible advantages and had just ignored all objections. They admitted that their staff members were still upset.

Both the supervisors who agreed with the policy and those who did not suffered from functional diffusion: They were unclear about their functions as supervisors in such conflicts and so had missed an opportunity to be helpful. I assured participants that functional diffusion was not a terminal illness and that, with a bit of clarification, they could recover easily.

The group began by tuning in to the feelings of the workers: Why did they react so strongly? One of the supervisors, reflecting on his earlier experiences in assessing client fees, suggested that it might be because they were uncomfortable with talking about money, including income and setting fees, which can be a taboo topic. Many of the workers may have simply felt uncomfortable about not knowing how to handle it in an interview. One of the supervisors who had tried to promote the idea said that this was where he had gone wrong: He had missed the underlying concerns and had seen only the resistance. The supervisor who had presented the example opposed the fees, and he admitted that he had been so quick to agree with his workers that he had overlooked the reasons for their stance.

In the workshop work that followed (role playing and discussion), the group developed an approach that both supervisors who opposed the new rule and those who had accepted it could use to open up the question, be honest about their own points of view, and try to understand the objections of their staffs. All these were essential because there is usually some truth to the immediate concerns, and the supervisor who simply addresses the underlying issues, while ignoring the objections, will be resented. They also practiced how to identify the hidden issues.

Here is the report of an encounter with his staff that one supervisor presented at a follow-up session:

I began by telling them I wanted to discuss the support payment issue again. I told them I was not satisfied with how I had handled it before, in that I had agreed with the policy change and had simply tried to sell it. They had some important objections, and I wanted to go over them again. Frank (the internal leader) began to raise the problems he could see in terms of client resistance. He felt they would resent having to make payments, and it would just be another barrier. I told them I could appreciate that the job was hard enough already, and they probably were not too happy about its being made harder in their view.

Theresa agreed with Frank but then went on to say she didn't believe it would do any good to argue, because the decision had already been made. I agreed that they had to follow the policy, but that did not mean we could not raise our concerns with the administration, and if we felt strongly enough, perhaps we could keep some documentation on how this was received by clients and then report back to the administration. I told them I was not sure it would help, but if they felt strongly enough, we should give it a try.

Frank wanted to know if I had changed my mind and was no longer supporting the policy. I told him I still held the same views on the matter, but I was open to examining the experience to see what came of it. I went on to say that in the last analysis, what really mattered was how they felt about this policy, because unless they could see some benefit, they would not be able to implement it with enthusiasm, and that would guarantee its failure. Most of the staff group nodded in agreement.

I asked if a subcommittee of staff could be set up to discuss ways of monitoring the experience, gathering data, and preparing feedback for the administration. There were three volunteers, including Frank. I then said I had been thinking about their reactions and wondered if in part they were also worried about how to handle that part of the interview with the parents. I said I could see how they would be worried about the problems it could create. Minnie said she dreaded the first one she had to deal with, and it was coming up that afternoon. I asked what she was worried about, and that began a discussion on the technical aspect of conducting the interview: how they would feel, how the client might feel, and how they would introduce the idea. The discussion was a good one, with most staff joining in. We role played Minnie's interview that afternoon, trying to help her (and all of us) find the right words.

In another example of working with the staff group, a supervisor was helping the staff get ready to meet with an administrator to discuss their reactions to a policy change. The group consisted of members of a nursing staff who were upset at a change in shift hours that had been implemented in what they regarded as an arbitrary manner by the administrator. The staff had developed a system of working longer hours a number of days in a row and then taking off a sizable block of time. This routine had been tried for a number of months, but the administration had decided it was not working well, and staff efficiency was falling after too many working hours on consecutive days. The administration had issued a memorandum requiring a return to the old system, and the staff was furious as much at the way it was announced as at the change itself.

The nursing supervisor had already met with the administrator to prepare her for the session. The following excerpt is her report of how she prepared the staff members to make their argument. After helping them set down their views in point-by-point fashion, with their supporting data, she focused on the process of the encounter:

> I asked who would make the presentation. Louise said she would start it off, but wouldn't mind others helping as well—so she wouldn't feel alone. I wondered if they were worried about Miss Pomeroy's reaction. Carol felt we had to make the case, and make it strongly, and if that made her upset, there was nothing we could do. I reminded them that I had already spoken to her, so that what they said would not come as too much of a surprise. I had also let her know they were angry, and my guess was that she was as worried about speaking to them as they were about speaking to her. They laughed at this, and then went on to select a few more people to make the case.
>
> Tess wondered if we should be careful not to get too angry during the discussion, so angry that Miss Pomeroy might just storm out. I said it was a tough balance. On the one hand, they needed to let her know how they really felt, and they couldn't do that without getting angry. On the other, they did not want to back her in a corner so that she got too upset to hear anything. I told them I had told Miss Pomeroy that I would try to stay in the middle during the discussion, helping her make her points and them to make theirs. I would also get my own views in there, because, as they already knew, I had my own reservations about the long hours. However, I was much more concerned about how they and Miss Pomeroy handled this meeting, so I would concentrate on that part of it. They agreed that this would be helpful.

It was important that the supervisor clarified her role in the meeting so that the staff understood her interventions. By acknowledging their fears about the confrontation, she helped keep the discussion honest. If a supervisor does not bring these issues into the open, they often appear at the meeting itself in the form of long silences and evasions, as everyone waits for the supervisor to take the lead in the attack while they hold his or her coat. The record of the supervisor's preparatory work with the administrator for the joint meeting is presented in the next section.

Another example of the supervisor's work with a staff group illustrates the problems involved in helping staff members deal with a situation they cannot immediately influence. In this case, governmental reductions in a social agency budget had led to reclassifications and cutbacks in a large number of positions. Additional cutbacks were threatened but had been delayed, and the agency administration was carrying out a campaign

Interactional Supervision

against the budget. As a result, a number of workers without seniority were on temporary contracts, living from month to month without knowing what would happen next. The cutbacks and delays that had been going on for months were causing a general malaise among all the workers and supervisors.

When the problem was presented in a workshop, I could sense the supervisors' depression under their expressions of anger. I reached for those feelings and tried to empathize with the difficulties they faced. We discussed social action steps that could be taken on a political level, as individual citizens, and as members of professional organizations. Many of these were already in progress, but they had only little hope of effect. As the examples were presented, all of us, including myself, felt a deepening despair and sense of hopelessness and helplessness.

As is often the case in workshops, the participants let me know what they were up against by their behavior in the session. This is yet another example of the parallel processes between supervisor and workers and between worker and clients. It was important to model an approach that demonstrated the principle that there always is a next step. I acknowledged their feelings and shared my own as follows:

> Consultant: It's obvious to me that under all of this anger, you are all feeling a lot of frustration and depression. It's not hard to understand that, because after listening to you for the past little while I'm feeling it as well—and I go home tomorrow. You have to live with this problem.
> Supervisor: It wasn't easy before, but now it seems to be hopeless. You have to wonder what the use is of trying anything. (Others in the group nod in agreement.)
> Consultant: You know, you didn't bring me all the way here just so I could listen and feel what you're going through and then agree with you that it's hopeless. It may be that you can't immediately influence these cutbacks, although you all seem to be making the right efforts to do so. If that's true, then we can look at how you can try to provide services within the context of the cutbacks. It might help to examine what the impacts of the cutbacks are and how to deal with them best. I don't mean administratively—that's not appropriate in my workshop—but in terms of your supervision of staff and, in turn, their provision of service to clients. What are some of the effects on staff members, and how have you been handling them?

One common problem arose from an example presented of a temporary worker whose work was seriously slacking off. He was obviously depressed about the uncertainty of his job. It became clear that the supervisor had felt so guilty that she had not discussed his performance with him. We did some work on how she could overcome her apathy and begin to help him deal with his. She might, for example, confront him with the problem and examine how it was affecting his work with clients. I pointed out that his clients might sense the problem of his impermanence, and that would affect their response to him. The change in atmosphere in the consulting group was noticeable as the members harnessed their energies to efforts to understand the impact of these cutbacks on their supervision, their workers, and the staff's service to clients. This was one next step they could take. As one supervisor pointed out in the evaluation, I had modeled what they had to do with their workers—be supportive but at the same time demanding.

Work with the Administration

There is little question that effective work with the administration is one of the most difficult aspects of the supervisor's job. The concept of transference that has been so helpful to understanding both client–worker relationships and worker–supervisor relationships is just as useful at the supervisor–administrator level. Supervisors have a long history of dealing with people in authority—family members, teachers, previous administrators—and feelings and patterns of interaction from all those relationships can be easily transferred to current authority symbols. Past experiences with other agencies, the current agency, and other large bureaucracies also contribute to the attitudes supervisors have developed over the years.

Difficulties in Supervisor–Administrator Relationships

Numerous factors make it hard for supervisors to affect their own administrations. First, there are usually so many issues in any setting that even considering an attempt to have an impact on all of them is a bit overwhelming. As a result, supervisors may decide that nothing can be done about any of them. It's a bit like having a long list of chores to do on the weekend, so long that it becomes easy to decide not even to start. When we are serious about dealing with our chores, or with the agency issues affecting practice, our first step is to use the skill of partializing, breaking big problems into smaller components and then focusing on one issue at a time.

In addition to the scope and extent of the problems, supervisors have to deal with their own feelings about change. They may bring to their work situation an apathetic attitude that reflects their view of themselves as incapable of exerting meaningful influence. This is a product of our socialization experiences that generally have encouraged us to conform to the existing social structure. Families, schools, peer groups, and work settings often do not encourage individual initiative. All systems have a profound stake in encouraging members to make personal contributions by challenging the system and asserting their individuality. But not all systems have been aware of this need and have acted on it.

All too often, in fact, the system achieves the integration of its members at the expense of individual initiative. As a result of efforts to integrate individuals, system norms that encourage conformity may be developed. The life experiences of many supervisors produce a viewpoint that sees taking responsibility for professional impact as a major change in their relationship to systems in general and to people in authority in particular. Even if they are willing to take risks and involve themselves in attempts to make an impact on the administration, their experiences often discourage any further efforts. When they encounter resistance to their first attempts, they may fail to recognize the agency's potential for change. The potential is there, but change requires persistence. If supervisors regard agencies as dynamic systems, simultaneously open and resistant to change, then an initial rebuff does not necessarily mean failure. The timing of the change effort is also important. Supervisors are mistaken if they think their agencies are static. An attempt to deal with a problem at one point in an agency's life may be blocked, whereas at a later stage in the agency's development the same effort could be welcome.

Many supervisors are simply afraid to assert themselves. If the agency culture has discouraged previous efforts and if supervisors regarded as troublemakers suspect that their jobs will be in jeopardy, they will be wary of raising questions about services or policies. Certainly, there are times when these fears are well founded—for example, when administrators are extremely defensive or when there are political pressures on an agency. Supervisors in such situations have to decide for themselves, in light of their personal situations and their convictions about the professional and ethical issues involved in the problem, whether they think they can take the risk.

Other supervisors do not get involved because of stereotyped attitudes about an administration that they have never tested, rather than any actual experience in the agency that has led them to fear reprisals. In either case, the courage needed for making attempts at change should not be minimized. When the effort is risky, the wise supervisor makes sure that allies are ready to help.

Lack of time is also a serious factor. If supervisory loads are maintained at high levels, the prospect of becoming involved in an effort at agency or social change can seem completely unrealistic. In such settings, the first efforts might deal with the work situation itself. Often, outside organizations such as professional associations or unions are the best media for effecting such changes.

The complexity and magnitude of administration-related issues thus tend to discourage supervisors' attempts at professional impact. Their personal feelings about asserting themselves, as well as specific experiences in agencies, may deter them. Fear of losing their jobs or fear of other retribution may be an obstacle, and insufficient time can discourage such attempts. In spite of all of these obstacles, supervisors do attempt to influence their administrators and the agency system—and sometimes they even succeed.

Examples of Work with the Administration

The first example features the supervisor from an earlier section who helped her nurses plan a strategy for a meeting with their administrator. When the nurses' first strong reaction to the decision about changing the policy was evident, the supervisor went to see the administrator. This first excerpt illustrates how the initial resistance of Miss Pomeroy, which confirmed the supervisor's stereotype of the administrator, resulted in a nonproductive exchange.

> I told Miss Pomeroy that the nursing staff was very upset at the change and, in particular, at the way the change was announced. I said that she knew I had some reservations about how the longer shifts had been working, but, in spite of these, I could appreciate how the staff were feeling. I asked her what she would do about this. She was silent for a moment and then said that this would pass. The staff often get upset about policy changes such as these, but they cool down later. She told me there had been a great deal of discussion about this at the upper administrative levels, and she was under some pressure to straighten out the situation as quickly as possible.
>
> I was feeling a bit frustrated, and I told her I didn't think she understood just how strongly this had hit them. She told me that she had been an administrator for a long time, and after I had more experience I would realize that you couldn't please the staff all of the time. I felt really put down and angry at the comment, but I said nothing, just thanked her for her time (probably sounding bitter) and left.

The supervisor had started the session expecting trouble, and she found it. In discussing the encounter retrospectively, she could see how her own feelings of having been put on the spot by her staff had dominated her, so that she had not bothered to tune in to what the administrator might feel when hearing of the angry reaction. The administrator's denial of the difficulty could instead have been interpreted as signaling her difficulty with the problem.

In this case, the administrator began to share some of the problem as she revealed the pressures she was experiencing from other administrators. The supervisor, instead of jumping back in with her response, could have simply asked the administrator, "What kinds of pressures have you been under?" Of course, it is easy to propose this alternative after the fact, in the comfort of a workshop setting. It was understandable why the supervisor had responded as she did at the time, but she had to face the fact that at precisely the moment she was asking the administrator to understand how her staff felt, she was unable to empathize with the administrator's bind. With a bit of support and understanding, she might have been able to work with the administrator on how to handle the problem more effectively. As it was, she came across as all demand and no support, and this could partly explain why the administrator retaliated with the comment about her experience.

After she had tuned in, the supervisor tried again. Note the skills of clarifying purpose, containment, elaboration, empathy, sharing own feelings, and the demand for work in this second effort:

I told Miss Pomeroy I was glad she could see me again, because I knew this was a busy time. I told her that I did not think I had handled our last conversation about the hours problem as well as I could have and that I wanted to try again. I had been upset by the pressure I was feeling from the staff, and I simply dumped it in her lap, when she obviously had pressures as well. She nodded but remained silent. I said I wasn't asking for a change in policy but rather wanted to discuss ways she and I might be able to deal with the staff's reaction. I wasn't sure anything would help, and she might have been right; it may just have to go away by itself. But I wanted to at least try, if there were any ways to facilitate it. I would like her reactions to some of the thinking I had done about the problem.

She said that she would be glad to discuss it but that she didn't think she could offer any answers, because top-level administration felt the experiment had been tried and had failed. I asked her if she had run into a rough time defending this new policy, and she went on at some length to describe how it had been attacked at an executive-level meeting. Other departments were afraid it might be demanded by their staffs as well. She told me she had tried to defend the nurses' right to experiment but had found it difficult because she was not convinced it was such a great idea. I told her I knew what she meant, because I felt the same way and it was easier to fight for something you really supported.

She continued to talk about the communication problems on the executive level, and I listened, because it was obvious she needed someone to talk with. As I listened, I had some clearer insights into the difficulties she faced when she tried to protect the interests of the nursing staff. I shared this with her. I then tried to bring her back to the present problem by telling her I thought it might help a lot if the nursing staff knew about her efforts on their behalf. Also, she could have their direct feedback about this decision, which might be helpful to her in dealing with the executive committee. We might not resolve anything, but at least the staff would feel they had been heard, and they might appreciate hearing that she did fight for their interests. I said they have a distorted view of what goes on in administration, with all administrators simply lumped together as "them."

She said she wasn't sure a meeting would help. I asked her why, and she told me she didn't know how much she could share with the staff because she did not want to seem that she was separating herself from the rest of the administration. I told her I could appreciate the dilemma because I felt the same way, caught between her and the staff. I told her I had found it helpful to level with staff and that they seemed to be able to understand that I could be with the administration and, at the same time, try to be helpful to them. I pointed out that my talking to her right now was an example of what I meant, because they knew I supported the decision to change the policy. She nodded in agreement.

I then asked if she was also worried about what kind of encounter it would be. The staff was angry, and I wouldn't blame her for not wanting to face a bunch of angry staff. She said the worst problem with meetings like this is that nobody says anything; they just sit and glare at you. I told her that I had planned to meet with them before the meeting to help them prepare to share their reactions constructively. I thought they might be honest with her if they felt she really wanted to hear. I would be glad to concentrate on helping them level with her, as well as helping her get her ideas across to them. I thought they would very much appreciate her making the effort to meet with them, especially if they could get a better idea of her binds. She said she would give it some thought and get back to me. I told her I appreciated her time, and the meeting ended.

The record of the encounter between the staff and the nursing administrator is given as an example in the next section. All supervisors' conversations with administrators do not go as well as this one, however, even when they are handled skillfully. Some administrators resist so strongly that they cannot respond to the supervisor's overtures. Even in such cases, the supervisor who does not lose hope immediately and instead allows some time to pass may find a greater responsiveness a few days or a week later. Often it takes the administrator some time to reflect on the discussion and be ready to respond. The supervisor must respect the process and must not be disappointed at meeting resistance in difficult areas.

Other situations clearly call for advocacy and taking a stand by the supervisor. In one example, a supervisor of the dietician service at a large institution was faced with an edict that her service must cut back its budget by 10 percent, as part of an across-the-board cut for all departments. When we discussed this example in a workshop, another dietician suggested the cut be taken out of the administrator's entertainment budget, a suggestion received with great delight by the group. This supervisor's style and her security in her job dictated her response: to empathize with the administrator's problem and then refuse to cut her budget. She had argued at a department head meeting that across-the-board cuts merely penalized departments that had already effectively economized and had not padded their budgets. Because she felt this was true in her case, she demanded, and got, an agreement to have audits of all budgets so that cuts would be based on service-related decisions. All workshop participants did not believe they would be able to make such a strong stand, but for this supervisor it made sense.

Schwartz (1975) described the worker's professional impact on systems on behalf of clients in a videotape program titled *Private Troubles and Public Issues: One Job or Two?* At one point he says, "There is a time to speak softly and a time to speak loudly." The same is true of the supervisor's relations with the administration on behalf of the staff. In many examples, I have found that supervisors have either confronted before they have spoken softly or been too understanding when they needed to confront. Understanding correct timing is as difficult in supervision as it is in life.

Mediating the Staff–Administrator Encounter

Although a supervisor can be extremely effective as a conduit of communications between staff and administration, he or she can also help bring the two together whenever possible. Administrators become less of a stereotype to workers if both groups can communicate directly, and the feelings of the staff have greater effect when they are experienced at firsthand by administrators. It is useful to build in such contacts regularly in order to develop a working relationship over time. When such encounters take place only at times of stress, they are usually more difficult for all parties involved. Because our society has developed norms that restrict open communication of negative feedback and anger, most people have had little experience with such sessions, and they regard them with a considerable apprehension.

The example of the planned meeting between the nursing administrator, Miss Pomeroy, and the nursing staff illustrates this process. This problem was presented at a workshop for nursing supervisors who met biweekly for two months; thus, the supervisor was able to draw on the help of colleagues and the consultant in her preparation for each step of the process.

The group first used tuning in to sensitize the supervisor to potential themes of concern and the indirect ways in which they might arise. For example, because silence early in the session might be a sign of the staff's anxiety, the supervisor developed a strategy for reaching inside the silence if it occurred (for example, "I know it's not easy to begin, especially when there are some hot issues involved . . .").

It was also important to develop a simple contracting statement to start the session so that all the participants would begin with a clear sense of purpose and would be acquainted with the supervisor's role (for example, "The purpose of this session is to discuss both the change in policy on shifts, as well as the way in which the changes took place. Because we know there are some strong feelings about this, I thought it best if I concentrated on helping everyone talk to and listen to each other. Is that okay with all of you?").

Most important was the supervisor's tuning in to her own concerns and feelings about the session. It was clear that she was anxious, and she said that she was afraid the situation could get worse. Further discussion revealed that all the participants were worried about expressing strong feelings and then not being able to control them because they had as much difficulty with anger and other negative feelings as did the staff. Perhaps, they thought, it was better to let the matter rest. When I asked them to imagine the worst problems, the participants suggested that people might get into a shouting match, or they might cry. The meeting might fall flat and everyone would be quiet, or the staff might be vocal but Miss Pomeroy might silence them, all of which would make matters worse.

As the group took up these points and developed some idea of what the supervisor could do in each instance, the worst problems began to seem less threatening. If the staff members did lose their tempers, the supervisor could step in and point out how angry they felt but also how hard the anger was making it for them to hear each other. She could offer to act as a "traffic cop" to keep some sense of order. Most participants felt it would not come to that; in fact, the problem might be to get them to admit the anger. This has been my experience: Our behavior has been so conditioned against expressing angry feelings directly that sarcasm, passive resistance, and other more indirect means of communication are likely in sessions such as these.

During a mini role play of what might happen if people cried at the meeting, the supervisor became so full of emotion herself that she was at a loss as to how to help. I suggested that she could begin by being honest about her own feelings at the moment. Such directness often frees a person's energy, allowing greater regard for the feelings of others. As for the possibility of silences, the group explored their meaning, and the supervisor practiced how she might ask the staff and Miss Pomeroy to discuss how difficult the session was—why it was hard for them to talk together. Often a few minutes of such discussion reveals that both the administrator and the staff have the same fears and reluctance to be candid. Recognition of this obstacle may be all that is needed to overcome it. If Miss Pomeroy should have a defensive reaction, the supervisor practiced how she might encourage the staff's reaction to the defensiveness, while at the same time recognizing how hard such a meeting might be for the administrator (for example, "You know, I think with everyone coming on so strong, it must be putting Miss Pomeroy on the spot; she's really caught in the middle on this issue").

After reviewing each of the worst fears and developing some strategy for responding to them, the group considered the possibility that none of the anticipated problems would occur. I suggested that it was essential for the supervisor to have some faith in both her staff members and Miss Pomeroy; with her help in leading the discussion, they could find the strength to handle their parts. She replied that the preparation had helped somewhat, but she was still scared. The workshop participants agreed that the encounter would be a bit frightening, no matter how prepared they felt.

The following is a summary report of the meeting that the supervisor presented at the next workshop session:

> On the morning of the meeting at least three or four of my staff members made joking comments about the session (for example, "Well, are you ready for the showdown?"). Each time I laughed, and then acknowledged their concern, just as we had practiced in the workshop. This helped steady my nerves a bit, because I felt I was starting to work as planned. In fact, I was pleased with myself. When Miss Pomeroy arrived, the staff all sat on one side of the conference room table, and she sat on the other side, with

me at the head. I realized this was a first signal, but I simply passed it over. I made my opening statement, just as I had practiced it, and when I asked for their comments, there was a brief silence. I was ready to "reach inside" when Louise began listing some of their points, as we had planned. Miss Pomeroy sat tense and quiet, listening to their concerns and arguments. Most were already familiar to her, as I had shared them in our conference.

When she finished, I said it might help if we took up the issues one at a time. I wondered where Miss Pomeroy might want to start. She began by explaining the thinking in relation to the policy, why they felt the system had not worked, and why she had to make the change. To each of her points, different staff members countered with their views, and I began to feel like we were going around in circles.

It is common for the discussion to begin on the substantive issue— here, the question of shifts and hours—but there are often other issues related to the process that can make it difficult for the two sides to understand each other, reach a compromise, or change their positions. In this case, the staff members' feelings about how the change was made and their feelings that the administration did not really value them were all part of the mixture in the meeting. In turn, Miss Pomeroy felt concerns about service to patients. She was caught in the middle between the nurses and the hospital, and yet she understood some of the reasons the staff wanted the changes to be made.

To break the deadlock, it was important for the supervisor to voice her sense of "going in circles" and to bring up some of the other issues affecting the discussion. The group had anticipated this problem, and the supervisor was prepared to try to break the cycle. This skill could be called *calling attention to the process*.

I interrupted at this point and told them what I saw happening. I said I thought there were other concerns that were not being shared. For example, I knew that the staff felt that the change in policy was just another example of the administration not caring—but this was not being said. I also knew that Miss Pomeroy had worked hard to defend the experiment, to stick up for her nurses, but this was also not being discussed. Carol asked if it was true that Miss Pomeroy had stuck up for them. Miss Pomeroy shared some of the process that went into the decision. She was very clear about saying that she had reservations about the new shift system but that she had fought for the staff to have a chance to experiment. She tried to explain some of the problems in the system that created immense pressures when one area of the hospital tried to innovate. The staff was listening intently, obviously interested in this description of how the hospital administration actually ran.

In response, some of the staff members opened up about how upset they were about the fact that they were not consulted when the policy was changed. They felt left out and took this process as an indication that nobody cared about them. Miss Pomeroy said she had to own up to the blame for that, because she knew that they would be upset about the change, but, also, that there was nothing that could be done. She went on to say that she really had felt the new shifts had led to serious problems in patient care, and she asked if they hadn't also noticed some of the difficulty. Ann said that there were some problems for some of the staff, who were stretched pretty thin at the end of so many straight days on. She, and others, often had to cover for such staff. However, she didn't feel the whole idea needed to be abandoned, that it could work with some modifications. I remained quiet as Miss Pomeroy and the staff began to work out what compromises might be possible.

This meeting did not solve the problem of the shifts, nor did it solve the general morale problem. However, Miss Pomeroy was able to raise the question at an administrative meeting, and an agreement was reached for a modified version of the new plan to be implemented on a three-month trial basis. The nursing staff was still dissatisfied with some aspects of the modified plan but felt that a start had been made in dealing with their problems. The supervisor was encouraged because she felt this had been a helpful first step in opening up direct communications between staff and administration.

In my opinion, this was a positive start largely because of the preparatory work that had been done by the supervisor and because of her skill and courage in the actual sessions. In large dynamic systems, such as a hospital or an agency, once any change is made in the system, even a small one, the old quasi-equilibrium is upset (see chapter 3), and the impact is usually felt on the system as a whole. Thus, although an incident such as this one does not solve all of the system's problems, it can be an important first step.

RESEARCH FINDINGS

The item on the workers' questionnaire in Shulman, Robinson, and Luckyj's 1981 study of supervision skill that dealt with the supervisor's third-force role was stated as follows: "My supervisor will communicate my views to the administration about policy and procedures." The average score for the supervisors in the study was close to "a good part of the time." There was a significant positive correlation between this variable and supervisor helpfulness ($r = .65$).

Both supervisors and workers provided written comments on this issue. Some examples from the supervisors included the following:

- I feel frustrated as a supervisor because I feel powerless to stop the loss of good staff or to prevent burnout.
- One gets nervous and at times quite paranoid when one doesn't know what to expect.
- It's been a lonely experience—with being in the middle—I don't truly feel a part of the overall agency.

- A major concern for supervisors is handling of three forces that dictate his actions—client needs, staff needs, and the needs of senior management.

One supervisor summed up many comments by saying that "middle management provides opportunities for either satisfaction or ulcers." Workers also commented in writing on this issue:

- I feel my supervisor is very much a "company man."
- My supervisor supports and represents his staff and departmental issues exceptionally well.

Other research on supervision has consistently identified this area of a supervisor's task as crucial. For example, in the Olmstead and Christenson (1973) study, worker satisfaction was associated positively with adequate and effective communications in the agency. In the Kadushin (1973) study, the most frequently cited source of strong dissatisfaction with supervision, as indicated by 35 percent of the 384 social workers responding, was the supervisor's hesitancy to confront the administration. As for the supervisors in the same study, having to get workers to adhere to agency policies with which they disagreed was cited by 41 percent as a strong source of dissatisfaction. In contrast, one of the strong sources of satisfaction for 45 percent of the supervisors surveyed was the greater leverage the supervisory job provided for influencing agency change.

SUMMARY

In working with the system, the supervisor acts as a third force between staff members and the agency administration system. This mediating role allows the supervisor to help both the staff and the administration find their areas of common ground, even as they openly explore their areas of disagreement.

Supervisors help individual staff members deal with people in the system who carry authority (for example, doctors, administrators). They also help staff groups deal with the administration at points of conflict on policy and procedures. The tasks of working with the staff group and the administrator and of overseeing the encounter between the two make up the supervisor's mediating role in working with the system.

RECORDING PROCEDURES AND PROFESSIONAL COMPETENCE

This book has drawn on the practice illustrations of many supervisors. Process recordings, transcripts of audiotapes and videotapes, summary devices, and examples recalled from memory by workshop participants have provided insights into the moment-by-moment activities of supervisors interacting with individual workers, staff groups, and representatives of the system. This book could not have been written without these examples.

Unfortunately, the idea of paying attention to the details of work in the helping professions through the use of some form of process or audio–video recording has been losing favor. A number of years ago, the writing of process records was considered students' work, a task that was quickly dropped after graduation. New workers who requested help from supervisors with such recordings were often told to realize they were in the "real world," where such devices were luxuries, or even more devastating, they were accused of being "overly dependent." More recently, the trend has been to abandon the use of recording even in the professional school. A number of graduates comment in my workshops that they did not write a single process recording in their two years of training.

This state of affairs is both ironic and alarming. It is ironic because recording and attention to detail were very much a part of early professional practices at a time when the ability to conceptualize practice skills was still at an infant stage. Although practice was being examined in detail, often it was without the analytical tools required for the job. Now that many middle-range models of practice from a number of theoretical frameworks are available, the tendency seems to be to move away from examining practice. This trend is alarming, I believe, because it is not possible to develop practice skills in working with clients or supervision of staff without some ongoing means of examining the details of one's practice efforts.

One event that countered the trend was the publication of a book on guidelines for recording by Suanna J. Wilson (1980). This excellent addition to the literature examines a number of types of recording in some detail and provides many useful illustrations for supervisors who want to strengthen their workers' recording efforts. The book also provides a model that supervisors can adapt for recording their own supervision practice.

When I discuss the recording issue with supervisors in my workshops, their first response is usually to raise the problem of time. The argument is that neither workers nor supervisors have time to record all of their work in such detail. I agree with the point but suggest that selecting cases or supervision interviews for periodic recording is practicable. Most supervisors agree, but then they point out how time-consuming writing and reading full process recordings can be. This is also true, so I offer a shortened version of the process recording, described by Schwartz (personal communication, May 1976) as accordion style, in which the beginning, middle, and the ending of a session are written in detailed process and the summary descriptions provide the links. The term *accordion* describes the expansion and contraction of the detailed portions of the record. The total writing might be less than two pages. Most agree that this would be a more manageable device.

The next problem with recording that supervisors often raise is worker resistance. This initiates a discussion of the meaning of such resistance and how to handle it. Many supervisors admit they have had bad experiences themselves with recording—for instance, they have submitted records that the supervisor never read, or they have received from the supervisor detailed critical or punitive comments on the margins of their recordings. One supervisor said she had learned quickly to write down not what she had really said in an encounter but what she thought the supervisor wanted her to say. Certainly, such experiences cause ambivalent feelings about the procedure when the supervisor is faced with resistance to it from staff members.

One of the most serious concerns about introducing recording into the supervisory process was put this way by one supervisor: "If I ask my workers to write records, I'm going to have to come through and offer them help." This fear of not being equal to the task is common among supervisors who feel that they must provide answers to their workers rather than suggestions for a way of working. I try to reassure them that it is all right to be teaching and learning at the same time and that workers will still respect them when they honestly share their own struggles with recording events. One supervisor described how he was process recording his own conferences with workers so that he could become comfortable with the tool in his own work before he set expectations for recording on his workers. He had shared this with his workers and had even showed them his beginning efforts. They were impressed with his willingness to be vulnerable.

In my training workshops for field instructors, each supervisor takes a turn at videotaping a conference with a student for presentation. Unless there are severe problems with the student, he or she is invited to sit in on the session and be a resource for our discussions. For example, we might inquire what the students were really feeling at points in their conferences. They quickly relax when they realize that we are analyzing the supervisor's activities and that they are not being judged.

These sessions are always powerful learning devices for all concerned. When students are asked for their reactions at the end of the sessions, they invariably mention their surprise at discovering that their supervisors are still learning. They point out how much it relieves them to know that they do not have to have all the answers before they graduate. Field instructors also report that the experience has a marked impact on their supervision because it usually opens up communications dramatically. Many report that they continue to use discussions of audiotaped or videotaped conferences with their students for their own learning.

Although it is often painful for supervisors to allow colleagues to view tapes of their supervision (an issue that must be discussed at the start of each workshop), they should find that the benefits of mutual aid and support make it worthwhile. Professional practice at any level is difficult, and supervisors can use all the help they can get. Overcoming the fear of risking oneself with colleagues is a first step in gaining access to this support. It is also unfair to ask the worker to make this effort unless the supervisor does the same.

In addition to process recordings and audiotape or videotape analysis, supervisors can make use of feedback questionnaires to provide information on how their workers view their supervision. The supervisors in the study reported in the research findings sections of this book (Shulman, Robinson, & Luckyj, 1981) received confidential reports with their average scores for every item. For comparison purposes, they also were provided with the averages for the overall study and for their professional groups (for example, social workers, child care workers), as well as the averages for their agencies. With the use of a computer, larger agencies could build in such a feedback process as an aid to supervisory development.

Supervisors who adopt some forms of recording will probably find themselves going against the trend in the profession. At a time when supervisors are being described in many settings as managers, with a decreased emphasis on direct teaching and practice supervision, attention to the details of the work is seldom encouraged. It is easier to look for structural solutions, such as changing agency practices or staffing patterns, or for social policy solutions. Structural and policy changes can have an important impact on client service; however, in the last analysis, practice competence must also be addressed.

As one example, when I discussed my research findings on supervision with an administrator, his first question was, "Can you tell me from your findings who to hire?" The implication was that if he could only find the right people for the staff, the positive results would follow. Selection can have an important impact on the quality of supervision in an agency, but if my research and practice experience have taught me anything, it is that the hard part comes after selection.

Shortly before his death, I had a discussion with William Schwartz on ways to develop higher levels of interest in practice and supervision competency in the profession. We agreed that this was difficult in a society that did not value attention to method and, in fact, was somewhat ambivalent about the whole question of services to people in need. He made an observation that I found helpful and that may also be helpful to a supervisor who feels he or she is bucking the trend. Although in the last analysis, major changes in our service systems will depend on changes in our society's attitudes and values, it is important that professionals, even if in a minority, keep alive their interest in the details of how they do their work. I endorse this perspective. Not only will it help many workers and, in turn, their clients, but also it will provide a means for professionals to continue developing their understanding of the art and science of the practice as they work to create a climate in which it can flourish.

NOTES ON RESEARCH METHODOLOGY

This Appendix summarizes the research methodology used in the author's studies of supervision that are noted throughout this book. The findings of both studies should be viewed with consideration of the methodology used and the limitations of the designs. A more detailed discussion of the early study can be found in Shulman, Robinson, and Luckyj (1981). The full details of the more recent study are included in Shulman (1991).

One area of investigation included in both studies was an examination of the communication, relationship, and problem-solving skills of supervisors. My colleagues and I were interested in the associations between the use of the various skills and the supervisor's development of a positive working relationship with workers or the supervisor's helpfulness. In addition to examining the process of supervision, we were also interested in exploring both the structure and context in which supervision is set. Variables examined included individual or group sessions, the frequency of sessions, and the content of supervision (for example, case consultation, job management, or practice skills teaching). Additional variables included in the analysis were demographic factors for both the supervisors and the workers (for example, training, age, and experience), as well as their perceptions of the supervisor's time investment in various roles (for example, manager, case consultant, teacher). Attempts were also made to measure the supervisor's satisfaction with role demands, sense of job stress and job manageability, and estimates of ongoing training and emotional support received.

Following established research procedures, we started with a number of hypotheses about the effects of these factors on the outcomes of supervision, as suggested by a theoretical model. Then we developed a research design to obtain empirical data for testing these hypotheses; we used the findings to support, challenge, elaborate, or rethink some of the basic constructs. This, in turn, created a new set of theoretical generalizations that could provide hypotheses for further study. In this continuing research process, each step is preliminary to another step, and the findings are always tentative. Only when repeated research in a range of settings has replicated our findings can we move from tentative hypotheses to confirmed generalizations. It is important to understand this research stance to make a proper evaluation of the findings. A number of the core propositions supported in the early study (1981) were also supported in the replication (1991).

INSTRUMENT DEVELOPMENT AND TESTING

The major work in developing and testing instruments was completed during the 1981 study. A questionnaire was designed to be completed by workers and to provide data on their perceptions of their supervision. For example, the supervisory skill of articulating the worker's feelings (or putting them into words) was phrased thus: "My supervisor can sense my feelings without my having to put them into words"; the worker indicated the frequency of this behavior.

A number of items asked for percentage estimates, such as "Please indicate what percentage of time during supervisory sessions your supervisor spends on the following categories. This should add to 100 percent." Categories for this item included the following: (a) planning on individual cases, (b) practice skills, (c) discussion of information from research that may be helpful to you on the job, (d) your ongoing job performance, (e) how to meet the administrative requirements of your job, and (f) other (specify).

Items that were used as dependent (outcome) variables asked for the worker's perception of the working relationship with the supervisor ("In general, how satisfied are you with your working relationship with your supervisor?") and the helpfulness of the supervisor ("In general, how helpful is your supervisor?"). Four scale responses to the first question ranged from "not satisfied at all" to "very satisfied," and to the second from "not helpful" to "very helpful."

Demographic data were compiled on such variables as the worker's training, experience, age, and sex. In addition, scores from the nondemographic items on this questionnaire were combined into indexes, or scales, designed to measure various constructs. These were the worker's evaluation of (1) regularity of contact with the supervisor, (2) the supervisor's availability, (3) level of trust in the supervisor, (4) the supervisor's empathic skills, and (5) the supervisor's problem-solving skills. Another index combined the supervisor's relationship and helpfulness scores. Items included in the trust, empathic skills, problem-solving skills, and relationship–

helpfulness scales were adapted from a questionnaire I had developed for my earlier social work skill studies (Shulman, 1978, 1981).

Reliability and Validity of Workers' Questionnaire Items

A number of procedures were undertaken in the 1981 study to determine the reliability and validity of the workers' questionnaire. Early drafts were considered by workers, supervisors, child welfare consultants, students, social work faculty, and individuals with no experience in social work. These key informants reported that the questionnaire appeared valid with regard to relevance and clarity of expression and instructions. With this indication of face validity, a pretest involving three workers and one supervisor was undertaken. This resulted in some scaling modifications, and a second test was then conducted with the revised questionnaire. The test used a sample of 37 workers reporting on four supervisors in a regional office of the British Columbia Ministry of Human Resources in Vancouver. Both workers and supervisors were guaranteed confidentiality.

Stability

To obtain information on the reliability of responses over time, questionnaires were distributed to the same workers again one week later, as part of a test–retest design. Twenty-two workers mailed back the second questionnaire, and the stability results are based on this sample.

All data analysis for this study used the computer software program Statistical Package for the Social Sciences (SPSS), Version 8 (Nie, Hull, Jenkins, Steinbrenner, & Brent, 1975), on the University of British Columbia computer. Of the total of 43 items on the questionnaire, in 31 (72 percent) a significant correlation ($p \leq .05$) was obtained between the scores on the first and second administrations of the questionnaire. These correlations were generally high, ranging from .45 to .91. The items with the lower correlations were related to the content and role of supervision and to the item asking for worker level of satisfaction with how he or she got along with the supervisor. Generally, items dealing with communication and relationship skills, the use of research-generated knowledge, the rating of the supervisor's helpfulness, and the context of supervision were judged to have positive results.

The test–retest scores of computed scales such as the one for empathic skills were also examined. Using more than one item to measure a variable increased the reliability of that measure. The test–retest correlations on the computed scales were as follows: contact regularity (.76), supervisor availability (.75), trust in supervisor (.90), empathic skills (.89), problem-solving skills (.50), supervisor helpfulness and working relationship (.63), agency practices (.49), and the use of research and theory (.77).

Internal Consistency

To determine the internal consistency of the computed scales, Cronbach's (1951) alpha was computed as a measure of the interitem correlation on appropriate scales. The results were as follows: availability (.47), trust (.88), empathy (.82), problem solving (.78), relationship–helpfulness (.94), agency practices (.84), and the use of research and theory (.77). Results of the analyses of both the stability and the internal consistency of the scales were judged to be at acceptable levels of reliability.

Construct Validity

In addition to using a research design with face validity, as described earlier, other efforts were made to establish the validity of this question-naire. Construct validity was supported by analysis of correlations using the constructs of the practice theory stated in the hypotheses. For example, a good working relationship between the supervisor and worker would be expected to have a strong association with supervisor helpfulness—it did ($r = .89$). In addition, although content and context were considered important to supervision, the theoretical model guiding this research sug-gested that interactional skills would be central in determining a supervisor's effectiveness. It was expected that these skills would be the most highly correlated variables, as opposed to other factors such as supervisor stress, education, or experience. The findings in this study par-alleled those in my practice study (Shulman, 1981) and were replicated in the more recent study (Shulman, 1991): These variables were indeed found to be most highly correlated with helpfulness.

Additional construct validity was determined in the 1991 study by the use of causal path models in which supervisory skill was found to con-tribute to the development of a working relationship. The reader is referred to the full study (Shulman, 1991) for a discussion of causal path analysis.

Predictive Validity

Another form of validity, termed *predictive validity*, is one of the most important types because it determines the ability of a variable to predict an outcome measure. To explore this avenue in the first study, we selected those supervisors, out of the total of 109 participants, who were in the top 25 percent and the bottom 25 percent on the computed scales. The theo-retical model guiding this research led us to expect significant differences between the scores of these two groups on the relationship–helpfulness scale. Furthermore, the model suggested that the context and content scales should make some difference, although the process skills should be more important.

Our findings strongly supported predictive validity. Significant differences on the relationship–helpfulness scale between the two groups of supervisors were found for all scales as follows: contact regularity ($F = 13.71$; $df = 51$; $p = .001$), availability ($F = 18.22$; $df = 51$; $p = .000$), content satisfaction ($F = 5.8$; $df = 52$; $p = .02$), trust ($F = 83.00$; $df = 51$; $p = .000$), empathic skills ($F = 68.43$; $df = 52$; $p = .000$), and problem-solving skills ($F = 77.33$; $df = 54$; $p = .000$). When the trust, empathy, and problem-solving skills were combined into one score as an index of interactional skills, the difference in helpfulness was also found for the two groups ($F = 103.17$; $df = 51$; $p = .000$). As predicted, the context and content scales were important, but not as important as the process scales. The causal path analysis conducted in the later study (Shulman, 1991) also supported the predictive ability of these items.

In summary, reliability and validity for the Supervision Question-. naire: Workers' Version were supported in terms of stability and internal consistency, as well as face, construct, and predictive validity.

Reliability and Validity of Supervisors' Questionnaire Items

A separate questionnaire was developed to obtain information on supervision from the supervisors themselves (Supervision Questionnaire: Supervisors' Version). The procedures for developing the questionnaire were similar to those used with the workers' version, including conversations with key informants (supervisors, workers, social work faculty, administrators, and the like) to determine items that might be relevant to this study.

In addition to demographic data (age, educational level, experience, sex, and so forth), the questionnaire requested information on four major areas that were then computed into scales. One scale combined training and support; items for this scale measured level of education, preparation for the task ("I received adequate preparation for the tasks and problems I faced as a beginning supervisor"); ongoing training; emotional support ("I have access to ongoing emotional support from other staff in the agency which helps me to carry out my job as a supervisor"); and collegial support ("I can talk to my fellow supervisors about job-related concerns"). The response scale to most items was (1) "strongly agree," (2) "agree," (3) "uncertain," (4) "disagree," and (5) "strongly disagree."

Another scale was designed to measure the stress and manageability of the job. Items in this area ("My job as a supervisor is stressful" and "My job as a supervisor is manageable") had the following response categories: (1) "none of the time," (2) "a little of the time," (3) "sometimes," (4) "a good part of the time," (5) "most or all of the time," and (6) "undecided." Because supervisors had indicated that it was possible to reply that their job was stressful but at the same time manageable, we computed a stress–manageability index by combining these variables in a manner that allowed respondents to be scored on a scale ranging from low stress–high manageability to high stress–low manageability.

An index of role satisfaction was computed by examining the supervisors' perceptions of the percentage of time they allocated to various tasks—supervision and consultation, management, personnel work, coordinating, and other—and what percentage of time the supervisor would like to allocate to these tasks. The index of role satisfaction was computed by subtracting the preferred from the actual percentages for each task and then adding the absolute values for a final score.

The design used to obtain reliability and validity data for the supervisors' questionnaire was similar to the one used with the workers' version. Face validity was determined through a number of key-informant interviews with supervisors in the field, administrators, and social work faculty members.

Stability

Forty-five of the supervisors participating in the main study were sent second copies of the questionnaire one week after they had completed the first one. Of this group, 41 respondents provided data for the test–retest analysis.

There were 21 items on the questionnaire, excluding demographic questions. Significant correlations were obtained for all 21 (for 19, $p \leq .05$; for 2, $p \leq .06$). Correlations for the individual items reported on in this book ranged from .53 to .82 and were judged to be within acceptable limits.

Correlations for the four computed scales were as follows: supervisor support and training ($r = .78$, $p = .000$), supervisor job stress and manageability ($r = .53$, $p = .000$), supervisor role satisfaction ($r = .33$, $p = .02$), and agency child welfare practice ($r = .68$, $p = .000$). The levels for the first, second, and fourth scales were within acceptable limits; the lower level for the role satisfaction scale suggested the need for caution in interpreting data involving this scale. Examination of the data on test–retest scores for each of the percentage categories (for example, percentage of time spent providing consultation and percentage of time the supervisor would like to spend consulting) indicated high correlations on individual items (.59 to .82). The lower correlation for the scale may mean that the gap between what supervisors do with their time and what they would like to do with their time may vary from week to week, a variation that was reflected in the scores.

Internal Consistency

Analysis of internal consistency of three of the computed scales, based on the returns of all 109 supervisors and using Cronbach's alpha, revealed the following results: supervisor support and training (*alpha* = .68), job stress and manageability (*alpha* = .50), and agency child welfare practices (*alpha* = .81). In general, the results supported the questionnaire's reliability.

Criterion and Predictor Validity

For criterion and predictor validity, the theoretical model suggested that the individual variables constituting the scales—support and training, stress and manageability, and role satisfaction—would not, by themselves, be major factors affecting outcome measures such as the supervisor's working relationship and helpfulness as perceived by workers. This was supported; none of these variables was significantly correlated with the outcome measures.

As a test of predictive validity, scores were compared on the relationship–helpfulness scales for the top 25 percent and bottom 25 percent of the supervisors on each of the computed scales. As expected, on the three scales of support and training, stress and manageability, and role satisfaction the different groups of supervisors were not significantly different in their scores on the relationship–helpfulness scale. The data were as follows: support and training (F = 0.043; df = 42; p = .84), stress and manageability (F = 0.053; df = 48; p = .82), and role satisfaction (F = 0.196; df = 38; p = .20).

The significance of these possibly surprising findings is discussed in the text. They should be interpreted in the light of the limitations of the design described in the final section of this Appendix. In particular, the self-selection of supervisors for participation may have created a biased sample; perhaps those supervisors under greatest stress did not participate in the study. There is some evidence of this in the range of scores on the stress and manageability items. The mean score on the stress item was 3.53 on a five-point scale, indicating that the job was stressful from "sometimes" to "a good part of the time" for the average supervisor (SD = 0.74). For manageability, the mean score was 4.29 on the same scale, indicating that the job was manageable from "a good part of the time" to "most or all of the time" for the average supervisor (SD = 0.72).

However, these results do offer some support for criterion and predictor validity.

METHODOLOGY OF THE 1981 STUDY

The data-gathering procedures used for the first study (Shulman, 1981) included mailing questionnaires to 120 supervisors and all of their professional (for example, nonclerical) staff members. Although the study was originally designed to include only district office supervisors from the

British Columbia Ministry of Human Resources, interest expressed by other supervisors led to the study's expansion.

Workers and supervisors were provided with stamped envelopes addressed to the research team at the University of British Columbia. The instructions were that each participant was to complete the questionnaire, seal the envelope, and mail it directly to the project. There were no worker identification codes on the questionnaires, and the participants were informed that supervisors would receive only average scores from their units, to protect individual worker confidentiality. Although larger unit scores for regions, departments, or agencies were to be computed, these would also be provided in a way that maintained individual region, department, or agency confidentiality.

Study Sample

Of the 120 supervisors who were mailed questionnaires, 109 (91 percent) responded. These supervisors all had volunteered to participate in this study, and many of them had been participants in one of my two-day workshops on the skills of supervision. Some had participated in longer supervision training projects that had been offered for a number of years. The 55 participants from the British Columbia Ministry of Human Resources represented 46 percent of the total 120 potential supervisor participants in this agency. From the Ottawa Children's Aid Society, the 27 participating supervisors represented 84 percent of the 32 possible respondents in this agency. The largest group of nonreturns was from nursing supervisors, who may have thought that the questionnaire did not relate directly enough to their situation.

The final supervisor sample included 55 social work supervisors from child welfare settings in British Columbia (Ministry of Human Resources), two from Manitoba Children's Aid Societies, and 14 from the Ottawa Children's Aid Society. Seventy-one (65 percent) of the participating supervisors were involved in child welfare or child welfare and financial aid practice. The remainder of the sample consisted of 15 participants (13.8 percent) who were nursing supervisors, 13 (11.9 percent) who were residential treatment center supervisors, and 10 (9.2 percent) who were social work supervisors from non–child welfare settings such as hospitals or schools.

It was possible to generalize from the findings because the participating supervisors were from a number of areas of Canada and from different locations (rural, urban, and suburban), from various settings and different agencies, and with a variety of functions (for example, social workers, nurses). But the factors of self-selection, prior training experiences with the researcher, and the heavy weighting given to child welfare supervision suggest that the sample should be viewed as biased, a fact that has implications for its external validity.

There were more men than women among the supervisors surveyed; 66 (60.6 percent) were male and 43 (39.4 percent) were female. Their educational background included 18 (16.5 percent) with community college degrees, 16 (14.7 percent) with bachelor of arts (BA) degrees, 15 (13.8 percent) with bachelor of social work (BSW) degrees, 36 (33.0 percent) with master of social work (MSW) degrees, and 24 (22.0 percent) with "other" degrees such as bachelor of science in nursing. In terms of supervisory experience, 31 (28.4 percent) had two years or fewer, 22 (20.2 percent) had from three to five years, 34 (31.2 percent) had from five to 10 years, and 22 (20.2 percent) had been supervisors for more than 10 years.

Out of 1,078 workers who were sent questionnaires, 671 (62.2 percent) responded. Some of these worker responses, however, were associated with supervisors who did not return their questionnaires. These returns were not included in the findings because the unit of analysis was the supervisor. In the final worker sample, 270 (40.2 percent) of the workers identified themselves as in the child welfare field, 102 (15.2 percent) as dealing with financial assistance, and 59 (8.8 percent) as residential treatment workers. In addition, 138 (20.6 percent) said they were in nursing, 98 (14.6 percent) indicated other social work settings, and four (0.6 percent) did not provide this information.

In the workers' group, 210 (31.3 percent) were male, 450 (67.1 percent) were female, and 11 (1.6 percent) did not provide gender data. Answers to the education question indicated that 213 (31.7 percent) of the workers had community college training, 143 (21.3 percent) had BAs, 119 (17.7 percent) had BSWs, 57 (8.5 percent) had MSWs, and 135 (20.1 percent) had "other" degrees. Four (0.6 percent) did not respond to the question.

Like the supervisor sample, the worker sample represented a diverse population in terms of training, job function, setting, geographic area, and agency. Nevertheless, self-selection must be considered because the returns were from those workers who chose to respond. In a brief discussion with workers on factors that might influence nonresponse, it was clear that fear of being identified persisted with some workers, even though we attempted to provide reassurances of confidentiality. On a number of returns, identifying data were not provided, probably because of this concern. It might be inferred that return rates were affected in situations in which trust was low and fear of supervisor retaliation was high (perhaps against an entire staff group if individuals could not be identified); this situation resulted in sample bias.

Data Analysis

All data were entered by trained coders on computer coding sheets designed for this study. Coding and key punch checks were made at regular intervals to keep the data as clean as possible and within acceptable limits. Average scores for each supervisor were computed for each variable on the workers' questionnaires. These scores were then added to the supervisors' own returns in an SPSS system file in which the supervisor was the unit of analysis. Thus, all procedures were implemented with a sample of 109 supervisors.

A number of analyses were undertaken, including correlations, regression analysis, analysis of variance, and partial correlation. The results of these analyses and the researchers' interpretations are reported throughout the text, usually at the end of the relevant chapter. For a more technical report of the project, see the study report (Shulman et al., 1981).

Third-Variable Analysis

One of the analyses reported in the study involved examining the correlations between a number of supervision skills and the quality of the working relationship between the supervisor and the worker, as well as the help provided by the supervisor. This third-variable analysis, based on a technique described by Rosenberg (1968), uses the partial correlation procedure to examine what happens to the association between two variables if a third, supposedly related, variable is held constant.

In this analysis, we examined the simple correlation between each skill and helpfulness and then observed the change (if any) in the correlation when relationship was held constant. If a correlation dropped significantly when controlling for relationship, then it might be inferred that the skill actually contributed to relationship (an intervening variable), which in turn was associated with being helpful. Each skill was also correlated with relationship, with helpfulness controlled, to see if the reverse might be true. Thus, an effort was made to determine how a specific skill made its contribution to the process.

Limitations of the Study

The findings in the supervision study must be considered in light of the limitations in its design. Many participants were from child welfare agencies, and the setting can have a strong impact. To explore this factor, returns from the various groups of professionals were compared. No significant differences on the crucial variables of the study were found, but the weight of this limitation is still important because imperceptible effects may be at work.

Perhaps the most important limitation of this study is the self-selection factor for participants. In a follow-up discussion, a number of supervisors who chose not to participate gave various reasons, including lack of confidence in procedures for protecting confidentiality, anger at the agency resulting in refusal to participate in an agency-sanctioned project, fear of an agency "hidden agenda" in the research, or reactions to recent policies of budget restraint. Others said they were so overwhelmed with the job that there was no time to participate, or, with great candor, "I'm afraid to have my staff fill those forms out on me." Whatever their reasons for not participating, we believe the nonrespondents as a group might have had some impact on certain aspects of the study, such as the stress and manageability findings. Nonetheless, their participation might have even heightened the importance of other findings, such as the impact of the supervisor's availability. In general, self-selection may have made the sample more positive.

The research instruments must also be considered in reviewing limitations of the study. Although supporting data were found for their reliability and validity, the workers' and supervisors' questionnaires need to be used in other settings and with further tests before there can be sufficient confidence in them to consider them more than developmental. The parallel findings of the importance of similar items in this study and my study of social work practice skills are a step in this direction. The follow-up study on supervision, reported in Shulman (1991), also offers support.

METHODOLOGY OF THE 1991 STUDY

This second study was an effort to develop a holistic, grounded theory of social work practice. One subdesign of the study focused on the impact of supervision on practice. This study element built on the work of the 1981 study and included variables from those questionnaires. Thus, the supervision subdesign represented, in part, a replication of the original study.

The project was conducted with staff and clients from the same government child welfare agency in British Columbia, Canada, which provided most of the sample in the 1981 study. A complete account of the overall study see can be found in the report of the project (Shulman, 1991). Ten representative regions (45 percent) of 22 in the province were selected for inclusion in the study. Project staff reviewed family files that had been recently opened in 68 district offices. Of the 1,056 families identified as potential subjects, 348 (33 percent) agreed to participate. The final sample consisted of 305 families with 449 children served by 171 social workers in 68 district offices.

Most of the data were gathered during the first three months of the project. Home interviews were conducted with the parents. A mail survey of staff at all levels (workers, supervisors, managers, and so forth) was carried out at the same time. Project staff also read the participating clients' files. Much of the analysis was based on the data obtained during this time period. Follow-up data were obtained through surveys mailed to clients and staff at intervals over the subsequent 15-month period. The family files were also reviewed by project staff every three months.

Twenty-three questionnaires and interview guides were developed for this study. A number incorporated elements of earlier instruments that were tested in previous studies. Standard validity and reliability checks were undertaken before the study started. Summary statistics were computed for all variables, and a number of statistical analyses were used.[1] For those analyses in which the number of cases exceeded 200, a causal path analysis was used.

Staff Study Sample

Table A.1 provides a profile of the staff in this study. The five executive directors all had MSW degrees; however, only 60 percent of the regional managers, 44 percent of the district supervisors, and 20 percent of the social workers held that degree. When MSWs, BSWs, and other professional degrees were included, 90 percent of the managers, 73 percent of the supervisors, and 68 percent of the social workers held professional degrees.

Data Analysis

Coding and analysis of data from this study followed the basic procedures outlined for the 1981 research. A number of further analyses were undertaken, including correlations, regression analysis, and analysis of variance. A new analytic procedure used in this study was causal path analysis with the statistical program Lisrel 7. The reader should consult *Lisrel 7: A Guide to the Program and Applications* (Jöreskog & Sörbom, 1988a, 1988b) for a full discussion of this statistical program. The following is a summary of the procedures followed.

Path analysis is a technique used to assess the direct and indirect causal contributions of one variable or variables to another variable or set of variables. Lisrel considers the model as a system of equations and estimates all of the structural coefficients directly. A model consisting of X variables (predictor) and Y variables (outcomes) is created, with arrows suggesting the path of influence. An underlying theoretical model, based on the propositions in the theory, was used to guide the structure of the initial models.

Lisrel conducts some initial tests of the general model and of each parameter (the path between an X variable and a Y variable or the path

---

[1] When variables involving ordinal data, such as agreement scales (for example, "strongly agree," "agree"), were correlated with other ordinal variables, the Prelis program (Jöreskog and Sörbom, 1988c) was used to compute "polychoric" correlations. When ordinal data variables were correlated with continuous variables, such as the number of days a child spent in care, "polyserial" correlations were computed. Pearson product-moment correlations were computed when continuous variables were correlated with each other. Crosstabulation, analysis of variance, and regression analysis were also used.

Profiles of the Staff in the Study: Age, Gender, and Education

	Executives (N = 5)	Managers (N = 10)	Coordinators (N = 10)	Supervisors (N = 68)	Social workers (N = 171)	Family workers (N = 51)
Age (%)						
20–30	0	0	10	2	27	38
31–40	20	50	40	60	42	39
41–50	60	20	40	22	16	17
Older than 50	20	30	10	16	15	6
Gender (%)						
Male	100	80	30	70	35	44
Female	0	20	70	30	65	56
Education (%)						
Community college	0	0	0	2	5	18
Bachelor of arts	0	10	10	25	27	39
Bachelor of social work	0	10	30	16	36	12
Master of social work	100	60	60	44	20	0
Other	0	20	0	13	12	31

between two Y variables). If the model and each parameter pass these tests (are "identified") and if the results for the overall model indicate a "stability index" of less than one, then further analysis can proceed in pursuit of a final model. The final model is the best "fit" for the data providing direct and indirect path coefficients (measures of association) between the X variables and the Y variables.

In effect, path analysis is a more sophisticated approach to the analysis attempted in the 1981 study using third-variable approaches to examine the relation among predictor, intervening, and outcome variables. Path analysis allows the researcher to examine a number of such relations simultaneously while taking into account the interactions among all variables and producing more exact measures of prediction and direction of influence.

Limitations of the ᷍udy

The study is limited by the self-selection of the staff and families involved. However, when the participating and nonparticipating groups were compared on a number of variables, no significant differences between the groups were found.

The ability to generalize the findings to the broader practice of social work is limited by the setting of the study, namely child welfare. Future studies in other fields of practice are needed to determine which findings are universal and which may be particular to this setting and population.

Finally, a major limitation of the study was the introduction of cutbacks in staff and services six months after commencement of data gathering. Much of the study data were gathered during the months preceding these events and thus were not affected. The impact of these cutbacks was incorporated into the design.

REFERENCES

Ackerman, N. W. (1958). *Psychodynamics of family life.* New York: Basic Books.

Amacher, K. (1976). *Field Instructors' Guide.* Vancouver: UBC School of Social Work.

Arlow, J. A. (1963). The supervisory situation. *Journal of the American Psychoanalytic Association, 11,* 574–594.

Austin, L. N. (1956). An evaluation of supervision. *Social Casework, 37,* 375–382.

Austin, L. N. (1960). Supervision in social work. In R. H. Kurtz (Ed.), *Social work year book* (pp. 579–586). New York: National Association of Social Workers.

Austin, L. N. (1961). The changing role of the supervisor. *Smith College Studies in Social Work, 31,* 179–195.

Berenson, B. G., & Carkhuff, R. R. (Eds.). (1967). *Sources of gain in counselling and psychotherapy.* New York: Rinehart & Winston.

Bion, W. R. (1961). *Experiences in groups.* New York: Basic Books.

Borland, J. (1981). Burnout among workers and administrators. *Health and Social Work, 6,* 73–78.

Carkhuff, R. R. (1969). *Helping and human relations: A primer for lay and professional helpers: Vol. 1. Selection and training.* New York: Holt, Rinehart & Winston.

Charney, E. (1967). How well do patients take oral penicillin? Collaborative study in private practice. *Pediatrics, 40,* 188–195.

Copans, S., Krell, H., Gundy, J. H., Rogan, J., & Field, F. (1979). The stresses of treating child abuse. *Children Today, 8,* 22–35.

Cronbach, L. J. (1951). Coefficient alpha and the internal structure of tests. *Psychometrika, 16,* 297–334.

Daley, M. R. (1979). Preventing worker burnout in child welfare. *Child Welfare, 58,* 443–450.

Dewey, J. (1916). *Democracy and education: An introduction to the philosophy of education.* New York: Free Press.

Doehrman, M. J. (1972). *Parallel processes in supervision and psychotherapy.* Unpublished doctoral dissertation, University of Michigan, East Lansing.

Falconer, N. (1983). *Attack on burnout: The importance of early training.* Toronto: Children's Aid Society of Metropolitan Toronto.

Flanders, N. A. (1970). *Analyzing teaching behaviors.* Reading, MA: Addison-Wesley.

Freudenberger, H. J. (1974). Staff burn-out. *Journal of Social Issues, 30,* 159–165.

Galm, S. (1972). *Issues in welfare administration: Welfare—An administrative nightmare* (U.S. Congress, Subcommittee on Fiscal Policy of the Joint Economic Committee). Washington, DC: U.S. Government Printing Office.

Gitterman, A., & Gitterman, N. P. (1979, Fall). Social work student evaluation: Format and method. *Journal of Education for Social Work, 15,* 103–108.

Gondolfo, R., & Brown, R. (1987). Psychology intern ratings of actual and ideal supervision of psychotherapy. *Journal of Training and Practice in Professional Psychology, 1,* 15–20.

Heppner, P., & Roehlke, H. (1984). Differences among supervisees at different levels of training. *Journal of Counseling Psychology, 31,* 76–90.

Hollander, E. P. (1961). Emergent leadership and social influence. In L. Petrullo & B. M. Bass (Eds.), *Leadership and interpersonal behavior* (pp. 30–47). New York: Holt, Rinehart & Winston.

Holt, J. (1969). *How children learn.* New York: Pitman.

Jöreskog, K. G., & Sörbom, D. (1988a). *Lisrel 7: A guide to the program and applications.* Chicago: Statistical Package for the Social Sciences.

Jöreskog, K. G., & Sörbom, D. (1988b). *Lisrel 7: User's reference guide.* Morresville, IN: Scientific Software.

Jöreskog, K. G., & Sörbom, D. (1988c). *Prelis: A program for multivariate data screening and data summarization* (2nd ed.). Morresville, IN: Scientific Software.

Kadushin, A. (1973). *Supervisor–supervisee: A questionnaire study.* Madison: University of Wisconsin, School of Social Work.

Kadushin, A. (1974). Supervisor–supervisee: A survey. *Social Work, 19,* 288–298.

Kadushin, A. (1976). *Supervision in social work.* New York: Columbia University Press.

Lewin, K. (1935). *A dynamic theory of personality: Selected papers of Kurt Lewin.* New York: McGraw-Hill.

Lewin, K. (1951). Field theory in social sciences. In D. Cartwright (Ed.), *Frontiers in group dynamics* (pp. 221–233). New York: Harper & Row.

Mayer, J. E., & Rosenblatt, A. (1975). Objectionable supervisory styles: Students' views. *Social Work, 20,* 184–189.

Munson, C. E. (1981). Style and structure in supervision. *Journal of Education for Social Work, 17,* 65–72.

Nie, N. H., Hull, C. H., Jenkins, J. G., Steinbrenner, K., & Bent, D. (1975). *Statistical package for the social sciences: Version 8.* New York: McGraw-Hill.

Olmstead, J., & Christenson, H. E. (1973). *Effects of agency work contexts: An intensive field study* (Research Rep. No. 2). Washington, DC: Department of Health, Education, and Welfare, Social Rehabilitation Service.

Olyan, S. D. (1972). *An explanatory study of supervison in Jewish community centers as compared to other welfare settings*. Unpublished doctoral dissertation, University of Pittsburgh, Pittsburgh.

Pincus, J. D. (1986). Communication, job satisfaction and job performance. *Human Communication Research, 12,* 395–419.

Riggar, T. F., Godley, S. H., & Hafer, M. (1984). Burnout and job satisfaction in rehabilitation administrators and direct service providers. *Rehabilitation Counseling Bulletin, 27*(3), 151–160.

Robinson, V. (1936). *Supervision in social casework*. Chapel Hill: University of North Carolina Press.

Rogers, C. R. (1961). *On becoming a person*. Boston: Houghton-Mifflin.

Rosenberg, M. (1968). *Logic of survey analysis*. New York: Basic Books.

Sales, E., & Navarre, E. (1970). *Individual and group supervision in field instruction: A research report*. Ann Arbor: University of Michigan, School of Social Work.

Schwartz, W. (1960). *Content and process in the educative experience*. Unpublished doctoral dissertation, Teachers College, Columbia University, New York.

Schwartz, W. (1961). The social worker in the group. In B. Saunders (Ed.), *New perspectives on services to groups: Theory, organization, practice* (pp. 7–34). New York: National Association of Social Workers.

Schwartz, W. (1962, September). Toward a strategy of group work practice. *Social Service Review, 36,* 268–279.

Schwartz, W. (1964, January). *The classroom teaching of social work with groups*. Paper presented at the annual meeting of the Council on Social Work Education, Toronto, Canada.

Schwartz, W. (1968, October). Group work in public welfare. *Public Welfare, 26,* 322–368.

Schwartz, W. (1969). Private troubles and public issues: One social work job or two? In M. Branscombe (Ed.), *The social welfare forum, 1969* (pp. 22–43). New York: Columbia University Press.

Schwartz, W. (1975). *The helping process in social work: Theory, practice and research* [Film]. Produced by L. Shulman. Montreal: McGill University, Instructional Communications Centre. 55 minutes. VHS.

Schwartz, W. (1976). Between client and system: The mediating function. In R. W. Roberts & H. Northern (Eds.), *Theories of social work with groups.* (pp. 171–197). New York: Columbia University Press.

Schwartz, W. (1977). Social group work: The interactionist approach. In J. B. Turner (Ed.), *Encyclopedia of social work* (Vol. 2, p. 1259). New York: National Association of Social Workers.

Schwartz, W. (1979, March). *Education in the classroom*. Paper presented at the annual meeting of the Council on Social Work Education, Boston.

Schwartz, W., & Zalba, S. (1971). *The practice of group work*. New York: Columbia University Press.

Scott, W. R. (1969). Professional employees in the bureaucratic structure. In A. Etzioni (Ed.), *The semi-professions and their organizations* (pp. 82–140). New York: Free Press.

Shulman, L. (1967). Scapegoats, group workers and preemptive intervention. *Social Work, 12,* 37–43.

Shulman, L. (1969a). *A casebook of social work with groups: The mediating model.* New York: Council on Social Work Education.

Shulman, L. (1969b). Social systems theory in field instruction: A case example. In G. Hearn (Ed.), *The general systems approach: Contributions toward an holistic conception of social work* (pp. 37–44). New York: Council on Social Work Education.

Shulman, L. (1969c). Social work skill: The anatomy of a helping act. In *Social work practice* (pp. 29–48). New York: Columbia University Press.

Shulman, L. (1970). Client, staff and the social agency. In *Social work practice* (pp. 21–40). New York: Columbia University Press.

Shulman, L. (1972). *Group work and effective college teaching.* Unpublished doctoral dissertation, Temple University, Philadelphia.

Shulman, L. (1977). *The impact of reduced caseloads on preventative services.* Research report submitted to the Ontario Ministry of Community and Social Affairs, Canada.

Shulman, L. (1978). A study of practice skill. *Social Work, 23,* 274–281.

Shulman, L. (1981). *Identifying, measuring and teaching the helping skills.* New York: Council on Social Work Education and the Canadian Association of Schools of Social Work.

Shulman, L. (1991). *Interactional social work practice: Toward an empirical theory.* Itasca, IL: Peacock.

Shulman, L. (1992). *The skills of helping individuals, families and groups* (3rd ed.). Itasca, IL: Peacock.

Shulman, L., & Buchan, W. (1982). *The impact of the family physician's communication, relationship and technical skills on patient compliance, satisfaction, reassurance, comprehension and improvement.* Vancouver, Canada: University of British Columbia.

Shulman, L., Robinson, E., & Luckyj, A. (1981). *A study of supervision skill: Context, content and process.* Unpublished report, University of British Columbia School of Social Work, Vancouver, Canada.

Stoltenberg, C., Pierce, R., McNeill, N., & Brian, W. (1987). Effects of experience on counselor trainees' needs. *Clinical Supervisor, 5,* 23–32.

Strean, H. S. (1978). *Clinical social work theory and practice.* New York: Free Press.

Taft, J. (1933). Living and feeling. *Child Study, 10,* 100–112.

Taft, J. (1949). Time as the medium of the helping process. *Jewish Social Service Quarterly, 26,* 230–243.

Truax, C. B. (1966). Therapist empathy, warmth, and genuineness, and patient personality change in group psychotherapy: A comparison between interaction unit measures, time sample measures, and patient perception measures. *Journal of Clinical Psychology, 71,* 1–9.

Wilson, S. J. (1980). *Recording: Guidelines for social workers* (2nd ed.). New York: Free Press.

Worthington, E. L., & Roehlue, H. J. (1979). Effective supervision as perceived by beginning counselors in training. *Journal of Counseling Psychology, 26,* 64–73.

FURTHER READING

Abels, P. (1977). *The new practice of supervision and staff development: A synergistic approach*. Chicago: Association Press.

Abrahamson, A. C. (1959). *Group methods in supervision and staff development*. New York: Harper.

Amacher, K. (1977). *Explorations into the dynamics of learning in field work*. Unpublished doctoral dissertation, Smith College, Northhampton, MA.

Bennis, W. G., & Shepard, H. A. (1956). A theory of group development. *Human Relations, 9*, 415–437.

Berg, W. E. (1980). Effects of job satisfaction on practice decisions: A linear flowgraph analysis. *Social Work Research and Abstracts, 16*(3), 30–37.

Blumenfield, M. (1982). *Applied supervision in psychotherapy*. New York: Grune & Stratton.

Brager, G., & Holloway, S. (1978). *Changing human service organizations: Politics and practice*. New York: Columbia University Press.

Briar, S. (1966). Family services. In H. Maas (Ed.), *Five fields of social services: Reviews of the literature* (pp. 9–50). New York: National Association of Social Workers.

Briar, S. (1971). Family services and casework. In H. Maas (Ed.), *Research in the social services: A five-year review* (pp. 108–125). New York: National Association of Social Workers.

Burns, M. E. (1958). *The historical development of the process of casework supervision*. Unpublished doctoral dissertation, University of Chicago.

Cherniss, C. (1988). Observed supervisory behavior and teacher burnout in special education. *Exceptional Children, 5*, 449–454.

Constable, J., & Russel, T. (1986). The effect of social support and the work environment upon burnout among nurses. *Journal of Human Stress, 12*, 20–26.

Cooper, L., & Gustafson, J. P. (1985). Supervision in a group: An application of group theory. *Clinical Supervisor, 3*, 7–26.

Cowan, B., Dastyl, R., & Wichan, E. R. (1972). Group supervision as a

teaching–learning modality. *Social Worker—Travailleur Social, 40,*
256–261.

Dallinger, J. (1987). Interpersonal perceptual influences on organizational supervisor accessibility. *Communication Research Reports, 4,* 31–37.

Dawson, J. B. (1967). The case supervisor in a family agency. *Family, 6,*
293–295.

Dowling, S. (1986). Supervisory training: Impetus for clinical supervision. *Clinical Supervisor, 4,* 27–34.

Farmer, S. S. (1987). Conflict management and clinical supervision. *Clinical Supervisor, 5,* 5–28.

Fenton, K., Yoshida, R., Maxwell, J., & Kaufman, M. (1979). Recognition of team goals: An essential step toward rational decision making. *Exceptional Children, 30,* 638–644.

Freeman, E. (1985). The importance of feedback on clinical supervision: Implications for direct practice. *Clinical Supervisor, 3,* 24–35.

Freud, S. (1953). Freud's psychoanalytic procedure. In J. Strachey (Ed. and Trans.), *The standard edition of the complete psychological works of Sigmund Freud* (Vol. 7; pp. 249–254). London: Hogarth Press. (Original work published 1923)

Getzel, G. S., Goldberg, J. R., & Salmon, R. (1971). Supervising in groups as a model for today. *Social Casework, 52,* 154–163.

Harkness, D., & Portner, J. (1989). Research and social work supervision: A conceptual review. *Social Work, 34,* 115–118.

Harrison, W. D. (1980). Role strain and burnout in child protective service workers. *Social Service Review, 54,* 31–44.

Hawthorne, L. (1987). Teaching from recordings in field instruction. *Clinical Supervisor, 5,* 7–22.

Ho, M. K. (1977). An analysis of the dynamics of interdisciplinary collaboration. *Child Care Quarterly, 6,* 2779–2787.

Holloway, S., & Brager, G. (1989). *Supervising in the human services: The politics of practice.* New York: Free Press.

Holtzman, R. F. (1966). *Major teaching methods in field instruction in casework.* Unpublished doctoral dissertation, Columbia University, New York.

Jayarante, S., & Chess, W. A. (1983). Job satisfaction and burnout in social work. In B. Farber (Ed.), *Stress and burnout in the human service professions* (pp. 53–59). New York: Pergamon Press.

Jerrell, J., & Larsen, J. K. (1985). How community mental health centers deal with cutbacks and competition. *Hospital and Community Psychiatry, 36,* 1169–1174.

Kadushin, A. (1968). Games people play in supervision. *Social Work, 13,* 23–32.

Kane, R. (1975). The interprofessional team as a small group. *Social Work in Health Care, 1,* 19–32.

Kaslow, F. W. (1972). Group supervision. In F. W. Kaslow & Associates (Eds.), *Issues in human services* (pp. 115–141). San Francisco: Jossey-Bass.

Kaslow, F. W., & Associates. (1977). *Supervision, consultation, and staff training in the helping professions.* San Francisco: Jossey-Bass.

Kettner, P. M. (1973). *Some factors affecting use of professional knowledge and skill by the social worker in public welfare agencies.* Unpublished doctoral dissertation, University of Southern California, Los Angeles.

Kledaras, C. G. (1971). *A study of role conflict in supervision.* Unpublished doctoral dissertation, Catholic University of America, Washington, DC.

Koeske, G. F., & Koeske, R. D. (1989). Work load and burnout: Can social support and perceived accomplishment help? *Social Work, 34,* 243–248.

Kutzik, A. S. (1977a). The medical field. In F. W. Kaslow (Ed.), *Supervision, consultation, and staff development* (pp. 25–60). San Francisco: Jossey-Bass.

Kutzik, A. S. (1977b). The social work field. In F. W. Kaslow (Ed.), *Supervision, consultation, and staff development* (pp. 1–24). San Francisco: Jossey-Bass.

Levy, C. (1973). The ethics of supervision. *Social Work, 18*(2), 14–21.

Levy, L. (1983). Social work supervision: From models toward theory. *Journal of Education for Social Work, 19,* 55–62.

Marcus, G. (1927). How case work training may be adapted to meet workers' personal problems. In *Proceedings of the National Conference of Social Work* (pp. 382–397). Chicago: University of Chicago Press.

Marks, J., & Hixon, D. (1986). Training agency staff through peer group supervision. *Social Casework, 67,* 418–423.

McRay, R., Freeman, E., & Logan, S. (1986). Strategies for teaching students about termination. *Clinical Supervisor, 4,* 45–156.

Mercaitis, P., & Peaper, R. (1987). Factors influencing supervision evaluation by students in speech–language pathology. *Clinical Supervisor, 5,* 39–52.

Meyer, C. H. (1966). *Staff development in public welfare agencies.* New York: Columbia University Press.

Morton, T. D., & Kurtz, D. P. (1980). Educational supervision: A learning theory approach. *Social Casework, 61,* 240–246.

Munson, C. E. (1979a). Evaluation of male and female supervisors. *Social Work, 24,* 104–110.

Munson, C. E. (Ed.). (1979b). *Social work supervision: Classic statements and critical issues.* New York: Free Press.

Munson, C. E. (1983). *An introduction to clinical social work supervision.* New York: Haworth Press.

Munson, C. E. (Ed.). (1984). *Supervising student internships in human services.* New York: Haworth Press.

Muszynski, L. (1981). Coping with layoffs. *Perception, 4,* 13–17.

Pines, A., & Kafry, D. (1978). Occupational tedium in the social services. *Social Work, 23,* 499–507.

Reynolds, B. C. (1942). *Learning and teaching in the practice of social work.* New York: Farrar, Straus, & Giroux.

Rickards, L. D. (1984). Verbal interaction and supervisor perception in counselor supervision. *Journal of Counseling Psychology, 31,* 262–265.

Robinson, E. (1980). *Development of an instrument to measure the skills and knowledge of child welfare supervisors.* Unpublished manuscript, University of British Columbia, Vancouver, Canada.

Robinson, V. (1949). *The dynamics of supervision under functional controls.* Philadelphia: University of Pennsylvania Press.

Rogers, E. (1987). Professional burnout: A review of the concept. *Clinical Supervisor, 5,* 91–106.

Rosenblum, A. F., & Raphael, F. B. (1987). Students at risk in the field practicum: Implications for field teaching. *Clinical Supervisor, 5,* 53–64.

Shinn, M., Rosario, M., Morch, H., & Chestnut, D. (1984). Coping with job stress and burnout in the human services. *Journal of Personality and Social Psychology, 46,* 864–876.

Smith, K. J., & Anderson, J. L. (1982). Relationship of perceived effectiveness to verbal interaction/context variables in supervisory conferences. *Journal of Speech and Hearing Research, 25,* 252–261.

Toseland, R. W., Palmer-Ganeles, J., & Chapman, D. (1986). Teamwork in psychiatric settings. *Social Work, 31,* 46–52.

Towle, C. (1954). *The learner in education for the professions: As seen in education for social work.* Chicago: University of Chicago Press.

Videka-Sherman, L., & William, R. (1985). The structural clinical record: A clinical education tool. *Clinical Supervisor, 3,* 45–62.

Williamson, M. (1961). *Supervision: New patterns and processes.* New York: Association Press.

Wilson, S. J. (1980). *Field instruction techniques for supervisors.* New York: Free Press.

Worthington, E. L. (1984). Empirical investigation of supervision of counselors as they gain experience. *Journal of Counseling Psychology, 31,* 64–73.

SUBJECT INDEX

A

Abrasive workers, 71–73
Accordion, 312
Ackerman, N. W., 236, 237
Administration
  confrontation used to deal with, 295
  mediation of staff encounter with, 305–308
  supervisor's relationship with, 300–304
Affirmative action
  in hiring and promotion practices, 59–60
  problems arising from, 60–65
Amacher, K., 206
Ambivalence
  to change, 105
  existence of underlying, 111–112
Anger
  expressed within groups, 232
  expression of professional, 196
  feelings regarding expression of, 101–103
Arlow, J. A., 201
Audiotape analysis, 311, 313
Authority
  obligations and expectations related to, 41
  as obstacle to empathy, 93
  research on issue of, 135–137
  staff conflicts over, 290–292
  of staff over clients, 169–173

supervisors from outside the unit and issues of, 52–53, 57–59
  as taboo subject, 42, 51, 169
Authority theme
  control and power in, 251–252
  demand function of supervisor and, 124
  discussion of, 118–122
  limitations of supervisor and, 123–124
  new relationships and, 67
  supervisor as outsider and, 122–123, 252–253
  supervisor as source of demand and, 255–256
  supervisor as source of support and, 253–254
  supervisor's limitations and, 254–255
  supervisor's role and, 122
  supportive function of supervisor and, 123
Autocratic leaders, 228

B

Bion, W. R., 101
British Columbia Ministry of Human Resources, 322
Brown, R., 22
Buchan, W., 133
Burnout, 83, 259. *See also* Job stress

C

Calling attention to the process, 307
Career planning, 292–294
Case consultation, 222–225, 227
Challenges, in presentation of ideas, 129–131, 156–157
Change process, 104–106
Christenson, H. E., 134–136, 309
Clients
  ability to have empathy for, 177
  aiding new workers for working with, 68
  articulation of feelings of, 174–175
  authority of workers over, 169–173
  death of, 259–263
  need for workers to understand culture of Hispanic, 62, 63
  physically attacking workers, 265–266
  second, 233
  sharing data with. *See* Data sharing
  staff endings in relation to, 144–145
  supervision vs. work with, 35–36
  supervisor–worker discussion of interviews with, 177, 184–185
Communications, doorknob, 133
Community information, 67–68
Computer software, 317
Conflict
  situations involving staff–authority, 290–292
  within staff groups, 245–251
  with system, 287–289
Confrontation
  application of facilitative, 107–109, 188–190
  in dealing with authority issues, 292
  to illusion of work, 113
Construct validity, 318
Containment skills
  discussion of, 88–89
  use of, 181–182
Contracting
  in beginning phase, 41–43, 218–219
  example of, 43–45

explanation of, 40–41
sessional skills for, 79, 83–85, 180–181
skills for teaching, 164–169
within staff groups, 218–219. *See also* Staff groups used in adversarial situations, 171
Control, in group–supervisor relationships, 251–252
Controversial areas, 74. *See also* Taboo subjects
Cost containment
  affecting level of services, 270–274
  job loss resulting from, 274–278
  reorganization and combining offices as method of, 279–281
  types of, 269–270
Countertransference
  authority theme and, 119–120
  and development of relationships, 149–150
  discussed during in-service training, 227
  group help with problems of, 226
  of supervisor's feelings to relationships with workers, 171
Cronbach's alpha, 318, 320
Cues, indirect, 38, 44, 161–164

D

Data sharing
  importance of, 124–125
  monitoring learning process and, 126–129
  of relevant data, 125–126
  research regarding, 136
  in staff groups, 216
  use of, 196–198
  in way that is open to challenge, 129–131
Death
  of client, 259–263
  of staff member, 263–265
Defensiveness, 105
Deviant behavior
  as form of communication, 55

in group members, 237–240
misreading of, 49
Dewey, J., 157, 160
Doehrman, M. J., 55, 201
Doorknob communications, 84, 133

E

Educational function
    assumptions about teaching and learning
        and, 156–157
    effective learning and, 158–160
    monitoring skills development as element
        of, 199–200
    overview of, 155–156
    research findings regarding, 201
    teaching core practice skills and, 161–
        198. *See also individual skills*
    teaching professional performance skills
        as, 160
Elaborating skills
    containment as, 88–89
    focused listening as, 89–90
    importance of, 85
    modeling of, 181–187
    moving from general to specific as, 85–
        88
    questioning as, 90
    reaching inside silences as, 90–91, 182
Emotions. *See* Feelings
Empathic skills, 79. *See also* Feelings
    acknowledging feelings as, 96–97
    articulating workers' feelings as, 97–99
    barriers to use of, 93–95
    discussion of, 92–93
    importance of, 75–76
    reaching for feelings as, 95–96
    relevance of, 93
    teaching of, 173–179
    used in adversarial situations, 171
Empathy. *See also* Feelings
    ability of supervisor to have, 36, 44, 107
    explanation of, 44
    instructor's ability to show, 156

within staff groups, 217
Endings
    due to staff members leaving, 142–149
    due to supervisors leaving, 149–152
    dynamics of, 81
    in groups, 256
    sessional skills for, 79, 131–133
    types of, 141–142
Evaluation
    difficulty of, 205–206
    formative, 203, 209
    obstacles to effective, 203–205
    research findings regarding, 208–209
    steps in process of, 206–208
    types of, 203
Exit interviews, 142
Experienced workers, 69–71

F

Facilitative confrontation
    in demand for work, 188, 189
    discussion of, 107–109
Feedback
    importance of inviting, 45
    silences interpreted as negative, 91
    within staff groups, 218
Feelings. *See also* Empathic skills; Empathy
    acknowledging, 96–97, 174
    articulation of clients', 174–175
    articulation of workers', 97–99, 133
    concerns regarding showing, 103
    reaching for, 95–96, 174
    regarding taboo subjects, 115–118
    related to expression of anger, 101–103
    research regarding, 134
    tuning in to, 81–83
    use of sharing one's, 192–196
    vulnerability regarding showing of, 100–
        101
Fight/flight, 235
Focus, holding to, 111, 188–189
Focused listening skills
    discussion of, 89–90

R

Racism
  affirmative action issues and, 61–62
  support system to deal with, 64–65
Reaching inside silences, 90–91, 182
Recording, 311–313. *See also* Process
    recording
Reflection
  beneficial use of, 176
  used by supervisors, 94
Rehearsing
  as ending skill, 133
  within staff groups, 218
Research methodology
  instrument development and testing used
    in, 316–321
  overview of, 315–316
  used in 1981 study, 321–325
  used in 1991 study, 325–328
Resistance
  to change, 105
  of clients to workers, 188
  dynamic of continued, 50–52
  within staff groups, 227–228. *See also*
    Staff groups
Robinson, E., 208, 308
Robinson, V., 13
Roehlke, H., 22
Rogers, C. R., 92–93
Rosenberg, M., 324
Rosenblatt, A., 55, 135

S

Sales, E., 256
Scapegoats, 242–245
Schwartz, William, 5–7, 11, 14, 19, 20,
    36, 38, 41, 46, 67, 74, 105–106, 112,
    113, 118, 124–125, 130, 157, 160,
    187, 193, 243, 245, 251, 289, 304,
    312, 314
Scott, W. R., 201
Second client, 233
Self-disclosure, 100. *See also* Feelings
Sessional skills

for contracting, 79, 83–85, 180–181
  for endings, 79, 131–133
  for tuning in, 79, 81–83
Sexism, 179
Sexual abuse, 177–178
Sexuality, 115–117
Shulman, L., 27, 133, 136, 160, 201, 208,
    308
Silences, reaching inside, 90–91, 182
Skills, 12
Social relationships, 46–48
Social trauma, 281–283
Social work students, 73–75
Specific concerns, moving from general
    concerns to, 85–88, 182
Staff groups
  beginning phase of, 218–219
  conflict within, 245–251
  dynamics of work with, 213–216
  ending phase in, 256
  group culture in, 231–236
  mutual aid processes in work with, 216–
    218
  overview of, 213–214
  purposes of, 219–228
  relationship with new worker, 67
  research findings regarding, 256–257
  supervisor relationships with, 251–256
  supervisor's role with, 228–231, 295–
    300
  third-force function in working with,
    295–300
  types of individuals in, 236–245
Staff member endings. *See also* Endings
  common themes of, 142–143
  of negative relationships, 147–149
  of positive relationships, 144–147
  strategies for dealing with, 142–144
Staff members. *See also* New staff members
  chairing meetings, 229
  conflicts involving authority, 290–292
  death of, 263–265
  deviant, 237–240
  impact of traumatic events on. *See*
    Traumatic events

inexperienced, 65–68, 199–200
as internal leaders, 240
job manageability across levels of, 29
job stress across levels of, 28
monitoring skill development in, 199–201
partializing concerns of, 109–110, 135
as quiet group members, 240–242
resistance to recording, 312
as scapegoats, 242–245
social relationships between supervisors
and, 46–48
vulnerability of, 44–45
Statistical Package for the Social Sciences
(SPSS) Version 8, 317, 324
Stereotypes
avoidance of, 48–50
efforts to correct cultural and racial, 63
Strean, H. S., 119
Stress. *See* Job stress
Summarizing, 132
Supervision
assumptions regarding process of, 6–7
client work vs., 35–36
context of, 24–26
definition of, 13–14
group, 225–226
models of, 24
obstacles to worker–system interaction
and, 18–19
task definition for, 13–15
terminology used regarding, 11–13
worker–system interaction and, 15–18
Supervision phases
beginning, for new supervisors, 40–45
with new workers, 65–75. *See also* New
staff members
research findings regarding, 75–77
tuning in as preliminary, 36–40
work. *See* Work phase; Work-phase tasks
Supervision Questionnaire, 319–320
Supervisor endings. *See also* Endings
dynamics of, 149–150
illustration of, 150–151
resulting from promotion from within,
151–152

Supervisors
affirmative action issues in hiring and
promoting, 59–65
function of, 19–21, 94
job stress and job manageability for, 27–
30
limitations of, 254–255
mediation function of, 20–21, 287–289,
305–308
new. *See* New supervisors
as outsiders, 122–123, 252–253
problems faced by minority, 62
relationships with administration, 300–
304
relationships with groups, 227, 251–256.
See also Staff groups
research findings regarding skills of,
133–139
as role models, 113–114
role of, 21–24, 68, 228–231
as source of demand, 255–256
as source of support, 253–254
third-force function of, 294–308

T

Taboo subjects
authority as, 42, 51, 169
exploration of, 115–118
expressed indirectly, 161
within groups, 232, 236
research regarding, 134
varying views regarding, 217
violence against workers as, 265
Taft, J., 36, 92
Teaching, assumptions about, 156–158
Third-force function
explanation of, 294–295
research findings regarding, 308–309
Third-variable analysis, 324
Training programs
focus of present, 5
in-service, 226–227
Transference
authority theme and, 119–120

CASE EXAMPLE INDEX

L

Late staff member
  deviant member, 239
Loss of job
  traumatic event, 275–278

M

Mediating function
  group session, 230
Mediating role
  budget cutbacks, 298–299
  interdisciplinary conflict, 290–291
  policy conflict, 302
  staff–administration conflict, 295–296,
    297
  staff–administrator meeting, 305
  staff career planning, 292
  working with the administrator, 292, 302
Memory work
  case consultation, 222–223
Monitoring learning
  sharing data, 126–127
Moving from general to specific
  new worker, 185

N

Negative feedback
  authority theme, 120–121
  child welfare, 121–122
Negative feedback from staff
  sharing supervisor's feelings, 100
New building
  traumatic event, 279–281
New supervisor
  affirmative action, 59–60, 62–64
  avoiding stereotypes, 48–49
  catching a mistake, 54–55
  child welfare, 47–48
  confrontation, 50–51, 53, 62–65
  contracting, 41, 43, 47, 50–51, 55–59
  gender conflict, 50–51
  hospital, 37–38
  hospital setting, 43

mistaken tuning in, 38–39
  from outside, 53, 59–60
  promoted from within, 47–48
  residential, 53
  resistance, 50–51
  supervising friends, 48–49
  transition house, 55–59
  from within, 48–49
New worker
  contracting, 66
  inexperienced, 66

O

Outsider
  supervisor's role as, 122–123

P

Partializing
  overwhelmed client, 188–189
  worker anxiety, 109–110
Passive resistance
  challenging illusion of work, 114
Personal problems
  acknowledging feelings, 96–97
  articulating feelings, 97–98
  reaching for feelings, 95–96
Physical attack on staff member
  group support, 265–266
Policy issues
  staff–administration conflict, 293–294
Poor worker performance
  demand for work, 102–103, 107–108
Preparing staff
  staff–administration conflict, 297
Probation period
  demand for work, 107–108
Professional impact
  policy conflict, 302
  staff–administration conflict, 295–297
  staff–administrator meeting, 305–308
  staff career planning, 292–294
  staff conflict with doctor, 290–291
  working with one's administrator, 292
Public attack on agency policy, 266–269

ABOUT THE AUTHOR

Lawrence Shulman, MSW, EdD, is Dean and Professor, School of Social Work, at the University of Buffalo, State University of New York (SUNY). He is a practitioner — researcher who has developed the "interactional" model of practice and supervision building on the original work of William Schwartz.

Shulman is widely used as a trainer and consultant on direct practice with individuals, families, and groups, supervision and administration, field instruction, child welfare, and teaching. His research has focused on operationalizing and testing skills for helping professionals at all levels of an organization or agency. More recently, he has explored the impact of contextual factors such as agency policy, cost containment efforts, and traumatic events on the caseload to develop a grounded, holistic model.

Shulman has written or edited 13 books and monographs including books on supervision and management and a widely used social work practice text, *The Skills of Helping Individuals, Families, and Groups*, now in its fourth edition. His most recent research results are reported in *Interactional Social Work Practice: Toward an Empirical Theory*. He was the author of the consultation section in the 18th edition of the *Encyclopedia of Social Work* and has been a contributor to *The Social Work Dictionary*. Shulman is on the editorial boards of four major journals including *The Clinical Supervisor* and has published often in professional journals.

ORDER THESE FINE REFERENCE WORKS ON MANAGEMENT FROM THE NASW PRESS

Interactional Supervision, *by Lawrence Shulman.* Helps human services supervisors develop skills for working with staff individually and in groups. Presents practical strategies for formal and informal supervision.
ISBN: 0-87101-220-0. Item #2200. $34.95.

The Social Work Ethics Audit: *A Risk Management Tool,* Frederic G. Reamer. *The Social Work Ethics Audit* provides practitioners with a practical and easy-to-use tool that helps assess the adequacy of ethics-related policies, practices, and procedures related to clients, staff, documentation, and decision-making. This volume assists respondents in determining appropriate action steps and strategy to correct any inadequacies or lapses in ethical practices. It creates opportunity for intense self-evaluation and implementation of corrective measures for improved social work practice.
ISBN: 0-87101-328-2. Item #3282. October 2000. $31.99.

Skills for Effective Management of Nonprofit Organizations, *edited by Richard L. Edwards, John A. Yankey, and Mary A. Altpeter.* This practical guide offers a new, relevant approach to leadership in the nonprofit environment. You'll find guidance for all aspects of management, including board development, consulting, and developing strategic alliances.
ISBN: 0-87101-290-1. Item #2901. $34.95.

Building a Strong Foundation: *Fundraising for Nonprofits,* by Richard L. Edwards, Elizabeth A. S. Benefield, Jeffrey A. Edwards, and John A. Yankey. Addresses all the aspects necessary to raise funds successfully in a non-profit environment. Learn how to build the relationships that are central to successful fundraising activities.
ISBN: 0-87101-249-9. Item #2499. $27.95.

New Management in Human Services, *Second Edition,* edited by Leon Ginsberg and Paul R. Keys. Offers guidance on how to work with boards, boost staff morale, work with the media, improve service delivery, and more. It also gives advice to help managers stay focused, maintain a high energy level, and control stress.
ISBN: 0-87101-251-0. Item #2510. $31.95.

(Order form on reverse side)

ORDER FORM

Qty.	Title	Item #	Price	Total
___	Interactional Supervision	2200	$ 34.95	_____
___	The Social Work Ethics Audit	3282	$ 31.99	_____
___	Skills for Effective Management of Nonprofit Organizations	2901	$ 34.95	_____
___	Building a Strong Foundation	2499	$ 27.95	_____
___	New Management in Human Services, 2nd Edition	2510	$ 31.95	_____

Subtotal	_____
Postage and Handling	_____
DC residents add 6% sales tax	_____
MD residents add 5% sales tax	_____
Total	_____

POSTAGE AND HANDLING
Minimum postage and handling fee is $4.95. Orders that do not include appropriate postage and handling will be returned.

DOMESTIC: Please add 12% to orders under $100 for postage and handling. For orders over $100 add 7% of order.

CANADA: Please add 17% postage and handling.

OTHER INTERNATIONAL: Please add 22% postage and handling.

❏ **Check** or **money order** (payable to NASW Press) for $ _____.

❏ **Credit card**
    ❏ NASW Visa* | ❏ Other Visa | ❏ NASW MasterCard* | ❏ MasterCard | ❏ Amex

_____   _____
Credit Card Number   Expiration Date

Signature _____

Use of these cards generates funds in support of the social work profession.

Name_____

Address _____

City _____ State/Province _____

Country _____ Zip _____

Phone _____ E-mail _____

NASW Member # (if applicable) _____

(Please make checks payable to NASW Press. Prices are subject to change.)

NASW PRESS
P. O. Box 431
Annapolis JCT, MD 20701
USA

Credit card orders call
1-800-227-3590
(In the Metro Wash., DC, area, call 301-317-8688)
Or fax your order to 301-206-7989
Or order online at http://www.naswpress.org